JOHN CATT'S

Which School? for Special Needs
2016/17

JOHN
CATT®
EDUCATIONAL
LIMITED

25TH EDITION

Published in 2016 by
John Catt Educational Ltd,
12 Deben Mill Business Centre,
Woodbridge, Suffolk IP12 1BL UK
Tel: 01394 389850   Fax: 01394 386893
Email: enquiries@johncatt.com
Website: www.johncatt.com
© 2015 John Catt Educational Ltd

**A CIP catalogue record for this book is available from the
British Library.**

ISBN: 978 1 909717 76 3

Contacts
Editor
Jonathan Barnes

Advertising and School Profiles
Tel: +44 (0) 1394 389850
Email: sales@johncatt.com

Distribution/Book Sales
Tel: +44 (0) 1394 389863
Email: booksales@johncatt.com

Contents

How to use this guide

Here are some pointers on how to use this guidebook effectively

Which School? for Special Needs is divided into specific sections:

1. Editorial

This includes articles, written by experts in their fields, explaining various aspects of special needs education. There are also case studies and other interesting articles.

2. Profiles

Here the schools and colleges have been given the opportunity to highlight what they feel are their best qualities in order to help you decide whether this is the right school for your child. They are presented in sections according to the needs they specialise in:

- social interaction difficulties (autism, ASD & ASP)

- emotional, behavioural and/or social difficulties.

- learning difficulties (including dyslexia/SPLD)

- sensory or physical impairment

Within these sections, schools and colleges are listed by region in alphabetical order.

3. Directory

Here you will find basic up-to-date information about every independent or non-maintained special needs school and college, and further education colleges, in England, Northern Ireland, Scotland and Wales, giving contact details, size of school and which specific needs are catered for. (You will find a key to the abbreviations at the start of each directory section) The directory is divided into four sections:

- social interaction difficulties (autism, ASD & ASP)

- emotional, behavioural and/or social difficulties.

- learning difficulties (including dyslexia/SPLD)

- sensory or physical impairment

Within these sections, each establishment is listed by region in alphabetical order and those that have entries in the profiles section are cross-referenced to allow you to find further detailed information. Against each entry you will find a number of symbols indicating any SEN speciality, including an icon to indicate if the school is DfE approved.

4. Useful associations and websites

In this section we provide a list of useful organisations and websites relevant to special educational needs, which may be useful to parents looking for specific help or advice.

5. Maintained schools

Here we have included basic details of all maintained special schools in England, Northern Ireland, Scotland and Wales. They are listed according to their Local Authority.

6. Index

Page numbers preceded by a D indicate a school appearing in the directory, those without will be found in the profiles section.

How to use this guide effectively

John Catt's *Which School? for Special Needs* can be used effectively in several ways according to the information you are looking for. For example, are you looking for:

A specific school? If you know the name of the school but are unsure of its location simply go to the index at the back of the guide where you will find all schools listed alphabetically.

A particular type of school? Both the profiles and directories are divided into sections according to the type of provision. **See also the appendix on page 177**, which lists specific special needs and the schools that cater for them.

A school in a certain region? Look first in the relevant directory. This will give you the basic information about the schools in each region, complete with contact details and which specific needs are catered for. More detailed information can be found in the profiles section for those schools who have chosen to include a full entry.

More information on relevant educational organisations? At the end of the directories you will find a list of useful organisations and websites relevant to special educational needs.

Please note: regional divisions

To facilitate the use of this guide, we have included the geographical region 'Central & West'. This is not an officially designated region and has been created solely for the purposes of this publication.

One final thing, on the next page you will find a list of commonly used SEN abbreviations. This list can be found repeated at various points throughout the guide.

Abbreviations – a full glossary can be found at page 319

ACLD	Autism, Communication and Associated Learning Difficulties	HI	Hearing Impairment
ADD	Attention Deficit Disorder	LD	Learning Difficulties
ADHD	Attention Deficit and Hyperactivity Disorder	MLD	Moderate Learning Difficulties
		MSI	Multi-sensory Impairment
ASD	Autistic Spectrum Disorder	OCD	Obsessive Compulsive Disorder
ASP	Asperger Syndrome	PD	Physical Difficulties
AUT	Autism	PH	Physical Impairment
		Phe	Partially Hearing
BESD	Behavioural, Emotional and Social Difficulties	PMLD	Profound and Multiple Learning Difficulties
		PNI	Physical Neurological Impairment
CCD	Complex Communication Difficulties	SCD	Social and Communication Difficulties
CLD	Complex Learning Difficulties	SCLD	Severe to Complex Learning Difficulties
CP	Cerebral Palsy	SEBD	Severe Emotional and Behavioural Difficulties
D	Deaf		
DYS	Dyslexia	SEBN	Social, Emotional and Behavioural Needs
DYSP	Dyspraxia	SLD	Severe Language Difficulties
EBD	Emotional and Behavioural Difficulties	SLI	Specific Language Impairment
EPI	Epilepsy	SPLD	Specific Learning Difficulties
GLD	General Learning Difficulties	SP&LD	Speech and Language Difficulties
HA	High Ability	VIS	Visual Impairment

HESLEY HELPED ME TO HELP MYSELF.

We're one of the UK's leading independent providers of residential services, schools and colleges supporting people with autism and complex needs.

Our highly trained staff provide the highest quality, person-centred approach. Giving those who use our services the support, skills and tools they need to be as independent as possible.

Our unique **Hesley Enhancing Lives Programme (HELP)** is a big part of this.

Combining the latest techniques and practices, HELP is our successful value-based positive behaviour support programme. Based on the principles of Therapeutic Crisis Intervention which is accredited by the British Institute of Learning Disabilities, HELP reduces the need for high-risk interventions by taking an empathic and proactive approach. We focus on how our actions can positively shape the emotional well-being of all those who use our services. It's why all our staff are given HELP training to make sure it works in practice as well as theory.

Find out more about our schools and colleges visit www.hesleygroup.co.uk or call 0800 0556789.

'More opportunities than threats' as SEND provision evolves

Adam Boddison, chief executive of Nasen, provides a snapshot of the sector

I am delighted to be writing this foreword and I hope you find this guide to be a useful tool in comparing the provision of schools and colleges across Britain. British education is the envy of the rest of the world, but despite that we have seen in recent times constant change across the sector. Perhaps this because we want an education system that remains up to date and relevant for our children and young people or perhaps it is a reflection of the fact that our education professionals see that the job is never done and they have a willingness for learning and improvement. In either case, the most recent changes and ambitions present a set of unique opportunities and challenges for improving the quality of education received by our children and young people with Special Educational Needs or Disabilities (SEND).

The government's recent white paper, Educational Excellence Everywhere, set out the Department for Education's strategic plans. There has been much attention and debate in relation to the plan for all schools to have converted, or be in the process of converting, to become academies by 2020, but there is relatively little information about what this means for schools offering specialist provision. One perspective might be that in an increasingly market-based system, special schools will be well placed to grow and expand or to further specialise as appropriate to their regional contexts. However, there is a risk that when all schools have full control over their own admissions, students with additional needs are less likely to be admitted into some mainstream settings, thereby increasing pressures in other parts of the school system. This is a risk that must be mitigated so that children and young people with SEND are embraced as part of an inclusive educational system. SEND provision should be built into the system from the outset and not a bolted-on afterthought.

The white paper discusses the need to replace Qualified Teacher Status and to redraft the Teachers' Standards. This is an excellent opportunity for the professional SEND community to argue that what constitutes high quality teaching for children and young people with SEND constitutes high quality teaching for all children. Therefore, the revised standards could use this as their starting point putting inclusivity at the heart of classroom practice.

The past year has been a demanding time for SENCOs with many leading on the transition of children on statements to Education, Health and Care plans (EHCPs). Not only is the paperwork involved in this process vast and unwieldy, but for those schools with an intake spanning multiple Local Authorities, there are significant differences in process. Looking ahead, there may be good news for SENCOs since the High Needs Funding consultation is likely to identify gaps in funding, thereby encouraging the government to invest further in those children and young people with the highest levels of need. This builds on the additional £80m government investment made in January to support the implementation of the SEND reforms.

Whilst the 3% of children nationally who have EHCPs are generally well supported, a challenge facing both school leaders and parents is how to support the 12% of children who have a special education need that is

> 2016 will be a defining year in the history of SEND provision. The outcome of the European Referendum could have major implications for children and young people with SEND. In the event that Britain was to leave Europe, there are a number of European laws, for example the Human Rights Act, that may not apply any more.

not severe or complex enough to warrant an EHC plan. These children were formerly identified using the School Action and School Action Plus criteria, but where they are now identified as having special educational needs, SEN support will be provided based upon the effective use of the graduated approach. The responsibility for this process and for the progress and accountability of such children sits with the child's teacher. The perceived wisdom is that high quality teaching and differentiation should be sufficient to cater for the needs of these students, but in order for this to work, further training and support is needed for existing teachers to both identify needs early and to develop research-informed practices. Once again, the positive news here is that government funding has been made available to support training and development in this area.

In this new and developing world of Multi-Academy Trusts (MATs), there will be significant opportunities to realise innovative approaches to effective SEND provision. Alliances of special schools are forming MATs offering complementary provision and building on specialist knowledge and expertise. Similarly, MATs are forming with a combination of mainstream schools, special schools and alternative provision with the aim of maximising potential and minimising exclusions. It is unclear yet whether there will be as few as 1000 MATs or as many as 4000, but what is clear is that SEND peer review will be a key factor both within and between MATs.

Looking towards Scotland, Wales and Northern Ireland, there are parallel journeys taking place in relation to SEND reforms. There are of course some differences, but many of the core principles are aligned, not least the re-emphasis of the class teacher's responsibility for all children and young people, including those with SEND.

2016 will be a defining year in the history of SEND provision. The outcome of the European Referendum could have major implications for children and young people with SEND. In the event that Britain was to leave Europe, there are a number of European laws, for example the Human Rights Act, that may not apply any more. This would remove the legal levers that are currently used by a significant number of parents to get the necessary support for their children. We must also be mindful that law is an evolutionary concept, so even if an alternative to the lost legislation is put in place, it will take time for those laws to be tested in the courts and for precedents to be set.

Despite this rapidly changing educational landscape, there are more opportunities than threats. School leaders are well placed to shape the education system and move it forwards in a way that would not have been possible in the past. I hope that these opportunities are fully embraced and that the result is an improved educational experience for all children and young people.

For more information about Nasen, visit www.nasen.org.uk

Moving in the right direction

Douglas Silas, Principal of Douglas Silas Solicitors, says progress with new SEN legislation has been positive – if slow

Well, another year has gone by and the trepidation in September 2014 that surrounded changes to a new legal SEN framework, seems a long time ago now…

As I write this (in March 2016), we have just completed 18 months of changing from 'Statements of SEN' ('Statements') to 'Education, Health & Care (EHC) Plans'. Whilst there have been some teething problems and some problems are continuing, the general sense is that things now seem to be falling into place.

We have all also started using new terminology like: 'Outcomes', 'Transfer Reviews', 'Joint Commissioning' and 'Working Together'; but some people now say that the changes we hoped for have all been a bit of a damp squib as, whilst we were promised a lot of new things, many things have not really changed that much. It's like the 'Emperor's New Clothes' they say.

We were also led to believe that there other new things would make our lives easier, such as 'Local Offers', 'Personal Budgets' (with the promise of 'Direct Payments') and there being more of a focus now on getting the 'best possible outcomes' for a child or young person with SEN. I am afraid that many of these things have not really materialised yet.

That being said, after initial delays in transferring Statements to EHC plans because many Local Authorities (LAs) were in confusion (some even openly admitted to there being 'chaos' during the first academic year of changes in 2014/15), I have noticed that, in this past academic year (2015/16), many LAs now are trying to transfer as many Statements as possible.

The Transitional Guidance, issued just before the changes came into effect (in September 2014, but amended again in April 2015), made clear that the process of transition from a Statement to an EHC plan,

would start off with a 'Transfer Review' meeting (which would usually take place at the same time as the Annual Review of a Statement) and would then take 14 weeks to complete. But, by September 2015 (one year from the implementation of the changes), it became very clear that many LAs were struggling to comply with these legal timescales.

Therefore, the Government amended the statutory requirements to allow LAs a further 4 weeks from then to complete the process (i.e. 18 instead of 14 weeks). Yet, I am afraid that many LAs are still struggling at the present time to complete transfers within these new extended timescales. I am not saying that LAs are going over by just one or two weeks, but sometimes by more than one or two months. I have even had cases where Transfer Reviews have been started in one month in one year, but still not completed by the same month of the following year!

The fact is that the new SEN framework was supposed to create a new way of doing things. There was supposed to be more integrated 'Education', 'Health' and 'Care' provision but, most importantly, children and young people with SEN (and their families) were supposed to now be put at the heart of the process. But, whilst many people (both parents and professionals) like the idea of now focusing more holistically on a child or

We have to be pragmatic about what we can achieve and, instead of complaining, look at how we can make things better and better manage people's expectations. The shame is also that we are trying to undertake massive changes in a time of funding cuts.

young person's needs and the idea of 'working together' towards 'mutually agreed outcomes', which now include health and care as well as educational needs; in practice, many parents say that nothing has really changed and new things are really just part of a tick-box exercise.

Many also feel that, whereas before there were not enough meetings about their child with the LA represented, there are now too many meetings being held by LAs which hold up the process! Many schools (as well as parents) are now being asked to complete long 'standard' application forms when making assessment requests, but then finding that, having done all of this work which is time-consuming, requests are often turned down at the first hurdle. It can be quite soul-destroying and, obviously, wastes a lot of man-power.

A number of common problems have been flagged up:

- Reforms not bringing about the desired results;
- LAs using the opportunity of transferring statements to EHC plans, as a chance to reduce provision or make provision less specific;
- More assessments for children under 5 but few post-19 assessments taking place (but another main aim of the changes was the need to prepare young people for adulthood).

It is great in theory to have joined-up thinking (I wonder how many times I have heard that said before); but this also doesn't work practically without there being good joint local commissioning being in place.

I still remain positive and I am still optimistic that we have moved to a better system overall. I also think that we have to be realistic and realise that big changes are not going to happen overnight. We have to be pragmatic about what we can achieve and, instead of complaining, look at how we can make things better and better manage people's expectations. The shame is also that we are trying to undertake massive changes in a time of funding cuts.

> One thing that I have noticed is how every LA now has a different way of doing things (and sometimes those differences are significant). The irony, of course, is that each LA thinks they are doing things correctly and that it is other LAs who are wrong!

On the whole, I believe that we are moving in the right direction. I know that significant changes take time (especially large ones) and that sometimes the pendulum has swung too far one way and has to go back too far the other way before it settles in the middle. There also has to be enough time to effect a proper cultural change, both for parents and for LAs.

One thing that I have noticed is how every LA now has a different way of doing things (and sometimes those differences are significant). The irony, of course, is that each LA thinks they are doing things correctly and that it is other LAs who are wrong! This is completely nonsensical.

I remain hopeful that things will sort themselves out in the near future - who knows, we may even find ourselves in a better position!

Douglas Silas Solicitors specialise exclusively in SEN, whose website is www.SpecialEducationalNeeds.co.uk

Douglas is also the author of 'A Guide To The SEND Code of Practice (What You Need To Know)' which is available for all eBook readers. For further information visit: www.AGuideToTheSENDCodeOfPractice.co.uk

Providing a unique education solution for every pupil

TCES Group schools provide (LA funded) education for pupils aged 7-18 years whose Social, Emotional or Mental Health (SEMH) needs or Autism Spectrum Condition (ASC) has made it difficult for them to achieve success in a mainstream school. Pupil's co-morbid needs can be complex. Undiagnosed speech, language and communication needs (SLCN), sensory difficulties or learning difficulties can create barriers to learning that must be addressed before the pupil can settle into education. Our integrated approach to education, health and care takes each pupil on an individual journey that encourages a love of learning. We offer two options according to the needs of the pupil:

Option 1 Day School Provision

Tier 1 For pupils with SEMH needs or an ASC for whom the expectation is that they will be able to thrive in and integrate easily into a small group learning environment, which would include an internal induction period as standard. Once in school full time, the pupil would be supported by TCES Group's Team Around the Child approach.

Tier 2 There may be exceptional circumstances where a pupil may need additional support over a specified period to ensure they are able to engage with and thrive in their placement.

Tiers 1 and 2 Services are delivered and managed by the Leadership Teams in each of our schools – Head and Deputy Head Teachers and Inclusion Managers – in conjunction with Head of Clinical Services, Clinical and Therapy Team, School Improvement Team and Contracts and Commissioning Lead.

Option 2 Create Service

Tier 3 Pupils with SEMH or an ASC for whom integration into a class-based school placement is not indicated, which may be for a number of reasons. At best they will need a graduated programme into a small group learning environment. They may need 1:1 support in the medium to long term in tandem with TCES Group's Team Around the Child approach.

Tier 4 Pupils with SEMH or an ASC who either present high risk to themselves or others or who are extremely vulnerable and are therefore at high risk. Pupils' complex and additional needs (across education, health and care) negate their ability to be educated in any group setting.

Tiers 3 and 4 Services are delivered and managed by the Head Teacher and Case Co-ordinators in the Create Service, a parallel service to that of our schools, in conjunction with our Head of Clinical Services, Clinical and Therapy Team, School Improvement Team and Contracts and Commissioning Lead. Therapeutic education, assessment and monitoring is delivered through a highly specialised case co-ordination model. Pupils may attend one of Create's Therapeutic Hubs, be educated in safe community spaces or, in some cases, their own homes.

East London
Independent School

North West London
Independent School

www.tces.org.uk
0208 543 7878

Essex Fresh Start
Independent School

Create Service
Personalised Therapeutic Education

The importance of early years intervention in autism education

Gemma McCarthy, specialist teacher at The National Autistic Society's Radlett Lodge School, discusses how autistic children can profoundly benefit from early intervention in school

Pupils on the autism spectrum don't experience the world in the same way we expect of most children who are in the Early Years stage of development and learning. It's therefore critical that each pupil has a regular, predictable and structured learning environment in order to set them up for success as they move through school life.

Many of our pupils start at school still needing to learn skills such as sitting on a chair, tolerating the proximity of another person, concentrating on a task for more than a few seconds or 'shared attention', which is in fact important for many aspects of language development. .

In the Early Years Foundation Stage, autistic pupils often:

- do not absorb and acquire skills or learning through observing others
- need each skill, developmental step or type of play to be taught explicitly
- need visual cues to understand what is expected of them
- have limited success in learning through discovery and experimentation, as they may lack the imagination and flexibility of thought to do so
- demonstrate poor organisational skills
- struggle to predict how long an activity will last, so are unsure when to start and finish an activity – often repeating it as they're unaware it has ended
- have no way of knowing or anticipating the order in which demands will be made.

For these reasons, amongst others, early intervention for autistic pupils is vital. To cultivate the best learning conditions for each child, it's important to help and teach them to interpret their environment in ways that are meaningful to them, as this reduces levels of stress and anxiety. While many are able to develop and learn to at least the same level as their non-autistic peers, they will need differentiated support tailored to their strengths and difficulties.

Teaching children basic skills as soon as they enter the classroom enables them to live a more independent and more socially acceptable life as they grow into adults. As a class, much of our time is spent toilet training in the first few weeks of a child's education. We put a toileting programme into place and the psychology team analyses the data collected, complemented by meetings to monitor progress and make adaptations when necessary. This has continually proven to be a successful way to introduce pupils to an important stage of their development.

Young autistic pupils find having targets in place

highly supportive – for example, using a cup to drink or using a spoon and fork to eat their food, or how to sit at a table in order to eat a meal. Incorporating a large number of opportunities throughout the day to enable the children to practise dressing and undressing, including putting on their shoes and coats, helps to seamlessly introduce another important development skill.

Many of our pupils start at school still needing to learn skills such as sitting on a chair, tolerating the proximity of another person, concentrating on a task for more than a few seconds or 'shared attention', which is in fact important for many aspects of language development. Attention Autism is a programme in the Early Years setting which teaches the children how to share attention. Starting with learning how to sit and look at what the adult is doing alongside their peers, the child is gradually able to watch an activity then try it themselves. The children get excited to join the group and want to take part in their activity without adults prompting them to sit and look. We understand that the children need to secure these 'learning to learn' tools before they're able to utilise the more formal types of 'educational experiences' available to them. Ultimately, we aim to foster the development of each child's independence and self-control, and the ability to express feelings or communicate in a way that's understood by others.

At Radlett Lodge School, we are all specialists. We are practised in the full range of approaches to teaching autistic children, which is so important as it enables us to select the combination that best supports individual progress. We closely follow the framework for the Early Years Foundation Stage but adapt it in a way our children can access. Due to autistic children having an impairment of social imagination, social communication and social interaction as well as a range of sensory issues, we don't follow child-initiated learning in the traditional sense. Instead, we spend time teaching children basic play skills and then show them how to generalise these

skills. For example, if a child enjoys spinning a ball, we would teach them other things you can do with a ball, and give them a range of toys and items they can spin to address any sensory issues.

We follow the TEACCH programme (Treatment of and Education of Autistic and related Communication Handicapped Children) and its three main principles: structure, visual clarity and consistency. It's important for every child to know what they're doing, how they are told what they should be doing and how the environment is organised. TEACCH underpins how we modify the environment, structure our teaching and focus on emerging skills. We know that the earlier a child can benefit from this structured the support, the more receptive they are to developing these skills which they can continue to build on through their lives.

The SPELL framework (Structure, Positive approaches and expectations, Empathy, Low arousal, Links) as a basis for training and teaching is fundamental when supporting autistic children in education. Structure makes the world a more predictable, accessible place, and aids personal autonomy and independence by reducing

dependence on others. Equally important is establishing and reinforcing self-confidence and self-esteem by building on natural strengths, interests and abilities. Praise and positivity is crucial when doing this. Beginning from the child's perspective, we gather insights into how they see and experience their world, knowing what it is that motivates or interests them but importantly what may also frighten, preoccupy or otherwise distress them.

An holistic approach should be taken from the start, so open links and communication between all people involved with the child is essential. Particularly in the Early Years stage, it is important that we take our lead from the children's parents as to what they enjoy and learn. They're invited into the class to observe their child and have the opportunity to speak to a range of professionals on site or receive training themselves. We understand that parents are the most important educators of their child, so we enjoy sharing their child's learning journey with them.

With all these early interventions in place, we can ensure that each child feels safe to learn and achieve their full potential throughout their life at school, and into their adult life.

For more information about the National Autistic Society schools, see page 42

Mental wellbeing and emotional support for children with complex needs

Fiona Minion and Cynthia Skelcher share the success of their work tackling an unseen problem

"The best way to overcome undesirable or negative thoughts and feelings is to cultivate the positive ones."
William Walker Atkinson

One in ten children aged between 5 and 16 years (three in every classroom) has a mental health problem, and many continue to have these problems into adulthood. Half of those with lifetime mental health problems first experience symptoms by the age of 14.

This number rises significantly for those with a vision impairment, learning disability, autism and other complex needs. (Until quite recently, it was thought that people with learning disabilities did not have the same range of feelings and emotional needs as other people. It is now realised that it is very common for young people with learning disabilities to experience mental health issues.)

At RNIB Pears Centre for Specialist Learning, we offer individually-tailored education, care and therapies to children and young people with multiple disabilities and complex health needs who are blind or partially sighted.

Rebecca's story (Name changed to protect identity)

Rebecca has Optic Nerve Hypoplasia and is registered blind, this a congenital condition in which the optic nerve is underdeveloped. She has a multi diagnosis of Attention Deficit Disorder (ADHD), Autistic Spectrum Disorder (ASD) and Obsessive – Compulsive Disorder. She also has a Cognitive development delay. Rebecca displays challenging behaviour and engages in severe self-injurious behaviours.

Rebecca's placement in long term foster care had broken down; this we believe led to feelings of bereavement and uncertainty in her life. When Rebecca came to live and learn at RNIB Pears Centre she displayed self-injurious behaviours ranging from head banging on hard surfaces to biting her hands; the latter being so severe that Rebecca's hands needed reviewing by the paediatric plastic surgeons teams every fortnight. She wore a helmet to protect her face and head and both hands were bandaged this restricted the use of her fingers. She verbalized loudly when anxious and had short bouts of screaming. It was also noticed that Rebecca has good learning and engagement skills.

Shortly after coming to live at RNIB Pears Centre 'a team around the child' was formed. This team included a Behavioural Nurse Specialist, Occupational Therapist, Teacher and Team leader from the bungalow where Rebecca lived. Other staff, who were beginning to build a relationship with Rebecca, were also involved. A Consultant Psychologist was also commissioned for advice.

Advice was also sought from CAHMS Consultant Psychiatrist in Learning Disabilities (Children and Adolescents) team.

We decided to enable teams that support Rebecca to work proactively and, in collaboration, a Pears Positive Mental Health Plan was created to incorporate trauma response prevention, crisis intervention and positive identity development.

It was decided that emotional management for Rebecca is vital and should be an integral part of her day. This includes a set therapy session within her weekly school timetable. This gives Rebecca some 'talk time' allowing her to chat about her personal and previous experiences.

Rebecca may also need time to understand her feelings and develop appropriate responses to these, supported by staff who she trusts.

Our occupational therapist also developed a sensory diet that was incorporated throughout Rebecca's day. This includes:

- regular deep pressure activities, the use of a bear hug/ weighted lap pad or blanket.
- not overloading Rebecca with too many noises.
- providing a safe quiet area if noise became too much.

A Positive Mental Health Plan was written. This gave staff working with Rebecca a deeper understanding why she displayed behaviours and self harmed. It also showed staff what activities Rebecca liked for enjoyment and engagement; how they could integrate enjoyable activities into Rebecca's day.

Rebecca has now been at RNIB Pears Centre for about 18 months. In that time she has developed immensely. The main area of concern for staff, Rebecca's self-injurious behaviour, has seen a significant reduction, particularly in her injuring her hands. We have been able to remove the bandages on one hand whilst the other hand is still bandaged but she can use her fingers functionally. She will still bang her head but this is now used more for a communication or attention rather than hurting herself.

Rebecca's behaviour has improved greatly, however this is still work in progress and Rebecca will continue to have all the support required to enable her to grow into a confident and happy young woman.

Due to their complex needs, the young people we support may have trouble understanding and controlling or interpreting thoughts and feelings. This often leads to challenging behaviours which may disrupt learning.

Our in-house Disability Nurse brought together a group of staff who wanted to look at behaviours and what they mean to our young people. For example, what are they communicating? What are their emotions at any one time? How can we find out why they are having problems?

We set up emotional support sessions to help a young person to understand their feelings. We humans have six basic emotions – happiness, surprise, sadness, anger, fear and disgust. We also experience more complex feelings such as embarrassment, shame, pride, guilt, envy, joy, trust, interest, contempt and anticipation.

The aim of our work and sessions with some of our young people is to help them realise their sense of wellbeing, and to try and understand their feelings. Realising that being able to communicate with others can help ease, or solve any problems, lesson their anxieties and hopefully to manage their inner feelings of self-control.

Working alongside a Consultant Psychologist, the group started to look at Positive Psychology, as we all felt we should make a firm commitment to the emotional, mental and physical wellbeing of young people. We needed to look at their personal experiences and life history; and recognise the emotional upheaval of moving from place to place.

Looking at the Seligman's PERMA Model which has 5 core elements of psychological wellbeing and happiness, and using the mental health plan from trauma response within positive psychology, we have adapted the paperwork and information required to suit the needs of our unique young people here at RNIB Pears Centre. We have called it the 'Pears Positive Mental Health Plan'. The aims are:

- to see the whole person
- find out what positive emotions and engagement mean to the individual

- explore how can we assist them to form good relationships with those that are important to them
- understand what they perceive to be a meaningful existence.

Fiona Minion is Registered Nurse Learning Disabilities (RNLD) and Behaviour Specialist; and Cynthia Skelcher is Therapies Assistant at RNIB Pears Centre for Specialist Learning. For more information about RNIB schools, see page 44

Picture posed by model

What's in a label?

Bambi Gardiner tells a parent's story of facing difficult schooling decisions – and how a lack of resources for dyslexic pupils prompted her to take action

Is a 'label' a problem? Let's face it, deciding to move your child from a mainstream school to a special needs school could be quite a big label. But is a label always a bad thing?

Giving your child a 'label' as dyslexic, dyspraxic, autistic, or any other special educational needs (SEN), causes many a sleepless night for parents. Whilst many SEN children sit at the more extreme end of the spectrum, countless others find themselves right at the other end. They may not have major behavioural issues or physical disabilities to deal with, but they have learning differences all the same. Differences for any child can feel extreme.

For many of these children, being 'labelled' can provide relief, knowing there is a reason they find certain things tricky. They can learn to understand what leads them to behave in a certain way or why they find certain tasks more challenging. They may also begin to understand why they see the world in a different way and the benefits this may bring. Our daughter's reaction

to being diagnosed as dyslexic with a slow processing speed was 'So, I'm not actually stupid then?'. That was with a supportive family, good school and nice friends around her. But, kids are kids and are not always kind. It is not the label that is the issue, but the (mis)understanding that comes with it. No-one ever has a problem with their child being 'labelled' sporty, funny or bright.

Most of our children will start life in a mainstream school. The decision to change to an SEN school can be a difficult one to make. You will be looking at taking your child out of his or her friendship group, away from an environment they know and into a potentially unknown academic world. Ultimately, it is us, as parents or guardians, who know our children best. It is also our responsibility to make that decision. It is not one to leave to the 'experts' as they most likely do not really know the intricacies of your child.

So, when you are being told by teachers in Year 2, Year 3 and Year 4 that you need to "relax" and "not

worry" or "they all develop at their own pace", should you listen to them or to your inner voice? The easy option is to listen to the teachers. We did. The implication was that our daughter would catch up and that, with some effort and focus, she would be fine.

But, if you put a penguin and a hawk together and try to get them to fly, the penguin will still be sitting on the ground, no matter how hard it flaps its wings, long after the hawk has soared away. Sometimes the desire and effort just won't overcome physical or mental limitations.

Our own daughter would have undoubtedly benefitted from some time spent in a specialist dyslexia school. Academic life would have slowed down and teaching methods would have been more creative to meet her needs (providing we found the right school for her). That is not knocking the excellent help she has had at her school but the bottom line is that she spent her entire school life, right there, at the bottom. Day in and day out that is a tough place to be. Maybe we could have found a special school that would have enabled her to realise that gaining 12 A* GCSEs would not make her into an amazing person because she already was one? Perhaps she would have had much higher confidence levels because she was spending time with people who, to be blunt, were struggling even more than her?

We didn't take the decision to move our daughter; we were too worried about her being happy (which she seemed to be). By the time we reached the point that she was not happy because of the academic pressure, it was year 8 and really too late to change. Or was that just an excuse?

She struggled through her GCSEs. Even with a superb LS department to help her, life was tough and her self-confidence was certainly affected. She is now in Lower Sixth and will have navigated her way through school with far better than expected results and everything will be fine. However, I do question whether she would have found life easier had we given her even a couple of years of space and time to be in a different school. Perhaps a SEN school would have slowed the pace so she could have the time she needed to grasp the basics. She had to work incredibly hard to achieve results that others would not have been so thrilled with and she certainly worked much harder than many of her peers.

At one point I was told by a department head that 'Mrs Gardiner, we are dealing with a Mini engine here. It is not going to suddenly turn into a Rolls Royce.' Well that stopped me in my tracks. How dare he insinuate that my daughter had a very low academic ability? What's more, that she always would have, no matter what we did. That turned out to be not entirely true.

This throwaway comment fired my determination to develop resources that would meet her unique learning style. She was, and is, capable of learning the same information as an 'A' student, but she needs information packaged in a different way. A lack of resources led me to start Oaka Books, where we are passionate about creating revision resources to help struggling readers. I am so proud of my daughter for going on to achieve 2 As, 3Bs and a C. She was the student who progressed most in her year from mocks to exams, and this is down to the highly visual revision tools. Not too shabby for a Mini!

The reality is that this one teacher, who dared to poke a stick at the lioness in me, was absolutely right. But hindsight is a wonderful thing. Although we constantly hear the drum being banged for keeping SEN children in mainstream schools, the reality is that there is no 'one size fits all' solution and there never will be.

In researching this article, it became very apparent that for our SEN children, no matter how slight or extreme their differences, the best choice of school is very much a personal one. As parents, we need to make ourselves aware of our child's issues early on, not sweep them under the carpet. We need to take our responsibility as parents on board and challenge what we are being told by the 'experts'. We need to arm ourselves with knowledge and understanding of what options are available and what help we can get for our child as early as possible. We need to understand and embrace that our children are different. We need to be prepared to be their lion or lioness. We need to not be afraid of a label.

Hawks may be great at flying but they don't swim. Our penguin is swimming brilliantly thank you very much.

Bambi Gardiner is the founder of Oaka Books, publisher of Topic Packs for struggling readers and visual learners in KS1, KS2 and KS3. For more information please visit www.oakabooks.co.uk.

Positive behavioural support: putting pupils at the centre of teaching

Karla Hancock, of The Together Trust, describes a new method designed to unlock learning potential

A special school in Cheadle has been using new ways of working with young people with autism to change the lives of pupils and their families.

Unlike traditional methods used by many schools, the staff at Inscape House School are using Positive Behavioural Support (PBS) to encourage and reinforce more acceptable behaviours rather than drawing attention to negative actions – an approach which means that eventually positive behaviour becomes more common amongst the young people with complex needs.

The school is run by North West charity, the Together Trust, where PBS is being used across the organisation to put people at the centre of all that they do.

Along with providing specialist education, the charity offers care and support to young people and adults with behavioural problems, learning difficulties, physical disabilities and autism spectrum conditions.

Niall Wilson, Clinical & Specialist Educational Psychologist for the Together Trust, explains, "PBS is a total environment approach to supporting people with complex developmental needs which reduces behaviours that challenge by increasing the quality of life for the individual.

"Where the environment is accurately designed to proactively meet the unique core needs of a person, then typically we see a marked reduction in behaviours that challenge."

Joe, a 16-year-old pupil at Inscape House School who has autism, ADHD (Attention Deficit Hyperactivity Disorder) and a hearing impairment had previously struggled at the school.

Education Assistants, Gary Hughes and Suzie Birchall, then worked to create a different timetable and ways of teaching which would suit Joe more, using PBS to unlock his potential.

Some Challenges Need Ambitious and Innovative Solutions!

Ruskin Mill Trust transforms lives for people with ASD including Asperger Syndrome, learning difficulties and differences, mental health issues and challenging behaviour

"Since being at Freeman College my mental health has improved enormously with less negative thoughts and anxiety issues" **Ed at Work Experience, above, has successfully gone onto higher education.**

re-imagining potential

Our young people learn and achieve through practical, real-life activities and accredited courses to progress onto greater independence, further education, training and employment.

Ruskin Mill Trust's *Practical Skills Therapeutic Education* draws on the understanding that developmental delay can be addressed by the intentional re-connection of hand, head and heart. An integrated programme of practical skills, contemporary apprenticeship and home-care, enables learners and residents to undertake their own journey to re-imagine their potential.

To find out more about our innovative, holistic and personalised curriculum for day and residential students, delivered by trained and expert staff, contact our nearest provision or visit our website: www.rmt.org

Ruskin Mill Trust draws its inspiration from the insights of Rudolf Steiner, John Ruskin and William Morris. Charity No: 1137167

"I was beginning to have doubts about him staying at the school as Joe was becoming stressed and anxious but the turnaround over the past 5-6 weeks has been fantastic, Joe still has anxiety but he is able to talk about it before it gets too much. The change in timetable has been brilliant and I have been more involved in his education."
Joe's mother

Joe had been showing signs of aggressive behaviour and became verbally abusive, but really he was very anxious about many social situations. He often covered up his anxiety by talking in a street style manner which he had learnt from music and acted out a role that kept people at a distance.

Education Assistant, Suzie, said, "We rewrote Joe's class timetable to be 90% outside of the formal school building, an environment which he was struggling to succeed in. It was clear that as soon as he left the formal environment, his behaviour changed. Sticking to the ASDAN curriculum we started to focus on areas where Joe struggled.

"Often Joe would only do things if he felt like he was going to get something back, so Gary and I took him to Manchester one day to distribute food to the homeless to show him that selfless acts can be rewarding, which he really enjoyed."

There were a number of factors involved in this new way of working which focussed on Joe and what was best for his way of learning including flexibility, rewards, transparency and honesty and complete communication with all involved.

Gary added, "I learn things about myself every day from Joe about new ways I can help him and ensure that he feels valued in society."

By listening to Joe's likes and dislikes, Gary and Suzie can focus on the best ways for him to learn. Joe will soon be going to a studio to record music of his own. By focussing on Joe's interests, the group will be using this opportunity to do something that Joe loves to help him learn new skills.

Joe's mum, Bev, has been involved in the change in learning every step of the way, getting daily feedback of how he is getting on at school has allowed Bev to develop a continuity between school and home, allowing Joe to develop further.

Bev said, "I was beginning to have doubts about him staying at the school as Joe was becoming stressed and anxious but the turnaround over the past 5-6 weeks has been fantastic, Joe still has anxiety but he is able to talk about it before it gets too much.

"The change in timetable has been brilliant and I have been more involved in his education. Suzie and Gary have changed things and made it easier to relate to Joe's education. I can't thank these people enough, I finally feel like Joe is going in a good direction – feeling liked for Joe was a big thing and now he feels like he is especially in their group.

"When things were starting to look like they were going wrong for Joe, Gary and Suzie have done what's necessary to gain Joe's trust to work with us."

Inscape House School recognises the importance of sharing good practice to support all their students. Joe's Mum and his support team completed a presentation to the staff within the school demonstrating the level of success and achievement Joe has made. It also showed the difference this approach can have for all students within the school using Joe's journey provides a real life example.

Joe added, "I like that we go to different places and I stay away from situations that are negative. I like Gary and Suzie because we all get on and it's fun."

For more information on Inscape House School and the work of the Together Trust, visit www.togethertrust.org.uk or call 0161 283 4750.

The silent struggle

Ronda Fogel, founder of The Moat School, on why children with minor learning difficulties often face the biggest challenges

We all dream of our children excelling at school – in maths, English, sport or music, but for some children, just getting through the normal school day can be challenging enough.

With a bit of luck, a pupil's school will flag up any learning difficulties around Year 2 and suggest an assessment, although many children with specific learning difficulties (SpLD) can remain undiagnosed for much longer. Parents may have suspected their child was not keeping up even though his or her intelligence appeared 'normal' otherwise it could come as a bolt out of the blue. It is at this stage that parents usually wonder what they should be doing.

A good school will probably recommend an educational psychologist (EP) and this will be the next step to finding out what the difficulties are and how serious. You can access a good list of EPs through the BDA. An EP will assess the child by performing a series of tests designed to calculate verbal and non-verbal reasoning as well as general cognitive ability. Parents

will receive a report with the results of the administered tests and a recommendation on how to address the child's needs. The sort of difficulties identified by an educational psychologist cover a broad range from Dsylexia, Dyspraxia, Discalcula, Aspergers or ADHD/ADD (Attention Deficit Hyperactivity Disorder/Attention Deficit Disorder), all on the SpLD spectrum.

There are many independent schools that offer specialist teaching outside of the classroom, but for children with moderate to severe difficulties this minimal intervention is like 'papering over the cracks'. In many cases, there are children unable to cope in a mainstream school environment and who need something more specialist. For parents in the expat community this will be a particular concern, not only will their child have to cope with a completely new home environment and new friends, but also a new school. If confidence levels are low due to previous poor achievement, then this will add to the family's anxieties at an already stressful time.

Much of the difficult part of the transition can

be avoided by transferring a child to a school that specialises in the teaching of children who require more individual learning support. This is where the child will get a complete and individual programme of the help they need including occupational and speech and language therapy, as well as counselling where necessary, all incorporated into their school day.

Specialist schools like the Moat School in London provides children diagnosed with a SpLD the opportunity of receiving an academic education in a safe and supportive learning environment up to GCSE for children between the ages of 11 to 16 years. CReSTeD produces a useful handbook and their website gives a list of accredited schools.

It comes as no surprise to parents that their children often possess extraordinary talents and creativity and it is an important goal for these schools to identify and foster

this by providing additional courses in non-traditional subjects such as creative and performing arts, food technology, computer technology, art and design, media studies and design technology. Pupils will need individual timetables that address their needs and classes must be small with a high teacher/pupil ratio. Look for a school that offers an enrichment program that enhances the pupils' skills academically, emotionally and socially.

It is well known that progress of pupils at these type of holistic specialist schools are typically outstanding. This reinforces the belief that, given the opportunity and resources at the right age, despite their difficulties, these children can make meaningful improvements to the quality of their lives and their contributions to society.

Helping parents find their way through the minefield of special education is not easy, but follow these steps and you could put them on the right track:

1. Do some research, this will pay enormous dividends.
2. Get free advice from the numerous agencies there to help. In the UK this will be the British Dyslexia Association, CReSTeD, and the Helen Arkell centre.
3. Make sure there is an up to date assessment of the child's special needs.
4. Encourage research in possible schools in the country the families are relocating to.
5. Speak to professionals such as educational psychologists, therapists and specialist tutors.
6. Consider an educational consultant who will know and understand schools in the destination area of relocation and who will be able to follow a particular brief. Especially useful if there is no time for research.

There are many alternative therapies and treatments around, but it is the view of many professionals that repetitive and intensive teaching from qualified teachers experienced in the teaching of children with SpLD pays the best educational dividends. With proper diagnosis and tailored educational practises, children with SpLD can go on to achieve academically, reach their full potential and have successful careers and future lives.

The Moat School was established by the Constable Educational Trust, an incorporated charitable company limited by guarantee in 1998 and is London's first secondary day school for children with dyslexia and related specific learning difficulties.
For more information about The Moat School, see page 98

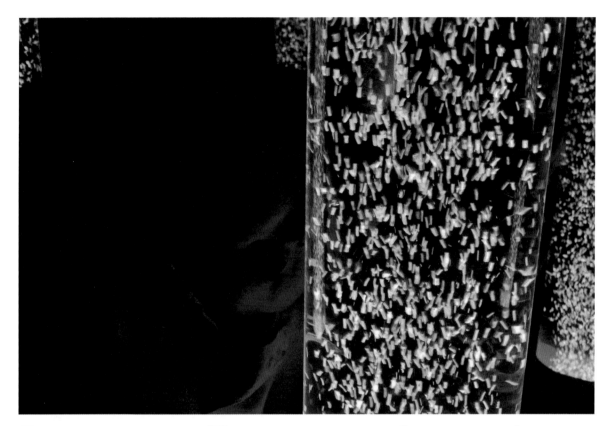

Does your multi-sensory environment follow the AAA principles?

Richard Hirstwood offers some thoughts for schools when considering a multi-sensory room

We've been thinking about the principles behind the design of a great multi-sensory room. Some designs I've seen are based on cost and/or standard company 'packages,' but the most successful designs are those based on the needs of the individuals who will use the space.

You need to consider – why do you need a sensory space? What is its function? What is the benefit for the learner, whatever their age? The beginning of this design process starts with the learner, not your new bit of technology! Here's where the 'AAA' principles of room design fit in – availability, appropriateness and achievability!

Availability

Your multi-sensory tools and equipment needs to be available when you need it – and to work first time. It's frustrating to reach a 'breakthrough' moment for it to be ruined when you can't find just the right tool or it doesn't work! Good storage and organisation is essential. Regular maintenance sessions to check your tools is perhaps not top of the excitement list – but they will save you time (no more disrupted sessions) and money (a stitch in time...) later on! Could this demonstrate a need for a multi-sensory room co-ordinator in school?

Appropriateness

Does your multi-sensory room really suit all of the learning styles and needs of all the pupils who use it? Is differentiation of the curriculum easy to achieve in your sensory room? As we know, some pupils/students need lots of sensory stimulation and others need just a single sensory experience. You may have a projector attached to your iPad projecting large images from Google Earth

Simplicity is often the best way forward – why have lots of complicated-to-use equipment (that no-one will) when you can have a few, easy to operate and effective multi-sensory tools which will be in continuous use?

for a geography lesson, but have you got the small tactile objects available for those kinaesthetic learners? Can you back project your images for the pupil with a visual impairment?

Achievability

Does the design of your multi-sensory room mean that it allows all practitioners to use the equipment without a vast technical knowledge? Is your sensory space a truly flexible, immersive space that can be changed in an instant? Simplicity is often the best way forward – why have lots of complicated-to-use equipment (that no-one will) when you can have a few, easy to operate and effective multi-sensory tools which will be in continuous use?

As well as simplicity, the key themes we promote at Hirstwood Training for successful multi-sensory room design are:

- creation of an exciting, innovative, multi-sensory studio/room, which may incorporate a more traditional environment.
- the development of a set of 'tools', which offer the practitioner an opportunity to engineer new learning experiences based on the learning styles of the pupils/students equipment which is easy to control and operate by the practitioner.
- a space which enables easy access to curriculum – at any level to establish a space to achieve simple control of sensory experiences – by pupils and staff alike.

So where else can a sensory room support the pupils/students that we work with?

Sensory approaches are essential to early stage literacy work to allow students to experience their environment, the people in their environments and the individual objects and artefacts that make up their world. For many students working at the levels of P1 to P3 we are working on providing stimulating experiences to develop awareness. We introduce consistent sensory experiences to develop some level of preferences, favourite activities to introduce making choices themselves, which will in turn necessitate some form of communication. This may be a regular expression when a favourite stimulus is presented or as complex as an eye point.

'Challenging behaviour' is a term all those working with pupils/students are familiar with. Everyone, at some point, will have asked the question "why do those we are trying to work with resort to such behaviour?" Everything we do is based on, stimulated by or is in response to our sensory experiences. Our senses provide us with the door to the world we live in. Using a controlled sensory room experiences help us to develop the ability of the pupils/students to take control of sensory stimuli – and to communicate acceptance or rejection of the sensory experience being offered.

Working with pupils/students with autism is often a challenge, but with massive rewards! Developing a Positive Sensory Plan for your pupils/students will be another 'tool' in your sensory 'toolkit,' which will enable staff to work successfully with the individual with autism. We need a strong sensory programme to use what we know about the individual's sensory preferences to create environments where the individual will be able to thrive, learn and relax. What individualised learning environment supports the pupil/student to be at their most successful for interacting and learning?

Hirstwood Training offer 'bespoke' in-house training packages and external courses to develop a great skill base in multi-sensory practice. For more information, visit www.hirstwood.com

How special schools found benefit in our books – to our surprise!

Publisher Ann Scott explains how a series of picture books have gained popularity in SEN classrooms

In 2009, I first published two of Patrick George's picture books. Patrick and I set up our publishing company to promote what we saw as a gap in the market for Patrick's quirky style of illustration, creating more challenging visuals than you'd typically expect to find in children's books. We initially took orders from school libraries and art galleries and were nominated for an illustration award. Since then, and with 18 books published, we have reached out internationally and seen the books' popularity grow, particularly for our 'acetate' series. Shortly after publication a teacher friend pointed out their validity in the classroom, but what I hadn't anticipated was a slow but steady growth in interest in the SEN community.

One of the disadvantages of being a tiny publishing house is that you cannot match the marketing resources and budgets of the bigger publishers to make an immediate impact upon publication. However, on the flip-side this allows us to reintroduce our backlist to new audiences over a longer period of time. Over the past six years we have received enough positive feedback from parents and teachers of children with learning difficulties to make us want to find out why. We decided to take a small space at last year's TES Special Education Needs Show. This was where I met Marilyn Tucknott (a consultant working with Local Authorities, schools, healthcare professionals and parents, and specialist in mental wellbeing in children), and Joanna Grace (a special educational needs and disabilities consultant and founder of The Sensory Project: **jo.element42.org**). Both were very enthusiastic about our books as were the teachers and parents who visited our stand and placed orders.

So why the attention? This was the question I too wanted to answer and, for the purposes of this article, I did some research. I interviewed an ASD SPD teacher, with ten years' experience teaching children with ASD

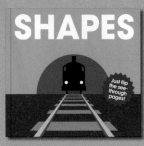

and speech and language difficulties, and an ASD SPD speech and language therapist. I also spent a day with Joanna Grace, author and lecturer of sensory stories and sensory coping strategies for children with ASD SPD and PMLD. All three have successfully used our books with their students.

I have thus learnt quite a lot in a short space of time: pictures are more effective than words; clear, contrasting images are great; concise text doesn't overburden the child or the reader and a clear message reinforces what is being taught; illustrations that are inclusive of all ages and abilities don't alienate; limited language input and a stimulating visual are good for discussion starters (with the more able students) and for eliciting language. I have learnt that repetition, consistency and clarity are all key to learning development.

The illustrations in all our books are bright, bold, uncluttered. The books are tactile and interactive (children love flipping the acetate back and forth, thus controlling the action) and the acetate page has the effect of 'magically' transforming the page underneath. This grabs their attention and is repeated throughout the book. While the books are designed for children, the imagery is not childish - which might alienate older children, and are therefore suitable from Early Years through to KS3.

A particularly popular book is 'Oh No!'. On the face of it, a frivolous book, it portrays a series of light-hearted accidents such as a ball being kicked through a window or a drink being spilt. The transparent page between each double-page spread, when turned from right to left, makes an accident happen. There are no words printed on the page but an exclamation of 'oh no!' is appropriate as each 'incident' occurs. This is repeated throughout the book with some situations more fanciful than others. Charlotte Wilson, speech and language therapist at the Stone Bay Special School in Broadstairs, uses this book on a daily basis with her ASD, SLD students. She pointed out that for children with limited communication, 'oh no!' is an extremely powerful thing to say. It can be used when something is not right, when someone needs help or feels vulnerable. It is an initial step on the journey to communication. The pictures are clean, the visual clues are very clear and the repetition reinforces the learning.

A KS3 teacher used 'Animal Rescue' with enormous success in her classroom. She gave me the following feedback: "My KS3 pupils with complex learning difficulties were completely absorbed by 'Animal Rescue'. Even those who rarely talk in class couldn't wait to talk about the pictures and ideas. They were motivated to write and draw their own afterwards". She went on to explain how difficult it can be to find the appropriate resources to teach more advanced topics

such as environmental issues without overburdening the children with complicated language. In the book, the animal on each spread is first seen in an unnatural situation: a tiger skin rug, for example, or an elephant in a circus, but by turning the acetate page, the child can 'rescue' the animal and put it back into the wild. As well as communicating a sophisticated message with ease, issues such as respect, empathy and the environment can be introduced. Again, there are no words in this book.

Joanna Grace of The Sensory Project has included 'Opposites' as part of her travelling resource pack. She says: "I travel with a Patrick George book in my luggage whenever I present a Sensory Stories training day in a special education setting. The clear layout and concise text lends itself beautifully to supporting the understanding of learners with additional needs. I highly recommend them."

Marilyn Tucknott, reviews our books on her website as follows:

"A delightful range of early years/Special Needs books with illustrations to delight the child and adult alike. A particular feature are the acetate pages that can be flipped between the right and left hand pages which are intended to amuse and provoke as children predict what will happen next. Great for storying and developing reasoning skills, particularly for those on the ASD spectrum." (**www.marilyntucknott.com**)

So where do we go from here? Well, we have four more acetate books in the pipeline for publication in 2017, which we hope will catch the attention of both mainstream and SEN teachers and I shall continue looking for other avenues to explore. If you are intrigued by our books please visit our website **patrickgeorge.com** for more information!

Choosing a special needs school

Educational psychologist and author Ruth Birnbaum offers practical advice on seeking effective education for children with special educational needs

No-one is prepared for having a special needs child and developmental difficulties know no boundaries. Parents are often in a quandary about whether a school is appropriate and suitable for their individual child and even whether they should travel the mainstream or special school route.

In writing my book, Choosing a School for a Child with Special Needs (2010), I hoped to demystify the process and empower parents to ask questions of schools when they visit, so that a more balanced view can be reached and an objective decision can be made. Parents need to work together with schools and other professionals to decide what their child needs and how their strengths can be realised in a school context. While parents live with their child every day and have much to offer, they also have to listen to advice. Weighing up what really matters is possible and choices can be made on the best evidence available.

Choosing a school is such an important decision that it cannot be left to chance.
Here are some helpful pointers:

1. Look at the primary area of need
The 2014 Code of Practice sets out four areas of special educational needs:
*   Communication and Interaction
*   Cognition and Learning
*   Social, Emotional and Mental Health
*   Sensory and Physical

2. Understand the Background
Understand the role of psychological assessment and draw up a list of schools which state they can meet the assessed need and then obtain the documents that will help you restrict your list to those schools that need to be visited.

3. Set up a Visit
Make sure a visit is set up with the right people; look at the general physical school environment, as well as the classroom environment. Make a record of the school visit. Look at the Local Offer in your Local Authority.

4. Look at Specific Provision/Intervention
Consider the type of provision in both mainstream and special schools. Probe and analyse what is available in reality and the professional support the child will receive.

What are the qualifications needed? What type of intervention could be available? Does the school offer help with Specific Learning Difficulties/Sensory Needs/ Autistic Provision; are different therapies available; eg Art Therapy; Music Therapy; Drama Therapy; Play Therapy or Psychotherapy. Does the school offer Counselling and Mentoring? Can the child access Speech and Language Therapy, Occupational Therapy and Physiotherapy?

5. Consider other important issues
Levels of Integration and Inclusion; Religious Beliefs; Co-Education; School Size; Small Classes; Transition; Equality and Discrimination. In all cases, there will be practical questions to ask.

6. Think about other School Models available
There can be a range of different school models to consider, depending on the need; such as mainstream, special units in mainstream, special schools, dual-placements, pupil referral units, residential schools, home education, hospital schools, studio schools and virtual schools.

7. Summarise your thoughts
Evaluate findings on a spreadsheet with your own comments and compare school visits. Trust your first impressions and feelings but be open to other views. Use websites, resources and organisations in the area you are researching. The Local Offer should help you understand

Parents need to work together with schools and other professionals to decide what their child needs and how their strengths can be realised in a school context. While parents live with their child every day and have much to offer, they also have to listen to advice. Weighing up what really matters is possible and choices can be made on the best evidence available.

what education, health and social care services can provide for your child.

Perhaps, a few selective questions from my book will offer some examples:

- A key question, when looking at special schools, is to determine whether all teachers share the specialism, or only some of them; eg if a child is placed in a specialist dyslexic school, will the child receive lessons in History and Geography at secondary level from specialist teachers in their subject area, who have also undertaken SpLD training? If not, one must consider whether the value of attending such a school outweighs a mainstream experience.
- What happens to the class work that the child misses when they are in the special unit? How do they catch up or will they be following the same curriculum in the unit? If the unit has a number of different aged children, are lessons taught across the age ranges in the unit or will children be taught separately?
- Is the Occupational Therapist trained or certified in the use of any standardised diagnostic tools that are used to assess children who might have sensory processing disorder?
- How often is the Speech and Language Therapist in school? Is the focus on individual or group therapy? Does the SaLT spend time in the classroom? How much time?
- In a special school, how many staff have a recognised qualification in the area of need? eg ASD.
- Is there any special equipment already being used in specific subjects; such as Food Technology, Maths, Science, PE, etc?
- In the classroom, note the class sizes and the physical space. Is there room for additional resources; eg a work station or wheelchair? Are the goals and objectives of the lessons clearly set out in a visual format and do the children understand them? Are different strategies used for children who cannot access the usual format?

By making a decision, based on factual evidence where possible, a parent should be able to accept or reject a school on the basis of impartial evaluation.

Using the combination of this guidebook and Choosing a School for a Child with Special Needs, parents will be able to make an informed choice and act as advocates for their child who may not be able to speak for themselves. The new Code of Practice (2014) now extends education for young adults up to 25 years and there is a clearer focus on the views, wishes and feelings of the child and young person and on their role in decision making, so take them on visits and ensure their views are heard whenever possible. It is important that the young person remains at the centre of decision making so that the best possible educational outcomes are achieved.

Ruth Birnbaum is an Educational Psychologist in independent practice with over 30 years' experience in education. She is a registered psychologist with the Health and Care Professions Council. She visits schools across the UK to consider provision and advise parents and consultants on which schools are most appropriate for which children. Website: www.ruthbirnbaum.co.uk

School groups

Cavendish Education

14 Waterloo Place,
London SW1Y 4AR
Tel: +44 (0)20 3696 5300
Email: info@cavendisheducation.com
Website: www.cavendisheducation.com

CAVENDISH
EDUCATION

Bredon School

Pull Court, Bushley, Tewkesbury, Gloucestershire GL20 6AH
Tel: 01684 293156
Fax: 01684 298008
Email: enquiries@bredonschool.co.uk
Website: www.bredonschool.org
FOR MORE INFORMATION SEE PAGE 52

Finches School

Levy Building, 80 East End Road, Finchley, London N3 2SY
Tel: +44 (0)208 343 0105
Email: info@finchesschool.co.uk
Website: www.finchesschool.co.uk
FOR MORE INFORMATION SEE PAGE 62

Gretton School

Manor Farm Road, Girton, Cambridge, Cambridgeshire CB3 0RX
Tel: 01223 277438
Email: info@grettonschool.com
Website: www.grettonschool.com
FOR MORE INFORMATION SEE PAGE 56

The Independent School (TIS)

23-31 Beavor Lane, Ravenscourt Park,
Hammersmith, London W6 9AR
Tel: 0203 086 8687
Email: admin@tis-london.org
Website: www.tis-london.org
FOR MORE INFORMATION SEE PAGE 97

Hesley Group

**Central Services, Hesley Hall
Tickhill, Doncaster, DH11 9NH
Tel: +44 (0)1302 866906
Fax: +44 (0)1302 861661
Email: enquiries@hesleygroup.co.uk
Website: www.hesleygroup.co.uk**

Fullerton House College

Tickhill Square, Denaby, Doncaster, South Yorkshire DN12 4AR

Tel: 01709 861663

Fax: 01709 869635

Email: enquiries@hesleygroup.co.uk

Website: www.hesleygroup.co.uk

FOR MORE INFORMATION SEE PAGE 72

Fullerton House School

Tickill Square, Denaby, Doncaster, South Yorkshire DN12 4AR

Tel: 01709 861663

Fax: 01709 869635

Email: enquiries@hesleygroup.co.uk

Website: www.fullertonhouseschool.co.uk

FOR MORE INFORMATION SEE PAGE 71

Wilsic Hall College

Wadworth, Doncaster, South Yorkshire DN11 9AG

Tel: 01302 856382

Email: enquiries@hesleygroup.co.uk

Website: www.hesleygroup.co.uk

FOR MORE INFORMATION SEE PAGE 72

Wilsic Hall School

Wadworth, Doncaster, South Yorkshire DN11 9AG

Tel: 01302 856382

Fax: 01302 853608

Email: enquiries@hesleygroup.co.uk

Website: www.wilsichallschool.co.uk

FOR MORE INFORMATION SEE PAGE 74

I CAN

31 Angel Gate (Gate 5), Goswell Road
London EC1V 2PT
Tel: 0845 225 4073
Fax: 0845 225 4072
Email: info@ican.org.uk
Website: www.ican.org.uk

helps children
communicate
REGISTERED CHARITY 210031

I CAN'S Dawn House School

Helmsley Road, Rainworth, Mansfield,
Nottinghamshire NG21 0DQ
Tel: 01623 795361
Fax: 01623 491173
Email: dawnhouse@ican.notts.sch.uk
Website: www.dawnhouseschool.org.uk
FOR MORE INFORMATION SEE PAGE 90

I CAN's Meath School

Brox Road, Ottershaw, Surrey KT16 0LF
Tel: 01932 872302
Fax: 01932 875180
Email: meath@meath-ican.org.uk
Website: www.meathschool.org.uk
FOR MORE INFORMATION SEE PAGE 99

Kisimul

**The Old Vicarage, 61 High Street,
Swinderby, Lincoln, Lincolnshire LN6 9LU
Tel: 01522 868279
Email: enquiries@kisimul.co.uk
Website: www.kisimul.co.uk**

Cruckton Hall

Cruckton, Shrewsbury, Shropshire SY5 8PR
Tel: 01743 860206
Fax: 01743 860941
Email: jo.burdon@cruckton.com
Website: www.cruckton.com
FOR MORE INFORMATION SEE PAGE 68

Kisimul School

The Old Vicarage, 61 High Street, Swinderby,
Lincoln, Lincolnshire LN6 9LU
Tel: 01522 868279
Fax: 01522 866000
Email: admissions@kisimul.co.uk
Website: www.kisimul.co.uk
FOR MORE INFORMATION SEE PAGE 88

Kisimul School – Woodstock House

Woodstock Lane North, Long Ditton, Surbiton, Surrey KT6 5HN
Tel: 020 8335 2570
Fax: 020 8335 2571
Email: admissions@kisimul.co.uk
Website: www.kisimul.co.uk
FOR MORE INFORMATION SEE PAGE 100

Kisimul Upper School

Acacia Hall, Shortwood Lane, Friesthorpe,
Lincoln, Lincolnshire LN3 5AL
Tel: 01673 880022
Fax: 01673 880021
Website: www.kisimul.co.uk

The National Autistic Society

393 City Road
London EC1V 1NG
Tel: +44 (0)20 7833 2299
Fax: +44 (0)20 7833 9666
Email: nas@nas.org.uk
Website: www.nas.org.uk

NAS Anderson School

Rookery Lane, Pilning, Bristol, BS35 4JN
Tel: 01454 632532
Fax: 01454 634907
Email: nasanderson@nas.org.uk
Website: www.andersonschool.org.uk
FOR MORE INFORMATION SEE PAGE 53

NAS Church Lawton School

Cherry Tree Avenue, Church Lawton, Stoke-
on-Trent, Staffordshire ST7 3EL
Tel: 01270 877601
Email: churchlawton@nas.org.uk
Website: www.churchlawtonschool.org.uk
FOR MORE INFORMATION SEE PAGE 70

NAS Daldorch House School

Sorn Road, Catrine, East Ayrshire KA5 6NA
Tel: 01290 551666
Fax: 01290 553399
Email: daldorch@nas.org.uk
Website: www.daldorchhouseschool.org.uk
FOR MORE INFORMATION SEE PAGE 75

NAS Daldorch Satellite School

St Leonards, East Kilbride, South Lanarkshire G74
Tel: 01355 246242
Fax: 01290 553399
Email: daldorch@nas.org.uk
Website: www.daldorchhouseschool.org.uk

NAS Helen Allison School

Longfield Road, Meopham, Kent DA13 0EW
Tel: 01474 814878
Fax: 01474 812033
Email: helen.allison@nas.org.uk
Website: www.helenallisonschool.org.uk
FOR MORE INFORMATION SEE PAGE 66

NAS Radlett Lodge School

Harper Lane, Radlett, Hertfordshire WD7 9HW
Tel: 01923 854922
Fax: 01923 859922
Email: radlett.lodge@nas.org.uk
Website: www.radlettlodgeschool.org.uk
FOR MORE INFORMATION SEE PAGE 57

NAS Robert Ogden School

Clayton Lane, Thurnscoe, Rotherham, South Yorkshire S63 0BG

Tel: 01709 874443

Fax: 01709 870701

Email: robert.ogden@nas.org.uk

Website: www.robertogdenschool.org.uk

FOR MORE INFORMATION SEE PAGE 73

NAS Sybil Elgar School

Havelock Road, Southall, Middlesex UB2 4NY

Tel: 020 8813 9168

Fax: 020 8571 7332

Email: sybil.elgar@nas.org.uk

Website: www.sybilelgarschool.org.uk

FOR MORE INFORMATION SEE PAGE 59

NAS Thames Valley School

Conwy Close, Tilehurst, Reading, Berkshire RG30 4BZ

Tel: 0118 9424 750

Email: thames.valley@nas.org.uk

Website: www.thamesvalleyschool.org.uk

FOR MORE INFORMATION SEE PAGE 67

RNIB

**105 Judd Street
London WC1H 9NE
Tel: 0303 123 9999
Website: www.rnib.org.uk**

supporting blind and
partially sighted people

RNIB College Loughborough

Radmoor Road, Loughborough, Leicestershire LE11 3BS
Tel: 01509 611077
Fax: 01509 232013
Email: enquiries@rnibcollege.ac.uk
Website: www.rnibcollege.ac.uk
FOR MORE INFORMATION SEE PAGE 116

RNIB Pears Centre for Specialist Learning

Wheelwright Lane, Ash Green, Coventry, West Midlands CV7 9RA
Tel: 024 7636 9500
Fax: 024 7636 9501
Email: pearscentre@rnib.org.uk
Website: www.rnib.org.uk/pearscentre
FOR MORE INFORMATION SEE PAGE 127

RNIB Sunshine House School and Residence

33 Dene Road, Northwood, Middlesex HA6 2DD
Tel: 01923 822538
Fax: 01923 826227
Email: sunshinehouse@rnib.org.uk
Website: www.rnib.org.uk/sunshinehouse
FOR MORE INFORMATION SEE PAGE 118

Ruskin Mill Trust

**Old Bristol Road, Nailsworth
Stroud GL6 0LA
Tel: 01453 837 521
Email: enquiries@rmt.org
Website: www.rmt.org**

Argent College

New Standard Works, 43-47 Vittoria Street,
Birmingham, West Midlands B1 3PE
Tel: 01384 399400
Fax: 01384 399401
Email: enquiries@argent.rmt.org
Website: www.rmt.org
FOR MORE INFORMATION SEE PAGE 106

Brantwood Specialist School

1 Kenwood Bank, Nether Edge, Sheffield, South Yorkshire S7 1NU
Tel: 0114 258 9062
Email: enquiries@brantwood.rmt.org
Website: www.rmt.org
FOR MORE INFORMATION SEE PAGE 84

Clervaux

Clow Beck Centre, Jolby Lane, Croft-on-Tees, North Yorkshire DL2 2TF
Tel: 01325 729860
Email: info@clervaux.org.uk
Website: www.clervaux.org.uk

Coleg Plas Dwbl

Mynachlog-ddu, Clunderwen, Pembrokeshire SA66 7SE
Tel: 01994 419420
Email: enquiries@plasdwbl.rmt.org
Website: www.rmt.org
FOR MORE INFORMATION SEE PAGE 114

Freeman College

Sterling Works, 88 Arundel Street, Sheffield,
South Yorkshire S1 2NG
Tel: 0114 252 5940
Fax: 0114 252 5996
Email: enquiries@fmc.rmt.org
Website: www.rmt.org
FOR MORE INFORMATION SEE PAGE 109

Glasshouse College

Wollaston Road, Amblecote, Stourbridge, West Midlands DY8 4HF
Tel: 01384 399400
Fax: 01384 399401
Email: enquiries@ghc.rmt.org
Website: www.rmt.org
FOR MORE INFORMATION SEE PAGE 107

Ruskin Mill College

The Fisheries, Horsley, Gloucestershire GL6 0PL
Tel: 01453 837500
Fax: 01453 837506
Email: enquiries@rmc.rmt.org
Website: www.rmt.org
FOR MORE INFORMATION SEE PAGE 86

TCES Group

**Park House, 8 Lombard Road, Wimbledon
London SW19 3TZ
Tel: +44 (0)20 8543 7878
Fax: +44 (0)20 8543 7877
Email: referrals@tces.org.uk
Website: www.tces.org.uk**

East London Independent School (ELIS)

Upper School, Ibex House, 1C Maryland Park, Stratford, London, E15 1HB

Tel: 020 8221 1247

Lower School, Stratford Marsh, Welfare Road, London, E15 4HT

Tel: 020 8555 6737

Custom House, 41 Varley Road, Newham, London, E16 3NR

Tel: 020 7540 9120

Email: referrals@tces.org.uk

Website: www.tces.org.uk

FOR MORE INFORMATION SEE PAGE 80

Essex Fresh Start Independent School (EFS)

Church Street, Witham, Essex CM8 2JL

Tel: 01376 780088

1 Wellesley Road, Clacton, Essex CO15 3PP

Tel: 01255 225204

Willowfield House, Tendring Road, Harlow, Essex CM18 6SE

Tel: 01279 410620

Email: referrals@tces.org.uk

Website: www.tces.org.uk

FOR MORE INFORMATION SEE PAGE 78

North West London Independent School (NWLIS)

85 Old Oak Common Lane, Acton, London W3 7DD

Tel: 020 8749 5403

Email: referrals@tces.org.uk

Website: www.tces.org.uk

FOR MORE INFORMATION SEE PAGE 81

WESC Foundation

**Topsham Road, Countess Wear
Exeter, Devon EX2 6HA
Tel: 01392 454200
Fax: 01392 428048
Email: info@wescfoundation.ac.uk
Website: www.wescfoundation.ac.uk**

The Specialist Centre for Visual Impairment

WESC Foundation – The Specialist College for Visual Impairment

Countess Wear, Exeter, Devon EX2 6HA

Tel: 01392 454200

Fax: 01392 428048

Email: info@wescfoundation.ac.uk

Website: www.wescfoundation.ac.uk

FOR MORE INFORMATION SEE PAGE 125

WESC Foundation – The Specialist School for Visual Impairment

Countess Wear, Exeter, Devon EX2 6HA

Tel: 01392 454200

Fax: 01392 428048

Email: info@wescfoundation.ac.uk

Website: www.wescfoundation.ac.uk

FOR MORE INFORMATION SEE PAGE 126

School profiles

Schools and colleges specialising in social interaction difficulties (Autism, ASD & ASP)

Bredon School

Pull Court, Bushley, Tewkesbury,
Gloucestershire GL20 6AH
Tel: 01684 293156
Fax: 01684 298008
Email: enquiries@bredonschool.co.uk

Website: www.bredonschool.org
Headmaster: Mr David Ward MA
School type:
Coeducational Boarding & Day
Age range of pupils: 3–18

'Come Alive and Thrive'

Bredon School in Gloucestershire is a mainstream independent school welcoming boys and girls of all abilities, from 3-18 years old.

Offering day and boarding facilities, the School is situated in an idyllic 84-acre rural estate and holds CReSTeD 'Dyslexia Specialist Provision' status; an accolade which recognises our outstanding provision for children with dyslexia and dyspraxia – including on-site Speech and Language Therapy, access to assistive technologies, and very highly-qualified, specialist staff.

We pride ourselves on our small class sizes and our warm and nurturing atmosphere.

All pupils, with or without additional learning needs, benefit from multi-sensory teaching methods, including access to a School Farm, where the students learn basic animal care and help to feed the livestock and maintain the estate. Agriculture, as a subject, can even be studied from Year 10 onwards providing a sound academic path for those interested in land based studies.

Younger pupils have the opportunity to learn outdoors also, on the School Farm, and in the dedicated woodland classroom learning basic bush craft skills and understanding more about nature and habitats.

A wide-ranging curriculum includes both traditional academic choices and practical vocational courses, leading to qualifications at GCSE, A Level and nationally accredited vocational levels including BTEC.

All pupils are able to make progress in the friendly and supportive environment, and students grow in self-confidence and self-belief; enabling them to achieve impressive academic results.

An array of extra-curricular activities, including overnight outdoor education trips, a Combined Cadet Force, the Duke of Edinburgh award scheme, clay and air rifle shooting, climbing, canoeing and traditional team sports, means every pupil can find their area in which to shine.

If you'd like to visit us to know more, please do get in touch.

Anderson School

NAS Anderson School
Rookery Lane, Pilning, Bristol BS35 4JN
T: 01454 632 532 | F: 01454 634 907
E: nasanderson@nas.org.uk | www.andersonschool.org.uk

Principal: Kim McConnell

School type: mixed independent school with day, weekly and year-round residential placements for children and young people on the autism spectrum

Catchment area: national
Age range: 7-19
Capacity: 24
Established: 2012

Anderson School is a small, nurturing specialist school providing tailored care for autistic students in a 24-hour learning environment. Our location on the outskirts of Bristol means students can enjoy being in a tranquil, spacious setting while engaging with the lively atmosphere and variety of enrichment activities offered by the city.

Working collaboratively with parents, local schools and services we provide pioneering autism education and care.

Our on-site facilities include therapy spaces, a student kitchen, library and music room as well as a secure garden, our own allotment and a play area with basketball courts. All our classrooms are set up with low sensory autism-friendly needs in mind.

Everything we do, in fact, is done with each autistic student we teach in mind. We follow the principles of **MyProgress®**, The National Autistic Society's overall strategy for working with children on the autism spectrum.

Drawing on many different approaches, we ensure that every student in our school has an education tailored entirely to them from start to finish.

Our provision is innovative; some students will remain with the school for the whole of their education, while others are supported to move back into mainstream education.

Placements are funded by your local authority.

The National Autistic Society

"It's a long time since I've seen my daughter smiling when coming home from school. She does now."

New parent, Anderson School

Prior's Court School

(Founded 1999)

Hermitage, Thatcham, West Berkshire
RG18 9NU
Tel: 01635 247202
Fax: 01635 247203
Email: mail@priorscourt.org.uk
Website: www.priorscourt.org.uk
Director of Education and Learning:
Sue Piper

Appointed: September 2011
School type: Independent Special School
Age range of pupils: 5–19
No. of pupils enrolled as at 01/01/2016: 59
Boys: 47 **Girls:** 12 **Sixth Form:** 26
No. of boarders: 55
Fees per annum as at 01/01/2016:
on application

Prior's Court School is an independent special school for students with autism aged from 5 to 19 years. The School offers day, weekly and termly places with 38, 44 and 52 week options. Students are on the autistic spectrum have moderate to severe learning difficulties and complex needs. They may have additional associated diagnoses. Some students exhibit challenging behaviours. All are working within P scales to lower national curriculum levels.

The School was opened in 1999. It is managed by Prior's Court Foundation, a registered, non-profit making charity which also runs a young adult provision and specialist autism training centre on the same site.

As an autism-specific school, Prior's Court is able to focus on meeting the special needs of its students in the most effective and consistent way to support their learning:

• A meaningful and functional curricu-

lum with individualised learning programmes used throughout the waking day is built around students' interests and skills.
• The environment is adapted to meet students' needs – it is highly structured, calm, low-arousal, safe and secure with space and physical exercise a key feature providing opportunities to learn, exercise, socialise and relax onsite. Set in over 50 acres, facilities include a stable yard and paddocks for

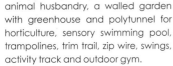

By combining autism expertise and best practice with a person-centred approach, the school aims to achieve the highest level of progress for each individual enabling them to self-manage behaviour, communicate, manage transitions, develop independent living and social skills, choice-making and advocacy and progress to building vocational skills and undertaking work-placement activities. Skills once taught and practiced onsite can then be generalised and undertaken successfully offsite. Frequent access to the nearby villages, towns and community facilities enable students to work towards inclusion as far as possible.

"The management team leads a culture in which staff strive to understand every child and young person and develop the best means for providing for their needs. Each resident therefore benefits from a personal package of care and many make significant progress as a result." Ofsted for Care Inspection 2015

"I am absolutely delighted with the progress being achieved. Teaching and house staff are superb, broadening our child's skills and experience. Improvement in speech and language has been very impressive, as has the ability to self-manage behaviour."

Parent at Prior's Court School

animal husbandry, a walled garden with greenhouse and polytunnel for horticulture, sensory swimming pool, trampolines, trim trail, zip wire, swings, activity track and outdoor gym.

- The school's strong focus on training means that staff are experienced in using a range of methodologies and strategies to support each individual's needs and development in all settings throughout the waking day.
- A large onsite multi-disciplinary team including Occupational therapy, Speech & Language therapy, Clinical Psychologists and Nurses as well as dedicated horticulture, animal hus-

bandry, swimming, activities and ICT instructors provide support throughout the school day and in residential settings as well as out in the community where appropriate. All staff (education, residential, night, multi-disciplinary and therapeutic as well as a team of flexible workers who provide cover for absence or injury) are trained from induction onwards ensuring the highest levels of knowledge and expertise. These dedicated staff work closely with families and professionals to create a co-ordinated and consistent programme of education and care whose success is recognised worldwide.

Gretton School

Gretton
School

Manor Farm Road, Girton, Cambridge,
Cambridgeshire CB3 0RX
Tel: 01223 277438
Email: info@grettonschool.com
Website: www.grettonschool.com

Head Teacher: Ms Tina Harris
School type:
Coeducational Day & Boarding
Age range of pupils: 5–19

'Where autism makes sense'

Gretton School is a small and friendly school, welcoming boys and girls from 5-19 years old, as weekly boarders or as day students.

Every student at Gretton has a diagnosis of autism or Asperger's syndrome and every student is different. As autism specialists, we provide a calm and purposeful atmosphere where consistent daily routines and staffing helps to keep anxiety at a minimum and ensures that our students feel safe and confident in their surroundings.

We have a high staff to student ratio and classes are small and personal. We know each of our students really well and employ the best strategies to support them in their everyday school life.

This positive approach, and the value we place on treating each of our students as an individual, means that whatever a child's past experience of education, they will enjoy learning with us.

The curriculum is enriched with real-life opportunities to learn with trips, visits and outings. And learning is extended beyond the National Curriculum through weekly

'Special Interests' sessions. We place an emphasis on the development of life and social skills too, meaning we are able to bring out the best in all our students, and provide them with opportunities to flourish.

Our highly-trained academic, care and therapy teams work together to help students feel supported and encouraged, and so when they are ready to leave us, they do so making the most of all the opportunities ahead of them.

We hope you will visit us to get to know us better.

Radlett Lodge School

NAS Radlett Lodge School
Harper Lane, Radlett, Herts WD7 9HW
T: 01923 854 922 | F: 01923 859 922
E: radlett.lodge@nas.org.uk | www.radlettlodgeschool.org.uk

Principal: Jo Galloway

School type: mixed independent school with day, weekly and termly residential placements for children and young people on the autism spectrum

Catchment area: national
Age range: 4-19
Capacity: 55
Established: 1974

At Radlett Lodge School, we are driven by our determination to provide the highest quality education to the children in our care and do the best we can for their families. Ofsted have recognised our pursuit for excellence by rating us Outstanding for both education and care for a number of years.

We get to know every pupil well, ensuring every element of their school life is personalised to them. We use the principles of The National Autistic Society's **MyProgress®** strategy to help your child to learn, develop and prepare for adult life to the very best of their ability – and we celebrate every achievement.

Radlett Lodge School caters for early years, primary, secondary and post-16 pupils. The school and our residential lodge are located on the same site, which supports a close-knit environment and easy transitions. Strong ties with our local community mean pupils apply their learning to the outside world, particularly when approaching adulthood in our post-16 unit. We also offer flexi-boarding to our pupils, and outreach support to external pupils.

In a structured and supportive learning environment and with the help of friendly, approachable staff, students develop social relationships and receive a broad and balanced education.

Placements are funded by your local authority.

The National Autistic Society

"Staff go above and beyond to reduce the barriers faced by children and young people. They work tirelessly to promote consistency, continuous care and stability."

Ofsted, 2016

Ofsted Outstanding 2013

Blossom Lower School and Upper House

Blossom Lower School, Christopher Place, London NW1 1JF
Tel: 020 7383 3834
Website: www.blossomchristopherplace.co.uk
Email: admincp@blossomhouseschool.co.uk

Blossom House School, Station Road Motspur Park, New Malden, London KT3 6JJ
Tel: 020 8946 7348
Fax: 020 8944 5848
Email: admin@blossomhouseschool.co.uk
Website: www.blossomhouseschool.co.uk

Principal: Joanna Burgess DipCST, MRCSLT, DipRSA, SpLD, PGCE, HPC
School type: Coeducational Day
Age range of pupils: 3–19
No. of pupils enrolled as at 01/01/2016: 214
Fees per annum:
On request

Blossom House School is a specialist school for children with speech, language and communication difficulties. Founded in 1989, the school continues to expand and we now have two separate sites, one in Central London and one in South West London.

Blossom Lower School, Christopher Place has pupils aged from 3-7 years, who will be moving up through the school to year 6. Blossom House, Motspur Park has pupils from 3-19 years and includes a post 16 'college links' provision.

Although many of our pupils have some associated difficulties such as fine motor problems or poor organisational skills, all are within the broadly average range of cognitive ability. We provide an integrated, holistic programme of learning and therapies in a caring and highly supportive environment, so that each child has the opportunity to fulfil his or her potential.

Blossom House has a unique atmosphere created by a dedicated, highly competent and wonderfully caring staff. Specific strengths are acknowledged and weaknesses supported, so that each child 'blossoms' and has the opportunity to fulfil his or her potential, whether that is remaining with us or returning to mainstream education.

The key aims of the school:

- To provide a communication centred environment where children with a range of speech, language and communication difficulties are supported in all areas of their learning.
- To provide a highly skilled team of specialist therapists, teachers and support staff who can work with the children in a range of learning environments.
- To provide support and advice for parents.

Sybil Elgar School

NAS Sybil Elgar School
Havelock Road, Southall, Middlesex, UB2 4NY
T: 020 8813 9168 | F: 020 8571 7332
E: sybil.elgar@nas.org.uk | www.sybilelgarschool.org.uk

Principal: Chloe Phillips

School type: mixed independent school with day, weekly term-time and 52-week residential placements for children and young people on the autism spectrum

Catchment area: national
Age range: 4-19
Capacity: 90
Established: 1965

As the first autism-specific residential school in the world, Sybil Elgar School is a pioneer in autism education. Having paved the way in autism education for over 50 years, we have the knowledge and experience to apply the tailored education and care each young person who learns with us will receive.

We have a highly specialised curriculum, and our dedicated staff closely support the learning of each pupil in communication, social, behavioural, emotional, sensory, physical and self-help skills. Our extensive performing arts curriculum complements this. Students can discover a new passion or enhance learning in other subjects through music, art and dance. They might play the drums in the school band and even perform at an international arts festival.

Our welcoming environment extends across our three school sites, which include a post-16 department and our year-round children's home, where all staff work together to ensure the safety, wellbeing and progress of all our students.

We follow the principles of The National Autistic Society's **MyProgress®** strategy to ensure each of our students has an experience with us that is truly personalised to them, their strengths, weaknesses and ambitions. And we recognise every achievement, helping our students value their successes and celebrate them.

Placements are funded by your local authority.

The National Autistic Society

"A school that looks good, has fine facilities and offers excellent care, understanding and education, centred round a core of communication and connectivity with people who understand the world of autism. 'It tastes good here,' said one child, and in the world of autism we doubt there is a higher accolade." **Good Schools Guide 2013**

Rainbow School
for Children and Young People with Autism (Part of BeyondAutism)

Rainb●wSchool
Part of Bey●ndAutism

(Founded 2000)
48 North Side, Wandsworth Common,
London, SW18 2SL

Tel: 020 3031 9700
Email:
rainbowschool@beyondautism.org.uk
Website: www.rainbowschool.org.uk
Head of Lower School: Bennie Lesch
Head of Upper School: David Anthony

School type: Independent Special School
Age range of pupils: 4–19 (Early Years/
Primary, Secondary and 6th Form)
Fees per annum as at 01/01/2016:
Available on request

Rainbow School is an Approved Independent Special School for children and young people aged 4-19 years with autism and related communication disorders. We provide an education that ensures each child and young person grows in confidence and autonomy. We make sure they feel safe and secure in their school environment and are empowered to lead fuller lives.

Rainbow School is run by BeyondAutism, a registered non-profit making charity. Based across two sites in Wandsworth, South West London, pupils are currently placed with us by 16 Local Authorities across London. The school offers 1:1 and small group teaching from 9.15am to 3.15pm at the primary school and from 9.30am to 3.30pm at the secondary school for 40 weeks per year.

Daily timetables include individual teaching sessions where pupils work on personalised speech and language, self-help, numeracy and literacy programmes, focussed social skills, independent living skills sessions and small group sessions, with 1:1 support as appropriate. Other activities include outdoor playtime, art, music, PE, yoga, and swimming. Depending on age, pupils may also participate in horse-riding and skiing. Regular community trips, library trips and other school and class outings are planned each term. All pupils participate in whole school weekly assemblies and there are further drama opportunities throughout the year including a Song Club and a full length musical production at Christmas.

How we teach

We offer a structured and individualised programme of intensive intervention using the principles of Applied Behaviour Analysis (ABA) and B F Skinner's Analysis of Verbal Behaviour (VB). ABA/VB targets the communication, academic, social and practical skills of children and young people. With these skills, they're better equipped to take advantage of educational and social opportunities in their communities, and to achieve their academic potential. We apply ABA/VB in teaching core skills from speech and language, self-care and motor skills right through to reading and writing. Teaching with ABA/VB also reduces challenging behaviour, which allows pupils to access a broad, balanced and specialised curriculum in line with the National Curriculum.

We use the framework of the National Curriculum and Early Years Foundation Stage Curriculum. Our teaching team includes the Speech and Language Therapist and the Occupational Therapist and our pupils' communication and sensory needs are developed daily across the curriculum.

Working together

We work closely with our pupils' families and offer parents information, training sessions, support and access to resources. The school meets regularly with parents to discuss progress, agree behaviour plans and support parents to manage their son or daughter's behaviour at home. A daily communication book also serves to strengthen the link between home and school.

Admissions

To be eligible for admission to Rainbow School pupils must:

- Be between 4 and 19 years of age.
- Have a diagnosis of autism or a related communication disorder.
- Have an EHCP or Statement of Special Educational Needs or be in the process of gaining one.
- Have agreement (in writing) from the LA to fund the placement.
- Have the appropriate age, skills and behaviour for the vacancy that exists.
- Live within a feasible commuting distance.

About BeyondAutism

BeyondAutism was founded by parents of children with autism in 2000 to empower people with autism to lead fuller lives through positive educational experiences, training for the people who work with them and support for their families and carers. We know that a specialist education is vital

and we understand that autism doesn't stop after leaving school. That's why we have developed a range of outreach, training and consultancy services which utilise the knowledge and experience of our highly skilled staff to deliver life changing outcomes for children and young people with severe autism in other schools and at home.

School Outreach

We can bring our support to you. BeyondAutism staff can make regular visits to other schools who are keen to develop their support for children with severe autism. We can deliver programmes to specific members of staff or train large groups in INSET training.

We also make individual visits to children in various settings. These can last throughout a child's time in school and beyond. In some cases, children may

need help and support at home.

Training

We offer training programmes to parents and carers so they can assist in their child's education. They cover topics such as:

- Managing challenging behaviour
- Teaching communication skills
- Eating Difficulties
- Sleeping difficulties
- Toilet training

BeyondAutism also runs day courses for professionals, including specialist ABA training. Our training team is made up of highly qualified BCBA Consultants and Teachers who are experts in the field of ABA and VB.

For further information on our outreach and training services please email info@beyondautism.org.uk or call 020 3031 9705. We are able to tailor all of our services to suit individual needs.

Finches School

FINCHES
SCHOOL

Levy Building, 80 East End Road, Finchley, London N3 2SY
Tel: +44 (0)208 343 0105
Email: info@finchesschool.co.uk

Website: www.finchesschool.co.uk
Headteacher: Mr Adrian Mahon
School type: Coeducational Day
Age range of pupils: 7–18

'Think differently'

Finches School is a small, warm and friendly school in North London for students with autism. We welcome boys and girls from 7 to 18 years old. Our campus is safe and secure, providing a comfortable and welcoming learning environment. With extensive grounds, we can provide access to the great outdoors onsite.

Every student at Finches has a diagnosis of autism or Asperger's syndrome and we understand how autism affects students, but we never label them: every student with autism is different.

When students come to us they often feel isolated and confused. They may think they'll never be able to cope with school. We reach out to them, taking our time and offering as much attention and understanding as they need. Gradually, they begin to see that they can enjoy learning and as they experience success, they understand that they have great potential.

We use a mix of teaching styles and recognised autism-specific approaches so that students feel calm, safe and confident in their learning.

At Finches, every student follows their own timetable, designed to meet their needs, interests and abilities. Our curriculum is broad and balanced, offering a range of academic subjects from the National Curriculum, extended learning outside the classroom, and vocational and work-based learning.

We offer a range of on-site therapy, appropriate to the individual needs, including speech and language therapy, occupational therapy, art, music and drama therapy. Our highly qualified, specialist staff team also includes an Educational Psychologist.

Students are encouraged to interact socially and to be an active part of the wider community. Building a solid basis of life skills is a key part of our approach.

If you'd like to know more, or would like to visit us, please do get in touch.

Riverston School

Riverston

(Founded 1926)

63-69 Eltham Road, Lee Green, London, SE12 8UF
Tel: 020 8318 4327
Fax: 020 8297 0514
Email: office@riverstonschool.co.uk
Website: www.riverstonschool.co.uk
Headmistress: Mrs S E Salathiel

School type: Independent Day School
Age range of pupils: 9 months–19 years
No. of pupils enrolled as at 01/01/2016: 215
Boys: 155 **Girls:** 60
Fees per annum as at 01/01/2016:
On application

Making the significant move away from mixed games to separate boys and girls was always going to have its own challenges. To insist that all sixty boys take part in rugby could be argued that the school was stuck in the dark ages, building up towards the traditional masters versus boys end-of-term match, something akin to Monty Python's Meaning of Life, as under-nourished boys are trampled into the mud, beaten into submission and left feeling broken and worthless. Readers will be delighted to hear that the reality was very different!

Breaking down the myths associated with rugby, teaching new skills, developing teamwork and instilling a passion for the game were at the heart of the staff delivering this bold new move. Given the additional needs of many of its pupils, was this a risk too great? Teaching the skills necessary to ensure safe play was essential, resulting in a contact tackle not even being considered in the first six weeks. In order to change attitudes, teaching had to be gentle, understanding and safe, whilst also exciting those who wanted to learn the tough stuff.

Despite the understandable concerns, progress has been steady, not only in the development of skills but in the changing outlook of so many of the children. Those who had previously thought of rugby as a treacherous game played by fearsome Welshmen have come to realise the poetic majesty of the game. Boys who had become accustomed to kicking the familiar round ball around the playground have swapped the traditional pig skin for the more beautifully-shaped oval of a Gilbert size 5. Six Nations fever, whilst not quite reaching Barclays Premiership levels, has taken a hold of our pupils and understanding is higher when we celebrate the efforts of every team on Super Saturday.

Whilst there remain some who do not like the game, opinions have been shifted and every one of those sixty has learned new skills and made inroads into the development of a sport that they had previously believed to be inaccessible.

As the strains of Bach's Toccata and Fugue drift across the playing fields, boys will be grateful to have been learning rugby today and not in the Python-inspired days of the 1970s.

The Holmewood School

The Holmewood School
London

(Founded 2010)

88 Woodside Park Road, London, N12 8SH
Tel: 020 8920 0660
Fax: 020 8445 9678
Email: enquiries@thsl.org.uk
Website: www.thsl.org.uk

Headteacher: Lisa Camilleri
School type: Coeducational Day
Age range of pupils: 7–19
Fees per annum as at 01/01/2016:
On request

The Holmewood School London caters for students with high functioning autism and Asperger's syndrome who may also have associated speech, language and social communication difficulties.

Our school offers a successful alternative to mainstream education. Class sizes are small with a high staffing ratio. Comprehensive programmes are planned and delivered by specialist staff to meet each child's needs.

Teaching ensures all learning styles are met and addresses our kinaesthetic, visual, auditory and multi-sensory learners so that maximum individual potential is achieved. A structured and tailored environment ensures students are supported and challenged in their learning and development.

The curriculum is designed using the National Curriculum up to GCSE. For those students more vocationally oriented we support a range of courses that develop interests, strengths and skills providing valuable career related experiences and qualifications.

Mainstream experiences with our link schools support teaching and learning. The Holmewood School is part of a global network of schools within the Dwight family of schools offering an international perspective.

Learning is enhanced through our social skills and life skills curriculum. Planning and reflection time built into each day emphasises the importance that we place on students' personal development. Our whole school focus on celebrating student achievement is reflected in our approach to positive behaviour and rewards.

Therapies and practice are cutting edge and delivered by our multidisciplinary team. Comprehensive programmes are designed and integrated within our curriculum. The school benefits from a unique sensory integration clinic.

Located in North London the school has access to the rich cultural and educational experiences that the capital provides. Excellent local transport services makes learning in the community accessible for our students. Educational visits and offsite activities are incorporated within our programmes so students can consolidate and generalise the learning that takes place in the classroom.

If you think The Holmewood School would be the right place for your child, please contact our admissions team on 020 8920 0660 or enquiries@thsl.org.uk.

West Kirby School and College

WEST KIRBY SCHOOL AND COLLEGE

(Founded 1881)

Meols Drive, West Kirby, Wirral, Merseyside
CH48 5DH
Tel: 0151 632 3201
Fax: 0151 632 0621
Website: www.wkrs.co.uk
Principal: Mr Iain Sim

School type: Coeducational Day &
Weekly Boarding
Age range of pupils: 5–19
No. of pupils enrolled as at 01/01/2016: 89
Fees per annum as at 01/01/2016:
On application

Changing Children's Lives, Building Better Futures

WKS is a Non Maintained Special School for pupils with a wide range of social, communication difficulties often linked with conditions such as Autism and additional complex learning needs.

The school prides itself on being able to help some very complex young people access the National Curriculum and work towards appropriate accreditation in all subjects including Open Awards, GCSEs and AS Levels. Staff are highly skilled in the understanding of the social and emotional needs of the pupils, as well as being able to personalise the academic work accordingly and provide high levels of support.

We believe the views of the pupils are paramount to success and the school offers opportunities for this through school council and individual discussion. Every pupil has an 'individual support plan' which they and staff contribute to. Differentiation and small classes with high levels of adult support have proven successful. We have excellent facilities, particularly for sport, music and other practical subjects.

The school has its own Therapy and Additional Support Services department which provides additional 'therapy' and educational support often necessary for the pupils to access the National Curriculum and fulfil their academic and personal potential. This department consists of: a Clinical Psychologist, SALT, Occupational, Behaviour and Reading support specialists/teams, a Learning Mentor and a Family Liaison Officer.

We have the option of day provision or flexible boarding provision on a termly basis, with pupils staying between one and four nights per week. Residential units include two houses in the locality and all are maintained to a high standard, with individual bedrooms and common areas for dining and recreation. We also offer 52 week options through a fostering support service.

We hold the International School Award and have forged strong links with schools in South Africa and China and an orphanage in India, where exchange visits have taken place over a number of years now, real experiences which most of our pupils would have considered beyond their reach.

Post 16 is based in an off-site annex. Each pupil has a study programme tailored to their individual needs, involving academic study, work related skills and further development of social and communication skills. The college is embarking on an ambitious building project to incorporate new facilities for courses in motor vehicles, construction and salon trades.

Staff are experienced at assisting pupils in the difficult process of transition from school to adult life. All pupils benefit from the strong pastoral ideal that runs through the school, to be aware both of themselves as individuals and within a group, increasing their respect for others, their self-esteem, emotional stability and self-regulation.

Our staff are well qualified, experienced professionals. Recruitment procedures are rigorous with exemplary professional development available for all, as evidenced through our Investors in People Silver award. Continued professional development is supported through an extensive range or partnerships with local schools, universities and other agencies.

The collective vision and drive, results in pupil's exceptional progress (Ofsted 2016 judged outstanding).

WKRS is a registered charity no. 207790.

Helen Allison School

NAS Helen Allison School
Longfield Road, Meopham, Kent DA13 0EW
T: 01474 814 878 | F: 01474 812 033
E: helen.allison@nas.org.uk | www.helenallisonschool.org.uk

Principal: Susan Conway

School type: mixed independent school with day and weekly term-time residential placements for children and young people on the autism spectrum

Catchment area: London, South East and East Anglia
Age range: 5-19
Capacity: 77
Established: 1968

At Helen Allison School we deliver a high quality, relevant and enjoyable education and use our expert knowledge of autism to find the best possible way for each student to learn to the best of their ability.

Following the principles of **MyProgress®**, The National Autistic Society's strategy for working with autistic students, we ensure they get the best start in life with an education tailored to them.

We believe in preparing our students for fulfilling adult lives, so our main curriculum is enhanced with a wide range of social activities and community-based learning.

Through our hub, older students partake in work experience, pursue formal qualifications or might even organise a football tournament with other local schools and colleges.

Rated 'Outstanding' for education, and 'Outstanding' for care under the new Ofsted criteria,

we are always pushing for excellence for our students, thinking creatively to adapt to their needs and aspirations.

As one of only a few schools with our own therapeutic team, your child will develop not only academically but foster strong social and communication skills so they can thrive alongside their peers.

Placements are funded by your local authority.

The National Autistic Society

"Through highly personalised support, students with complex needs resulting from autism make excellent progress."
Ofsted, 2015

Thames Valley School

NAS Thames Valley School
Conwy Close, Tilehurst, Reading, Berkshire RG30 4BZ
T: 0118 9424 750 | E: thames.valley@nas.org.uk
www.thamesvalleyschool.org.uk

Principal: Gary Simm

School type: mixed free school with day placements for children and young people on the autism spectrum

Catchment area: Reading, Berkshire and neighbouring local authorities
Age range: 5-16
Capacity: 50
Established: 2013

Thames Valley School is a high-achieving specialist school for children and young people on the autism spectrum. Our school has been purpose-built for us, meaning we could design it to be perfectly suitable for our students. We have calming pods where children can relax or read, independent rooms attached to every classroom, outdoor play areas for all ages and a state-of-the-art innovation hub, opening up opportunities for pupils to take on digital projects such as coding, social media and cyber security.

We have high expectations of our pupils, and through delivering the National Curriculum at all key stages, we expect the majority of our students to attain at least the same levels as their mainstream school peers. At age 16 our pupils take national qualifications, and our aim is for most to achieve five GCSEs at A to C or equivalent vocational qualifications.

Small classes, committed and experienced specialist teachers and a wonderful learning environment all contribute to making our school an exceptional place to be. We follow the principles of The National Autistic Society's **MyProgress®** strategy to give your child an education specific to them, so they can flourish.

Placements are funded by your local authority.

The National Autistic Society

"I think it's absolutely brilliant. It makes me feel happy knowing he's there: in mainstream I was always on edge."
Parent

Cruckton Hall
(part of the Kisimul Group)

(Founded 1981)

Cruckton, Shrewsbury, Shropshire SY5 8PR

Tel: 01743 860206

Fax: 01743 860941

Email: jo.burdon@cruckton.com

Website: www.cruckton.com

Head Teacher: Jo Burdon

School type: Boys' Residential

Age range of boys: 8–19

No. of pupils enrolled as at 01/01/2015: 80

Fees per annum as at 01/01/2015:

On application

Curriculum

For those pupils who are resident at Cruckton we provide a 24-hour approach. All boys at the school have an Individual Education Plan (IEP), an Individual Pupil Case Plan (IPCP), Health Plan and, from Year 9, a Transition Plan. The respective parts of these plans are discussed between the professionals at the school, the boy and his parents/carers. The school has a full range of specialist rooms to support all National Curriculum subjects. All pupils are prepared for GCSE examinations in English, maths and science. They can also choose to study for GCSE in history, geography, French, German, computer studies, art, home economics, music and design technology. In addition, we also offer ECDL, AQA Skills for Life Awards and a variety of Entry Level certificates.

Assessment and entry requirements

Entry is by interview and assessment. The multi-disciplinary team of professionals will carry out a baseline assessment on each student within the first six weeks of admission. Cruckton has a visiting consultant child and adolescent psychiatrist who visits the boys on a regular basis, as required. The multi-disciplinary team consists of a consultant educational psychologist, systemic psychotherapist, two speech and language therapists and an occupational therapist. They provide a variety of interventions and therapies to minimise the anxieties and maximise the development of our young people.

The wider environment

The hall is a listed building surrounded by ten acres of gardens that include woods, playing fields and play areas.

The site is located within a friendly rural community, in beautiful countryside, four miles from the market town of Shropshire. The Welsh Marches provide a stunning backdrop and a rich source of options for our regular trips and adventures. The town of Shrewsbury offers excellent amenities for the school and is now linked to the motorway network of the West Midlands, greatly improving access.

Residential environment and activities

The structure that provides success for the boys in the classroom environment is replicated in the residential area and boys have a range of recreational activities provided, which reflect their needs and encourage their specialisms. Many boys choose an active leisure programme. This can be provided by activities such as skateboarding, swimming, football and cricket, and in the summer the Adventure Camp encourages team work amongst our student group through activities such as orienteering, mountain biking, rock climbing and raft building. For the more studious, a range of activities from *Warhammer* to chess club are provided. Links with local clubs and societies include the local stables, local army cadet force, Jiu Jitsu, Laser Quest, bowling alley, street dancing and swimming are well-established. The links between the IEP targets are shared across the 24-hour approach, both in the home and education setting, with a huge variety of enrichment activities and programmes. Forest school, Lego therapy, robotics, stable management, mountain biking, Blists Hill Museum and work experience are all part of the enrichment programme.

Behaviour management

It is accepted that many boys come to Cruckton Hall School exhibiting both

difficult and challenging behaviour. The structural consistency of various approaches, combined with a consistent nurturing environment, has a track record of providing the boys with the ability to be accepted within social settings of their choice. The basis of the approach is to foster the following qualities: self-respect, respect for other students, respect for staff, courtesy, politeness, patience, tolerance and motivation to work. Boys will be encouraged and supported to meet as many of these expectations as is possible. Attendance at school is a non-negotiable requirement of a boy's placement at Cruckton Hall. School uniform is always worn.

Aims and philosophy

Cruckton Hall School aims to provide a warm, structured and caring learning environment in which each boy feels safe and secure, can succeed, is treated as an individual and is able to develop his skills and talents in order that he leaves school as an active participant in, and a positive contributor to, society.

"Cruckton Hall School's new curriculum has had a positive impact on improving and accelerating pupils' progress. Pupils develop the skills they need to learn effectively in lessons and to be prepared for the next stage of their education, training or employment."

"There is provision for pupils' spiritual, moral, social and cultural development by a particular emphasis on improved social skills, respect and tolerance and a better understanding of right and wrong." *Ofsted 2016*

Church Lawton School

NAS Church Lawton School, Cherry Tree Avenue, Church Lawton, Stoke-on-Trent, Staffordshire ST7 3EL
T: 01270 877 601 | E: church.lawton@nas.org.uk
www.churchlawtonschool.org.uk

Principal: Paul Scales

School type: mixed free school with day placements for children and young people on the autism spectrum

Catchment area: Cheshire East and surrounding authorities, including Stoke-on-Trent and Staffordshire

Age range: 4-19
Capacity: 60
Established: 2015

Church Lawton School is The National Autistic Society's second free school providing tailored care for local autistic students. We opened in 2015 and offer a highly specialised learning environment to our pupils on our brand new, purpose-built site.

With large open classrooms and an average class size of six, our pupils have the space and attention they need to reach their full potential.

Combined with well-resourced classrooms for music, art, design and technology, science and food technology, our building is equipped for academic excellence, and so we aim for our pupils to perform well in GCSEs, A Levels and more.

We follow the principles of **MyProgress®**, The National Autistic Society's overall strategy for working with children on the autism spectrum. Systematic and thorough, we work with you and your child to create the best education for them.

We equip pupils with the skills and knowledge to support them as they move into further study and adult life. They get to know their community and, as they move through the school, have the opportunity to take part in work experience or study in local colleges and universities. Above all we are dedicated to making sure every one of our pupils is given the tools they need to thrive.

Placements are funded by your local authority.

The National Autistic Society

"I have never come across a school that is as kind, caring and understanding about its pupils."

A visiting parent

Fullerton House School

(Founded 1990)

Tickill Square, Denaby, Doncaster, South Yorkshire DN12 4AR

Tel: 01709 861663
Fax: 01709 869635
Email: enquiries@hesleygroup.co.uk
Website: www.fullertonhouseschool.co.uk
General Manager: Michael Cavan
Appointed: 2015
Head of Education: Michael Walsh

School type: Independent Specialist Residential School
Age range of pupils: 8–19
No. of pupils enrolled as at 01/01/2016:
Capacity: 36
Fees per annum as at 01/01/2016:
Available on request

A specialist residential school offering flexible education and care, which can include day and respite provision, for up to 52-weeks-per-year for people aged 8-19, all of whom have complex needs including behaviour that may challenge and a learning disability, often in association with autism.

Fullerton House School is situated in the heart of the village of Denaby Main, near Doncaster. Its central location provides easy access by road, rail or air. Our mission is to enhance the lives of the young people entrusted to us by focusing on their specific needs, capabilities and aspirations.

Education: Each person has a carefully designed Individual Learning Plan based on their specific needs in line with the National Curriculum, which supports their positive progress in a range of areas.

Extended learning: During evenings, weekends and school holidays a wide range of extra-curricular activities are on offer to ensure that people are fully engaged with stimulating and meaningful experiences both on and off-site.

Professional services: A dedicated on-site team including carers, teachers, tutors, communication, behaviour and occupational therapy , psychology and other specialists ensure that people have ready access to the services they require.

High-quality accommodation: Single person and small group occupancy of high-quality accommodation is provided at Fullerton House School. Each person has their own bedroom, the majority of which have en-suite bathrooms. We also have a range of on-site facilities to complement and enrich the lives of those who come to live and learn with us.

Keeping in contact: We understand that while we may offer a very positive option for the person, we may not be on your doorstep. Keeping in touch with loved ones is essential. Everyone has a plan to support optimum contact with family/carers and friends whether this be by phone, letter, email or Skype.

Independent Specialist Colleges

(Founded 2013)

Fullerton House College

Tickhill Square, Denaby, Doncaster, South Yorkshire DN12 4AR

Tel: 01709 861663

Fax: 01709 869635

Wilsic Hall College

Wadworth, Doncaster, South Yorkshire DN11 9AG

Tel: 01302 856382

Fax: 01302 853608

Email: enquiries@hesleygroup.co.uk

Website: www.hesleygroup.co.uk

Head: Richard Webster

Appointed: 2016

School type: Independent Specialist Residential College

Age range of pupils: 18–25

No. of pupils enrolled as at 01/01/2016:

Fullerton House College Capacity: 12

Wilsic Hall College Capacity: 9

Fees per annum as at 01/01/2016:

On request

Specialist residential colleges offering flexible education care and support for up to 52 weeks per year for young people aged 18-25, who have complex needs including behaviour that may challenge and a learning disability, often in association with autism.

At Wilsic Hall College, everyone lives within a beautiful rural setting with ready community access and at Fullerton House College in the heart of the community, in an urban setting with many local facilities including a sports centre, restaurants and shops.

Mission

Our Independent Specialist Colleges (ISCs) support young people with their transition into adult life by focusing on their specific needs, capabilities and aspirations.

Education: Everybody has a highly personalised programme of learning, equipping them with skills they will need for adult life.

Extended learning: During evenings, weekends and college holidays a wide range of extra-curricular activities are on offer to ensure people are fully engaged with stimulating experiences both on and off site providing further, meaningful learning opportunities.

Professional services: A dedicated multi-disciplinary therapeutic team including college tutors, college support workers, consultant clinical psychologist, consultant psychiatrist, applied behaviour analysts, speech and language therapists, occupational therapists, registered manager, care and support staff work together to support each individual's progress.

High quality accommodation: College accommodation includes individualised bedrooms, quality living spaces that promote independence and progressive skills development assisted by the appropriate use of specialist/adaptive technology. We also have a range of on-site and off-site facilities that offer progressive learning opportunities for young people with a range of needs and wishes.

Keeping in contact: We work to develop relationships between staff and families that are strong, positive and mutually respectful. People are supported to be in contact with their friends and family; we welcome visits to the colleges at any time. Everyone has a plan that will include the best means for them to maintain this contact whether by 'phone, letter, email or Skype.

Robert Ogden School

NAS Robert Ogden School
Clayton Lane, Thurnscoe, South Yorkshire S63 0BG
T: 01709 874 443 | F: 01709 807 701
E: robert.ogden@nas.org.uk | www.robertogdenschool.org.uk

Principal: Lorraine Dormand

School type: mixed independent school with day, weekly term-time and 52-week residential placements for children and young people on the autism spectrum

Catchment area: national
Age range: 5-19
Capacity: 127
Established: 1976

One of the largest schools in the UK for autistic children and young people, Robert Ogden School offers an environment where students can feel safe, supported and encouraged to achieve beyond their expectations. Following the principles of **MyProgress®**, The National Autistic Society's strategy for working with your child, we create a tailor-made experience for each student so they reach their full potential.

We are autism experts, with a specialist team dedicated to providing the highest quality care and education to our students. Our Inclusive Learning Hub is run by a highly skilled group of staff who ensure pupils with particularly complex needs, requiring a non-directive approach, get the individualised curriculum and attention they need to thrive alongside their peers.

With autism-friendly buildings and facilities, your child will comfortably settle into school life. We even have a pottery room, several sensory and soft play rooms, a purpose-built primary unit and a teaching flat for independent living skills. Our students have every opportunity to develop the skills they will need for adult life, which is why we have a student-run café and shop, an award-winning fudge making enterprise project and a partnership with local charity shops. We give our students the help they need to make the best of their strengths and build upon them.

Placements are funded by your local authority.

The National Autistic Society

"You have achieved what many others could not… I am so grateful for Robert Ogden, no wonder so many parents are fighting for a place, it truly is a magnificent school with magnificent staff."

Sarah, parent

Wilsic Hall School

(Founded 1996)
Wadworth, Doncaster, South Yorkshire
DN11 9AG

Tel: 01302 856382
Fax: 01302 853608
Email: enquiries@hesleygroup.co.uk
Website: www.wilsichallschool.co.uk
Head: Geoff Turner
Appointed: 2008

School type: Independent Specialist Residential School
Age range of pupils: 11–19
No. of pupils enrolled as at 01/01/2016:
Capacity: 31
Fees per annum as at 01/01/2016:
Available on request

A specialist residential school offering flexible education and care, which can include day and respite provision, for up to 52-weeks-per-year for people aged 11-19, all of whom have complex needs including behaviour that may challenge and a learning disability, often in association with autism.

Wilsic Hall School is situated in its own 14-acre site approximately five miles south of Doncaster. Its central location provides easy access by road, rail or air. Our mission is to enhance the lives of the people entrusted to us by focusing on their specific needs, capabilities and aspirations.

Education: Each person has a carefully designed Individual Education Plan based on their specific needs in line with the National Curriculum, which supports their positive progress in a range of areas.

Extended learning: During evenings, weekends and school holidays a wide range of extra-curricular activities are on offer to ensure that people are fully engaged with stimulating and meaningful experiences both on and off-site.

Professional services: A dedicated team including carers, teachers, tutors, behaviour, communication and occupational therapy, psychology and other specialists ensure that each person has ready access to the services they require.

High-quality accommodation: Single person and small group occupancy of high-quality accommodation is provided at Wilsic Hall School. Each person has their own bedroom, the majority of which have en-suite bathrooms. We also have a range of on-site facilities to complement and enrich the lives of those who come to live and learn with us.

Keeping in contact: We understand that while we may offer a very positive option for the person, we may not be on your doorstep. Keeping in touch with loved ones is essential. Everyone has a plan to support optimum contact with family/carers and friends whether this be by phone, letter, email or Skype.

Daldorch House School

NAS Daldorch House School
Sorn Road, Catrine, East Ayrshire, Scotland KA5 6NA
T: 01290 551 666 | F: 01290 553 399
E: daldorch@nas.org.uk | www.daldorchhouseschool.org.uk

Principal: Bernadette Casey

School type: mixed independent school with day, weekly, termly and 52-week residential placements for children and young people on the autism spectrum

Catchment area: national
Age range: 8-21
Capacity: 64
Established: 1998

At Daldorch House School we work compassionately with each of our pupils, while challenging them to achieve to the best of their ability. Our 11 acre site is in a beautiful rural setting, while being only an hour from the bustle of Glasgow city centre.

Our classrooms are designed to suit the needs of all our pupils, and each lesson is arranged according to those learning in it.

Developing communication, social and life skills is at the core of our 24-hour curriculum at Daldorch, and we enrich each pupil's learning by capitalising on their interests and expanding their understanding of the world.

We also have a satellite school in East Kilbride, offering a year-round residential provision for families living in the South Lanarkshire local authority area, meaning your child can live and learn close to home in an area they know well.

Our curriculum is relevant, engaging and designed to develop each child's independence as they mature, our focus on lifelong learning strengthening as they approach adult life. With a blended approach to learning through The National Autistic Society's **MyProgress®** strategy, your child will have an education at Daldorch that is entirely personalised to them.

Placements are funded by your local authority.

The National Autistic Society

"The school has excellent systems for identifying the strengths of young people and the difficulties they face."
Education Scotland

Schools and colleges specialising in emotional, behavioural and/or social difficulties (EBSD)

Essex Fresh Start Independent School (EFS)

Essex Fresh Start
Independent School

(Founded 2007)

Church Street, Witham, Essex CM8 2JL
Tel: 01376 780088
1 Wellesley Road, Clacton, Essex CO15 3PP
Tel: 01255 225204
Willowfield House, Tendring Road, Harlow,
Essex CM18 6SE
Tel: 01279 410620

Email: referrals@tces.org.uk
Website: www.tces.org.uk
Schools' Proprietor: Thomas Keaney
Appointed: 2007
Head Teacher: Cheryl Rutter
School type: Coeducational Day
Age range of pupils: 7–18

Essex Fresh Start (EFS) is a TCES Group school, providing LA funded day school education for pupils aged 7-18 years whose social, emotional and mental health needs or Autism Spectrum Condition has made it difficult for them to achieve success in a mainstream school. Our pupils often have additional undiagnosed learning or sensory needs and speech, language and communication needs which create a complex set of barriers that must be addressed before they can settle into education.

Pupils attending EFS often require highly personalised learning programmes, focusing on developing their independent study skills. In addition, our Post-16 programmes of study specialise in developing independence, preparation for adult life and life after school.

We know that it is only when pupils enjoy their school that they make real progress. We offer a structured routine in a safe, comfortable environment, which encourages mutual respect and tolerance.

We nurture each child's ambitions by accrediting them with as many achievements as possible to help them make positive choices for their future careers. As a result, 80% of our leavers happily go straight into work, education or training.

In addition to counselling, nurture groups and art and drama therapy, we offer speech and language intervention from our own Speech and Language Therapists, plus clinical assessments for our more hard-to-reach pupils whose needs may need further assessment.

Pupils who need this bespoke intervention are supported through referral to a Clinical Psychologist and a Paediatrician at Consultant level (a service we retain).

A parallel service to our schools, Create Service, offers therapeutic education, delivered through a case co-ordination model, to pupils who present (or are at) significant risk to themselves or others and cannot be educated in a school setting.

At EFS, 'Every Child Really Matters'. We delight in seeing our pupils make progress, gain qualifications and achieve skills they never before thought possible.

To find out more about the school and its facilities please come and visit us! In the first instance please contact us on referrals@tces.org.uk or 020 8543 7878.

Kingsdown Secondary School

112 Orchard Road, Sanderstead,
Croydon, Surrey CR2 9LQ
Tel: 020 8657 1200
Fax: 020 3252 2088
Website: www.kingsdownsse.com

Headteacher: Ms Carole Nicholson
School type: Coeducational Boarding
Age range of pupils: 11–16
No. of pupils enrolled as at 01/01/2016: 12

We are a very small school for boys with extreme SEBD. All of our pupils have typically experienced a number of exclusions from mainstream, PRU and Special School settings and require a highly structured and personalised approach within a very small group setting in order to experience educational success.

Under the old SEN Code of Practice our boys' primary need is identified as SEBD and they have a range of diagnoses including ADHD, ASD, ODD, anxiety and conduct disorders. The majority also have a degree of Learning Difficulty (typically dyslexia and global delay) and/or communication difficulties. In the proposed new Code of Practice we anticipate that all of our boys will have Education, Health and Care Plans and that their primary need will fall into the social, emotional and mental health category of need.

All of our pupils are extremely complex and we pride ourselves on:

- Promoting the best possible achievement for pupils referred to us – we do not lose focus on the importance of educational attainment for promoting long term positive outcomes for children and young people.
- Working very closely with parents and carers to support them to support their sons/wards.
- Liaising and working with all the agencies and professionals involved with the young person including CAMHS, Social Care, Youth Offending Services and Youth Support Services. We have a full time Head of Welfare who ensures that coordination between the school and other agencies is tight.

We aim to re-engage young people in the learning process, to encourage and enable them to aspire to becoming independent and ethical citizens who are economically independent and who recognise the values of work and progression as well as functioning as productive members of society with an understanding of right and wrong.

East London Independent School (ELIS)

East London
Independent School

Upper School, Ibex House, 1C Maryland Park, Stratford, London, E15 1HB
Tel: 020 8221 1247
Lower School, Stratford Marsh, Welfare Road, London, E15 4HT
Tel: 020 8555 6737
Custom House, 41 Varley Road, Newham, London, E16 3NR

Tel: 020 7540 9120
Email: referrals@tces.org.uk
Website: www.tces.org.uk
Schools' Proprietor: Thomas Keaney
Acting Head Teacher: Simon Cartwright
School type: Coeducational Day
Age range of pupils: 7–18

East London Independent School (ELIS) is A TCES Group school, providing LA funded day school education for pupils aged 7-18 years whose social, emotional or mental health needs or Autism Spectrum Condition has made it difficult for them to achieve success in a mainstream school. Pupils will often have additional undiagnosed learning or sensory needs and speech, language and communication needs which create a complex set of barriers to learning that must be addressed before the pupil can settle into education.

The school is situated across three sites: Upper School, Lower School and Custom House – ELIS' stand-alone dedicated provision for pupils with an Autism Spectrum Condition whose primary autism needs may be part of a complex array of co-morbid diagnoses.

Pupils attending ELIS often require highly personalised learning programmes and can remain for Post-16 programmes of study; specialising in developing independence, preparation for adult life and life after school (including study at college or preparation for the world of work).

Running as a parallel service to ELIS, TCES Group's Create Service offers therapeutic education, delivered through a case co-ordination model, to pupils who present (or are at) significant risk to themselves or others, meaning they cannot be educated in the school environment.

Our pupils are provided with the opportunities and support necessary to develop their self-esteem, interpersonal and social skills as well as making positive behaviour choices both in and out of school. We firmly believe our pupils will become successful members of society through the knowledge, values and thinking skills learned in the classroom.

Many of our pupils have experienced difficulties, trauma and rejection in their previous school life. We offer the stability that is a necessary pre-requisite for reflecting on their experience and gaining insight, emotional literacy, resilience and empathy with others so their future can be brighter and happier.

To find out more about the school and its facilities please come and visit us! In the first instance please contact us on referrals@tces.org.uk or 020 8543 7878.

North West London Independent School (NWLIS)

North West London
Independent School

(Founded 2008)

85 Old Oak Common Lane, Acton, ,
London W3 7DD

Tel: 020 8749 5403

Email: referrals@tces.org.uk

Website: www.tces.org.uk

Schools' Proprietor: Thomas Keaney

Head Teacher: Nicole Teakle **School type:**
Coeducational Day

Age range of pupils: 7–18

No. of pupils enrolled as at 01/01/2016: 69

North West London Independent School (NWLIS) is a TCES Group school, providing LA funded day-school education for pupils aged 7-18 years whose social, emotional or mental health needs or Autism Spectrum Condition has made it difficult for them to achieve success in a mainstream school. Our pupils' co-morbid needs can be complex. Undiagnosed speech, language and communication needs (SLCN), sensory difficulties or learning difficulties can create barriers to learning that must be addressed before the pupil can settle into education. Our integrated approach to education, health and care takes each pupil on an individual journey that encourages a love of learning.

Our pupils are taught in groups of up to six to ensure each individual receives an intensive level of support, with a Teacher and TA as minimum. TCES Group's Inclusion Model is embedded at NWLIS, delivered by the Inclusion Manager and Pastoral Co-ordinator: tutor support, key work, group process, nurture groups and drama therapy, speech and language intervention and clinical assessments are part of the core offer.

The school delivers TCES Group's 5 Part Curriculum, which includes access to support from the Clinical and Therapy Team on an as-needs basis. SALT, OT, Counselling, Drama and Art Therapy are delivered by our in-house team and access to Clinical Psychology and a Paediatrician at Consultant level can be arranged for those pupils whose needs require further investigation.

Pupils attending NWLIS often need highly personalised learning programmes and can remain for Post-16 programmes

of study, specialising in developing independence, preparation for adult life and life after school.

We provide a well-structured routine in a safe, calm and happy environment which promotes tolerance and respect throughout our school community. We nurture ambition and work with each child to provide them with the life skills, accreditation and certification needed to achieve future careers.

A parallel service to our schools, TCES Group's Create Service offers therapeutic education, delivered through a case co-ordination model, to pupils who present (or are at) significant risk to themselves or others, who cannot be educated in a school setting.

To find out more about the school and its facilities please come to visit us! In the first instance please contact us on referrals@tces.org.uk or 020 8543 7878.

Early Intervention Works

Therapeutic Care and Education for Younger Children

Appletree
treatment centre
growing & learning together
www.appletreeschool.co.uk

Over 20 years' experience specialising in therapeutic care and education for girls and boys 6 to 12 years old with emotional, health, social and associated learning difficulties, who have suffered: Trauma, Neglect, Physical, Emotional, Sexual abuse.

Therapy in Action - Not Therapy in a Vacuum

Qualified, Experienced Psychologists and Therapists provide individual therapy for our children, clinical input for each childs' programme, clinical consultation and training for our care, teaching and support teams.

Therapeutic Relationships, Structured 24 hour Programme
Our therapeutically informed teams are skilled at helping our children form healthy attachments, build emotional resilience and confidence, increasing their self-esteem, helping them acquire the skills needed to succeed at home, in life and in school.

Stability and Felt Security are Key to our Children's Success
Once a child is placed with us we will not exclude them, they will only experience planned moves forward. This stability and security helps them develop meaningful relationships, build self esteem and develop resilience.

Successful reintegration to families

After an average of just 2 years and 6 months with us 91% of our leavers in the last 5 years were able to leave residential care/special school provision and return to families or foster families and day schools. The remaining 9% of our leavers continued in residential care to facilitate increased and appropriate contact with their families.

We work alongside adoptive, foster and birth families

All children engage in individual therapy, most continue throughout their stay with us

Close to 100% attendance in education with no unauthorized absence

Appletree

Fell House

Willow Bank

Appletree Treatment Centre has three children's homes

Appletree for up to 12 children

Fell House for up to 8 children

Willow Bank for up to 4 children

We provide high quality therapeutic care and education. We help children who are vulnerable and require a nurturing environment.

Appletree and Fell House each have their own school on site, Willow Bank children attend Appletree school

tel 015395 60253 - Natland, Kendal Cumbria LA9 7QS - **email clair.davies@appletreeschool.co.uk**

Everyone within Appletree Treatment Centre has a responsibility for, and is committed to, safeguarding and promoting the welfare of children and young people and for ensuring that they are protected from harm.

Philpots Manor School

(Founded 1959)

West Hoathly, East Grinstead, West Sussex
RH19 4PR

Tel: 01342 810268

Email: info@philpotsmanorschool.co.uk

Website: www.philpotsmanorschool.co.uk

Education Co-ordinator:
Ms Linda Churnside BEd

School type: Coeducational Boarding

Age range of pupils: 7–19

No. of pupils enrolled as at 01/01/2016: 32

Boys: 21 **Girls:** 11

Fees per annum as at 01/01/2016:

Day: £65,000

Weekly Boarding: £65,000

Founded in 1959 and set in the heart of the Sussex countryside, Philpots Manor School is an independent residential school and training centre offering an academic and social education to children and young adults from 7 to 19 years of age.

The emotional, behavioural, social and communication problems that most of our students display may stem from a learning difficulty, social deprivation, abuse or from a recognised clinical condition, such as epilepsy, a development disorder or autism. Students need to have the potential to function in a social situation. Because of this we do not admit students with severe learning difficulties, severe psychological problems, or with extreme behavioural problems.

Classes usually contain a maximum of six students with one class teacher and at least one class assistant. Our residential units can accommodate either up to six or nine residential students, depending on the size of the unit. We also cater for day students. We offer a 36 week curriculum with residential children returning home at weekends. As well as offering a wide range of academic subjects we also offer horse-riding, pottery, gardening, weaving, art and music. Most pupils are entered for examination at GCSE or Entry Level in English, Maths, Science and Art at a time that is appropriate for each. Up to six GCSE subjects are offered.

OCN courses for Post-16 pupils accredit a wide range of subjects that most pupils study. Continuous assessment by the teachers avoids examinations for those pupils who least benefit from additional stress in their lives. Current courses include stable management and land-based studies.

We have play therapy, counselling, speech, music, Eurythmy and Bothmer Gym as well as a visiting osteopath.

For further information, please visit our website at:

www.philpotsmanorschool.co.uk

or telephone 01342 810268

Brantwood Specialist School

1 Kenwood Bank, Nether Edge, Sheffield,
South Yorkshire S7 1NU
Tel: 0114 258 9062
Email: enquiries@brantwood.rmt.org
Website: www.rmt.org

Headteacher: Jenni Rosenbrock
School type: Independent
Coeducational Day & Residential
Age range of pupils: 7–19

Brantwood is an independent specialist school for children and young people aged 7-19 with complex difficulties, particularly Autistic Spectrum Condition, including Asperger Syndrome, attachment disorder, PDA (Pathological Demand Avoidance), ADHD and those deemed 'hard to engage'. The school offers daytime and residential provision up to 52 weeks and respite care subject to availability. The school is set in a quiet, leafy neighbourhood with secure grounds and has been graded by Ofsted as 'Good' education provision and 'Outstanding' Care provision.

Curriculum

The curriculum has four distinct strands:

Steiner Waldorf Education provides a holistic and inclusive approach to the development of the young person, which emphasises the importance of the distinct ways in which humans relate to the world through their intellectual, emotional and physical activity.

Practical Skills Therapeutic Education (PSTE) enables people to develop transferable skills through real-life purposeful activities, gain confidence through achievement in school, engage in the wider community and achieve a wide range of qualifications according to their interests and skills.

The National Curriculum ensures that students can achieve appropriate nationally-recognised qualifications, including NOCN, BTEC, GCSE and A level.

Individual Therapies, such as Speech and Language, Movement (Eurythmy), Massage, Art and Occupational Therapies, are incorporated into each young person's education plan as appropriate. The team of therapists work closely with staff and parents/carers at all times.

Brantwood Specialist School provides:

- Small class sizes and house groups of five students or fewer according to a student's ability and need
- Healthy organic food and nutritional education
- Engagement with the local community and help in planning leisure time and outdoor activities
- Involvement in festivals, other celebrations and social and cultural events
- Opportunities to develop and improve living skills for both day and residential students

Residential

Residential provision is in the school's central location within the local community, providing consistency, warmth and positive role modelling to develop the young person's skills and potential. Students are actively engaged in leisure activities, community participation and planning and cooking a healthy organic diet.

'Young people in this provision make exceptional progress in all areas of their development. The home is personalised to meet each young person's very complex needs'. Ofsted 2015

Admissions

For enquiries or Admissions, contact Karen on 07812 234 339, Laura on 07813 234 696 or email admissions@brantwood.rmt.org. School placements are available throughout the year.

Brantwood Specialist School Registered No: 373/6002. Children's Home Registered No: SC423753. Ruskin Mill Trust is an educational charity No: 1137167.

Schools and colleges specialising in learning difficulties (including dyslexia/SPLD)

Ruskin Mill College

The Fisheries, Horsley, Gloucestershire
GL6 0PL
Tel: 01453 837500
Fax: 01453 837506
Email: enquiries@rmc.rmt.org

Website: www.rmt.org
Principal: Dan Alipaz
School type: Coeducational Day & Residential
Age range of pupils: 16–25

Ruskin Mill College, a long-standing and successful independent college in Gloucestershire, offers over 100 places to young people with complex learning and behavioural difficulties, mental health issues and autistic spectrum disorders, including Asperger Syndrome.

Practical Skills Therapeutic Education

Set in 140 acres including a biodynamic farm, woodlands and a fishery, the college is operated by Ruskin Mill Trust, whose internationally renowned Practical Skills Therapeutic Education method offers young people a unique opportunity to learn and develop transferable skills through meaningful, hands-on, real-life activities and accredited courses. Our experienced Pathways team works with each student and the relevant Local Authority assisting them to undertake work experience and prepare each student for their transition back into their respective communities. The Pathways team will stay in touch with the student for a further six months for continuity purposes.

The college provides an extensive range of nutritional, therapeutic and medical support. Each core element of the educational cycle is designed to establish active and positive relationships with nature, people and the community through a holistic approach to human development and supports three key stages: overcoming barriers to learning, becoming skilled, and being ready to engage and give back to the community.

Integrated Learning for Living and Work

The college offers a personalised pre-entry assessment leading to an individualised learning and development programme to work towards agreed outcomes. A rich and varied curriculum offers exciting opportunities to develop communication, social, work and living skills, leading to increased independence. Activities include practical land-based

and traditional craft activities including animal husbandry, fish farming, woodland management, horticulture, catering, drama and art, with communication and functional skills embedded throughout the day and residential provision. At Gables Farm and the market garden, students help to grow and harvest healthy biodynamic food and prepare meals in the college canteens, café and households.

Accreditation and Transition

Courses are accredited through the Regulated Qualifications Framework and students will also prepare for work competency through a wide range of internal and external work experience. Qualifications include NVQs and BTECs. The college's cultural programme offers students further opportunities to develop their social and work skills. Throughout their placement, students work with a dedicated transition team and engage with their acquired transferable skills to

prepare for life after college.

Residential Provision

Students live in family or team houses in the local community which offer the consistency, warmth and positive role modelling that some young adults need to develop their living skills, achieve greater independence and re-imagine their potential. Students can progress onto placements in training flats or semi-independent living, where they have the opportunity to take greater responsibility for themselves. Ruskin Mill College takes referrals throughout the year and offers up to 52-week placements.

Admissions

For all initial enquiries please contact the Admissions Team on 01453 837502 or by email: admissions@rmc.rmt.org

Ruskin Mill Trust is an educational charity and draws its inspiration from the insights of Rudolf Steiner, John Ruskin and William Morris. Charity No: 1137167.

The Unicorn School

(Founded 1991)

20 Marcham Road, Abingdon,
Oxfordshire OX14 1AA
Tel: 01235 530222
Email: info@unicornoxford.co.uk
Website: www.unicornoxford.co.uk

Headteacher: Mr. Andrew Day BEd (Hons) University of Wales (Cardiff)
School type: Coeducational Day
Age range of pupils: 6–16
No. of pupils enrolled as at 01/01/2016: 64
Fees per annum as at 01/01/2016:
Information on application.

The Unicorn School is a leading, specialist day school for pupils aged 6 years and up, who have dyslexia, dyspraxia, dyscalculia, or who need support with Speech and Language. The school is introducing GCSE education from September 2016, making it unique as the only dyslexia-specialist day school in Oxfordshire to provide GCSE education.

The Unicorn School provides a nurturing environment in which every pupil is helped to build self-confidence, appreciate their learning difficulties and develop their own personal learning style. Our teachers are specialists in working with dyslexia and related difficulties, equipping our pupils with the strategies for learning that will enable them to succeed in their future education and beyond.

The Unicorn School has a proven record of providing specialist education for both girls and boys from Year 2 and above, and pupils will now have the opportunity to complete their secondary education at our school. We are delighted to have opened our dedicated senior school building and we hope that you will share our enthusiasm.

We warmly welcome you to visit us at The Unicorn School to discuss how we can support your child's needs. To join us at our upcoming open mornings, or to book an individual visit please contact our Registrar on 01235 530222, or registrar@unicornoxford.co.uk.

Kisimul School

(Founded 1977)

The Old Vicarage, 61 High Street,
Swinderby, Lincoln, Lincolnshire LN6 9LU
Tel: 01522 868279
Fax: 01522 866000
Email: admissions@kisimul.co.uk
Website: www.kisimul.co.uk
Director of Education:

Mr Danny Carter BA(Hons), MA, MEd
School type: Coeducational
Independent Residential Special School
Age range of pupils: 8–19
No. of pupils enrolled as at 01/01/2016: 60
Fees per annum as at 01/01/2016:
On application

Kisimul School is one of the UK's leading independent residential special schools, offering a homely and safe environment for children who have severe learning difficulties, challenging behaviour, autism and global developmental delay.

Kisimul School offers residential education, care and leisure programmes at both our upper and lower school, for up to 52 weeks of the year, for pupils aged 8 to 19 years. The school is registered with the Department for Education and Ofsted. Limited day placements are also offered at both school sites.

The name Kisimul, pronounced 'kishmul', was taken from Kisimul Castle, which overlooks one of the safest harbours in the British Isles. Like its namesake, Kisimul School offers a safe haven, providing care and protection for its pupils whilst preparing them for the journey ahead into adulthood.

Kisimul School was founded in 1977 in a comfortable Georgian house (known today as the Old Vicarage) set in four acres within the small Lincolnshire village of Swinderby. Facilities at the Old Vicarage include an indoor heated swimming pool, large playground, soft play areas with ball pool and multi-sensory rooms for relaxation and stimulation.

In 2003, our upper school, Acacia Hall opened, offering the same standard of exceptional care and education within grounds adapted and utilised in a way to reflect the older age group. Acacia Hall offers riding stables, an adventure playground, collection of small farm animals and an area dedicated to horticulture.

Kisimul School has opened an additional school, Woodstock House, in Long Ditton, Surrey. Woodstock House received its first pupils in April 2008, and

again offers the same quality of care and education for pupils aged 8 to 19 years. Kisimul School has developed this site to be a mirror image of its existing school operations, using the same teaching methods and ethos.

Kisimul School's mission is to continuously strive for excellence in the care and education of its pupils, with a vision to have the best assisted living environment.

The school provides a caring, consistent, safe and supportive environment in which its young people can flourish and develop their skills in order to fully realise their individual potential. Residential and school staff work closely together to enable the pupils to progress in their personal development and learning. The 24-hour approach incorporates a wide range of activities to enrich the learning experiences of all pupils, helping them to learn to communicate and cooperate more effectively with others and enabling them to grow in confidence, self-esteem and independence.

The highly structured school curriculum aims to address the very specific needs of our pupils, by providing every opportunity for them to enjoy their education and develop their skills, knowledge and understanding through practical and functional learning experiences.

Classes are small and matched to learning profiles alongside the dynamics of peers. There is a high staffing ratio which reflects the complex needs of learners. The curriculum incorporates the National Curriculum (lower school) and an accreditation based vocational learning model is a feature at the upper school. An integrated therapeutic programme includes Psychology, Speech and Language, Music Therapy and Occupational Therapy (Sensory

Integration) is part of the core provision of the school.

A key priority is to develop our pupils' communication skills and since many are non-verbal we teach the alternative and augmentative systems of Makaton signing and PECS (Picture Exchange Communication System) alongside vocalisations and speech.

External accreditation is gained through a wide variety of ASDAN 'Towards Independence' programmes and the Duke of Edinburgh's Award Scheme.

Kisimul School works closely with the parents, carers and professionals from its placing authorities to ensure the highest possible standards of care and education.

Kisimul School is committed to the view that all people are entitled to equality of opportunity regardless of ability or disability, gender or chosen gender, age, status, religion, belief, nationality, ethnic origins or sexual orientation.

For further information, including exciting job opportunities within Kisimul School, please visit our website at www.kisimul.co.uk or contact us at the address above.

I CAN'S Dawn House School

helps children
communicate
REGISTERED CHARITY 210031

(Founded 1974)

Helmsley Road, Rainworth, Mansfield, Nottinghamshire NG21 0DQ
Tel: 01623 795361
Fax: 01623 491173
Email: dawnhouse@ican.notts.sch.uk
Website: www.dawnhouseschool.org.uk
Principal: Angela Child

School type: Coeducational Day & Residential
Age range of pupils: 5–19
No. of pupils enrolled as at 01/01/2016: 79
Fees per annum as at 01/01/2016:
On request

I CAN's Dawn House School is a specialist speech, language and communication school for children and young people aged 5-19 years. We are committed to the highest quality education, therapy and care for pupils with severe and/or complex speech, language and communication difficulties or Asperger's Syndrome.

At Dawn House School the pupils receive the specialist intensive support that they need. We are able to cater for a number of other difficulties which are commonly associated with communication difficulties, including: learning difficulties, behavioural difficulties, problems with attention and memory, motor dyspraxia, sensory difficulties, autistic spectrum difficulties and emotional problems.

Pupils' individual needs are assessed and addressed through curriculum planning and assessment and IEP planning. Speech and language therapists and teachers plan lessons that meet two sets of targets: curriculum learning objectives and specific speech and/or language aims. For pupils who need more specific focused work to develop their speech and language skills, individual or small group sessions are timetabled during the school day.

Our school makes use of Makaton to support children's learning. The school also promotes the use of a range of voice output devices to support individual pupil's communication.

A full-time Occupational Therapist and OT assistants work within some lessons and with individual pupils on more focused, intensive work where necessary. The Family and Community Liaison Worker supports pupils' families and is a key link between home and school.

Residential Care at Dawn House School aims to ensure the emotional and physical well-being of our boarding pupils through an extended curriculum. The school can provide opportunities for non-residential young people to benefit from extended days and overnight stays. The care staff organise a range of activities out of school hours.

Dawn House was rated as an 'Outstanding' school by Ofsted in March 2014 and January 2015, its residential care inspection also gained an 'Outstanding' rating in February 2016. The inspectors found pupils at the school achieve exceptionally well and all pupils make outstanding progress whatever their individual needs or disabilities.

The Further Education department caters for students (16-19 years) who have a communication difficulty or Asperger's Syndrome. The provision is based at the Dawn House site but has very close partnerships with Vision West Notts and Portland two local FE colleges, local employers and training providers.

Dawn House School is part of I CAN, the children's communication charity (www.ican.org.uk).

Blossom Lower School and Upper House

Blossom Lower School, Christopher Place,
London NW1 1JF
Tel: 020 7383 3834
Website:
www.blossomchristopherplace.co.uk
Email: admincp@blossomhouseschool.
co.uk

Blossom House School, Station Road
Motspur Park, New Malden, London
KT3 6JJ
Tel: 020 8946 7348
Fax: 020 8944 5848
Email: admin@blossomhouseschool.co.uk
Website: www.blossomhouseschool.co.uk

Principal: Joanna Burgess DipCST,MRCSLT,
DipRSA,SpLD,PGCE,HPC
School type: Coeducational Day
Age range of pupils: 3–19
No. of pupils enrolled as at 01/01/2016: 214
Fees per annum:
On request

Blossom House School is a specialist school for children with speech, language and communication difficulties. Founded in 1989, the school continues to expand and we now have two separate sites, one in Central London and one in South West London.

Blossom Lower School, Christopher Place has pupils aged from 3-7 years, who will be moving up through the school to year 6. Blossom House, Motspur Park has pupils from 3-19 years and includes a post 16 'college links' provision.

Although many of our pupils have some associated difficulties such as fine motor problems or poor organisational skills, all are within the broadly average range of cognitive ability. We provide an integrated, holistic programme of learning and therapies in a caring and highly supportive environment, so that each child has the opportunity to fulfil his or her potential.

Blossom House has a unique atmosphere created by a dedicated, highly competent and wonderfully caring staff. Specific strengths are acknowledged and weaknesses supported, so that each child 'blossoms' and has the opportunity to fulfil his or her potential, whether that is remaining with us or returning to mainstream education.

The key aims of the school:

- To provide a communication centred environment where children with a range of speech, language and communication difficulties are supported in all areas of their learning.
- To provide a highly skilled team of specialist therapists, teachers and support staff who can work with the children in a range of learning environments.
- To provide support and advice for parents.

Pield Heath House School

(Founded 1901)

Pield Heath Road, Uxbridge, Middlesex
UB8 3NW
Tel: 01895 258507
Fax: 01895 256497
Email: admin@pieldheathschool.org.uk
Website: pieldheathschool.org.uk
Executive Principal: Sister Julie Rose

School type: Co-educational Day and
Short Break/Residential
Age range of pupils: 7–19
No. of pupils enrolled as at 01/01/2016: 83
Fees per annum as at 01/01/2016:
Upon application

Pield Heath House is a non-maintained school in West London for young people aged 7-19. Judged 'Outstanding' by Ofsted at our last three inspections we offer day, residential and short break provision for those with moderate to severe learning difficulties, complex learning and behavioural needs, including autistic spectrum disorders and associated speech, language and communication difficulties.

Each of our students has a personalised education programme which addresses their specific needs to live a fulfilled life in a challenging and changing world. Our multi-disciplinary team facilitates the learning process both in classroom settings and in the home environment for those who are resident.

Therapies: our therapeutic service includes Music, Dance, Speech and OT and the team of experienced therapists work alongside educational and residential staff in supporting the development of each individual student.

Curriculum: a comprehensive programme based on the National Curriculum is offered at Key Stage 2 and 3. Small class groups, with a high level of staff support, enable our students to access a suitably individualised curriculum. Statutory requirements at Key Stage 4 include the core subjects of English, Maths, ICT, RE, Citizenship and Science.

For students aged 14-19, the curriculum is structured to enable them to acquire the necessary skills to develop independence in their adult lives. Programmes are designed to promote their personal, social and vocational skills, and they have the opportunity to access nationally accredited programmes including ASDAN, OCR , NOCN and Btec qualifications. Performing Arts is a key element of the post 16 curriculum offer.

Inclusion Hub: for those students who are unable to access learning in a classroom environment we have an Inclusion Hub which provides individual spaces for learning. Each student is supported with a highly personalised timetable and follows an individualised curriculum, closely related to their interests and abilities. Here staff provide support to develop the skills to allow the student to reintegrate, over time, back into the classroom.

Thrive: we are proud to be a Thrive accredited school and follow its principles to help support the emotional and social development of our students. Our Inclusion Support Team works with staff, therapists and parents to deliver a programme for each student to help improve their confidence, behaviour and social interactions.

Pield Heath House accommodates a wide range of learning requirements; the provision is flexible and tailored to optimise individual rates of progress and attainment. This encourages the development of confident, well adjusted, sensitive and independent young people able to live life to the full.

The Link Primary School

(Founded 1964)
138 Croydon Road, Beddington, Croydon, Surrey CR0 4PG
Tel: 020 8688 5239
Fax: 020 8667 0828
Email: office@linkprim.co.uk

Website: www.linkprim.co.uk
Head Teacher: Mrs Beverley Dixon CertEd, ASE, NPQH
School type: Coeducational Day
Age range of pupils: 4–11
No. of pupils enrolled as at 01/01/2016: 45

The Link Primary School provides specialist teaching and therapy for up to 45 children aged 4 to 11 years whose primary need is speech, language and communication. Some pupils may also have additional learning, sensory or physical needs. The School has been recognised by Ofsted as 'outstanding' since 2008 and draws upon over 50 years of experience.

The School has a warm, safe, friendly and nurturing environment which helps children to learn, express their ideas, communicate, develop friendships and become confident citizens. Small classes with high adult to child ratio enable children to settle quickly, move confidently around the school and learn the daily routines which form an integral part of school life.

Children enjoy a wide range of school facilities including an ICT suite, library, fully equipped hall, food technology room, art room and music room. During playtime they have access to climbing frames, sandpit, trikes and other outdoor toys and games.

A brand new teaching block with facilities for enhanced therapy was completed in September 2015 and also provides the children with larger classrooms and additional outdoor learning opportunities including a sensory garden and kitchen allotment.

We foster close relationships with our local community to enable our children to gain valuable life experiences and encourage children to play an active role in extra-curricular activities such as dance and athletics club. A range of off-site activities are available including horse riding and for the older children the opportunity to experience a residential educational visit.

Working with parents
Establishing and developing relationships with parents and carers is a central part of our philosophy. Children learn best when the school and parents work together and we value the contribution that parents make to our school and endeavour to provide many opportunities where parents are involved in school life.

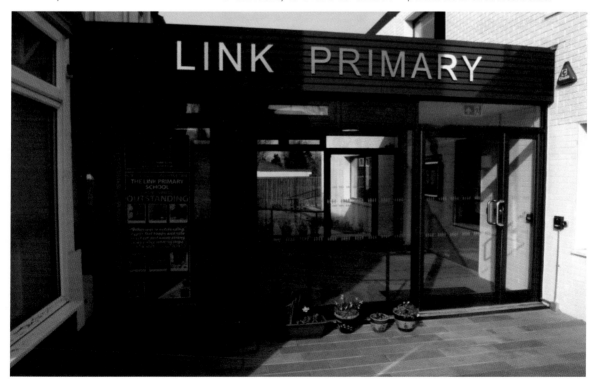

Frederick Hugh House

48 Old Church Street, London, SW3 5BY
Tel: 0207 349 8833
Email: info@frederickhughhouse.com
Website: www.frederickhughhouse.com

Headteacher: Miss Tanya Jamil
School type: Coeducational Day
Age range of pupils: 10–16

This is an exciting and unique venture; a school built around celebrating the individual strengths of each pupil. Frederick Hugh House is an independent, special day school in the Royal Borough of Kensington and Chelsea, imbued with inspiration, aspiration and innovation.

We opened our doors in 2010 providing an all through, specialist education for children who require individualised, integrated educational and therapeutic programmes within a small class and a small school setting. Frederick Hugh House provides a personalised education with a rich, broad and balanced curriculum which is collaboratively planned, updated and delivered by a team of professionals made up of teachers, physiotherapist, occupational therapist, speech and language therapist and teaching assistants. Each child's special educational needs are addressed through the collaborative teaching approach, incorporating sensory, speech and language, physical, psychological and educational needs into one uniquely delivered programme. Each child's programme involves 1:1, paired, small group, class and whole school teaching.

We aim to ensure that each child's first crucial steps at Frederick Hugh House, whatever their age, are compelling and exciting, so as to draw them into a world of lifelong learning. We do this in our purpose built school with its well resourced classrooms, ICT suite, Dance Hall, Therapy rooms, Science room and Multi-sensory 'Journey Room'. As the students grow and mature, we have the capability to adapt the physical environment to meet their changing needs. Building on our Primary school curriculum with an emphasis on Literacy and Maths, the practical based secondary programmes including Biology, Physics and Chemistry, Photography, ICT, Food Technology, SRE and ASDAN programmes supports students to develop into independent young individuals with the confidence to express themselves. Students are offered a rich arts programme which includes drama, choir and orchestra alongside individual and small group musical instrument tuition. Students also participate in horse riding, climbing and swimming.

We believe we have a duty to unlock the strengths in every child so they can achieve their best in all aspects of their lives, as independently as possible. Come in and see for yourself!

Limespring School

Park House, 16 High Road, East Finchley,
London N2 9PJ
Tel: 020 8444 1387
Email: info@limespringschool.co.uk

Website: www.limespringschool.co.uk
Principal: Denise Drinkwater
School type: Coeducational Day
Age range of pupils: 7–11

Led by Principal Denise Drinkwater, Limespring School is a small, independent junior school that opened in January 2012 in East Finchley, North London for children with specific learning differences such as Dyslexia and Dyspraxia. We offer a proven approach to learning tailored to the needs of your child. The experience is one that every child enjoys in which they feel confident to engage with their learning, to demonstrate their own achievements and emerge, feeling a pride in their success. High expectations are the norm for all children and individual talents and aspirations celebrated. Your child will shine.

Limespring School is based in lovely, safe premises next to Cherry Tree woods and park and directly opposite East Finchley underground station: the first school of its type for children in this part of north London. The school provides a personalised approach that supports the development of a child's learning and social competence

in a warm, positive, stress-free environment. This is achieved by maintaining a small school in which everyone is well known and small learning groups.

Our focus is on the individual strengths and learning needs of each child. Programmes of work are tailored to ensure that children thrive in school and are able to develop the skills and awareness of their own approaches to learning enabling them to confidently move into the next phase of their education.

The school provides a range of different services, recognising that children and parents will benefit from more than a single or standard package.

Full-time: Places are available for children from year 3-6. This is provided for up to 32 children in small class sizes. We like to meet the child and offer a trial and low key assessment so that we can understand needs and expectations.

Limespring time: An intensive one or two-

term programme aimed at children who would benefit from the boost, provided one or more mornings a week, by intensive and specialist support from specialist teaching staff trained and experienced in meeting the individual needs of children with learning differences such as dyslexia, dyspraxia and dyscalculia, unlocking their potential. The child returns to their main school at lunchtime.

Boosters: Week-long summer boosters in maths and literacy are provided over the Summer. These confidence-building boosters will set your child up for the new school term.

Touch-typing: keyboards are common in all aspects of our lives and mastery is a particularly useful for children with learning differences such as dyslexia and dyspraxia. Often the ability to get thoughts down quickly leads to much greater confidence. Five hour long sessions are run on week nights after school.

Parayhouse School

New Kings School Annex, New Kings
Road, Fulham, London, SW6 4LY
Tel: 020 7751 0914
Fax: 020 7751 0914
Email: a.sullivan@parayhouse.com
Website: www.parayhouse.com

Head: Mrs Sarah Jackson CertEd,
DipEd(Complex Learning Handicap)
Appointed: 1983
School type: Non-Maintained Special
School
Age range of pupils: 7–16

No. of pupils enrolled as at 01/01/2016: 46
Boys: 35 **Girls:** 11
Fees per annum as at 01/01/2016:
Day: £27,540 (Less £10,000 if in receipt of
EFA funding)

Parayhouse was established in 1983 as a school for students with moderate learning difficulties as well as those with speech, language and communication needs. 30 years later we continue to provide a specialist education for students from 14 Local Education Authorities across Greater London.

We focus our work on preparing students with special needs for the challenges they will meet when leaving school. We recognise that it is the development of social, language and thinking skills which enable our students to express themselves, to understand and to function optimally in the world. We also believe in the power of collaborative practice. Together, we face challenges, celebrate achievement and aspire to do our very best.

We deliver our mission in three essential ways. **Firstly**, we provide a safe and nurturing environment where students feel secure and are confident and eager to learn. **Secondly**, we create a highly specialised and individualised curriculum with speech and language at its heart, empowering students to learn. **Thirdly**, we establish close working relationships between parents, carers, students and staff to support learning and behaviour at home as well as at school.

We are committed to providing a safe, nurturing environment for our students, many of whom are educationally fragile and arrive at Parayhouse with low self-confidence, undeveloped basic skills and behavioural problems. We have high expectations of our students and our tight-knit family atmosphere provides the happy and supportive environment they need to develop the same expectations of themselves as well as a love of learning.

At Parayhouse School we understand that language is integral to learning. Therefore speech and language therapy

at Parayhouse is not simply an "add on." Speech and Language Therapy provides the underpinning for learning, thinking and the development of social skills. Our exemplary collaborative practice between teachers and therapists ensures that our students develop the necessary language skills needed to fully access the curriculum and optimise each student's learning potential.

We tailor the curriculum to meet the individual needs of students. We consistently encourage and challenge them to learn and to develop independence so that they are able to make wise choices and succeed in life.

Staff, parents and students collaborate to establish and review termly targets for individual students. To meet their individual learning levels, students follow a differentiated form of the National Curriculum.

All Parayhouse teachers and LSAs have a thorough understanding of the language levels of our students. Our therapists also have been trained to understand the P–level and national curriculum requirements expected from school-aged students. Together the language and learning team tailor a curriculum to meet the individual learning needs of each student.

The Independent School (TIS)

23-31 Beavor Lane, Ravenscourt Park, Hammersmith, London W6 9AR
Tel: 0203 086 8687
Email: admin@tis-london.org

Website: www.tis-london.org
Principal: Ms Tanya Moran
School type: Coeducational Day
Age range of pupils: 11–16

'**Independence of thought, independence of mind, independence of learning… achieving independence beyond our doors'.**

The Independent School, London, is a small, friendly, mainstream secondary school for boys and girls aged 11-16 years old.

The School offers a close-knit community and the opportunity to learn in a modern, bright and inspiring environment. We have a staff-to-student ratio of 1:4 and a maximum class size of 8 students. This ensures that each individual's needs are catered for and that their progress is carefully monitored.

We welcome students with mild specific learning needs such as dyslexia and dyspraxia, together with those who perform better in a more individualised environment. We believe that learning differences should never be seen as a barrier to academic success.

Through individually tailored teaching, together with the TIS Enriched Skills Programme, the School aims to equip every student, regardless of learning style, with the confidence, skills and self-belief necessary to fulfil their potential at GCSE and beyond.

We provide guidance and support with personal organisation skills, such as touch typing, study skills and time management, and each student benefits from a designated teacher mentor that they meet with regularly to reflect on their learning, set targets and importantly, to ensure that their time at The Independent School is happy and productive.

We have a strong focus on the development of Information Technology (IT) skills, making the curriculum more accessible and engaging. Students are linked to our IT structure via their own individual tablet, enabling us to draw on the best IT educational resources available.

We help all our students build the confidence, skills and self belief necessary to achieve independence beyond our doors.

If you'd like to find out more, we'd love to hear from you.

The Moat School

The MOATSCHOOL
All dyslexic children can be helped to achieve

(Founded 1998)

Bishops Avenue, Fulham, London, SW6 6EG

Tel: 020 7610 9018
Email: office@moatschool.org.uk
Website: www.moatschool.org.uk
Head: Ms Clare King
Appointed: January 2013
School type: Coeducational Day

Age range of pupils: 9–16
No. of pupils enrolled as at 01/01/2016:
Boys: 54 **Girls:** 13
Fees per annum as at 01/01/2016:
Day: £28,800

An inspirational London day school for children with specific learning difficulties
Founded in 1998, The Moat School is London's first co-educational secondary day school for children with specific learning difficulties (primarily dyslexia). We offer an intensive and structured learning programme teaching the National Curriculum.

A fundamental aim of The Moat is to identify and nurture talent to enable pupils to flourish, experience success and fulfil their potential. Teachers at The Moat School are not only subject specialists but also hold a post graduate specialist qualification in teaching pupils with SpLDs. In addition to our teaching staff and Learning Support Assistants, we have a team of experienced therapists including Speech and Language, Occupational Therapy and a School Counsellor. The Moat School is an ISA school and CReSTeD registered and has been described as the 'Gold Standard' in SpLD education.

The Moat School Offers

- A whole-school approach to learning for pupils aged 9 to 16 years (year groups 5-11)
- Specialist teaching with highly-trained staff
- Structured and individual learning programmes
- Class sizes based on a maximum of 10 pupils with individual and smaller group teaching as appropriate
- An embedded, whole-school therapeutic approach
- Development of organisational and study skills, and advanced use of Information & communication Technology (ICT)
- Access to the National Curriculum and GCSE qualifications
- A wide range of sporting and extra-curricular enrichment activities

In terms of adding value, The Moat School has continued to perform in the top 5% of schools nationally since 2005 – *Analysis of MidYIS by the Durham University's Centre for Evaluation and Monitoring*

The Good Schools Guide says: *'Something special. Not for children wanting to be cosseted and comforted, but a hardworking haven for bright, determined dyslexics and dyspraxics who know what they want from life and will achieve when given a chance.'*

The Moat School, come and see for yourself!

I CAN's Meath School

helps children
communicate

REGISTERED CHARITY 210031

(Founded 1982)

Brox Road, Ottershaw, Surrey KT16 0LF
Tel: 01932 872302
Fax: 01932 875180
Email: meath@meath-ican.org.uk
Website: www.meathschool.org.uk
Headteacher: Janet Dunn OBE, MA, AdvDipSpecEduc

Appointed: September 2003
School type: Coeducational Day & Residential
No. of pupils enrolled as at 01/01/2016: 56
Fees per annum as at 01/01/2016: On request

I CAN's Meath School is a residential (weekly) and day school providing teaching, therapy and care to children aged 4-11 years, whose primary difficulty is speech, language and communication, including Asperger's Syndrome. Meath School is a unique, dynamic, specialised learning community. The school and care settings have been recognised by Ofsted as continuously 'outstanding' since 2008 and are on the Ofsted Outstanding Providers list.

Children with associated difficulties including some degree of learning difficulty, attention control, fine and gross motor co-ordination problems, mild visual and/or hearing impairments, medical needs and social interaction problems may also benefit from the provision.

Learning and achieving

All pupils are taught within a broad, balanced and relevant curriculum, including the new National Primary Curriculum for 2014 (except Modern Foreign Languages) which is differentiated, modified and tailored for pupils with severe and complex speech, language and communication needs. Strong processes for assessment, planning, teaching and reviewing ensure that each pupil makes outstanding progress in language skills and learning.

Classes are primarily based on pupils' language comprehension levels, also taking account of curriculum attainments, learning and social needs. In this way we know behaviour and progress are maximised.

Class groups can include between eight and twelve pupils, across year groups and Key Stages.

Each class has a core team of teacher, speech and language therapist and at least one learning support assistant. The speech and language therapy team and occupational therapist department are an important and integral part of the pupils' education. Specialist teaching is offered in music, art, craft, design and PE.

Partnership with parents

Meath School staff collaborate closely with parents, sharing successes and helping with any concerns or difficulties at home. The Family Support Worker acts as a link between home and school and will visit families where needed.

The School

Meath School is housed in fine Victorian buildings and the site includes a modern teaching block, gym, music, art and cookery rooms, ICT suite, small swimming pool, school field, activity play areas and a woodland park with bike track. The school has a programme of lunch clubs, after school clubs, trumpet tuition and a summer holiday club.

Meath School is part of I CAN, the children's communication charity (www.ican.org.uk), and is an integral part of the I CAN Centre in Surrey. It belongs to a local confederation of mainstream schools. The Centre offers a holistic multi-disciplinary independent two day specialist assessment services.

Kisimul School – Woodstock House

(Opened 2008)

Woodstock Lane North, Long Ditton,
Surbiton, Surrey KT6 5HN
Tel: 020 8335 2570
Fax: 020 8335 2571
Email: admissions@kisimul.co.uk
Website: www.kisimul.co.uk
Director of Education:

Mr Danny Carter BA(Hons), MA, MEd
School type: Coeducational
Independent Residential Special School
Age range of pupils: 8–19
No. of pupils enrolled as at 01/01/2016: 40
Fees per annum as at 01/01/2016:
On application

Kisimul School is one of the UK's leading independent residential special schools, offering a homely and safe environment for children who have severe learning difficulties, challenging behaviour, autism and global developmental delay.

Kisimul School offers residential education, care and leisure programmes at both our upper and lower school, for up to 52 weeks of the year, for pupils aged 8 to 19 years. The school is registered with the Department for Education and Ofsted. Limited day placements are also offered at both school sites.

The name Kisimul, pronounced 'kishmul', was taken from Kisimul Castle, which overlooks one of the safest harbours in the British Isles. Like its namesake, Kisimul School offers a safe haven, providing care and protection for its pupils whilst preparing them for the journey ahead into adulthood.

The original Kisimul School was founded in 1977 in a comfortable Georgian house (known today as the Old Vicarage) set in four acres within the small Lincolnshire village of Swinderby. Facilities at the Old Vicarage include an indoor heated swimming pool, large playground, soft play areas with ball pool and multi-sensory rooms for relaxation and stimulation.

In 2003, our upper school, Acacia Hall opened, offering the same standard of exceptional care and education within grounds adapted and utilised in a way to reflect the older age group. Acacia Hall offers riding stables, an adventure playground, collection of small farm animals and an area dedicated to horticulture.

Woodstock House received its first pupils in April 2008, and again offers the same quality of care and education for pupils aged 8 to 19 years. Kisimul School has

developed this site to be a mirror image of its existing school operations, using the same teaching methods and ethos.

Woodstock House is situated within 8.1 acres of tranquil countryside, offering space to develop in a safe and secure environment. Woodstock House is within easy access from the M25 via the A3.

Kisimul School's mission is to continuously strive for excellence in the care and education of its pupils, with a vision to have the best assisted living environment.

The school provides a caring, consistent, safe and supportive environment in which its young people can flourish and develop their skills in order to fully realise their individual potential. Residential and school staff work closely together to enable the pupils to progress in their personal development and learning. The 24-hour approach incorporates a wide range of activities to enrich the learning experiences of all pupils, helping them to learn to communicate and cooperate more effectively with others and enabling them to grow in confidence, self-esteem and independence.

The highly structured school curriculum aims to address the very specific needs of our pupils, by providing every opportunity for them to enjoy their education and develop their skills, knowledge and understanding through practical and functional learning experiences.

Classes are small and matched to learning profiles alongside the dynamics of peers. There is a high staffing ratio which reflects the complex needs of learners. The curriculum incorporates the National Curriculum (lower school) and an accreditation based vocational learning model is a feature at the upper school. An integrated therapeutic programme includes Psychology,

Speech and Language, Music Therapy and Occupational Therapy (Sensory Integration) is part of the core provision of the school.

A key priority is to develop our pupils' communication skills and since many are non-verbal we teach the alternative and augmentative systems of Makaton signing and PECS (Picture Exchange Communication System) alongside vocalisations and speech.

External accreditation is gained through a wide variety of ASDAN 'Towards Independence' programmes and the Duke of Edinburgh's Award Scheme.

Kisimul School works closely with the parents, carers and professionals from its placing authorities to ensure the highest possible standards of care and education.

Kisimul School is committed to the view that all people are entitled to equality of opportunity regardless of ability or disability, gender or chosen gender, age, status, religion, belief, nationality, ethnic origins or sexual orientation.

For further information, including exciting job opportunities within Kisimul School, please visit our website at www. kisimul.co.uk or contact us at the address above.

St Catherine's School

St Catherine's School
For Speech, Language and Communication Needs

(Founded 1983)
Grove Road, Ventnor, Isle of Wight
PO38 1TT
Tel: 01983 852722

Fax: 01983 857219
Email: general@stcatherines.org.uk
Website: www.stcatherines.org.uk
Principal: Mrs R Weldon
Appointed: September 2016
School type: Coeducational Boarding

Age range of pupils: 7–19
No. of pupils enrolled as at 01/01/2016: 55
Boys: 41 **Girls:** 14 **Sixth Form:** 28
No. of boarders: 36
Fees per annum as at 01/01/2016:
On request

St Catherine's offers specialist education, therapy and residential care to young people with **speech, language, communication** and associated needs such as **autism, Asperger Syndrome, dyspraxia** and **dyslexia**. In 2014, Ofsted rated our education provision as Good and our care provision was rated Outstanding in December 2015.

Our small school provides a nurturing environment. Our students – who are a mixture of day students, and weekly or termly boarders – come from across the UK and abroad. Student places can be funded by local authorities or privately. As highlighted in our recent Ofsted report our students make excellent progress across all areas of their lives.

Students are taught a modified National Curriculum in small classes, with high staff-to-student ratios incorporating a teacher, a speech and language therapist, an occupational therapist and a learning support assistant. Each student has their own individual educational and care programme, which integrates speech and language therapy and occupational therapy.

Students have the opportunity to gain a variety of qualifications according to individual abilities and preferences including Entry Level exams, GCSEs, BTECs and Functional Skills. From age 14 we provide students with a range of work-related experiences including accredited courses at our vocational training unit, work experience and taster courses at our local college.

Our therapy team are integral to St Catherine's and support the school's Total Communication approach by using a range of communication methods including sign-supported English. The speech and language and occupational therapists provide in-depth assessments, individualised therapy programmes, small group therapy sessions, intervention in the classroom and residential support.

We provide a home from home experience for our residential students, who each have their own bedroom and

are supported to pursue leisure activities as well as learn independence skills. Our location at the heart of a small town gives our students everyday opportunities to develop their life skills including independent travel.

St John's School & College

ST. JOHN'S
EMPOWERING VOICE ENABLING CHOICE

Business Centre, 17 Walpole Road,
Brighton, East Sussex BN2 0AF
Tel: 01273 244000

Fax: 01273 602243
Email: admissions@st-johns.co.uk
Website: www.st-johns.co.uk
Principal & Chief Executive:
Mr Mark Hughes
Appointed: September 2010
School type: Coeducational Boarding
& Day

Age range of pupils: 7–25
No. of pupils enrolled as at 01/01/2016: 97
Boys: 78 **Girls:** 19
No. of boarders: 47
Fees per annum as at 01/01/2016:
Day: £50,000 approx
Full Boarding: £95,000 approx

St. John's is a non-maintained special school and independent specialist college, working with learners who have complex learning disabilities; including some learners who may have difficulties resulting from behavioural, emotional and social difficulties, Autistic Spectrum Conditions, Asperger's Syndrome and Pathological Demand Avoidance Syndrome.

St. John's is a place where learning is shaped around your hopes and aspirations; where our courses are tailored to meet your goals and where you are supported by a highly skilled staff team who respect your choices and lifestyle.

St. John's innovative curriculum provides a full range of exciting, challenging and meaningful learning experiences (both accredited and non-accredited) that prepare each learner with relevant vocational and personal skills that will significantly impact on their future lives.

Our focus on vocational skills is carried out through real, work based learning, which allows our learners to work within and support the services and functions of our organisation, our own enterprises and community work experience placements.

Maths, English, Communications and ICT are embedded or are timetabled sessions along with PSHE, sport, termly options and community access.

Learners at St. John's have access to a variety of vibrant and age appropriate learning environments that reflect their needs. These include: our cafés providing real work experience, theatre for performing arts, fully equipped music and recording studio, construction workshop, community printing enterprise, IT and project hub and sensory areas.

Throughout their journey at St. John's learners are supported by our qualified and experienced Wellbeing team, who provide communication therapy, occupational therapy, behaviour support, nursing and counselling.

We also have a dedicated transitions team who support learners in visiting potential services for their future lives. The team works closely with the Wellbeing team in preparing learners for life beyond St. John's.

St Joseph's Specialist School & College

(Founded 1950)

Amlets Lane, Cranleigh, Surrey GU6 7DH

Tel: 01483 272449
Fax: 01483 276003
Email: admissions@
st-josephscranleigh.surrey.sch.uk
Website:
www.st-josephscranleigh.surrey.sch.uk
Principal: Mrs Annie Sutton

Appointed: April 2016
School type: Coeducational Day & Residential
Age range of pupils: 5–19
No. of pupils enrolled as at 01/01/2016: 75
Fees per annum as at 01/01/2016:
Day: £57,905 **Full Boarding:** £83,898

The School

St Joseph's Specialist School & College is recognised by Ofsted as an "Outstanding" well established day school and Children's Home providing care over 52 weeks of the year for children and young people with special needs from ages 5 to 19 years.

Currently with 85% of learners on the Autistic Spectrum we also specialise in a range of complex needs including Speech & Language difficulties, moderate to severe learning difficulties, social communication disorders and challenging behaviours. Autism Accredited by the National Autistic Society, St Joseph's is a proven solution for both families and Local Authorities seeking the next step for education, care and therapy.

With Specialisms in Communication Interaction and the Creative Arts, we offer tailor made teaching and learning styles, environment, therapies, and professional standards to meet all the needs of ASD learners through personalised learning programmes based on an integrated curriculum, functional communication, visual structure and positive behaviour management. These programmes incorporate a number of methods recognised for working with ASD learners: TEACHH, Intensive Interaction, PECS, Social Stories and MAKATON signing and symbols. By focusing on learning and behavioural needs, as well as personal preferences, ensures a truly bespoke and personalised approach is taken to ensure success. Information is carefully gathered from a wide range of sources including: the statement of specials needs or Education Health Care Plan; the diagnosis; developmental history; educational records and assessments; medical records; parents, care staff and observations.

The school is situated close to Cranleigh Village, which retains a great sense of 'community' with a range of amenities including a Leisure Centre, library, shops, cafes, Arts Centre, churches, sports and social clubs. With good transport links to both Horsham and Guildford where more leisure and social facilities including cinemas, theatre and indoor bowling can be found. The school is an active member of the local community and all learners are encouraged to take an active part in community life, to maximise their potential and engage with local people.

Strong leadership, teaching, care and therapeutic intervention combine to deliver positive outcomes to meet high expectation and aspirations of

both learners and families. A calming environment takes into account a wide variety of complex sensory issues and uses a variety of techniques – photographs, symbols and visual clues – children feel comfortable in their surroundings and cope easily with daily routines.

We specifically adapt the curriculum to meet each child's individual needs and focus on the development of personal social and communication along with independent living skills, especially for those aged 16+ years.

By maintaining routines within a structured environment and promoting functional communication we enable learners to stay motivated, maximise their potential and work towards positive learning outcomes, whilst seeing a reduction in both anxiety and challenging behaviours.

Therapies

We have our own dedicated team of integrated therapists who work within both class and residential settings to enhance and complement the education and care of all learners. Our Head of Therapies co-ordinates and leads a department which includes Speech and Language, Occupational Therapy, Music, Arts, Equine and Drama.

We believe communication underpins successful learning, self-esteem, positive behaviour and opportunities for life. All learners are assessed and a therapy programme devised based on their individual needs. To ensure learning is transferred to real life situations, our therapists accompany our children and young people into the community on a regular basis to access local facilities and activities.

Flexible Residential Options

Registered as a Children's Home, we provide care, education and therapies for up to 52 weeks a year. Alternatively, we can offer a variety of Residential options to meet the needs of Local Authorities, Learners and families.

We offer an environment where each learner is supported and able to develop those skills needed to maximise personal independence. Each residential group is staffed on an individual basis and well equipped to give a homely atmosphere. Our last Ofsted Inspection rated the Children's home as "Outstanding". By maintaining a waking day curriculum we

believe our learners benefit greatly from a consistency of approach.

Fully integrated into our community we ensure all our learners' skills are transferred and managed in realistic settings and reflects their levels of need. A Speech and Language therapist also visits all the residential groups to ensure consistency across the day.

Supported Living

We also provide Supported Living for young people aged 19+. Springvale in Cranleigh and Long Barn in Beare Green offer accommodation for adults with learning difficulties where each young person has their own tenancy and is supported by a tailored individual support package reflecting their own lifestyle choices and activities.

Argent College

New Standard Works, 43-47 Vittoria Street,
Birmingham, West Midlands B1 3PE
Tel: 01384 399400
Fax: 01384 399401
Email: enquiries@argent.rmt.org

Website: www.rmt.org
Executive Principal: Oliver Cheney
School type: Coeducational Day
Age range of pupils: 16–25

Argent College was launched in 2015 as a satellite of Glasshouse College (established in 2000 and awarded 'Good' by Ofsted) and based in the centre of Birmingham. Argent College offers up to 60 places to young people with a wide range of complex and comorbid learning, emotional and behavioural difficulties, mental health issues, ASD and Asperger Syndrome.

Practical Skills Therapeutic Education

Set within the heritage Jewellery Quarter of central Birmingham, Argent College is operated by Ruskin Mill Trust, whose internationally renowned Practical Skills Therapeutic Education method offers young people a unique opportunity to learn and develop transferable skills through meaningful real-life activities and accredited courses in both day and residential settings.

The college provides a focussed and safe learning environment and is part of the wider educational, vocational and social enterprise schemes at the New Standard Works. It benefits from an extensive range of nutritional, therapeutic and medical support within Glasshouse College. Each core element of the educational cycle is designed to establish active and positive relationships with nature, people and the community through a holistic approach to human development and supports three key stages: overcoming barriers to learning, becoming skilled, and being ready to engage and give back to the community.

Integrated Learning for Living and Work

A personalised pre-entry assessment leads to an individualised learning and development programme. A rich and varied curriculum offers exciting opportunities to develop communication, social, work and living skills. This includes two newly refurbished state-of-the-art visitor centres at nearby Glasshouse

College which offer students exceptional opportunities to develop social and vocational skills in professional and public environments.

Activities at Argent College include jewellery-making, leatherwork, textiles, photography, living skills, catering, horticulture and candle-making, with numeracy, communication, social and functional skills embedded throughout the provision. The development of a roof garden, a bakery, café and cultural programmes at the New Standard Works will offer a wide range of work-based and vocational skills opportunities.

Accreditation and Transition

Argent College delivers a range of BTEC courses within the varied curriculum

which are accredited through the Regulated Qualifications Framework. Access to work experience is available in the local community and will be expanded upon at the New Standard Works as social enterprises become available. Throughout their placement, students work with a dedicated team to consolidate their transferable skills and prepare for transition.

Admissions

For all initial enquiries, please contact the Admissions Team on 01384 399437 or by email at: admissions@ghc.rmt.org.

Ruskin Mill Trust is an educational charity and draws its inspiration from the insights of Rudolf Steiner, John Ruskin and William Morris. Charity No: 1137167.

Glasshouse College

Wollaston Road, Amblecote, Stourbridge, West Midlands DY8 4HF
Tel: 01384 399400
Fax: 01384 399401
Email: enquiries@ghc.rmt.org

Website: www.rmt.org
Executive Principal: Oliver Cheney
School type: Coeducational Day & Residential
Age range of pupils: 16–25

Glasshouse College, awarded 'Good' by Ofsted and 'Good' by Care Quality Commission, offers over 145 places to young people with a wide range of complex and comorbid learning, emotional and behavioural difficulties, mental health issues, ASD and Asperger Syndrome.

Practical Skills Therapeutic Education

Set within the heritage glassmaking district of Stourbridge, including 46 acres of farm and woodlands and its new campus, Argent College, in Birmingham's jewellery quarter, Glasshouse College is operated by Ruskin Mill Trust, whose internationally renowned Practical Skills Therapeutic Education method offers young people a unique opportunity to learn and develop transferable skills through meaningful real-life activities and accredited courses in both the day and residential settings.

The college provides an extensive range of nutritional, therapeutic and medical support. Each core element of the educational cycle is designed to establish active and positive relationships with nature, people and the community through a holistic approach to human development and supports three key stages: overcoming barriers to learning, becoming skilled, and being ready to engage and give back to the community.

Integrated Learning for Living and Work

A personalised pre-entry assessment leads to an individualised learning and development programme. A rich and varied curriculum offers exciting opportunities to develop communication, social, work and living skills. Two newly refurbished state-of-the-art visitor centres, the Glasshouse Arts Centre and the Ruskin Glass Centre, offer students exceptional opportunities to develop social and vocational skills in professional and public environments.

Activities include traditional glassmaking, jewellery-making, land-based and traditional craft activities, animal husbandry, woodland management, bow-making, archery, mountain biking, catering, working a narrowboat, music, art and drama, with numeracy, communication and functional skills embedded throughout the day and residential provision. The college's farm and gardens help students to grow and harvest healthy biodynamic food and then prepare meals in our canteens, cafés and households.

Accreditation and Transition

Courses are accredited through the Regulated Qualifications Framework and include OCNs, NVQs, BTECs, and GCSE and AS levels in partnership with local providers. Work competency is gained through a wide range of internal and external work experience. Throughout their placement, students work with a dedicated team to consolidate their transferable skills and prepare for transition.

Residential Provision

Students live in family or team houses in the local community, which offer the consistency, warmth and positive role-modelling that some young adults need to develop living skills, achieve greater independence and re-imagine their potential. Training flats offer even more opportunities to take greater responsibility for themselves. Glasshouse College and Argent College accept referrals throughout the year and offer up to 52-week placements, as well as respite care.

Admissions

For all initial enquiries, please contact the Admissions Team on 01384 399437 or by email at: admissions@ghc.rmt.org.

Ruskin Mill Trust is an educational charity and draws its inspiration from the insights of Rudolf Steiner, John Ruskin and William Morris. Charity No: 1137167.

Overley Hall School

(Founded 1979)
Overley, Wellington, Telford, West
Midlands TF6 5HE
Tel: 01952 740262
Fax: 01952 740875

Email: info@overleyhall.com
Website: www.overleyhall.com
Headteacher: Mrs Beverley Doran
Appointed: September 2013
School type: Coeducational Residential

Age range of pupils: 8–19
No. of pupils enrolled as at 01/01/2016: 20
Boys: 16 **Girls:** 4
No. of boarders: 20

Overley Hall School is an independent, residential special school and Children's Home, providing education and care to children and young adults aged from eight to 19 years who have a wide range of complex needs including autism, epilepsy and severe learning disabilities. The school is committed to offering each child a wide range of good quality experiences; this occurs through partnerships with parents/carers, teachers and therapists in the delivery of a waking day curriculum by a dedicated team.

Our therapy team is comprised of language and communication and occupational therapists and a clinical psychologist.

The school/residential home is set in a quiet, rural location which provides a calm and nurturing learning and living environment for young people in our care. Our school building, alongside the residential house, stands in 13 acres of lawn, walled kitchen garden and woodland.

Other facilities within the campus and grounds include a lifeskills room, indoor sensory hydropool, soft play space, art and craft workshops, sensory lodge, cinema room, farm shop, recreational and relaxation areas.

Our registered 'Forest School' operates within the woodland areas, and is led by qualified practitioners from Overley Hall School; this offers pupils opportunities for multi-sensory outdoor learning and recreation experiences throughout the seasons.

Freeman College

Sterling Works, 88 Arundel Street, Sheffield,
South Yorkshire S1 2NG
Tel: 0114 252 5940
Fax: 0114 252 5996
Email: enquiries@fmc.rmt.org

Website: www.rmt.org
Principal: Perdita Mousley
School type: Coeducational Day &
Residential
Age range of pupils: 16–25

Freeman College, awarded 'Good' by Ofsted, offers over 90 places to young people with complex learning and behavioural difficulties, mental health issues and ASD, including Asperger Syndrome.

Practical Skills Therapeutic Education

Based in the illustrious metalworking district of Sheffield, the college is operated by Ruskin Mill Trust whose internationally renowned Practical Skills Therapeutic Education method offers young people a unique opportunity to learn and develop transferable skills through meaningful real-life activities and accredited courses in both the day and residential programmes.

Freeman College provides an extensive range of nutritional, therapeutic and medical support. Each core element of the educational cycle is designed to establish active and positive relationships with nature, people and the community through a holistic approach to human development and supports three key stages: overcoming barriers to learning, becoming skilled, and being ready to engage and give back to the community.

Integrated Learning for Living and Work

A personalised pre-entry assessment leads to an individualised learning and development programme. A rich and varied curriculum is designed to offer opportunities to develop lifelong communication, social, work and living skills. Activities include traditional metal crafts such as spoon forging, copper-work, pewter-work and jewellery, as well as land-based and traditional crafts, animal husbandry, horticulture, catering and hospitality, music, art and drama, with communication and functional skills embedded throughout the day and residential provision. Healthy food is grown and harvested at the college's 9-acre market garden (using the biodynamic method) and prepared with students in the canteens, café and households.

Accreditation and Transition

Courses are accredited through the Regulated Qualifications Framework and include OCNs, NVQs, BTECs, as well as GCSE and AS-levels delivered in partnership with local providers. Work competency is gained through a wide range of internal and external work experience including through its arts and crafts shop, the Academy of Makers, cultural and events programmes, workshops and award-winning café. Throughout their placement, students collaborate with a dedicated transition team to hone their transferable skills and prepare for life after college.

Residential Provision

Students live in family or team houses in the local community, which offer the consistency, warmth and positive role-modelling that some young adults need to develop their living skills, achieve greater independence and re-imagine their potential. Students can progress onto placements in training flats where they have the opportunity to take greater responsibility for themselves.

Freeman College takes referrals throughout the year and offers up to 52-week placements.

Admissions

For all initial enquiries please contact the Admissions Team on 0114 252 5953 or by email: admissions@fmc.rmt.org.

Ruskin Mill Trust is an educational charity and draws its inspiration from the insights of Rudolf Steiner, John Ruskin and William Morris. Charity No: 1137167.

Independent Specialist Colleges

(Founded 2013)

Fullerton House College

Tickhill Square, Denaby, Doncaster, South Yorkshire DN12 4AR

Tel: 01709 861663

Fax: 01709 869635

Wilsic Hall College

Wadworth, Doncaster, South Yorkshire DN11 9AG

Tel: 01302 856382

Fax: 01302 853608

Email: enquiries@hesleygroup.co.uk

Website: www.hesleygroup.co.uk

Head: Richard Webster

Appointed: 2016

School type: Independent Specialist Residential College

Age range of pupils: 18–25

No. of pupils enrolled as at 01/01/2016:

Fullerton House College Capacity: 12

Wilsic Hall College Capacity: 9

Fees per annum as at 01/01/2016:

On request

Specialist residential colleges offering flexible education care and support for up to 52 weeks per year for young people aged 18-25, who have complex needs including behaviour that may challenge and a learning disability, often in association with autism.

At Wilsic Hall College, everyone lives within a beautiful rural setting with ready community access and at Fullerton House College in the heart of the community, in an urban setting with many local facilities including a sports centre, restaurants and shops.

Mission

Our Independent Specialist Colleges (ISCs) support young people with their transition into adult life by focusing on their specific needs, capabilities and aspirations.

Education: Everybody has a highly personalised programme of learning, equipping them with skills they will need for adult life.

Extended learning: During evenings, weekends and college holidays a wide range of extra-curricular activities are on offer to ensure people are fully engaged with stimulating experiences both on and off site providing further, meaningful learning opportunities.

Professional services: A dedicated multi-disciplinary therapeutic team including college tutors, college support workers, consultant clinical psychologist, consultant psychiatrist, applied behaviour analysts, speech and language therapists, occupational therapists, registered manager, care and support staff work together to support each individual's progress.

High quality accommodation: College accommodation includes individualised bedrooms, quality living spaces that promote independence and progressive skills development assisted by the appropriate use of specialist/adaptive technology. We also have a range of on-site and off-site facilities that offer progressive learning opportunities for young people with a range of needs and wishes.

Keeping in contact: We work to develop relationships between staff and families that are strong, positive and mutually respectful. People are supported to be in contact with their friends and family; we welcome visits to the colleges at any time. Everyone has a plan that will include the best means for them to maintain this contact whether by 'phone, letter, email or Skype.

Fullerton House School

(Founded 1990)

Tickill Square, Denaby, Doncaster, South Yorkshire DN12 4AR

Tel: 01709 861663

Fax: 01709 869635
Email: enquiries@hesleygroup.co.uk
Website: www.fullertonhouseschool.co.uk
General Manager: Michael Cavan
Appointed: 2015
Head of Education: Michael Walsh

School type: Independent Specialist Residential School
Age range of pupils: 8–19
No. of pupils enrolled as at 01/01/2016:
Capacity: 36
Fees per annum as at 01/01/2016:
Available on request

A specialist residential school offering flexible education and care, which can include day and respite provision, for up to 52-weeks-per-year for people aged 8-19, all of whom have complex needs including behaviour that may challenge and a learning disability, often in association with autism.

Fullerton House School is situated in the heart of the village of Denaby Main, near Doncaster. Its central location provides easy access by road, rail or air. Our mission is to enhance the lives of the young people entrusted to us by focusing on their specific needs, capabilities and aspirations.

Education: Each person has a carefully designed Individual Learning Plan based on their specific needs in line with the National Curriculum, which supports their positive progress in a range of areas.

Extended learning: During evenings, weekends and school holidays a wide range of extra-curricular activities are on offer to ensure that people are fully engaged with stimulating and meaningful experiences both on and off-site.

Professional services: A dedicated on-site team including carers, teachers, tutors, communication, behaviour and occupational therapy , psychology and other specialists ensure that people have ready access to the services they require.

High-quality accommodation: Single person and small group occupancy of high-quality accommodation is provided at Fullerton House School. Each person has their own bedroom, the majority of which have en-suite bathrooms. We also have a range of on-site facilities to complement and enrich the lives of those who come to live and learn with us.

Keeping in contact: We understand that while we may offer a very positive option for the person, we may not be on your doorstep. Keeping in touch with loved ones is essential. Everyone has a plan to support optimum contact with family/carers and friends whether this be by phone, letter, email or Skype.

Wilsic Hall School

(Founded 1996)

Wadworth, Doncaster, South Yorkshire

DN11 9AG

Tel: 01302 856382

Fax: 01302 853608

Email: enquiries@hesleygroup.co.uk

Website: www.wilsichallschool.co.uk

Head: Geoff Turner

Appointed: 2008

School type: Independent Specialist Residential School

Age range of pupils: 11–19

No. of pupils enrolled as at 01/01/2016:

Capacity: 31

Fees per annum as at 01/01/2016:

Available on request

A specialist residential school offering flexible education and care, which can include day and respite provision, for up to 52-weeks-per-year for people aged 11-19, all of whom have complex needs including behaviour that may challenge and a learning disability, often in association with autism.

Wilsic Hall School is situated in its own 14-acre site approximately five miles south of Doncaster. Its central location provides easy access by road, rail or air. Our mission is to enhance the lives of the people entrusted to us by focusing on their specific needs, capabilities and aspirations.

Education: Each person has a carefully designed Individual Education Plan based on their specific needs in line with the National Curriculum, which supports their positive progress in a range of areas.

Extended learning: During evenings, weekends and school holidays a wide range of extra-curricular activities are on offer to ensure that people are fully engaged with stimulating and meaningful experiences both on and off-site.

Professional services: A dedicated team including carers, teachers, tutors, behaviour, communication and occupational therapy, psychology and other specialists ensure that each person has ready access to the services they require.

High-quality accommodation: Single person and small group occupancy of high-quality accommodation is provided at Wilsic Hall School. Each person has their own bedroom, the majority of which have en-suite bathrooms. We also have a range of on-site facilities to complement and enrich the lives of those who come to live and learn with us.

Keeping in contact: We understand that while we may offer a very positive option for the person, we may not be on your doorstep. Keeping in touch with loved ones is essential. Everyone has a plan to support optimum contact with family/carers and friends whether this be by phone, letter, email or Skype.

The New School

BUTTERSTONE

(Founded 1992)

Butterstone, Dunkeld, Perth & Kinross
PH8 0HA
Tel: 01350 724216
Fax: 01350 724283
Email: info@thenewschool.co.uk
Website: www.thenewschool.co.uk
Head of School: Mr Scott Gordon
Appointed: January 2015

School type: Coeducational Day & Boarding
Age range of pupils: 11–19
No. of pupils enrolled as at 01/01/2016: 25
Boys: 21 *Girls:* 4
Fees per annum as at 01/01/2016:
Available on request

Education should be enjoyable and meaningful – we believe all young people are able to develop and achieve their potential. Through a range of educational opportunities across the 24 hour curriculum we help to prepare for life beyond school.

We have clear expectations and the relaxed, flexible and supportive environment of The New School encourages our young people to feel comfortable with who they are, and to flourish as individuals.

We are a Theraputic Learning Community. Our provision is aimed at those young people who find mainstream education difficult to access. The New School specialises in education for fragile learners in general, for young people with Aspergers/Autistic Spectrum condition, ADHD, Tourette's syndrome and Foetal Alcohol syndrome. Skilled teaching and care staff support young people who have had interrupted learning, dissatisfying school experiences, or simply those who learn differently. We are a truly inclusive school.

The New School curriculum is broad, coherent and highly varied – meeting the different needs of each and every one of our young people. Our classes are small, with an average of five. Our students are encouraged to follow interests – making the learning motivating, relevant and meaningful for them, regardless of academic ability. We deliver a full menu of SQA accredited courses, from Curriculum for Excellence National 2 up to Higher level in most subjects. ASDAN accreditation system units and courses are offered to some students, helping them to develop independence, skills for work and skills for life. Speech and language therapy is offered to all students, if required. Our sector-leading 'Showcase' eprofile recording system ensures that the student population recognise and celebrate their own achievements – both academic and more broadly throughout their time here, evidence is gathered across the 24-hour curriculum. We are passionate about outdoor learning, and utilise the beautiful school situation to promote this in various ways. Our trained staff deliver full Duke of Edinburgh's Award up to Gold level.

Coleg Plas Dwbl

Mynachlog-ddu, Clunderwen,
Pembrokeshire SA66 7SE
Tel: 01994 419420
Email: enquiries@plasdwbl.rmt.org
Website: www.rmt.org

Principal: Paul Garnault
School type: Coeducational Day &
Residential
Age range of pupils: 16–25

Coleg Plas Dwbl offers places to young people with complex learning and behavioural difficulties, mental health issues and autistic spectrum disorders, including Asperger Syndrome.

Practical Skills Therapeutic Education

Coleg Plas Dwbl is based in 100 acres of biodynamic farm and woodlands. Coleg Plas Dwbl is operated by Ruskin Mill Trust, whose internationally renowned Practical Skills Therapeutic Education method offers young people a unique opportunity to learn and develop transferable skills through meaningful real-life activities and accredited courses, helping them to prepare for adulthood. The college provides a range of nutritional and therapeutic support. Each core element of the educational cycle is designed to establish active and positive relationships with nature, people and the community through a holistic approach to human development and supports three key stages: overcoming barriers to learning, becoming skilled, and being ready to engage and give back to the community.

Integrated Learning for Living and Work Programme

Coleg Plas Dwbl offers a personalised pre-entry assessment leading to an individualised learning and development programme. A rich and varied curriculum offers exciting opportunities to develop communication, social, work and living skills. Activities include practical land-based and traditional craft activities, animal husbandry, woodland management, horticulture, catering and drama with social, communication and functional skills embedded throughout the day and residential curriculum. Students help to work the farm producing, harvesting and preparing healthy organic food, and supplying local outlets.

Accreditation and Transition

Courses are accredited through the Regulated Qualifications Framework and students will also prepare for work competency through a wide range of internal and external work experience. Qualifications include Agored Cymru, LANTRA Awards and the Welsh Baccalaureate. The curriculum is also supported by additional sessions and activities which help students to understand and explore the culture and history of the area and try local crafts. Throughout their placement, students are supported by staff to focus on transition and engage with the many transferable skills acquired to prepare for life after college.

Residential Provision

Students live in family houses or team houses which offer the consistency, warmth and positive role modelling that some young adults need to develop their living skills, achieve greater independence and re-imagine their potential. When appropriate, students can then progress to placements in training flats where they have the opportunity to take greater responsibility for themselves. Coleg Plas Dwbl takes referrals throughout the year and offers placements for up to 52 weeks.

Admissions

For all initial enquiries please contact the Admissions Team on 01994 419420 or by email at: admissions@plasdwbl.rmt.org

Ruskin Mill Trust is an educational charity and draws its inspiration from the insights of Rudolf Steiner, John Ruskin and William Morris. Charity No: 1137167.

Schools and colleges specialising in sensory or physical impairment

RNIB College Loughborough

RNIB College Loughborough

(Founded 1989)

Radmoor Road, Loughborough,
Leicestershire LE11 3BS
Tel: 01509 611077
Fax: 01509 232013
Email: enquiries@rnibcollege.ac.uk
Website: www.rnibcollege.ac.uk

Principal: June Murray
School type: Coeducational College and residence
Age range of pupils: 16–65
No. of pupils enrolled as at 01/01/2016: 109

We are a friendly residential college supporting young people and adults with a wide range of disabilities to achieve their goals. Our programmes are designed to develop independence skills for involvement in community life.

Education and skills

Choose us for your Further Education and you'll learn practical skills and gain work experience within our enterprises — our Café, eBay business, Conference Centre, Arts Centre, Shop and Office. You could also choose a course at our partner mainstream college located next door.

If you are a young adult wanting to gain the skills and confidence to progress into independent or supported living, you may want to apply for our Bridge programme. It's a one-year residential programme which will help you to build your independence. You'll be encouraged and supported to do things you've previously had help for, making you ready to move into your own home.

Also on offer is Flexible Futures, our daytime activities programme. You could spend time in each of our different enterprises, providing a vital role in these real businesses and being part of college life. You could also go out and enjoy the local community.

Accommodation

Our Stan Bell Centre offers modern, purpose built, safe accommodation. Learners are encouraged to be as independent as possible; however we recognise that some people will always need a little more support. Our residence is staffed 24 hours a day.

Wider services

We offer a range of other services too, including short courses for adults, and training for professionals and organisations that support people with sight loss.

Visit us!

The best way to find out more about our college is to come and have a look round. Call us today to arrange your visit!

Royal School for the Deaf Derby

(Founded 1894)

Ashbourne Road, Derby, Derbyshire

DE22 3BH

Tel: 01332 362512

Fax: 01332 299708

Email: enquiries@rsdd.org.uk

Website: www.rsd-derby.org

Headteacher: Helen Shepherd

School type: Coeducational Day & Boarding

Age range of pupils: 3–19

No. of pupils enrolled as at 01/01/2016: 125

Boys: 81 **Girls:** 44

Day: £21,912

Weekly Boarding: £33,807

Royal School for the Deaf Derby is a non-maintained residential special school with a national catchment area.

The school prides itself on being a warm and inclusive environment providing both day and weekly residential places. Language is developed using the learner's preferred method of communication. The broad range of subjects offered is delivered using an individualised approach tailored to the language profile of each child. An Audiologist and Speech and Language Therapists, who specialise in working with deaf children, provide expert support. The Health Centre provides comprehensive support to pupils and a 'Complex Needs SENCO' gives additional input where the needs of the learner are not straightforward.

The inviting and stimulating range of equipment in Early Years Foundation Stage includes an all weather outdoor learning area. Children in Primary Department are taught in small groups by qualified teachers of the deaf with education assistant support.

In Secondary Department we strive for best academic achievement according to individual potential and starting points. Our high expectations challenge every pupil to raise their aspirations and develop their confidence. Deaf and hearing staff work throughout the department allowing pupils to access an environment rich in both BSL and English. External examinations offered include Entry Level, GCSE, DiDA, BTEC and BSL.

Our Post 16 Department works in partnership with local mainstream secondary schools and colleges to offer vocational courses with full support from RSDD staff for students up to the age of 19. Specialist teachers and teachers of the deaf continue to develop students' numeracy and literacy skills. Courses lead to a full range of recognised qualifications.

Residential life in purpose built accommodation offers a rich environment where both BSL and English are valued.

For further information, contact Helen Shepherd or Anne Muller at the School.

Royal School for the Deaf Derby is a Registered Charity (No. 1062507) whose object is the education of deaf children aged 3 to 19.

RNIB Sunshine House School and Residence

33 Dene Road, Northwood, Middlesex
HA6 2DD
Tel: 01923 822538
Fax: 01923 826227
Email: sunshinehouse@rnib.org.uk

Website: www.rnib.org.uk/sunshinehouse
Head: Jackie Seaman
School type: Coeducational
Age range of pupils: 2–14

RNIB Sunshine House School and Residence, in Northwood, Middlesex, is a specialist school, children's home and service for families supporting blind and partially sighted children with significant learning difficulties and disabilities.

Boasting a range of specialist indoor and outdoor facilities, Sunshine House provides a safe and supportive environment for children to meet their full potential.

Education and Curriculum
Everyone at Sunshine House is treated as an individual with their own specific needs and learning goals. Working together with parents and specialists we ensure that achievements go beyond the classroom into everyday life.

Our specialist school educates children and young people from two to 14 years who have a range of physical, learning and sensory needs. Children follow an individually tailored curriculum supporting their special education needs. Most children are working between P levels 1 and 8. Each class has no more than eight children with a minimum support ratio of two adults for every three children.

Therapies and Healthcare
Our team of in-house therapists combine their work with a child's learning, making therapies a part of everyday school life. We also have a paediatric community nurse who ensures that all health needs are met.

Short Stays
Our children's home offers a range of flexible day care, overnight and short stay options, where children and young people aged between two and 16 years can stay up to four nights per week (Monday to Thursday) for up to 50 weeks per year during the school term and holidays. We welcome children who attend school elsewhere, providing we can meet their needs.

Visit us!
The best way to find out more about the school and residence is to come and have a look round. Call us today to arrange your visit!

Chailey Heritage School

(Founded 1903)

Haywards Heath Road, North Chailey, Lewes, East Sussex BN8 4EF
Tel: 01825 724444
Fax: 01825 723773
Email: office@chf.org.uk
Website: www.chf.org.uk
Charity Chief Executive: Helen Hewitt
Headteacher: Simon Yates

Director of Social Care: Denise Banks
School type: Coeducational Boarding & Day
Age range of pupils: 3–19
19–25
No. of pupils enrolled as at 01/01/2016: 73
Fees per annum as at 01/01/2016:
Please contact the school for details

Chailey Heritage School, part of Chailey Heritage Foundation, is a non-maintained special school for children and young people aged 2-19 with a wide range of complex physical, communication, sensory and learning difficulties and health needs.

Chailey Heritage School was judged to be 'Outstanding' by Ofsted in October 2014 for a third consecutive time. Chailey Heritage Residential is a registered children's home and offers flexible care packages from short breaks through to 52 weeks of the year.

Meeting children's health and therapy needs

Chailey Heritage School's unique on-site partnership with Chailey Heritage Clinical Services, part of Sussex Community NHS Trust. Working with our expert teachers, the pupils' health and therapy needs are met in a holistic way by a highly skilled team that includes Paediatric Medical Consultants and Doctors, a full range of Therapists, residential Nursing team and Rehabilitation Engineers.

Experts in promoting independence through powered mobility and communication

Every young person has the opportunity to experience appropriate forms of powered mobility. The award-winning Chailey Heritage Foundation engineering team have developed a range of advanced assistive technologies to develop driving skills and allow progression.

All pupils at Chailey Heritage School have some level of communication difficulty. We always strive to meet every individual's need and their right to communicate and be listened to. By working closely alongside Speech and Language Therapists, we develop a wide variety of Alternative and Augmentative Communication (AAC) approaches to meet personal needs.

Purposeful learning

Chailey Heritage School has developed its own curriculum driven by the individual learners needs. This means every learner has their own curriculum built specifically for them based on their skills and desired outcomes, it is broad, in that it covers all aspects of their development and it is balanced in that it weighs up, specifically for them, the input that is needed. Above all it is meaningful to each child and their family.

Support for parents and families at every step in any way we can

We work in partnership with parents and families at every step of their Chailey Heritage journey, providing support at difficult times and celebrating achievements together.

Chailey Heritage Residential

Chailey Heritage Residential is a nationally recognised, registered children's home for 3 to 19 year olds with complex physical disabilities and health needs. We offer flexible residential provision ranging from short breaks to 52 weeks a year.

Find out more

We take great pride in and celebrate the achievements of our young people. Whatever your role in our school is or might be – as a parent, potential parent, grandparent, governor, volunteer, fundraiser, supporter – we would be delighted to show you around. Please get in touch now to arrange a visit and in the meantime visit our website at www.chf.org.uk

Chailey Heritage School and Chailey Heritage Residential are part of Chailey Heritage Foundation, registered charity number 1075837, registered in England as a charitable company limited by guarantee No. 3769775

Moor House School & College

(Founded 1947)

Mill Lane, Hurst Green, Oxted, Surrey
RH8 9AQ
Tel: 01883 712271
Fax: 01883 716722
Email:
admissionsteam@moorhouseschool.co.uk;
info@moorhouseschool.co.uk
Website: www.moorhouseschool.co.uk

Principal: Mrs H A Middleton
School type: Coeducational Day &
Residential
Age range of pupils: 7–19
No. of pupils enrolled as at 01/01/2016: 121
Fees per annum as at 01/01/2016:
On request

"Quality of teaching: Outstanding" – Ofsted 2014
Moor House is a special school and college for children and young people with language difficulties and related communication difficulties. Students come to Moor House from our local area as well as from across the UK. Their fees are paid by their Local Authorities.

The school, believed to be the first of its kind, has provided inspiration for other schools both in the UK and abroad, and continues to lead in areas of specialist education, therapy and research. Moor House shares its expertise and research findings to support children in the wider community and professionals at Moor House publish their work to share our innovative and evidence based methods internationally.

"... Pioneering work in many areas of speech and language therapy and in teaching methods continues to place Moor House School at the forefront of research, development and practice in the education of children with severe, specific speech and language impairments." The Bercow Report

Learning
Students are empowered to reach their potential in classroom learning and independence, and to develop communication skills, friendships and self-belief. We offer a highly specialist, safe, caring and stimulating learning environment. Students are taught in small classes by teachers with experience of working with children with language difficulties. Adapted language and visual approaches are used so that children can understand and develop the language that they need for learning.

Speech and language therapists (SLTs) work closely with teachers to understand and support each child's difficulties and strengths. Taking a holistic approach to learning, the teachers and SLTs plan and deliver English and Science lessons collaboratively, to ensure that children gain maximum benefit.

The curriculum
An adapted National Curriculum is taught at Moor House, with the core curriculum of English, Maths, Science and ICT being taught along with Geography, History, Art (including 3D Design), Music, Design & Technology, Food Technology, PSHCE, P.E. and Religious Education.

Progress and Qualifications
Our results show that overall our students make excellent progress. Students take qualifications that match with their skills and level of development. Many students take GCSE qualifications, which we offer in English Language, English Literature, Mathematics, Science, ICT, History, Fine Art and Ceramics. We also offer Functional Skills qualifications in English and Maths, vocational qualifications such as Home Cooking Skills at Levels 1 and 2, the AQA Unit Award Scheme in Science, and Entry Level qualifications in subjects such as English, Maths, ICT, DT and Music.

Therapy
Speech and language therapy is an essential part of a student's week at Moor House and is integrated throughout their day. The SLTs work with students individually, in groups, as well as in the classroom where lessons such as English are jointly planned and delivered.

All students are supported through the school by occupational therapy programmes which include functional class support and life skills training.

For some students who have more

specific occupational therapy needs, we provide additional weekly individual, paired or group work delivered by an Occupational Therapist (OT).

Residential Care

Our Residential Care has been classed as Outstanding by Ofsted in each of the last four years. The Care team work to provide our students with a homely environment whilst they stay with us. The team also works closely with the teaching and therapy staff to ensure that each child receives the support needed.

College (Sixth Form) Curriculum

"The sixth form is outstanding and prepares students exceptionally well for the next stage in their adult lives" Ofsted 2014

The College's objective is to support each student to gain vocational qualifications, make confident and appropriate life choices and to be prepared for the next stage of their adult life. Students are supported by the Moor House specialist staff to enable them to access our local partner college courses. Students also access our specialist support to achieve additional qualifications in Maths and English and develop important

skills for life and employment. Teaching and residential care staff work jointly with SLTs and OTs to provide individual study programmes and after college support.

Learning at the Partnership Colleges

Students can access vocational courses on offer at the partnership colleges such as painting and decorating, child care, media studies, art and design,

catering, sport and active leisure and animal management, to name a few. Achievement ranges from Foundation and Level 1 in Year 12 to as high as Level 4 at the end of Year 14. As well as providing support directly to the students, the MHC Therapy department offers training and student specific advice to teaching staff running the partner college courses.

St Mary's School & 6th Form College

Making a difference
st.marys
Special School & College Bexhill

(Founded 1922)
Wrestwood Road, Bexhill-on-Sea, East
Sussex TN40 2LU
Tel: 01424 730740
Fax: 01424 733575
Email: admin@stmarysbexhill.org

Website: www.stmarysbexhill.org
Principal: Amanda Clugston
School type:
Coeducational Boarding & Day
Age range of pupils: 7–19
No. of pupils enrolled as at 01/01/2016: 73

Making a difference

We are an inspirational School and 6th Form College for young people aged 7-19 with speech, language and communication disabilities, many of whom have other complex needs. We are committed to providing integrated therapy, education and care tailored to each young person's abilities and aspirations.

The children and young people are taught in small groups and follow an exciting broad and balanced curriculum, which is adapted to meet individual needs and is delivered by highly qualified teachers and support staff with the integrated support of therapists for a truly holistic approach.

Children receive individual therapy programmes which may include specialist support from: Speech and Language Therapists, Physiotherapists, Occupational Therapists, Well-being Team and Educational Psychologist.

Other specialist professionals include an Audiologist and Teacher of the Deaf, Sign Language Tutors, Social Worker, visiting Doctor (GP) and onsite Nursing Team.

Here at St Mary's, we support each child to develop and maximise their communication skills. Parent signing classes are offered on site or via Skype to ensure families can communicate with their child as effectively as possible.

At St Mary's our residences are warm and caring places, creating a 'home from home' feel. In nurturing and stimulating environments we work with our children and young people to develop life skills and encourage everyone to learn and live with each other. Opportunities to take part in a wide range of activities are available every day, with children and young people accessing the local community on a daily basis.

Our fantastic facilities include:

- Sensory Room
- Physiotherapy Room
- Adventure Playground
- Swimming and Hydrotherapy pool
- Sensory Integration Room
- Traversing Wall
- Nature Trail
- Music & Drumming Room
- Outdoor Tennis Courts
- Science Lab
- ICT Suite
- Horticultural area & Polytunnel

The Children's Trust School
Non-Maintained Special School

The Children's Trust
For children with brain injury

(Founded 1985)

Tadworth Court, Tadworth, Surrey
KT20 5RU
Tel: 01737 365810
Fax: 01737 365819
Email: school@thechildrenstrust.org.uk
Website:
www.thechildrenstrust.org.uk/school

Head Teacher: Samantha Newton
School type: Coeducational Boarding
Age range of pupils: 3–19
No. of pupils enrolled as at 01/04/2016: 51
Fees per annum as at 01/01/2016:
On application

At The Children's Trust School our aim is to provide high quality education and expertise to meet each pupil's individual special educational needs and to celebrate all achievements in a happy, secure environment.

As a non-maintained special school, we pride ourselves on seeing the 'whole' child and delivering integrated, holistic, education, therapy and care for pupils with profound and multiple learning difficulties providing day and residential education for pupils aged 3 to 19.

We focus on developing pre-intentional learning into intentional and formal stages of learning with an aim of supporting pupils to improve their understanding of the world around them.

Individualised learning opportunities relevant to each pupil are created to support the development of their communication, language and literacy skills, their cognitive development, physical skills, environmental control and social, emotional and personal well-being.

Working alongside teachers and core class staff, we have on-site professionals including play therapists, music therapists, physiotherapists, occupational therapists, speech and language therapists and paediatric nurses. Pupils also have access to health services including GPs, consultants and clinics such as orthotics.

We provide stimulating educational opportunities, supported by unparalleled expertise delivering significant outcomes for our pupils.

Treloar School

Treloar's
Enabling Education

(Founded 1908)

Holybourne, Alton, Hampshire GU34 4GL
Tel: 01420 547400
Email: admissions@treloar.org.uk
Website: www.treloar.org.uk
Head: Jo McSherrie
Principal: John Stone
School type:
Coeducational Boarding & Day

Religious Denomination: Non-denominational
Age range of pupils: 2–19 yrs
No. of pupils enrolled as at 01/01/2016: 95
Boys: 50 *Girls:* 45 *Sixth Form:* 31
No. of boarders: 54
Fees per annum as at 01/01/2016:
As per assessment

Treloar Nursery and School provide education, care, therapy, medical support and independence training to children and young people from 2 to 19 years of age with complex physical disabilities. Provision is both day and residential and we accept students from across the UK and overseas. In addition our College, based on the same site, offers continued education and care up to the age of 25 years. Our aim is to prepare physically disabled young people for adult life, giving them the confidence and skills they need to achieve their full potential, and also become socially and economically active in their communities.

We have an on site medical centre and weekly doctors surgeries in addition to on site provision for occupational therapy, physiotherapy, speech and language therapy, educational psychology, visual and hearing impairment, assistive technology plus dieticians and counsellors. Timetables are integrated with classroom and daily living activities to ensure the most beneficial use of the student's time.

Entry Requirement

Admission is considered on the basis of the particular student's needs following discussion and assessment with education, medical, therapy and care staff. All offers are tailor made to provide the maximum benefit for each student and we strive to be flexible. Part time placements, limited time placements and respite for day students are all available. We pride ourselves on our strong parental links and have been awarded the nationally recognised Leading Parent Partnership Award.

Life on Campus

We are situated in a beautiful rural location on the edge of Alton in Hampshire with a good road and rail network. We ensure a varied range of out of school activities including sports, art, drama, clubs and extensive visits off site utilising our own specialist fleet of vehicles. On site facilities include a swimming pool, all weather sports facilities, a hydrotherapy pool and social club.

Treloar Trust is a registered charity which supports Treloar School and College (Charity No 1092857).

WESC Foundation – The Specialist College for Visual Impairment

The Specialist College for Visual Impairment

(Founded 1838)
Countess Wear, Exeter, Devon EX2 6HA
Tel: 01392 454200
Fax: 01392 428048
Email: info@wescfoundation.ac.uk
Website: www.wescfoundation.ac.uk

Principal: Mrs Tracy de Bernhardt-Dunkin
School type: Non-maintained Special School and College
Age range of pupils: 16+–
Fees per annum as at 01/01/2017:
On request

WESC Foundation provides a wide range of post-16 academic and vocational courses and specialist training and support to help young people with a visual impairment make a successful transition to adult life. Many learners from the school move directly to the college.

Tailored to the needs of the individual, our courses contain employability and work experience modules and are supported by work placements in our own social enterprise firms (shops and eBay centre) or with partner organisations.

We also work in partnership with other colleges of further education to provide our students with a unique academic and vocational experience.

The college offers:
- Specialist support tailored to the needs of each learner
- A challenging curriculum
- A wide range of nationally accredited awards and qualifications
- Work placements with local employers
- Professional specialists: speech and language therapists, physiotherapists, occupational therapists, music therapists, mobility tutors, qualified nurses and care staff
- Qualified and experienced teachers of the visually and multi-sensory impaired
- Individual learning plans
- High staff:learner ratio
- Purpose-built accommodation: from fully supervised to self-contained houses
- Day and residential placements
- Broad-based leisure programmes
- Specialist sensory environments.

College accommodation comprises of comfortable bedrooms with well-equipped areas for socialising with friends and visitors. Maple Lodge and Ash Lodge benefit from larger bedrooms and extra wide access for wheelchairs. Lodges feature adjustable height kitchen and bathroom appliances, talking kitchen equipment and an accessible laundry room. The latest technologies, equipment and fittings help develop and support independent living skills. Campus facilities include: pool, gym, library, bar and social area.

Situated on the outskirts of Exeter the campus offers access to a huge range of activities and experiences. Extended curricular activities include trips to the beach, park, ten pin bowling and even residential trips abroad.

Please call or email for more information on assessment and admissions quoting WHM/17.

Registered charity no. 1058937.

WESC Foundation – The Specialist School for Visual Impairment

The Specialist School for Visual Impairment

(Founded 1838)

Countess Wear, Exeter, Devon EX2 6HA
Tel: 01392 454200
Fax: 01392 428048
Email: info@wescfoundation.ac.uk
Website: www.wescfoundation.ac.uk
Chief Executive: Mrs Tracy de Bernhardt-Dunkin

School type: Non-maintained Special School and College
Age range of pupils: 5–16
Fees per annum as at 01/01/2017:
On request

WESC Foundation specialises in meeting the needs of young people with visual impairment, including many with complex needs. The school offers an adapted curriculum that follows the National Curriculum. Each learner receives mobility and therapy sessions where a need has been identified (occupational therapy, physiotherapy, speech and language therapy, music therapy, etc.). Specialist ICT equipment and adapted access technology is tailored for each learner.

The school residences offer homely, comfortable accommodation for weekly boarders and those wishing to stay occasionally. Accommodation comprises of comfortable bedrooms and areas for socialising with friends and visitors. Groundfloor areas are wheelchair accessible and suitable adaptations are made for individuals.

Our 14-acre campus provides space for pupils to enjoy the sensory garden, swimming pool, gym and adapted playing areas. Situated on the outskirts of Exeter the campus offers access to a huge range of activities and experiences. Extended curricular activities include trips to the beach, park, ten pin bowling and even residential trips abroad.

Learners are totally involved in planning for their future with many of them continuing their studies and development at our college, which is situated on the same campus.

Candidates for both the school and college need to come for an assessment. This is free and is usually held over a period of two days. The assessment process is an opportunity for you to take an in-depth look at what we have to offer and allows our specialist staff to determine how best to meet a young person's needs. Please call or email for more information on assessment and admissions quoting WHM/01/17.

Registered charity no. 1058937

RNIB Pears Centre for Specialist Learning

RNIB

Pears Centre

(Founded 1957)

Wheelwright Lane, Ash Green, Coventry, West Midlands CV7 9RA
Tel: 024 7636 9500
Fax: 024 7636 9501
Email: pearscentre@rnib.org.uk
Website: www.rnib.org.uk/pearscentre

Headteacher: Emily Hopkins-Hayes
Appointed: September 2007
School type: Coeducational day school and Children's Home
Age range of pupils: 2–19
No. of pupils enrolled as at 01/01/2016: 29

At RNIB Pears Centre, we provide a stimulating, creative and purpose-built setting for children and young people with multiple disabilities, complex health needs and vision impairment to live, learn and grow.

We support children to make progress, to develop their independence, and to make their own choices.

Education and outreach

If you're looking for a specialist school, our education celebrates a child's abilities and stimulates all of their senses. Our broad, balanced and relevant curriculum is tailored to meet individual learning needs.

Ofsted rated our school as 'Outstanding'! This shows that we're very effective in helping children to make progress in their learning and development.

Our national outreach service – "Periscope" – offers practical support to pupils and educational advice and guidance to professionals and parents. We can also mentor students and provide braille tuition.

Therapies

Our in-house therapy team offers specialist expertise in vision impairment and learning disabilities, physiotherapy, speech and language therapy, behaviour management and mobility/habilitation. Water and music therapies, clinical psychology and occupational therapy are also part of our provision.

Specialist care and leisure

Sometimes, the chance to share the care of a child can help to relieve pressure on families. Our children's home offers 24-hour care all year round, with waking night staff in spacious bungalows.

Each young person living with us has their own bedroom, which is made safe and personal to them. We support children to access a range of activities and community events, like pop concerts and swimming.

If a young person has high health and medical needs, our nursing care offers rehabilitation and a real alternative to long stays in hospital.

Visit us!

The best way to find out more about what we offer is to come and have a look round. Call us today to arrange your visit!

The Royal National College for the Blind (RNC)

Great Britain's leading specialist college for people who are blind or partially sighted

The Royal National College for the Blind

Education, employment and empowerment

(Founded 1872)

Venns Lane, Hereford, Herefordshire

HR1 1DT

Tel: 01432 376621

Fax: 01432 842979

Email: info@rnc.ac.uk

Website: www.rnc.ac.uk

Principal: Mr Mark Fisher

School type: Coeducational Boarding & Day

Age range of pupils: 16–65

students from all–over the UK

No. of pupils enrolled as at 01/01/2015:

No. of boarders: 150

Fees per annum as at 01/01/2015:

Funded via Local Authorities (younger students) or Department for Work and Pensions (adults):

The Royal National College for the Blind (RNC) is the UK's leading specialist residential college of further education for people aged 16+ with a visual impairment.

We have created a vibrant and supportive community, valuing personalised learning plans that help students achieve their future ambitions whilst developing their self-confidence and independence.

We offer a wide range of study programmes at levels to suit each individual including A Levels, BTECs, ITECs, NVQs and OCRs in subjects from humanities, massage and languages to IT and media production.

RNC is home to the UK's first VI Sports Academy and Cisco Networking Academy, offering tailored training in both the sporting and technology industries. Students also gain independence and mobility skills to support their transition to adulthood.

Many students go on to university or into employment or self-employment, having engaged not just academically but socially in a safe yet dynamic environment. Among the many clubs and activities on offer are Duke of Edinburgh Awards, angling, Young Enterprise, arts, horticulture and sports from novice to elite level.

In 2011, Ofsted awarded RNC 'outstanding' as a specialist residential provider. In 2013 we maintained our 'good' with outstanding elements rating as a Further Education and Skills provider. Teachers were praised as being skilled at providing an accessible learning environment in which students with little or no sight participate fully.

RNC also offers services to a diverse audience including businesses, universities and professionals working with people with a visual impairment. The College is a member of Natspec and holds the Investors in Diversity Award, ranked sixth in the UK.

Prospective students can visit the College and speak with specialist staff, or attend a free Have a Go weekend, trying out different courses in a relaxed atmosphere. Contact Student Enquiries for more information on 01432 376 621 or visit www.rnc.ac.uk.

Doncaster School for the Deaf

Doncaster School for the Deaf

(Founded 1829)

Leger Way, Doncaster, South Yorkshire
DN2 6AY

Tel: 01302 386733

Fax: 01302 361808

Email: principal@ddt-deaf.org.uk or secretary@ddt-deaf.org.uk

Website: www.deaf-trust.co.uk

Executive Principal: Mr Alan W Robinson

School type: Non-maintained (Special) Coeducational Boarding and Day

Age range of pupils: 4–19

No. of pupils enrolled as at 01/01/2016: 29

Boys: 20 **Girls:** 9

No. of boarders: 5

Fees per annum as at 01/01/2016:

Fees on request

We offer a broad and balanced curriculum which is accessible to all our pupils, providing smooth progression and continuity through all Key Stages.

The language and communication policy at Doncaster School for the Deaf is a pupil-centred approach, based on their method of preferred communication. We aim to meet the needs of pupils who communicate through British Sign Language (BSL) or English.

The School has a full-time Audiologist, Speech and Language Therapists and a team of Teaching Assistants as well as an on-site fully qualified Nurse. Most teachers are experienced and qualified teachers of the deaf.

Provision for resident pupils is in a modern comfortable house sympathetically converted to provide high standards of living accommodation.

Qualifications include A Levels, AS Levels, GCSE, Entry Level Certificate of Achievement, ASDAN and Signature (BSL). The school believes that the school curriculum should be broad, balanced and personalised in order to reflect the needs of each pupil and to nurture a lifelong desire to learn. In addition to curriculum subjects pupils access speech therapy, BSL lessons and Deaf Studies. Some KS4 and KS5 pupils are able to access vocational courses as part of the 14-19 curriculum.

The School works in partnership with Little Learners Day Nursery and Communication Specialist College Doncaster (formerly Doncaster College for the Deaf) which share the same campus.

We have close links with parents, and other professionals.

The school occupies a large, pleasant site. A superb sports hall, heated indoor swimming pool and extensive playing fields. The school welcomes visitors.

St John's Catholic School for the Deaf

(Founded 1870)
Church Street, Boston Spa, Wetherby,
West Yorkshire LS23 6DF
Tel: 01937 842144
Fax: 01937 541471

Email: info@stjohns.org.uk
Website: www.stjohns.org.uk
Headteacher: Mrs A Bradbury BA(Hons),
MSc, NPQH
School type: Coeducational Boarding & Day

Age range of pupils: 4–19
No. of pupils enrolled as at 01/01/2016: 68
Fees per annum as at 01/01/2016:
On application

St John's is a non-maintained residential and day school offering bespoke education to deaf, multi-sensory impaired (MSI) and language impaired children. We were founded almost 150 years ago and although the school is based on a Catholic ethos, we welcome children from other faiths or none. Some pupils have additional and complex needs which may include dyslexia, dyspraxia, learning difficulties, ASD, ADHD, and physical disabilities. Our pupils are aged from 4 to 19 years and come to us from all parts of the UK.

St John's is an oral school, where pupils are taught by specialist teachers of hearing impaired children. We place great emphasis on developing each child's potential for understanding and using spoken and written language, as well as reading and writing. Our unique

approach has gained us a national and international reputation for promoting linguistic, academic and personal growth, enabling pupils to make their contribution to a wider world.

In our Speech and Language Department we have specialist therapists so pupils can receive intensive individual speech therapy. Our teachers are qualified teachers of hearing impaired children with additional qualifications in areas such as MSI and dyslexia and we also have qualified intervenors. Close liaison and joint planning across staff teams helps to provide well-coordinated provision, including support from the York Deaf CAMHS team.

We offer a vibrant curriculum with a wide range of qualifications that include GCSEs as well as creative and vocational courses, to meet the needs of the individual pupils.

The development of communication skills has special emphasis at St John's and we have a dedicated Expressive Arts Centre which is designed for drama, music, and dance. We have specialist music and drama teachers, one to one music tuition and have a soundproof recording booth for pupils to create their own compositions.

Our other facilities include three different sensory rooms to support pupils with dual or multi sensory impairments to maximise their use and integration of all their senses.

Our Post 16 students attend mainstream colleges, supported by our own note takers and a teacher of the deaf. Students receive additional tutorial support at school as well as continuing with speech therapy and courses in English and Maths.

Residential life at St John's supports pupils' communication, social and life skills.

Students grow in confidence and maturity, leaving St John's so well prepared for adult life that Ofsted has judged the care pupils receive as outstanding.

If you would like to visit and experience first-hand, the education and care we offer our pupils, please contact our Pupil Admissions Co-ordinator Mandy Dowson on 01937 842144 or email info@stjohns.org.uk.

The Royal Blind School

ROYAL BLIND
THE ROYAL BLIND SCHOOL
(Founded 1835)
43-45 Canaan Lane, Edinburgh, EH10 4SG
Tel: 0131 446 3120
Fax: 0131 447 9266

Email: office@royalblindschool.org.uk
Website: www.royalblind.org/education
Head Teacher: Elaine Brackenridge (BEd)
School type: Coeducational, National Grant Aided Special School

Age range of pupils: 5–19
No. of pupils enrolled as at 25/02/2016: 39
Boys: 26 **Girls:** 13
Fees per annum as at 25/02/2016:
Available on request

The Royal Blind School was founded on compassionate and forward thinking principles in 1835. It is run by Scotland's largest visual impairment charity, Royal Blind, and is regulated by Education Scotland and the Care Inspectorate. We are a grant-aided special school supported by the Scottish Government.

The school, situated in the Morningside area of Edinburgh, is Scotland's only residential school specialising in the care and education of visually impaired young people, including those with complex needs.

Places are paid for through fees from local authorities or privately.

- We offer day and weekly residential places. Our residential houses are fully accessible and designed to be a home from home.
- We enrol pupils from P1 to S6 and in addition there is a free pre-school playgroup held on Friday mornings during term time.

The Royal Blind School has a high ratio of staff to pupils. Each child follows an individualised education programme underpinned by the Curriculum for Excellence and Getting It Right for Every Child (GIRFEC). We deliver a broad general education and offer qualifications and accreditation by the Scottish Qualifications Authority (SQA), Junior Awards Scheme Scotland, Personal Achievement Awards and ASDAN in the senior phase.

Our approach is inclusive and pupil-centred, providing many opportunities for experience and achievement. We strive to make learning enjoyable, fun, challenging and self-affirming. We offer a full curriculum of subjects including Art, Drama, Outdoor Education, Craft, Design and Technology, ICT, Home Economics, PE/Swimming, social subjects, Music and Mindfulness.

We deliver independent living skills, building self-confidence and self-esteem by providing a greater awareness of the wider environment through mobility and orientation to ensure that all pupils become as independent as possible.

Pupils in the fourth, fifth and sixth year have the opportunity to undertake work experience. Some pupils are involved in a Coffee Shop Enterprise Project. This activity gives young people the opportunity to develop a valuable range of life skills such as social interaction, handling money,

planning, shopping and baking.

Outreach Support

We also provide an education outreach service offering support, training, resources and advice to staff in mainstream schools who are working with visually impaired pupils through our Learning Hub, www.royalblind.org/learninghub.

For more information please visit our website www.royalblind.org/education or telephone 0131 446 3120, or email office@royalblindschool.org.uk.

Scottish Charity No. SC 017167.

Directory

Schools and colleges specialising in social interaction difficulties (Autism, ASD & ASP)

Abbreviations

ACLD	Autism, Communication and Associated Learning Difficulties
ADD	Attention Deficit Disorder
ADHD	Attention Deficit and Hyperactive Disorder (Hyperkinetic Disorder)
ASD	Autistic Spectrum Disorder
ASP	Asperger Syndrome
AUT	Autism
BESD	Behavioural, Emotional and Social Difficulties
CCD	Complex Communication Difficulties
CLD	Complex Learning Difficulties
CP	Cerebral Palsy
D	Deaf
DEL	Delicate
DYS	Dyslexia
DYSP	Dyspraxia
EBD	Emotional and Behavioural Difficulties
EBSD	Emotional, Behavioural and/or Social Difficulties
EPI	Epilepsy
GLD	General Learning Difficulties
HA	High Ability
HI	Hearing Impairment
HS	Hospital School
LD	Learning Difficulties
MLD	Moderate Learning Difficulties
MSI	Multi-sensory Impairment
OCD	Obsessive Compulsive Disorder
PD	Physical Difficulties
PH	Physical Impairment
Phe	Partially Hearing
PMLD	Profound and Multiple Learning Difficulties
PNI	Physical Neurological Impairment
PRU	Pupil Referral Unit
SCD	Social and Communication Difficulties
SCLD	Severe and Complex Learning Difficulties
SEBD	Severe Emotional and Behavioural Disorders
SEBN	Social, Emotional and Behavioural Needs
SLD	Severe Learning Difficulties
SLI	Specific Language Impairment
SPLD	Specific Learning Difficulties
SP&LD	Speech and Language Difficulties
SLCN	Speech Language & Communication Needs
VIS	Visually Impaired

Key to Symbols

Type of school:

(icon)	Boys' school
(icon)	Girls' school
(icon)	International school

School offers:

(A)	A levels
(icon)	Boarding accommodation
(16)	Entrance at 16+
(icon)	Vocational qualifications
(icon)	Learning support
(✓)	This is a DfE approved independent or non-maintained school under section 342 or 347(1) of the 1996 Education Act

Please note: Unless otherwise indicated, all schools are coeducational day schools. Single-sex and boarding schools will be indicated by the relevant icon.

Central & West

Bristol

NAS ANDERSON SCHOOL
For further details see p. 53
Rookery Lane, Pilning,
Bristol BS35 4JN
Tel: 01454 632532
Email: nasanderson@nas.org.uk
Website:
www.andersonschool.org.uk
Principal: Kim McConnell
Age range: 7–19
No. of pupils: 24
Special needs catered for:
ASD, ASP, AUT

Gloucestershire

BREDON SCHOOL
For further details see p. 52
Pull Court, Bushley, Tewkesbury,
Gloucestershire GL20 6AH
Tel: 01684 293156
Email: enquiries@
bredonschool.co.uk
Website:
www.bredonschool.org
Headmaster: Mr David Ward MA
Age range: 3–18

Oxfordshire

LVS Oxford
Spring Hill Road, Begbroke,
Oxfordshire OX5 1RX
Tel: 01865 595170
Head Teacher: Mrs Louisa
Allison-Bergin
Age range: 11–19
Special needs catered for:
ASD, ASP, AUT

Swalcliffe Park School Trust
Swalcliffe, Banbury,
Oxfordshire OX15 5EP
Tel: 01295 780302
Principal: Mr Kiran Hingorani
Age range: B11–19
No. of pupils: 45
Special needs catered for: ADHD,
ASD, BESD, DYS, DYSP, MLD, SP&LD

West Berkshire

PRIOR'S COURT SCHOOL
For further details see p. 54
Hermitage, Thatcham,
West Berkshire RG18 9NU
Tel: 01635 247202
Email: mail@priorscourt.org.uk
Website: www.priorscourt.org.uk
**Director of Education and
Learning:** Sue Piper
Age range: 5–19
No. of pupils: 59 VIth26
Special needs catered for:
AUT, CLD, EPI, MLD, SCLD

Wiltshire

Farleigh Further Education
College Swindon
Fairview House, 43 Bath Road, Old
Town, Swindon, Wiltshire SN1 4AS
Tel: 01793 719500
Principal/Manager: Mr
Martin Bentham
Age range: 16–25
No. of pupils: 63
Special needs catered for: ASP, LD

Stratford Lodge
4 Park Lane, Castle Road,
Salisbury, Wiltshire SP1 3NP
Tel: 0800 288 9779
Head: Sue King BA(Hons), PGCE
Dip in Adv Ed Studies SEN, NPQH
Age range: 16–19
Special needs catered for:
ADHD, ASD, ASP

East

Cambridgeshire

GRETTON SCHOOL
For further details see p. 56
Manor Farm Road,
Girton, Cambridge,
Cambridgeshire CB3 0RX
Tel: 01223 277438
Email: info@grettonschool.com
Website:
www.grettonschool.com
Head Teacher: Ms Tina Harris
Age range: 5–19
Special needs catered for:
ASD, AUT, LD

On Track Training Centre
Enterprise House, Old Field Lane,
Wisbech, Cambridgeshire PE13 2RJ
Tel: 01945 580898
Headteacher: Mrs Sharon Claydon
Age range: 11–18
Special needs catered for:
ADHD, ASP, EBD

Park House
Wisbech Road,
Thorney, Peterborough,
Cambridgeshire PE6 0SA
Tel: 01733 271187
Head: Mr Alan Crossland
Age range: 4–16
Special needs catered for: AUT

Essex

The Yellow House School
1 Alderford Street, Sible
Hedingham, Halstead,
Essex CO9 3HX
Tel: 01787 462504
Age range: 13–17
No. of pupils: 11
Special needs catered for:
ADHD, ASP, EBD

Hertfordshire

NAS RADLETT
LODGE SCHOOL
For further details see p. 57
Harper Lane, Radlett,
Hertfordshire WD7 9HW
Tel: 01923 854922
Email: radlett.lodge@nas.org.uk
Website:
www.radlettlodgeschool.org.uk
Principal: Jo Galloway
Age range: 4–19
No. of pupils: 55
Special needs catered for:
ASD, ASP, AUT

Norfolk

Acorn Park School
Mill Road, Banham, Norwich,
Norfolk NR16 2HU
Tel: 01953 888656
Head Teacher: Mr John Shaw
BEd(Hons), DipEdMan
Age range: 4–19
Special needs catered for:
ASD, AUT, CLD, EPI, LD, MLD,
SCD, SCLD, SLD, SPLD

St Andrews School
Lower Common, East Runton,
Cromer, Norfolk NR27 9PG
Tel: 01263 837927
Headteacher: Ms Gillian
Baker BSc(Hons), BA, CertEd,
PGC-Asperger Syndrome
Age range: 6–17
No. of pupils: 17
Fees: Day £40,000
Special needs catered for:
ADD, ADHD, ASD, ASP, AUT, DYS,
DYSP, SCD, SLD, SP&LD, SLI

Social interaction difficulties (Autism, ASD & ASP)

East Midlands

Derbyshire

High Grange School
Hospital Lane, Mickleover,
Derby, Derbyshire DE3 0DR
Tel: 01332 412777
Headteacher: Marisa Kelsall
Age range: 8–19
Special needs catered for:
ASD, ASP, AUT
⑯ ✔

Leicestershire

Sketchley Horizon
Manor Way, Sketchley, Burbage,
Leicestershire LE10 3HT
Tel: 01455 890023
Principal: Ms Sarah-Jane Astbury
Age range: 8–19
No. of pupils: 30
Special needs catered for:
ASD, ASP, AUT
⑯ ✔

Northamptonshire

Alderwood
302 Wellingborough Road,
Rushden, Northamptonshire
NN10 6BB
Tel: 01933 359861
Head: Mrs Jacqueline Wadlow
Special needs catered for:
ASD, AUT
⚐ ⑯ ✔

Hill Farm College
c/o The Manor House,
Squires Hill, Rothwell,
Northamptonshire NN14 6BQ
Tel: 01536 711111
Principal: Jo Morris
Age range: 14–19
No. of pupils: 12
Special needs catered for:
ADHD, ASD, ASP
⚐ ⑯

Potterspury Lodge School
Towcester, Northamptonshire
NN12 7LL
Tel: 01908 542912
Executive Head: Ms Lise Sugden
BSc(Hons), PGCE, NPQH
Age range: B8–18
No. of pupils: 40 VIth8
Special needs catered for:
ADD, ADHD, ASD, ASP, AUT,
DYS, DYSP, EBD, SCD, SP&LD
⚐ ⚐ ⑯ ✔

Rutland

Wilds Lodge School
Stamford Road, Empingham,
Rutland LE15 8QQ
Tel: 01780 767254
Age range: 5–18
Special needs catered for:
ASD, MLD, SEBD
⑯

Greater London

Kent

Baston House School
Baston Road, Hayes,
Bromley, Kent BR2 7AB
Tel: 020 8462 1010
Principal: Steve Vincent
Age range: 3–19
Special needs catered for: ASD
⑯ ✔

Middlesex

NAS SYBIL ELGAR SCHOOL
For further details see p. 59
Havelock Road, Southall,
Middlesex UB2 4NY
Tel: 020 8813 9168
Email: sybil.elgar@nas.org.uk
Website:
www.sybilelgarschool.org.uk
Principal: Chloe Phillips
Age range: 4–19
No. of pupils: 90
Special needs catered for:
ASD, ASP, AUT
⚐ ⑯ ✔

Surrey

BLOSSOM LOWER SCHOOL AND UPPER HOUSE
For further details see p. 91
Station Road, Motspur Park,
New Malden, London KT3 6JJ
Tel: 020 8946 7348
Email: admin@
blossomhouseschool.co.uk
Website: www.blossomhouse
school.co.uk
Principal: Joanna Burgess
DipCST,MRCSLT,DipRS
A,SpLD,PGCE,HPC
Age range: 3–19
No. of pupils: 214
Special needs catered for:
ADD, ADHD, ASP, DYS,
DYSP, SCD, SP&LD, SPLD
⑯ ✔

Link Secondary Day School
82-86 Croydon Road, Beddington,
Croydon, Surrey CR0 4PD
Tel: 020 8688 7691
Headteacher: Miss P
Ridgwell BEd, NPQH
Age range: 11–19
No. of pupils: 48 VIth9
Special needs catered for:
ASD, ASP, SP&LD, SLI
✔

'the little group'
c/o St Josephs Catholic
Primary School, Rosebank,
Epsom, Surrey KT18 7RT
Tel: 01372 720218
Head Teacher: Judy Gilham
Age range: 2–5+
Special needs catered for:
ASD, AUT

London

North London

FINCHES SCHOOL
For further details see p. 62
Levy Building, 80 East End Road,
Finchley, London N3 2SY
Tel: +44 (0)208 343 0105
Email: info@finchesschool.co.uk
Website:
www.finchesschool.co.uk
Headteacher: Mr Adrian Mahon
Age range: 7–18
Special needs catered for:
ASD, AUT
⑯

Kestrel House School
104 Crouch Hill, London N8 9EA
Tel: 020 8348 8500
Headteacher: Kerry Harris
Age range: 4–16
Special needs catered for: ASP, AUT
✔

THE HOLMEWOOD SCHOOL
For further details see p. 64
88 Woodside Park Road,
London N12 8SH
Tel: 020 8920 0660
Email: enquiries@thsl.org.uk
Website: www.thsl.org.uk
Head of School: Headteacher
Lisa Camilleri
Age range: 7–19
Special needs catered for:
ASP, AUT, DYS, DYSP, SP&LD
Ⓑ ⑯ ✔

TreeHouse School
Woodside Avenue, London N10 3JA
Tel: 020 8815 5424
Head: Julie O'Sullivan
Age range: 3–19
No. of pupils: 67
Special needs catered for:
ASD, AUT
⑯ ✔

South-East London

RIVERSTON SCHOOL
For further details see p. 63
63-69 Eltham Road, Lee
Green, London SE12 8UF
Tel: 020 8318 4327
Email: office@
riverstonschool.co.uk
Website:
www.riverstonschool.co.uk
Headmistress: Mrs S E Salathiel
Age range: 9 months–19 years
No. of pupils: 215
Special needs catered for:
ASD, ASP, AUT, LD

South-West London

RAINBOW SCHOOL
For further details see p. 60
48 North Side, Wandsworth
Common, London SW18 2SL
Tel: 020 3031 9700
Email: rainbowschool@
beyondautism.org.uk
Website:
www.rainbowschool.org.uk
**Head of Lower
School:** Bennie Lesch
Age range: 4–19 (Early
Years/Primary, Secondary
and 6th Form)
Special needs catered for:
ASD, ASP, AUT, SCD

**The Chelsea Group
of Children**
The Hall, Waynflete Street,
London SW18 3QG
Tel: 020 8946 8330
Director: Libby Hartman
Age range: 4–8
Special needs catered for: ADHD,
ASP, AUT, LD, MLD, SP&LD, SPLD

The Priory Lodge School
Priory Lane, London SW15 5JJ
Tel: 020 8392 4410
Principal: Pancho Martinez
Age range: 7–19
No. of pupils: 40
Special needs catered for:
ASD, ASP, AUT, LD

North-East

Durham

Priory Hurworth House
38 The Green, Hurworth-on-Tees,
Darlington, Durham DL2 2AD
Tel: 01325 720424
Principal: Mr John Anderson
Age range: 7–19
No. of pupils: 30
Special needs catered for:
AUT, BESD, EBD

Tyne & Wear

ESPA College
6-7 The Cloisters, Ashbrooke,
Sunderland, Tyne & Wear SR2 7BD
Tel: 0191 510 2600
Principal (Acting): Mrs C Pickup
Age range: 16–25
No. of pupils: 100
Special needs catered for:
ASD, ASP, AUT

Thornhill Park School
21 Thornhill Park, Sunderland,
Tyne & Wear SR2 7LA
Tel: 0191 514 0659
Head Teacher: Margaret Burton
Age range: 4–19
No. of pupils: 74
Fees: Day £33,752–£45,806
FB £117,433–£204,986
Special needs catered for:
ASD, ASP, AUT

North-West

Cheshire

Royal College Manchester
Seashell Trust, Stanley Road,
Cheadle, Cheshire SK8 6RQ
Tel: 01616 100100
Age range: 19–25
No. of pupils: 70
Special needs catered for:
ASD, D, MSI, PD, PMLD, VIS

Royal School Manchester
Seashell Trust, Stanley Road,
Cheadle, Cheshire SK8 6RQ
Tel: 01616 100100
Age range: 2–19
No. of pupils: 45
Special needs catered for:
ASD, D, HI, MSI, PMLD

Cumbria

Lindeth College
The Oaks, Lindeth, Bowness on
Windermere, Cumbria LA23 3NH
Tel: 01539 446265
Principal/Manager: Ms
Shirley Harrison
Age range: 16–25
No. of pupils: 30
Special needs catered for: ASP, LD

Greater Manchester

Fairfield House School
59 Warburton Lane, Partington,
Manchester, Greater
Manchester M31 4NL
Tel: 0161 7762827
Headteacher: Ms Melanie Sproston
Age range: 8–19
Special needs catered for: ASD

Inscape House Cheadle
Schools Hill, Cheadle, Greater
Manchester SK8 1JE
Tel: 0161 283 4750
Headteacher: Liz Loftus
Age range: 5–16
No. of pupils: 55
Special needs catered for: AUT

Lancashire

Bracken School
1 Harbour Lane, Warton,
Preston, Lancashire PR4 1YA
Tel: 01772 631531
Headteacher: Paul Addison
Age range: G11–16
No. of pupils: 5
Special needs catered for:
ADHD, DYS, MLD

Oliver House
Hall Gate, Astley Village,
Chorley, Lancashire PR7 1XA
Tel: 01257 220011
Principal: Ms Wendy Sparling
Age range: 6–19
No. of pupils: 28
Special needs catered for:
ASD, ASP

Red Rose School
28-30 North Promenade,
St Annes on Sea, Lytham St
Annes, Lancashire FY8 2NQ
Tel: 01253 720570
Principal: Colin Lannen
Age range: 5–16
Special needs catered for:
ASD, DEL, SPLD

Rossendale School
Bamford Road, Ramsbottom,
Bury, Lancashire BL0 0RT
Tel: 01706 822779
Headteacher: Mr David Duncan
Age range: 7–18
Special needs catered for:
ADD, ADHD, ASD, ASP, AUT,
BESD, CLD, DYS, DYSP, EBD, EPI,
HA, SCD, SEBD, SLD, SPLD

Trax Academy
Riverside Park, Wallend Road,
Preston, Lancashire PR2 2HW
Tel: 0330 0240 170
Headteacher: Mr Edward Sloane
Age range: 11–18
No. of pupils: 12
Special needs catered for:
ADHD, EBD

Westmorland School
Weldbank Lane, Chorley,
Lancashire PR7 3NQ
Tel: 01257 278899
Head Teacher: Mrs S M Asher
BSc (Hons), PGCE, NPQH
Age range: 5–11
No. of pupils: 44
Special needs catered for:
ADHD, ASD, ASP, AUT, BESD,
MLD, SP&LD, SPLD

Merseyside

Arden College
40 Derby Road, Southport,
Merseyside PR9 0TZ
Tel: 01704 534433
Principal/Manager: Mr
Mark Musselle
Age range: 16–25
No. of pupils: 53
Special needs catered for: ASP, LD

Social interaction difficulties (Autism, ASD & ASP)

Lakeside School
Naylors Road, Huyton, Liverpool,
Merseyside L27 2YA
Tel: 0151 4877211
Head Teacher: Mrs V I Size
BEd(Hons), MEd(Autism)
Age range: 5–13
No. of pupils: 24
Special needs catered for: ADD,
ADHD, ASD, ASP, AUT, BESD, CLD,
DEL, DYS, DYSP, EPI, HA, HI, LD, MLD,
PH, SCD, SP&LD, SPLD, SLI, VIS
✔

Peterhouse School for Pupils with Autism & Asperger's Syndrome
Preston New Road, Southport,
Merseyside PR9 8PA
Tel: 01704 506682
Headteacher: Janet Allan
Age range: 5–19
No. of pupils: 51 VIth20
Fees: Day £38,190
WB £90,896 FB £120,045
Special needs catered for:
ASD, ASP, AUT
🏫 16+ ✔

WEST KIRBY SCHOOL AND COLLEGE
For further details see p. 65
Meols Drive, West Kirby, Wirral,
Merseyside CH48 5DH
Tel: 0151 632 3201
Website: www.wkrs.co.uk
Principal: Mr Iain Sim
Age range: 5–19
No. of pupils: 89
Special needs catered for:
ADHD, ASD, SCD, SEBD, SLI
🏫 ✔

South-East

Berkshire

Heathermount, The Learning Centre
Devenish Road, Ascot,
Berkshire SL5 9PG
Tel: 01344 875101
Headteacher: Ms Ruth Bovill
Age range: 5–19
No. of pupils: 25
Special needs catered for:
ASD, ASP, AUT
16+ ✔

NAS THAMES VALLEY SCHOOL
For further details see p. 67
Conwy Close, Tilehurst,
Reading, Berkshire RG30 4BZ
Tel: 0118 9424 750
Email: thames.valley@nas.org.uk
Website: www.thamesvalley
school.org.uk
Principal: Gary Simm
Age range: 5–16
No. of pupils: 50
Special needs catered for:
ASP, AUT

East Sussex

Rookery Hove
22-24 Sackville Gardens,
Hove, East Sussex BN3 4GH
Tel: 01273 202 520
Principal/Manager: Mr Loz Blume
Age range: 18–35
No. of pupils: 13
Special needs catered for:
ASD, ASP
16+ 🏫

Step by Step School for Autistic Children
Neylands Farm, Grinstead Lane,
Sharpethorne, East Sussex RH19 4HP
Tel: 01342 811852
Headteacher: Mrs Faye Palmer
Age range: 4–11
No. of pupils: 12
Special needs catered for: AUT
✔

Hampshire

Grateley House School
Pond Lane, Grateley, Andover,
Hampshire SP11 8TA
Tel: 0800 288 9779
Head: Mrs Sue King BA(Hons),
PGCE, DAE (SEN) NPQH
Age range: 9–19
Special needs catered for:
ASD, ASP
🏫 16+ ✔

Hill House School
Rope Hill, Boldre, Lymington,
Hampshire SO41 8NE
Tel: 0800 288 9779
Head of School: Ms Kate Landells
BSc (open), CertSocSci(open)
NVQ3 HSC, PTLLS(L4)
Age range: 11–19
Special needs catered for:
ASD, AUT, SCD, SCLD, SLD
🏫 16+ ✔

Southlands School
Vicars Hill, Boldre, Lymington,
Hampshire SO41 5QB
Tel: 0800 288 9779
Head: Ms Naomi Clarke
BEd DipEd, SEN, AMBDA
Age range: B7–16
Special needs catered for:
ASD, ASP
👤 🏫 16+ ✔

Tadley Horizon
Tadley Common Road, Tadley,
Basingstoke, Hampshire RG26 3TB
Tel: 01189 817720
Principal: Phil Jonas
Age range: 5–19
No. of pupils: 67
Special needs catered for:
ASD, ASP, AUT
🏫 16+ ✔

Kent

Blue Skies School
126 Maidstone Road,
Chatham, Kent ME4 6DQ
Tel: 01634 357770
Head of School: Mr
Jonathan Higgins
Age range: 11–19
No. of pupils: 17
Special needs catered for:
ASD, ASP, AUT
16+ ✔

NAS HELEN ALLISON SCHOOL
For further details see p. 66
Longfield Road, Meopham,
Kent DA13 0EW
Tel: 01474 814878
Email: helen.allison@nas.org.uk
Website:
www.helenallisonschool.org.uk
Principal: Susan Conway
Age range: 5–19
No. of pupils: 77
Special needs catered for:
ASD, ASP, AUT
🏫 16+ ✔

The Quest School
Church Farm, Church Road, The
Old Stables, Offham, Kent ME19 5NX
Tel: 01732 522700
Headteacher: Mrs Anne Martin
Age range: 4–14
No. of pupils: 8
Special needs catered for:
AUT, EBD
✔

Surrey

Eagle House School (Mitcham)
224 London Road, Mitcham,
Surrey CR4 3HD
Tel: 020 8687 7050
Head Teacher: Alan Simons
Age range: 4–11
Special needs catered for: ASD,
ASP, AUT, MLD, SCD, SLD
✔

Eagle House School (Sutton)
95 Brighton Road, Sutton,
Surrey SM2 5SJ
Tel: 020 8661 1419
Head Teacher: Mr Tom Coulter
Age range: 11–19
Special needs catered for: AUT
16+ ✔

Jigsaw CABAS® School
Building 20, Dunsfold Park, Stovolds
Hill, Cranleigh, Surrey GU6 8TB
Tel: 01483 273874
Executive Head: Ms Kate Grant
Age range: 4–19
No. of pupils: VIth17
Fees: Day £49,900–£52,732
Special needs catered for:
ASD, AUT
16+ ✔

Papillon House School
Pebble Close, Tadworth,
Surrey KT20 7PA
Tel: 01372 363663
**Headteacher and
Director:** Mrs Gillian Hutton
Age range: 4–16
Fees: Day £45,000
Special needs catered for:
ASD, AUT
✔

Unsted Park School
Munstead Heath Road,
Godalming, Surrey GU7 1UW
Tel: 01483 892061
Principal: Mr Steve Dempsey
Age range: 7–19
No. of pupils: 55
Special needs catered for:
ASD, ASP, AUT
🏫 16+ ✔

West Sussex

LVS Hassocks
London Road, Sayers Common,
Hassocks, West Sussex BN6 9HT
Tel: 01273 832901
Head Teacher: Kira Brabanec
Age range: 8–19
Special needs catered for:
ASD, ASP, AUT
16+

South-West

Cornwall

Three Bridges Education Centre
East Hill, Blackwater, Truro, Cornwall TR4 8EG
Tel: 01872 561010
Headteacher: Rebecca Edwards
Age range: 11–19
No. of pupils: 8
Special needs catered for: ASD, ASP, AUT
16+ ✓

Devon

Cheltham Senior School
Bere Alston, Yelverton, Devon PL20 7EX
Tel: 01822 840379
Principal: Mr John Steward
Age range: 7–19
No. of pupils: 63
Special needs catered for: ADHD, ASD, ASP, AUT, BESD, CLD, EBD, GLD, MLD, SCD, SCLD
🏛 16+ ✓

Coombe House
Coleford, Crediton, Devon EX17 5BY
Tel: 01363 85910
Principal: Pat Dingle
Age range: 16–30
No. of pupils: 16
Special needs catered for: ASD
16+ 🏛

Dorset

Portfield School
Parley Lane, Christchurch, Dorset BH23 6BP
Tel: 01202 573808
Headteacher: Mr Tyler Collins
Age range: 3–19
No. of pupils: 59
Special needs catered for: ASD, AUT
🏛 16+ ✓

Purbeck View School
Northbrook Road, Swanage, Dorset BH19 1PR
Tel: 0800 288 9779
Head: Susan Harvey CQSW Ex Dip in Management
Age range: 7–19
Special needs catered for: ASD, AUT
🏛 16+ ✓

The Forum School
Shillingstone, Blandford Forum, Dorset DT11 0QS
Tel: 0800 288 9779
Head: Mr Adrian J A Wylie BED PG DIP (Autism) NPQH
Age range: 7–19
Special needs catered for: ASD, AUT
🏛 16+ ✓

The Wing Centre
126 Richmond Park Road, Bournemouth, Dorset BH8 8TH
Tel: 0800 288 9779
Head: Janette Morgan MA, BA, NPQH, PGCert in AS, CM CIPD
Age range: B16–19
Special needs catered for: ASD, ASP
🏃 🏛 16+

Somerset

3 Dimensions
Chardleigh House, Chardleigh Green, Wadeford, Chard, Somerset TA20 3AJ
Tel: 01460 68055
Education Manager: Ms Nita Ellul
Age range: B11–16
No. of pupils: 5
Special needs catered for: ADHD, AUT, EBD
🏃 🏛 ✓

Farleigh College Mells
Newbury, Nr Mells, Frome, Somerset BA11 3RG
Tel: 01373 814980
Principal: Ms Sharon Edney
Age range: 11–19
No. of pupils: 52
Special needs catered for: ADD, ADHD, ASD, ASP, AUT, DYS, DYSP
🏛 16+ ✓

Farleigh Further Education College Frome
North Parade, Frome, Somerset BA11 2AB
Tel: 01373 475470
Principal/Manager: Mr Alun Maddocks
Age range: 16–25
No. of pupils: 87
Special needs catered for: ASP, LD
16+ 🏛

North Hill House
Fromefield, Frome, Somerset BA11 2HB
Tel: 01373 466222
Principal: Ms Sharon Edney
Age range: B7–18
No. of pupils: 62
Special needs catered for: ADD, ADHD, ASD, ASP, AUT
🏃 🏛 16+ ✓

West Midlands

Shropshire

CRUCKTON HALL
For further details see p. 68
Cruckton, Shrewsbury, Shropshire SY5 8PR
Tel: 01743 860206
Email: jo.burdon@cruckton.com
Website: www.cruckton.com
Head Teacher: Jo Burdon
Age range: B8–19
No. of pupils: 80
Special needs catered for: ADD, ADHD, ASP, AUT, DYS, EBD, PMLD, SPLD
🏃 Ⓐ 🏛 ✓

Higford School
Higford Hall, Higford, Shifnal, Shropshire TF11 9ET
Tel: 01952 630600
Headteacher: Anne Adams
Age range: 8–19
Special needs catered for: ASD, AUT, CLD, DYS, DYSP, EPI, GLD, HA, LD, MLD, MSI, PMLD, SCLD, SLD, SP&LD, SPLD
🏛 16+ ✓

Staffordshire

NAS CHURCH LAWTON SCHOOL
For further details see p. 70
Cherry Tree Avenue, Church Lawton, Stoke-on-Trent, Staffordshire ST7 3EL
Tel: 01270 877601
Email: churchlawton@nas.org.uk
Website: www.churchlawtonschool.org.uk
Principal: Paul Scales
Age range: 4–19
No. of pupils: 60
Special needs catered for: ASD, AUT
16+

Priory Highfields
9 & 11 Highfields Road, Chasetown, Burntwood, Staffordshire WS7 4QR
Tel: 01543 672 173
Principal: Ms Joan Pearson
Age range: 18–25
No. of pupils: 10
Special needs catered for: ASD
16+ 🏛

Rugeley Horizon
Blithbury Road, Blithbury, Rugeley, Staffordshire WS15 3JQ
Tel: 01889 504400
Principal: Ms Joan Pearson
Age range: 5–19
No. of pupils: 48
Special needs catered for: ASD, ASP, AUT
🏛 16+ ✓

Strathmore College
Unit 7 Imex centre, Technology Park, Bellringer Road, Trentham Lakes South, Stoke-on-Trent, Staffordshire ST4 8LJ
Tel: 01782 647384
Principal/Manager: Ms Kate Ward
Age range: 16–25
No. of pupils: 37
Special needs catered for: ASP, BESD, CLD, GLD, LD, MLD, SLD
16+ 🏛

Warwickshire

Avon Park School
St John's Avenue, Rugby, Warwickshire CV22 5HR
Tel: 01788 524448
Head Teacher: Sophie Garner B.Ed, M.Ed (Oxon), NPQH
Age range: 6–16
No. of pupils: 19
Special needs catered for: ADD, ADHD, ASD, ASP, BESD, CLD, DYSP, LD, SCD, SEBD, SP&LD

West Midlands

The Island Project School
Diddington Hall, Diddington Lane, Meriden, West Midlands CV7 7HQ
Tel: 01675 442588
Principal: Sarah Gallagher
Age range: 6–19
Special needs catered for: ASD, AUT
✓

Worcestershire

AALPS Midlands
The Rhydd, Hanley Castle,
Worcestershire WR8 0AD
Tel: 01684 312610
Registered Manager: Darren
Goodwin
Age range: 16–25
Special needs catered for: ASD
16· 🏛 16·

Yorkshire & Humberside

Lincolnshire

Barton School
Barrow Road, Barton-upon-
Humber, Lincolnshire DN18 6DA
Tel: 01652 631280
Headteacher: Mark Eames
Age range: 8–19
Special needs catered for:
ASD, ASP, AUT, CLD, DYS,
DYSP, GLD, HA, LD, MLD, MSI,
PMLD, SCLD, SLD, SPLD
🏛 ✔

The Bridge@Barton School
Barrow Road, Barton-upon-
Humber, Lincolnshire DN18 6DA
Tel: 01652 631280
Head of School: Mr Mark Eames
Age range: 8–19
Special needs catered for:
🏛

North Lincolnshire

AALPS North
Winterton Road, Roxby,
Scunthorpe, North
Lincolnshire DN15 0BJ
Tel: 01724 733777
Centre Head: Mr Russell Leese
Age range: 16–30
Special needs catered for: ASD
16· 🏛 16·

Demeter House
98-100 Oswald Road, Scunthorpe,
North Lincolnshire DN15 7PA
Tel: 01724 277877
Headteacher: Mrs L Wardlaw
Age range: B5–14
No. of pupils: 5
Special needs catered for:
ADD, EBD
🧍 🏛 ✔

South Yorkshire

FULLERTON HOUSE SCHOOL
For further details see p. 71
Tickill Square, Denaby,
Doncaster, South
Yorkshire DN12 4AR
Tel: 01709 861663
Email: enquiries@
hesleygroup.co.uk
Website: www.fullertonhouse
school.co.uk
General Manager: Michael
Cavan
Age range: 8–19
Special needs catered for:
ASD, ASP, AUT, CLD, DYS, DYSP,
GLD, LD, MLD, SCLD, SLD, SPLD
🏛 16· ✔

FULLERTON HOUSE COLLEGE
For further details see p. 72
Tickhill Square, Denaby,
Doncaster, South
Yorkshire DN12 4AR
Tel: 01709 861663
Email: enquiries@
hesleygroup.co.uk
Website:
www.hesleygroup.co.uk
Head: Richard Webster
Age range: 18–25
Special needs catered for:
ASD, ASP, AUT, CLD, DYS, DYSP,
GLD, LD, MLD, SCLD, SLD, SPLD
🏛

NAS ROBERT OGDEN SCHOOL
For further details see p. 73
Clayton Lane, Thurnscoe,
Rotherham, South
Yorkshire S63 0BG
Tel: 01709 874443
Email: robert.ogden@nas.org.uk
Website:
www.robertogdenschool.org.uk
Principal: Lorraine Dormand
Age range: 5–19
No. of pupils: 127
Special needs catered for:
ASD, ASP, AUT
🏛 16· ✔

WILSIC HALL COLLEGE
For further details see p. 72
Wadworth, Doncaster,
South Yorkshire DN11 9AG
Tel: 01302 856382
Head: Geoff Turner
Age range: 19–25
No. of pupils: 3
Special needs catered for:
ASD, ASP, AUT, CLD, DYS, DYSP,
GLD, LD, MLD, SCLD, SLD, SPLD
🏛

WILSIC HALL SCHOOL
For further details see p. 74
Wadworth, Doncaster,
South Yorkshire DN11 9AG
Tel: 01302 856382
Email: enquiries@
hesleygroup.co.uk
Website:
www.wilsichallschool.co.uk
Head: Geoff Turner
Age range: 11–19
Special needs catered for:
ASD, ASP, AUT, CLD, DYS, DYSP,
GLD, LD, MLD, SCLD, SLD, SPLD
🏛 16· ✔

Scotland

East Ayrshire

NAS DALDORCH HOUSE SCHOOL
For further details see p. 75
Sorn Road, Catrine, East
Ayrshire KA5 6NA
Tel: 01290 551666
Email: daldorch@nas.org.uk
Website: www.daldorchhouse
school.org.uk
Principal: Bernadette Casey
Age range: 8–21
No. of pupils: 64
Special needs catered for:
ASD, ASP, AUT
🏛 16·

Moray

Troup House School
Gamrie, Banff, Moray AB45 3JN
Tel: 01261 851 584
Principal: Mr David McNally
Age range: 8–16
No. of pupils: 12
Special needs catered for:
AUT, BESD
🏛

South Lanarkshire

NAS Daldorch Satellite School
St Leonards, East Kilbride,
South Lanarkshire G74
Tel: 01355 246242
Principal: Shona Pinkerton
Age range: 5–19
No. of pupils: 5
Special needs catered for:
ASD, ASP, AUT
🏛 16·

Wales

Carmarthenshire

Coleg Elidyr
Rhandirmwyn, Llandovery,
Carmarthenshire SA20 ONL
Tel: 01550 760400
The College Manager: Contact
Age range: 18–25
No. of pupils: 43
Special needs catered for:
ADD, ADHD, ASD, ASP, AUT,
BESD, CLD, DEL, DYSP, EBD, EPI,
GLD, LD, MLD, Phe, SCD, SLD

Flintshire

AALPS Cymru
Llanerch-y-mor, Holywell,
Flintshire CH8 9DX
Tel: 01745 562570
Registered Manager: Shian Thomas
Age range: 18+
Special needs catered for: ASD

Kinsale School
Kinsale Hall, Llanerch-y-Mor,
Holywell, Flintshire CH8 9DX
Tel: 01745 562500
Head of Service: Mr Mark Williams
Age range: 8–19
Special needs catered for:
ASD, AUT, CLD, DYS, DYSP, EPI,
GLD, LD, MLD, MSI, PH, PMLD,
SCLD, SLD, SP&LD, SPLD

Torfaen

Priory Coleg Wales
Coleg Gwent, Pontypool
Campus, Blaendare Road,
Pontypool, Torfaen NP4 5YE
Tel: 01495 762609
Principal/Manager: Mr Simon Coles
Age range: 16–25
No. of pupils: 11
Special needs catered for: ASP, LD

Vale of Glamorgan

Beechwood College
Hayes Road, Penarth, Vale
of Glamorgan CF64 5SE
Tel: 029 2053 2210
Principal: Mr Darren Jackson
Age range: 16+
No. of pupils: 66
Special needs catered for:
ASD, ASP, SLD

Wrexham

Priory Coleg North Wales
67 King Street, Grove Park
Road, Wrexham LL11 1HR
Tel: 01978 366 006
Principal/Manager: Mr Simon Coles
Age range: 16–25
No. of pupils: 5
Special needs catered for: ASP, LD

Schools and colleges specialising in emotional, behavioural and/or social difficulties (EBSD)

Abbreviations

ACLD	Autism, Communication and Associated Learning Difficulties
ADD	Attention Deficit Disorder
ADHD	Attention Deficit and Hyperactive Disorder (Hyperkinetic Disorder)
ASD	Autistic Spectrum Disorder
ASP	Asperger Syndrome
AUT	Autism
BESD	Behavioural, Emotional and Social Difficulties
CCD	Complex Communication Difficulties
CLD	Complex Learning Difficulties
CP	Cerebral Palsy
D	Deaf
DEL	Delicate
DYS	Dyslexia
DYSP	Dyspraxia
EBD	Emotional and Behavioural Difficulties
EBSD	Emotional, Behavioural and/or Social Difficulties
EPI	Epilepsy
GLD	General Learning Difficulties
HA	High Ability
HI	Hearing Impairment
HS	Hospital School
LD	Learning Difficulties
MLD	Moderate Learning Difficulties
MSI	Multi-sensory Impairment
OCD	Obsessive Compulsive Disorder
PD	Physical Difficulties
PH	Physical Impairment
Phe	Partially Hearing
PMLD	Profound and Multiple Learning Difficulties
PNI	Physical Neurological Impairment
PRU	Pupil Referral Unit
SCD	Social and Communication Difficulties
SCLD	Severe and Complex Learning Difficulties
SEBD	Severe Emotional and Behavioural Disorders
SEBN	Social, Emotional and Behavioural Needs
SLD	Severe Learning Difficulties
SLI	Specific Language Impairment
SPLD	Specific Learning Difficulties
SP&LD	Speech and Language Difficulties
SLCN	Speech Language & Communication Needs
VIS	Visually Impaired

Key to Symbols

Type of school:

⚹	Boys' school
⚹	Girls' school
🌐	International school

School offers:

Ⓐ	A levels
🏫	Boarding accommodation
16+	Entrance at 16+
⚙	Vocational qualifications
✎	Learning support
✓	This is a DfE approved independent or non-maintained school under section 342 or 347(1) of the 1996 Education Act

Please note: Unless otherwise indicated, all schools are coeducational day schools. Single-sex and boarding schools will be indicated by the relevant icon.

Central & West

Buckinghamshire

Benjamin College
4 Wren Path, Fairford Leys,
Aylesbury, Buckinghamshire
HP19 7AR
Tel: 01296 483584
Principal: Mr Jeremy Yelland
Age range: 12–18
Special needs catered for: BESD

Gloucestershire

Cotswold Chine School
Box, Stroud, Gloucestershire
GL6 9AG
Tel: 01453 837550
Headteacher: Maureen
Smith MA(Ed), PGCertSpLd,
PGCE, BA(Hons)
Age range: 9–19
No. of pupils: 48
Special needs catered for:
ADD, ADHD, ASP, AUT, DYS,
DYSP, EBD, EPI, MLD, SP&LD

Oxfordshire

Action for Children Parklands Campus
Chardleigh House, Near Appleton,
Abingdon, Oxfordshire OX13 5QB
Tel: 01865 390436
Principal: Mr. Sean Cannon
Age range: 11–19
No. of pupils: 7 VIth2
Fees: Day £50,000 FB £192,000
Special needs catered for: ADD,
ADHD, ASD, ASP, AUT, BESD,
EBD, LD, MLD, SEBD, SPLD

Chilworth House School
Thame Road, Wheatley, Oxford,
Oxfordshire OX33 1JP
Tel: 01844 339077
Head Teacher: Mr Dave
Willcox BEd (Hons)
Age range: 4–11
No. of pupils: 29
Special needs catered for: ADHD,
ASD, ASP, BESD, EBD, MLD, SCD, SLD

Chilworth House Upper School
Grooms Farm, Thame Road,
Wheatley, Oxfordshire OX33 1JP
Tel: 01844 337720
Head Teacher: Mr Kevin
Larsen BEd(Hons), MA,
PGCE ED Management
Age range: 11–16
No. of pupils: 59
Special needs catered for: ADD,
ADHD, ASD, ASP, AUT, BESD,
DEL, GLD, HI, LD, MLD, Phe, SCD,
SCLD, SEBD, SP&LD, SPLD

Hillcrest Park School
Southcombe, Chipping Norton,
Oxford, Oxfordshire OX7 5QH
Tel: 01608 644621
Headteacher: David
Davidson MA(Hons), PGCE
Age range: 7–18
Special needs catered for: ADD,
ADHD, ASD, ASP, BESD, DYS, DYSP,
EBD, GLD, MLD, SCD, SEBD

Mulberry Bush School
Standlake, Witney,
Oxfordshire OX29 7RW
Tel: 01865 300202
Director: John Turberville BSc, MA
Age range: 5–12
No. of pupils: 36
Special needs catered for: EBD

East

Bedfordshire

Advanced Education - Walnut Tree Lodge School
Avenue Farm, Renhold
Road, Wilden, Bedford,
Bedfordshire MK44 2PY
Tel: 01234 772081
Headteacher: Mr John Boslem
Age range: 11–16
Special needs catered for: EBD

Cambridgeshire

Advanced Education - Wisbech School & Vocational Centre
Old Session House, 32 Somers Road,
Wisbech, Cambridgeshire PE13 1JF
Tel: 01945 427276
Headteacher: Mr Mick Coleman
Age range: 9–16
Special needs catered for:
EBD, SEBD

Chartwell House School
Goodens Lane, Newton, Wisbech,
Cambridgeshire PE13 5HQ
Tel: 01945 870793
Head: Mrs D A Wright
No. of pupils: 8
Fees: FB £67,600
Special needs catered for:
DYS, EBD

The Old School House
March Road, Friday Bridge,
Wisbech, Cambridgeshire PE14 0HA
Tel: 01945 861114
Manager: Rick Ogle-Welbourn
Age range: B7–13
Special needs catered for: EBD

Essex

Advanced Education - Essex School
Unit 7 Woodgates Farm, Broxted,
Dunmow, Essex CM6 2BN
Tel: 01279 850474
Headteacher: Julie Barnes
Age range: 11–16
Special needs catered for: BESD

Continuum School Whitewebbs
Whitewebbs, Molehill Green,
Takely, Stansted, Essex CM22 6PQ
Tel: 01279 850474/07966 543931
Headteacher: Mr David Flack
Age range: 11–18
Special needs catered for: EBD

Donyland Lodge School
Fingringhoe Road, Rowhedge,
Colchester, Essex CO5 7JL
Tel: 01206 728869
Director: Lesley Woodhouse
Age range: 11–18
Special needs catered for: EBD

ESSEX FRESH START INDEPENDENT SCHOOL (EFS)
For further details see p. 78
Church Street, Witham,
Essex CM8 2JL
Tel: 01376 780088
Email: referrals@tces.org.uk
Website: www.tces.org.uk
Schools' Proprietor: Thomas
Keaney
Age range: 7–18
Special needs catered for:
ASD, BESD

Hopewell School
Harmony House, Baden Powell
Close, Dagenham, Essex RM9 6XN
Tel: 020 8593 6610
Headteacher: Ms Sharina Klaasens
Age range: 5–18
Special needs catered for:
EBD, MLD, SEBD

Jacques Hall
Harwich Road, Bradfield,
Manningtree, Essex CO11 2XW
Tel: 01255 870311
Principal: Mr Paul Emmerson
Age range: 11–18
No. of pupils: 21
Special needs catered for:
ADHD, BESD, EBD, MLD, SEBD

The Ryes College & Community
New Road, Aldham,
Colchester, Essex CO6 3PN
Tel: 01206 243473
Headteacher: Miss Jackies Shanks
Age range: 7–24
Special needs catered for:
ADD, ADHD, ASD, ASP, AUT,
BESD, EBD, SCD, SEBD

Norfolk

Avocet House
The Old Vicarage, School Lane,
Heckingham, Norfolk NR14 6QP
Tel: 01508 549320
Principal: Mr Jonathan Lees
Age range: B8–16
No. of pupils: 8
Special needs catered for:
EBD, SEBD, SPLD

Future Education
168b Motum Road, Norwich,
Norfolk NR5 8EG
Tel: 01603 250505
Headteacher: Mr Dennis Freeman
Age range: 14–16
Special needs catered for: BESD

Sheridan School
Thetford Road, Northwold,
Thetford, Norfolk IP26 5LQ
Tel: 01366 726040
Interim Principal: Mr John Steward
Age range: 8–18
No. of pupils: 40
Special needs catered for: ADD,
ADHD, ASD, ASP, BESD, EBD, SEBD
⚥ 16+ ✓

Suffolk

Bramfield House
Walpole Road, Bramfield,
Halesworth, Suffolk IP19 9AB
Tel: 01986 784235
Head: Mrs D Jennings
Age range: B10–18
No. of pupils: 51
Special needs catered for:
ADD, ADHD, BESD, DEL, EBD
⚥ ⚥ ✓

Greenfield School
Four Elms, Norwich Road, Stonham
Parva, Stowmarket, Suffolk IP14 5LB
Tel: 01449 711105
Head: Raymond Saunders
Age range: B11–16
No. of pupils: 11
Special needs catered for:
EBD, MLD
⚥ ⚥ ✓

**On Track Education
Centre (Mildenhall)**
82E & F Fred Dannatt Road,
Mildenhall, Suffolk IP28 7RD
Tel: 01638 715555
Headteacher: Mrs Ruth Durrant
Age range: 11–18
Special needs catered for: EBD
16+ ✓

East Midlands

Derbyshire

Eastwood Grange School
Milken Lane, Ashover, Chesterfield,
Derbyshire S45 0BA
Tel: 01246 590255
Principal: Mr Ray Scales
Age range: B9–16+
No. of pupils: 34
Special needs catered for: ADD,
ADHD, BESD, DYS, EBD, HA, SCD
⚥ ⚥ ✓

**The Linnet Independent
Learning Centre**
107 Mount Pleasant Road,
Castle Gresley, Swadlincote,
Derbyshire DE11 9JE
Tel: 01283 213989
Head Teacher: Jan Sullivan
Age range: 5–16
No. of pupils: 13
Fees: Day £74,250
Special needs catered for: ADD,
ADHD, ASD, ASP, BESD, CLD,
DEL, DYS, DYSP, EBD, GLD, LD,
MLD, SCD, SEBD, SP&LD, SPLD
✓

The Meadows
Beech Lane, Dove Holes,
Derbyshire SK17 8DJ
Tel: 01298 814000
Headteacher: Ms Rachel Dowle
Age range: 11–16
Special needs catered for: EBD
✓

Leicestershire

Claybrook Cottage School
Frolesworth Lane, Claybrook
Magna, Lutterworth,
Leicestershire LE17 5DA
Tel: 01455 202049
Headteacher: Mrs
Jennifer Collighan
Age range: 8–16
Special needs catered for: BESD
✓

Gryphon School
Slater Street Lodge, Abbey Park,
Leicester, Leicestershire LE1 3EJ
Tel: 07833 623420
Headteacher: Miss Christina Church
Age range: 11–17
Special needs catered for: EBD
✓

Lewis Charlton School
North Street, Ashby-De-La-
Zouch, Leicestershire LE65 1HU
Tel: 01530 560775
Head: Ms Georgina Pearson
Age range: 11–16
No. of pupils: 20
Special needs catered for: EBD
⚥ ✓

**Meadow View
Farm School**
c/o Brookland Farm House, Kirby
Road, Barwell, Leicestershire LE9 8FT
Tel: 01455 840 825
Headteacher: Mr J Read
Age range: 6–11
Special needs catered for:
ASD, BESD, SCD
✓

Oakwood School
20 Main Street, Glenfield,
Leicester, Leicestershire LE3 8DG
Tel: 0116 2876218
Headteacher: Mrs.
Jennifer Collighan
Age range: 8–18
No. of pupils: 18
Special needs catered for: EBD
✓

Trinity College
Moor Lane, Loughborough,
Leicestershire LE11 1BA
Tel: 01509 218906
Headteacher: Mr Adam Brewster
Age range: 9–16
No. of pupils: 36
Fees: Day £36,075
Special needs catered for:
EBD, MLD
✓

Lincolnshire

Broughton House
Brant Broughton,
Lincolnshire LN5 0SL
Tel: 0800 288 9779
Head of Service: Mr
Michael Semilore
Age range: 16–25
Special needs catered for: AUT,
BESD, LD, SCD, SCLD, SEBD, SLD
16+ ⚥

Northamptonshire

**Advanced Education -
Northampton School**
67 Queens Park Parade,
Kingsthorpe, Northampton,
Northamptonshire NN2 6LR
Tel: 01604 719711
Headteacher: Rob Bilbe
Age range: 11–16
Special needs catered for:
EBD, MLD
✓

Ashmeads School
Buccleuch Farm, Haigham
Hill, Burton Latimer, Kettering,
Northamptonshire NN15 5PH
Tel: 01536 725998
Headteacher: Joyce Kuwazo
Age range: 11–16
No. of pupils: 12
Special needs catered for: EBD
✓

Belview School
124b Midland Road,
Wellingborough,
Northamptonshire NN8 1NF
Tel: 01933 441877
Headteacher: Ms Candy Shaw
Age range: 11–17
No. of pupils: 4
Special needs catered for: BESD
✓

Thornby Hall School
Thornby Hall, Thornby,
Northampton,
Northamptonshire NN6 8SW
Tel: 01604 740001
Director: Ms Rene Kennedy
CertEd, DipArt Therapy
Age range: 12–18
No. of pupils: 20
Fees: FB £106,177
Special needs catered for: EBD
⚥ 16+ ✓

Nottinghamshire

Freyburg School
The Poppies, Greenmile
Lane, Babworth,
Nottinghamshire DN22 8JW
Tel: 01777 709061
Headteacher: Mr David Carr
Age range: B11–16
Special needs catered for: BESD
⚥ ✓

Hope House School
Barnby Road, Newark,
Nottinghamshire NG24 3NE
Tel: 01636 700 380
Headteacher: Mrs Teri
Westmoreland
Age range: 4–19
No. of pupils: 3
Fees: Day £135,000–£155,000
FB £160,000–£180,000
Special needs catered for:
ADD, ADHD, ASD, ASP, AUT,
BESD, DEL, EBD, SCD, SEBD
16+ ✓

**Wings School,
Nottinghamshire**
Kirklington Hall, Kirklington, Newark,
Nottinghamshire NG22 8NB
Tel: 01636 817430
Principal: Dr John Flint
Age range: 9–17
Special needs catered for:
ADD, ADHD, ASP, BESD, EBD
⚥ ✓

Rutland

**The Grange
Therapuetic School**
Knossington, Oakham,
Rutland LE15 8LY
Tel: 01664 454264
Director: Dr A J Smith MA,
MEd, PhD, CPsychol, AFBPs
Age range: B8–16
No. of pupils: 75
Special needs catered for: EBD
⚥ ⚥ 16+ ✓

Greater London

Essex

Barnardos
Tanners Lane, Barkingside,
Ilford, Essex IG6 1QG
Tel: 020 8550 8822
Special needs catered for:
AUT, EBD, MLD, PH, PMLD,
SLD, SP&LD, SPLD
♿ 16+

Middlesex

Unity School
62 The Ride, Hounslow,
Middlesex TW8 9LA
Age range: 11–16
No. of pupils: 4
Special needs catered for: EBD
♿

Surrey

Cressey College
Croydon, Surrey CR0 6XJ
Tel: 020 86545373
Headteacher: Ms Adrienne Barnes
Age range: 11–17
Special needs catered for:
BESD, EBD, SCD
✔

KINGSDOWN SECONDARY SCHOOL
For further details see p. 79
112 Orchard Road, Sanderstead,
Croydon, Surrey CR2 9LQ
Tel: 020 8657 1200
Website:
www.kingsdownsse.com
Headteacher: Ms
Carole Nicholson
Age range: 11–16
No. of pupils: 12
Special needs catered for:
ASD, ASP, EBD, SPLD
♿ ✔

London

East London

EAST LONDON INDEPENDENT SCHOOL (ELIS)
For further details see p. 80
Upper School, Ibex House,
1C Maryland Park, Stratford,
London E15 1HB
Tel: 020 8221 1247
Email: referrals@tces.org.uk
Website: www.tces.org.uk
Schools' Proprietor: Thomas
Keaney
Age range: 7–18
Special needs catered for:
ASD, BESD
16+ ✔

Leaways School London
Theydon Road, Clapton,
London E5 9NZ
Tel: 020 8815 4030
Headmaster: Richard Gadd
Age range: 10–17
Special needs catered for: SEBD

North-West London

Gloucester House the Tavistock Children's Day Unit
33 Daleham Gardens,
London NW3 5BU
Tel: 020 77943353
Headteacher: Ms
Ellenore Nicholson
Age range: B5–12
Special needs catered for: BESD
♿ ✔

South-East London

Cavendish School
58 Hawkstone Road, Southwark
Park, London SE16 2PA
Tel: 020 7394 0088
Headteacher: Mrs Sara Craggs
Age range: 11–16
No. of pupils: 42
Special needs catered for: EBD
✔

Octavia House School, Vauxhall
Vauxhall Primary School, Vauxhall
Street, London SE11 5LG
Tel: 02036 514396
Executive Head: Mr James Waite
Age range: 5–14
No. of pupils: 65
Special needs catered for: ADD,
ADHD, BESD, EBD, SCD, SEBD

Octavia House School, Walworth
Larcom House, Larcom
Street, , London SE17 1RT
Tel: 02036 514396
Head of School: Mr James Waite

Trinity School
4 Recreation Road, Sydenham,
London SE26 4ST
Headteacher: Mr Philip Lee
Age range: 11–16
Special needs catered for: BESD
✔

West London

Insights Independent School
3-5 Alexandria Road,
Ealing, London W13 0NP
Tel: 020 8840 9099
Headteacher: Ms Barbara Quartey
Age range: 7–18
No. of pupils: 62
Special needs catered for: ADD,
ADHD, ASD, ASP, BESD, DYS,
EBD, GLD, MLD, SCD, SPLD
16+ ✔

NORTH WEST LONDON INDEPENDENT SCHOOL (NWLIS)
For further details see p. 81
85 Old Oak Common Lane,
Acton, London W3 7DD
Tel: 020 8749 5403
Email: referrals@tces.org.uk
Website: www.tces.org.uk
Schools' Proprietor: Thomas
Keaney
Age range: 7–18
No. of pupils: 69
Special needs catered for:
ASD, BESD
16+ ✔

North-East

Durham

Highcroft School
The Green, Cockfield, Bishop
Auckland, Durham DL13 5AG
Tel: 077 02916189
Headteacher: Mr David Laheney
Age range: 11–16
No. of pupils: 3
Special needs catered for: BESD
✔

Priory Pines House
Middleton St George,
Darlington, Durham DL2 1TS
Tel: 01325 331177
Principal: Mr John Anderson
Age range: 7–16
No. of pupils: 16
Special needs catered for: EBD
♿

East Riding of Yorkshire

Advanced Education - Beverley School
Units 19-20 Priory Road Industrial
Estate, Beverley, East Riding
of Yorkshire HU17 0EW
Tel: 01482 307830
School Manager: Melanie Jackson
Age range: 10–18
Special needs catered for: EBD, LD
16+ ✔

Hartlepool

Advanced Education - Hartlepool School & Vocational Centre
Sovereign Park, Brenda Road,
Hartlepool TS25 1NN
Tel: 01429 224965
Headteacher: Mr Paul Barnfather
Age range: 11–16
No. of pupils: 10
Special needs catered for: EBD
✔

Emotional, behavioural and/or social difficulties (EBSD)

Northumberland

Cambois House School
Cambois, Blyth,
Northumberland NE24 1SF
Tel: 01670 857689
Headteacher: Mr David Smith
Age range: 11–16
No. of pupils: 8
Special needs catered for:
BESD, EBD
✔

Tyne & Wear

Talbot House School
Hexham Road, Walbottle,
Newcastle upon Tyne,
Tyne & Wear NE15 8HW
Tel: 0191 229 0111
Director of Services: A P James
DAES, BPhil, CRCCYP
Age range: 7–18
No. of pupils: 40
Special needs catered for: ADD,
ADHD, ASD, BESD, EBD, MLD
✔

Thornbeck College
14 Thornhill Park, Sunderland,
Tyne & Wear SR2 7LA
Tel: 0191 5102038
Principal: Ms Christine Dempster
Special needs catered for: ASP, AUT

West Yorkshire

Broadwood School
252 Moor End Road, Halifax,
West Yorkshire HX2 0RU
Tel: 01422 355925
Headteacher: Mrs Deborah Nash
Age range: 11–18
No. of pupils: 38
Special needs catered for: EBD
✔

Meadowcroft School
24 Bar Lane, Wakefield,
West Yorkshire WF1 4AD
Tel: 01924 366242
Head of School: Miss
Lynette Edwards
Age range: 10–19
Special needs catered for: EBD
16+ ✔

North-West

Cheshire

Advanced Education - Warrington School
2 Forrest Way, Gatewarth
Industrial Estate, Warrington,
Cheshire WA5 1DF
Tel: 01925 237580
Headteacher: Olufemi Onasanya
Age range: 11–18
No. of pupils: 10
Special needs catered for:
BESD, EBD, SEBD
16+ ✔

Halton School
33 Main Street, Halton Village,
Runcorn, Cheshire WA7 2AN
Tel: 01928 589810
Headteacher: Emma McAllester
Age range: 7–14
No. of pupils: 14
Special needs catered for: EBD
✔

High Peak School
Mudhurst Lane, Higher Disley,
Stockport, Cheshire SK12 2AP
Tel: 01663 721 731
Principal: David Glaves
Age range: 9–19
Special needs catered for: SEBD
🏛

Hope Corner Academy
70 Clifton Road, Runcorn,
Cheshire WA7 4TD
Tel: 01928 580860
Head of School: Rev. D Tunningley
Age range: 14–16
Special needs catered for:
ASD, BESD, MLD

Cumbria

APPLETREE SCHOOL
For further details see p. 82
Natland, Kendal,
Cumbria LA9 7QS
Tel: 015395 60253
Email: admin@
appletreeschool.co.uk
Website:
www.appletreeschool.co.uk
Head of Education: Mr R
Davies BEd, MSpED
Age range: 6–12
Special needs catered for: ADD,
ADHD, BESD, DEL, DYS, DYSP, EBD,
GLD, HA, LD, MLD, SCD, SEBD
🏛 ✔

Eden Grove School
Bolton, Appleby, Cumbria CA16 6AJ
Tel: 01768 361346
Principal: Mr John McCaffrey
Age range: 8–19
No. of pupils: 65
Special needs catered for:
ADHD, ASP, AUT, BESD, CP, DYS,
EBD, EPI, MLD, PH, SP&LD
🏛 16+ ✔

Eden Park Academy
119 Warwick Road, Carlisle,
Cumbria CA1 1JZ
Tel: 01228 631770
Headteacher: Miss Kerry Maynard
Age range: 11–16
No. of pupils: 6
Special needs catered for: EBD

Fell House School
Grange Fell Road, Grange-
Over-Sands, Cumbria LA11 6AS
Tel: 01539 535926
Headteacher: Mr Rob Davies
Age range: 7–12
No. of pupils: 8
Special needs catered for: EBD
🏛 ✔

Kirby Moor School
Longtown Road, Brampton,
Cumbria CA8 2AB
Tel: 016977 42598
Headteacher: Mrs
Catherine Garton
Age range: B10–18
Special needs catered for:
BESD, CLD, EBD
🚹 🏛 16+ ✔

Underley Garden School
Kirkby Lonsdale, Carnforth,
Cumbria LA6 2DZ
Tel: 01524 271569
Headteacher: Ellie Forrest
Age range: 9–19
No. of pupils: 43
Special needs catered for:
ADD, ADHD, ASP, SLD, SP&LD
🏛 ✔

Whinfell School
110 Windermere Road,
Kendal, Cumbria LA9 5EZ
Tel: 01539 723322
Headteacher: Mr R D Tyson
Age range: B11–19
No. of pupils: 5
Special needs catered for:
AUT, EBD
🚹 🏛 16+ ✔

Wings School, Cumbria
Whassett, Milnthorpe,
Cumbria LA7 7DN
Tel: 01539 562006
Principal: Donagh McKillop
Age range: 11–17
Special needs catered for:
ADD, ADHD, ASP, BESD, EBD
🏛 ✔

Witherslack Hall School
Witherslack, Grange-Over-
Sands, Cumbria LA11 6SD
Tel: 01539 552397
Head Teacher: Mr. Robin Adams
Age range: B10–19
No. of pupils: 41
Special needs catered for:
ADHD, ASD, ASP, AUT,
BESD, EBD, MLD, SPLD
🚹 🏛 ✔

Greater Manchester

Acorns School
19b Hilbert Lane, Marple, Stockport,
Greater Manchester SK6 7NN
Tel: 0161 449 5820
Headteacher: Naseem Akhtar
Age range: 5–17
No. of pupils: 40
Special needs catered for: EBD
✔

Ashcroft School (CYCES)
Schools Hill, Cheadle, Greater
Manchester SK8 1JE
Tel: 0161 283 4832
Principal: Stephen
Grimley MA, CertEd
Age range: 8–16
No. of pupils: 40
Special needs catered for: BESD
✔

Birch House School
98-100 Birch Lane, Longsight,
Manchester, Greater
Manchester M13 0WN
Tel: 0161 2247500
Headteacher: Mr Bilal Mahmud
Age range: 11–16
No. of pupils: 22
Special needs catered for:
BESD, EBD, SEBD
✔

Lime Meadows
73 Taunton Road, Ashton-Under-
Lyne, Greater Manchester OL7 9DU
Tel: 0161 3399412
Head of School: Mr W Baker
Age range: B14–19
No. of pupils: 5
Special needs catered for: EBD
🚹 🏛 16+ ✔

Nugent House School
Carr Mill Road, Billinge, Wigan,
Greater Manchester WN5 7TT
Tel: 01744 892551
Principal: Miss W Sparling
BA(Hons), QTS, MA(SEN),
PG Dip (Autism), NPQH
Age range: B7–19
No. of pupils: 65
Fees: Day £63,036–£84,048
Special needs catered for: EBD

St John Vianney School
Rye Bank Road, Firswood, Stretford,
Greater Manchester M16 0EX
Tel: 0161 8817843
Age range: 4–19
No. of pupils: 80
Fees: Day £7,155
Special needs catered for: MLD

Lancashire

Belmont School
Haslingden Road, Rawtenstall,
Rossendale, Lancashire BB4 6RX
Tel: 01706 221043
Headteacher: Mr M J Stobart
Age range: B10–16
No. of pupils: 70
Special needs catered for:
ADD, ADHD, ASD, ASP, AUT,
BESD, DEL, EBD, SCD, SEBD

Cedar House School
Bentham, Lancaster,
Lancashire LA2 7DD
Tel: 015242 61149
Headteacher: Ms Kathryn
Taylor BEd (Hons)
Age range: 7–18
No. of pupils: 63
Special needs catered for:
ADD, ADHD, ASD, ASP, BESD,
DYSP, EBD, EPI, GLD, LD, MLD,
SCD, SEBD, SP&LD, SPLD

Crookhey Hall School
Crookhey Hall, Garstang
Road, Cockerham, Lancaster,
Lancashire LA2 0HA
Tel: 01524 792618
Headteacher: Mr D P Martin
Age range: B11–16
No. of pupils: 64
Special needs catered for: ADD,
ADHD, BESD, DEL, EBD, SCD, SEBD

Cumberland School
Church Road, Bamber Bridge,
Preston, Lancashire PR5 6EP
Tel: 01772 284435
Head Teacher: Mr Nigel Hunt
BSc (Hons), PGCE (SEN), NPQH
Age range: 11–18
No. of pupils: 57
Special needs catered for:
ADHD, ASP, BESD, MLD, SP&LD

Darwen School
3 Sudell Road, Darwen,
Lancashire BB3 3HW
Tel: 01254 777154
Headteacher: Mr Sean Naylor
Age range: 7–16
No. of pupils: 10
Special needs catered for: EBD

Egerton Street Independent School
48/50 Egerton Street, Heywood,
Rochdale, Lancashire OL10 3BG
Tel: 01706 625982
Manager: Dave Edwards
Age range: 11–16
Special needs catered for: EBD

Elland House School
Unit 7, Roman Road, Royton,
Lancashire OL2 5PJ
Tel: 0161 6283600
Headteacher: Mrs Jan Murray
Age range: 11–16
Special needs catered for: BESD

Keyes Barn
Station Road, Salwick, Preston,
Lancashire PR4 0YH
Tel: 01772 673672
Headteacher: Mr Gary Holliday
Age range: 5–12
Special needs catered for: EBD

Learn 4 Life
Quarry Bank Community Centre,
364 Ormskirk Road, Tanhouse,
Skelmersdale, Lancashire WN8 9AL
Tel: 01695 768960
Head of School: Ms
Catherine Briggs
Age range: 11–16
No. of pupils: 4
Special needs catered for:
ADD, ADHD, ASD, ASP, AUT,
BESD, DYS, EBD, GLD, SCD

Moorlands View Children's Home and School
Manchester Road, Dunnockshaw,
Burnley, Lancashire BB11 5PQ
Tel: 01282 431144
Head Teacher: Wayne Carradice
Age range: 11–16
No. of pupils: 12
Special needs catered for: EBD

Primrose Cottage
c/o Northern Care, 214 Whitegate
Drive, Blackpool, Lancashire FY3 9JL
Tel: 01253 316160
Head of Education: Valerie
Gardener
Age range: G11–16
No. of pupils: 6
Special needs catered for:
EBD, MLD

Roselyn House School
Moss Lane, Off Wigan Road,
Leyland, Lancashire PR25 4SE
Tel: 01772 435948
Headteacher: Miss S Damerall
Age range: 11–16
No. of pupils: 21
Special needs catered for:
AUT, EBD

The Brambles
159 Longmeanygate, Midge Hill,
Leyland, Lancashire PR26 7BT
Tel: 01772 454826
Head of School: Mr Alan Rainford
Age range: B11–16
Special needs catered for: EBD

The Willows at Oakfield House School
Station Road, Salwick, Preston,
Lancashire PR4 0YH
Tel: 01772 672630
Headteacher: June Redhead
Age range: 5–11
No. of pupils: 23
Special needs catered for:
EBD, SLD

Waterloo Lodge School
Preston Road, Chorley,
Lancashire PR6 7AX
Tel: 01257 230894
Headteacher: Mrs J Taylor
Age range: 11–16
No. of pupils: 45
Fees: Day £29,649
Special needs catered for: ADD,
ADHD, BESD, DEL, EBD, SCD, SEBD

Merseyside

Balmoral Independent School
41 Balmoral Road, Newsham Park,
Liverpool, Merseyside L6 8ND
Tel: 0151 2910787
Manager: Alison Morris
Age range: 10–16
Special needs catered for: EBD

Clarence High School
West Lane, Freshfield,
Merseyside L37 7AS
Tel: 01704 872151
Head: Ms Carol Parkinson
Age range: 7–17
Special needs catered for: EBD

Olsen House School
85-87 Liverpool Rd, GT. Crosby,
Liverpool, Merseyside L23 5TD
Tel: 0151 924 0234
Headteacher: Jeremy Keeble
Age range: 9–16
Special needs catered for: SEBD

Warrington

Chaigeley
Thelwall, Warrington WA4 2TE
Tel: 01925 752357
Principal: Mr Antonio Munoz Bailey
Age range: B8–16
No. of pupils: 75
Special needs catered for:
ADD, ADHD, ASD, ASP, AUT,
BESD, DYS, EBD, GLD, HA, LD,
MLD, SCD, SEBD, SLD, SP&LD

Cornerstones
2 Victoria Road, Grappenhall,
Warrington WA4 2EN
Tel: 01925 211056
Head: Ms Caron Bethell
Age range: B7–18
No. of pupils: 11
Special needs catered for:
AUT, EBD

South-East

Berkshire

Cressex Lodge (SWAAY)
Terrace Road South, Binfield, Bracknell, Berkshire RG42 4DE
Tel: 01344 862221
Headteacher: Ms Sarah Snape
Age range: B11–16
No. of pupils: 9
Special needs catered for: BESD

High Close School
Wiltshire Road, Wokingham, Berkshire RG40 1TT
Tel: 0118 9785767
Head: Mrs Zoe Lattimer BSc(Hons), PGCE
Age range: 7–18
Special needs catered for: ADHD, ASD, ASP, BESD, EBD, MLD

Buckinghamshire

Unity College
150 West Wycombe Road, High Wycombe, Buckinghamshire HP12 3AE
Tel: 077 02916189
Headteacher: Mrs Lois Hubbard
Age range: 11–16
No. of pupils: 12
Special needs catered for: BESD, MLD, SEBD

East Sussex

Headstart School
Crouch Lane, Ninfield, Battle, East Sussex TN33 9EG
Tel: 01424 893803
Headteacher: Ms Nicola Dann
Age range: 7–18
Special needs catered for: BESD

Springboard Education Junior
39 Whippingham Road, St Wilfred\'s Upper Hall, Brighton, East Sussex BN2 3PS
Tel: 01273 885109
Headteacher: Elizabeth Freeman
Age range: 7–13
Special needs catered for: ADHD, BESD

The Lioncare School
87 Payne Avenue, Hove, East Sussex BN3 5HD
Tel: 01273 734164
Headteacher: Mrs J Dance
Age range: 7–16
No. of pupils: 9
Special needs catered for: EBD

The Mount Camphill Community
Faircrouch Lane, Wadhurst, East Sussex TN5 6PT
Tel: 01892 782025
Head of Education: Mr Julian Ritchie
Age range: 16–24
No. of pupils: 35
Special needs catered for: ADD, ADHD, ASD, ASP, AUT, BESD, CLD, CP, DEL, DYS, DYSP, EBD, EPI, GLD, HI, LD, MLD, MSI, PD, Phe, PH, PNI, SCD, SLD, SP&LD, SPLD, SLI

Hampshire

Coxlease Abbeymead
Palace Lane, Beaulieu, Hampshire SO42 7YG
Tel: 02380 283 633
Principal: Mr Rick Tracey
Age range: 9–16
No. of pupils: 5
Special needs catered for: EBD

Coxlease School
Clay Hill, Lyndhurst, Hampshire SO43 7DE
Tel: 023 8028 3633
Principal: Mr Rick Tracey
Age range: 9–18
No. of pupils: 55
Special needs catered for: BESD, MLD

Hillcrest Jubilee School
84-86 Jubilee Road, Waterlooville, Hampshire PO7 7RE
Tel: 03458 727477
Head of School: Alice Anstee
Age range: 8–16
Special needs catered for: BESD, SEBD

St Edward's School
Melchet Court, Sherfield English, Romsey, Hampshire SO51 6ZR
Tel: 01794 885252
Head: L Bartel BEd(Hons)
Age range: B9–18
No. of pupils: 38
Special needs catered for: ADD, ADHD, ASD, ASP, AUT, BESD, DYS, EBD, MLD, SCD, SEBD, SPLD

The Serendipity Centre
399 Hinkler Road, Southampton, Hampshire SO19 6DS
Tel: 023 8042 2255
Head Teacher: Dr. Michele Aldridge
Age range: G9–18
No. of pupils: 15
Special needs catered for: SEBD

Kent

Brewood Middle School
146 Newington Road, Ramsgate, Kent CT12 6PT
Tel: 01843 597088
Head of School: Mr Daniel Radlett
Age range: 5–13
No. of pupils: 8
Fees: Day £23,863
Special needs catered for: ADD, ADHD, ASD, ASP, AUT, BESD, CLD, DEL, EBD, EPI, GLD, HA, HI, LD, MLD, PH, SCD, SLD, SP&LD, SLI

Brewood Secondary School
86 London Road, Deal, Kent CT14 9TR
Tel: 01304 363000
Head of School: Mr Daniel Radlett
Age range: 11–18
No. of pupils: 12
Fees: Day £23,863
Special needs catered for: ADD, ADHD, ASD, ASP, AUT, BESD, CLD, DEL, EBD, EPI, GLD, HA, HI, LD, MLD, PH, SCD, SLD, SP&LD, SLI

Browns School
Cannock House, Hawstead Lane, Chelsfield, Orpington, Kent BR6 7PH
Tel: 01689 876816
Headteacher: Mr M F Brown
Age range: 7–12
No. of pupils: 32
Special needs catered for: EBD, SPLD

Caldecott Foundation School
Hythe Road, Smeeth, Ashford, Kent TN25 6PW
Tel: 01303 815678
Acting Head: Mrs Valerie Miller
Age range: 5–18
No. of pupils: 56
Special needs catered for: EBD

Esland School
Units 12-13, Oare Gunpowder Works, Off Bysingwood Road, Faversham, Kent ME13 7UD
Tel: 01795 531730
Head of School: Mr M Colvin
Age range: 12–17
No. of pupils: 9
Special needs catered for: BESD

Greenfields School
Tenterden Road, Biddenden, Kent TN27 8BS
Tel: 01580 292523
Director: Gary Yexley
Age range: 5–11
No. of pupils: 13
Fees: Day £29,004
Special needs catered for: EBD

Heath Farm School
Egerton Road, Charing Heath, Ashford, Kent TN27 0AX
Tel: 01233 712030
Head: Liz Cornish
Age range: 5–16
No. of pupils: 70
Special needs catered for: EBD

Hope View School
Station Approach, Chilham, Canterbury, Kent CT4 8EG
Tel: 01227 738000
Head of School: Ms Carla Kaushal
Age range: 11–17
No. of pupils: 16
Special needs catered for: ADD, ADHD, ASD, ASP, BESD

Hythe House Education
Power Station Road, Sheerness, Kent ME12 3AB
Tel: 01795 581006
Headteacher: Mr Robert Duffy
Age range: 11–16
No. of pupils: 20
Special needs catered for: EBD

ISP Sittingbourne School
Church Street, Sittingbourne, Kent ME10 3EG
Tel: 01795 422 044
Headteacher: Craig Walter
Age range: 11–16
Special needs catered for: BESD, SCD, SEBD

Learning Opportunities Centre
Ringwould Road, Ringwould, Deal, Kent CT14 8DN
Tel: 01304 381906
Headteacher: Mrs Diana Ward
Age range: 11–16
No. of pupils: 40
Special needs catered for: EBD

Little Acorns School
London Beach Farm, Ashford Road, St Michael's, Tenterden, Kent TN30 6SR
Tel: 01233 850422
Headteacher: Miss Angela Flynn
Age range: 4–14
No. of pupils: 7
Special needs catered for: EBD

Meadows School and Meadows 16+
London Road, Southborough, Kent TN4 0RJ
Tel: 01892 529144
Principal: Mike Price BEd(Hons), DipSEN, MA
Age range: 11–19
No. of pupils: 45
Special needs catered for: ADHD, ASP, AUT, DYS, DYSP, EBD, MLD, SEBD

Ripplevale School
Chapel Lane, Ripple,
Deal, Kent CT14 8JG
Tel: 01304 373866
Principal: Mr Ted Schofield CRSW
Age range: B9–16
No. of pupils: 30
Special needs catered for: ADD,
ADHD, ASD, ASP, AUT, BESD, CLD,
DYS, DYSP, EBD, GLD, HA, LD, MLD,
PMLD, SCD, SCLD, SP&LD, SPLD

The Ashbrook Centre
8 Almond Close, Broadstairs,
Kent CT10 2NQ
Tel: 01843 482 043
Principal: Mr Nigel Troop
Age range: 5–18
No. of pupils: 5
Special needs catered for:
BESD, SEBD

The Davenport School
Princess Margaret Avenue,
Ramsgate, Kent CT12 6HX
Tel: 01843 589018
Headteacher: Mr Franklyn Brown
Age range: B7–12
Special needs catered for: EBD

The New School at West Heath
Ashgrove Road, Sevenoaks,
Kent TN13 1SR
Tel: 01732 460553
Principal: Mrs Christina Wells
Age range: 10–19
No. of pupils: 120 B87 G33 VIth40
Fees: Day £46,583 WB £31,245
Special needs catered for:
ADD, ADHD, ASD, ASP, BESD,
DEL, EBD, SCD, SP&LD, SPLD

The Old Priory School
Priory Road, Ramsgate,
Kent CT11 9PG
Tel: 01843 599322
Head: Jack Banner
Age range: B10–15
Special needs catered for: EBD

The Old School
Capel Street, Capel-le-Ferne,
Folkestone, Kent CT18 7EY
Tel: 01303 251116
Headteacher: Martyn Jordan
Age range: B9–17
No. of pupils: 24
Special needs catered for: EBD

Surrey

Cornfield School
53 Hanworth Road, Redhill,
Surrey RH1 5HS
Tel: 01737 779578
Headteacher: Mrs Jayne Telfer
Age range: G11–18
No. of pupils: 25
Special needs catered for: EBD

Grafham Grange School
Nr Bramley, Guildford,
Surrey GU5 0LH
Tel: 01483 892214
Headteacher: Ms Debra Henderson
Age range: B10–19
Special needs catered for:
ADHD, ASD, BESD, EBD, SP&LD

Tudor Lodge School
92 Foxley Lane, Woodcote,
Purley, Surrey CR8 3NA
Tel: 020 8763 8785
Headteacher: Ms Patricia Lines
Age range: 12–16
No. of pupils: 7
Special needs catered for: SEBD

West Sussex

Brantridge School
Staplefield Place, Staplefield,
Haywards Heath, West
Sussex RH17 6EQ
Tel: 01444 400228
Headteacher: Gina Wagland
Age range: B6–13
No. of pupils: 27
Special needs catered for:
ADHD, ASD, ASP, BESD, EBD, LD

Farney Close School
Bolney Court, Bolney,
West Sussex RH17 5RD
Tel: 01444 881811
Head: Mr B Robinson MA, BEd(Hons)
Age range: 11–16
No. of pupils: 78
Fees: Day £55,222.10
Special needs catered for: ADHD,
ASP, DYS, EBD, MLD, SP&LD

Hillcrest Slinfold School
Stane Street, Slinfold, Horsham,
West Sussex RH13 0QX
Tel: 01403 790939
Principal: Ms Sarah Olliver
Age range: B11–17
Special needs catered for: ADD,
ADHD, ASD, ASP, BESD, DYS, DYSP,
EBD, GLD, MLD, SCD, SEBD

Muntham House School Ltd
Barns Green, Muntham Drive,
Horsham, West Sussex RH13 0NJ
Tel: 01403 730302
Principal: Mr R Boyle
MEd, BEd, AdvDipSE
Age range: B8–18
No. of pupils: 51 VIth12
Special needs catered for:
ADD, ADHD, ASD, BESD, DYS,
EBD, MLD, SP&LD, SPLD

PHILPOTS MANOR SCHOOL
For further details see p. 83
West Hoathly, East Grinstead,
West Sussex RH19 4PR
Tel: 01342 810268
Email: info@
philpotsmanorschool.co.uk
Website: www.philpotsmanor
school.co.uk
Education Co-ordinator: Ms
Linda Churnside BEd
Age range: 7–19
No. of pupils: 32
Fees: Day £65,000 WB £65,000
Special needs catered for:
ADD, ADHD, ASD, ASP, AUT,
BESD, DEL, DYS, EBD, EPI,
GLD, LD, MLD, SCD, SP&LD

Springboard Education Senior
55 South Street, Lancing,
West Sussex BN15 8HA
Tel: 01903 605980
Head Teacher: Mr Simon
Yorke-Johnson
Age range: 11–18
No. of pupils: 10
Special needs catered for: ADD,
ADHD, ASD, ASP, AUT, BESD, EBD

South-West

Devon

Advanced Education - Devon School
Oaklands Park, Oaklands Road,
Buckfastleigh, Devon TQ11 0BW
Tel: 01364 644 823
Headteacher: Swavek
Nowakiewicz
Age range: 10–16
Special needs catered for:
ASP, AUT, EBD, SEBD

Chelfham Mill School
Chelfham, Barnstaple,
Devon EX32 7LA
Tel: 01271 850448
Principal: Mrs K T Roberts
BEd, BPhil(EBD)
Age range: B9–16
No. of pupils: 40
Special needs catered for:
ADD, ADHD, ASP, DYS, DYSP,
EBD, GLD, LD, MLD

Oakwood Court
7/9 Oak Park Villas, Dawlish,
Devon EX7 0DE
Tel: 01626 864066
Principal: J F Loft BEd,
BPhil(SEN), HNDHIM
Age range: 16–25
Special needs catered for: ADHD,
ASP, DYS, DYSP, EBD, EPI, MLD, SLD

The Libra School
Edgemoor Court, South Radworthy,
South Molton, Devon EX36 3LN
Tel: 01598 740044
Headteacher: Ms J E Wilkes
Age range: 8–18
Special needs catered for: EBD

Dorset

Ivers College
Ivers, Hains Lane, Marnhull,
Sturminster Newton, Dorset DT10 1JU
Tel: 01258 820164
Principal: Linda Matthews
Age range: 18+
No. of pupils: 23
Special needs catered for:
EBD, LD, MLD, SCD

Gloucestershire

Marlowe Education Unit
Hartpury Old School,
Gloucester Road, Hartpury,
Gloucestershire GL19 3BG
Tel: 01452 700855
Head Teacher: Diane McQueen
Age range: 8–16
No. of pupils: 8
Special needs catered for:
EBD, MLD

Somerset

Advanced Education - Somerset School
Westport House, Langport Road, Hambridge, Somerset TA10 0BH
Tel: 01460 281216
Headteacher: Mr Will Houghton
Age range: 10–16
Special needs catered for: AUT, EBD, HI, SEBD
✔

Aethelstan College
Newton Road, North Petherton, Somerset TA6 6NA
Tel: 01278 662377
Headteacher: Mrs Ros Hagley
Age range: 11–16
Special needs catered for: EBD
✔

Inaura School
Moorview House, Burrowbridge, Bridgwater, Somerset TA7 0RB
Tel: 01823 690211
Headteacher: Dr Adam Abdelnoor
Age range: 8–18
No. of pupils: 24
Fees: Day £45,954
Special needs catered for: ADHD, ASD, BESD, CLD, EBD, LD, SCD
16+ ✔

Newbury Manor School
Nr Mells, Frome, Somerset BA11 3RG
Tel: 01373 814 980
Head of School: Mr. Andy Holder
Age range: 7–19

Somerset Progressive School
Bath House Farm, West Hatch, Taunton, Somerset TA3 5RH
Tel: 01823 481902
Headteacher: Mr Neil Gage
Age range: 9–19
No. of pupils: 20
Special needs catered for: EBD
16+ ✔

The Marchant-Holliday School
North Cheriton, Templecombe, Somerset BA8 0AH
Tel: 01963 33234
Head Teacher: Mr T J Kitts MEd, BEd(Hons), DPSE(SEN)
Age range: B5–13
No. of pupils: 38
Special needs catered for: ADD, ADHD, ASD, ASP, BESD, DYS, DYSP, EBD, SCD
♦ ♠ ✔

Wiltshire

The Faringdon Centre
School Lane, Salisbury, Wiltshire SP1 3YA
Tel: 01722 820 970
Head of School: Ms Rebecca Peacock
Age range: 11–16
No. of pupils: 8
Special needs catered for: EBD, MLD

Wessex College
Wessex Lodge, Nunney Road, Frome, Wiltshire BA11 4LA
Tel: 01373 453414
Head of School: Mr Nigel Troop
Age range: 11–16
No. of pupils: 6
Special needs catered for: EBD
✔

West Midlands

Cheshire

Aidenswood
48 Parson Street, Congleton, Cheshire CW12 4ED
Tel: 01260281353
Head of School: Ms Marion Goodwin
Age range: B13–17
No. of pupils: 6
Special needs catered for: EBD, MLD
♦ ♠ ✔

Herefordshire

Cambian Hereford School
Coningsby Road, Leominster, Herefordshire HR6 8LL
Tel: 0800 1381184
Head of School: Ms Kate Reeves
Age range: 11–19
Special needs catered for: EBD
16+ ✔

Queenswood School
Callows Hills Farm, Hereford Road, Ledbury, Herefordshire HR8 2PZ
Tel: 01531 670632
Principal: Mr James Imber
Age range: 11–19
No. of pupils: 15
Special needs catered for: BESD, SEBD
♠ 16+ ✔

Shropshire

Acorn School
Dale Acre Way, Hollinswood, Telford, Shropshire TF3 2EN
Tel: 01952 200410
Head: Ms Sarah Morgan
Age range: 11–16
No. of pupils: 16
Special needs catered for: EBD
✔

Care UK Children's Services
46 High Street, Church Stretton, Shropshire SY6 6BX
Tel: 01694 724488
Director: Simon W Rouse BA(Hons), CSS, DipPTh
Age range: 10–18
No. of pupils: 24
Special needs catered for: EBD
16+

Ditton Priors School
Station Road, Ditton Priors, Bridgnorth, Shropshire WV16 6SS
Tel: 01746 712985
Headteacher: Mr Stephen Piper
Age range: 11–16
No. of pupils: 10
Special needs catered for: BESD, EBD
✔

Gateway VTEC
Unit 1-4, Sleap, Harmer Hill, Shrewsbury, Shropshire SY4 3HE
Tel: 01939 233042
Education Manager: Jan Rogers
Special needs catered for: EBD

Smallbrook School
Smallbrook Lodge, Smallbrook Road, Whitchurch, Shropshire SY13 1BX
Tel: 01948 661110
Headteacher: Peter Sinclair
Age range: 11–19
No. of pupils: 15
Special needs catered for: EBD
16+ ✔

Young Options College
Lamledge Lane, Shifnal, Shropshire TF11 8SD
Tel: 01952 468220
Head Teacher: Ms Julia Saint
Age range: 7–19
Special needs catered for: ADD, ADHD, ASP, BESD, DEL, EBD, SCD, SEBD
♠ ✔

Staffordshire

Bloomfield College
Bloomfield Road, Tipton, Staffordshire DY4 9AH
Tel: 0121 5209408
Headteacher: Mr Andrew Harding
Age range: 11–16
Special needs catered for: EBD
✔

Draycott Moor College
Draycott Old Road, Draycott-in-the-Moors, Stoke-on-Trent, Staffordshire ST11 9AH
Tel: 01782 399849
Headteacher: Mr David Rutter
Age range: 11–16
Special needs catered for: EBD
✔

Hillcrest Oaklands College
Alrewas Road, Kings Bromley, Staffordshire DE13 7HR
Tel: 01543 473772
Principal: Mr David Biddle MAEd, BA (HONS), CertEd
Age range: G12–19
Special needs catered for: ADD, ADHD, ASD, ASP, BESD, DYS, DYSP, EBD, GLD, MLD, SCD, SEBD
♦ ♠ 16+ ✔

Longdon Hall School
Longdon Hall, Rugeley, Staffordshire WS15 4PT
Tel: 01543 491051
Headteacher: Mr Matt Storey
Age range: 7–18
Special needs catered for: BESD, EBD
16+ ✔

The Roaches Independent School
Tunstall Road, Knypersley, Stoke-on-Trent, Staffordshire ST8 7AB
Tel: 01782 523479
The Principal: Head of Education
Age range: 7–16
No. of pupils: 16
Fees: Day £30,780 FB £103,740
Special needs catered for: EBD
♠ ✔

Young Options Pathway College Stoke
Phoenix House, Marlborough Road, Longton, Stoke-on-Trent, Staffordshire ST3 1EJ
Tel: 01782 320773
Headteacher: Mel Callaghan-Lewis
Age range: 11–19
No. of pupils: 11
Special needs catered for: ADD, ADHD, ASP, AUT, BESD, CLD, DEL, DYS, DYSP, EBD, GLD, HA, LD, MLD, MSI, PMLD, SCD, SEBD, SLD, SPLD
16+ ✔

Warwickshire

Arc School - Ansley
Ansley Lane, Ansley, Nuneaton, Warwickshire CV10 9ND
Tel: 01676 543 810
Headteacher: Mr Christian Williams
Age range: 7–16
Special needs catered for: ADHD, ASD, SEBD

Arc School - Church End
Church End, Ansley, Nuneaton, Warwickshire CV10 0QR
Tel: 024 7639 4801
Headmistress: Pauline Garret
Age range: 7–11
No. of pupils: 30
Special needs catered for: BESD
(symbols)

Arc School - Napton
Vicarage Road, Napton-on-the-Hill, Warwickshire CV47 8NA
Tel: 01926 817 547
Acting Head Teacher: Cathal Lynch
Age range: 7–16
Special needs catered for: ADHD, ASD

Wathen Grange School
Church Walk, Mancetter, Atherstone, Warwickshire CV9 1PZ
Tel: 01827 714454
Head of Education Service: Mr Chris Nock
Age range: 11–16
No. of pupils: 15
Special needs catered for: EBD
(symbol)

West Midlands

Blue River Academy
36 Medley Road, Greet, Birmingham, West Midlands B11 2NE
Tel: 0121 7667981
Age range: B14–16
Special needs catered for: BESD
(symbols)

Oaklands School
215 Barrows Lane, Yardley, Birmingham, West Midlands B26 1QS
Headteacher: Ms Rebecca Hill
Age range: 11–16
No. of pupils: 4
Special needs catered for: BESD
(symbol)

The Collegiate Centre for Values Education for Life
51-54 Hockley Hill, Hockley, Birmingham, West Midlands B18 5AQ
Tel: 0121 5230222
Headteacher: Mrs Val Russell
Age range: 11–17
No. of pupils: 25
Special needs catered for: BESD
(symbol)

Yorkshire & Humberside

East Riding of Yorkshire

Horton House School
Hilltop Farm, Sutton Road, Wawne, Kingston upon Hull, East Riding of Yorkshire HU7 5YY
Tel: 01482 875191
Head: Mr Matthew Stubbins
Age range: 8–23
Fees: Day £25,000–£50,000 WB £75,000–£150,000 FB £180,000
Special needs catered for: ADD, ADHD, ASD, ASP, AUT, BESD, CLD, DYS, DYSP, EBD, EPI, GLD, LD, MLD, SCD, SCLD, SEBD, SLD, SPLD
(symbols)

North Yorkshire

Advanced Education - Scarborough School
Unit 11, Plaxton Park, Cayton Low Road, Eastfield, Scarborough, North Yorkshire YO11 1JR
Tel: 01723 581 475
Headteacher: Ms Anne Wood
Age range: 8–16
Special needs catered for: SEBD
(symbol)

Breckenbrough School
Sandhutton, Thirsk, North Yorkshire YO7 4EN
Tel: 01845 587238
Headmaster: Geoffrey Brookes BEd
Age range: B9–19
No. of pupils: 49
Special needs catered for: ADD, ADHD, ASP, BESD, DEL, DYS, EBD, HA
(symbols)

Clervaux
Clow Beck Centre, Jolby Lane, Croft-on-Tees, North Yorkshire DL2 2TF
Tel: 01325 729860
Strategic Lead: Bonny Etchell-Anderson
Age range: 16–25+
Special needs catered for: ASD, ASP, AUT, BESD, CLD

Spring Hill School
Palace Road, Ripon, North Yorkshire HG4 3HN
Tel: 01765 603320
Principal: Linda Nelson
Age range: 9–19
No. of pupils: 31
Special needs catered for: ADHD, ASP, AUT, CP, DEL, DYS, DYSP, EBD, EPI, MLD, SLD, SP&LD
(symbols)

South Yorkshire

BRANTWOOD SPECIALIST SCHOOL
For further details see p. 84
1 Kenwood Bank, Nether Edge, Sheffield, South Yorkshire S7 1NU
Tel: 0114 258 9062
Email: enquiries@brantwood.rmt.org
Website: www.rmt.org
Headteacher: Jenni Rosenbrock
Age range: 7–19
Special needs catered for: ADD, ADHD, ASD, ASP, BESD, CLD, EBD, GLD, LD, MLD, PMLD, SCD, SCLD, SEBD, SPLD
(symbols)

Chrysalis Therapeutic Educational Centre
48 Wostenholm Road, Nether Edge, South Yorkshire S7 1LL
Tel: 0114 2509455
Headteacher: Mrs Sarah Allkins
Age range: 8–14
No. of pupils: 4
Special needs catered for: BESD
(symbol)

Dove School
194 New Road, Staincross, Barnsley, South Yorkshire S75 6PP
Tel: 01226 381380
Headteacher: Mrs Helen Mangham
Age range: 9–16
Special needs catered for: BESD
(symbol)

West Yorkshire

Denby Grange School
Stocksmoor Road, Midgley, Wakefield, West Yorkshire WF4 4JQ
Tel: 01924 830096
Head: Miss Jennie Littleboy
Age range: 11–17
No. of pupils: 36
Special needs catered for: EBD, SCD
(symbol)

New Gables School
2 New Close Road, Shipley, West Yorkshire BD18 4AB
Tel: 01274 584705
Teacher-in-charge: Caroline Matson
Age range: 11–16
Special needs catered for: SEBD

The Grange School
2 Milner Way, Ossett, Wakefield, West Yorkshire WF5 9JE
Tel: 01924 378957
Headteacher: Phil Bennett
Age range: 7–14
No. of pupils: 12
Special needs catered for: BESD
(symbol)

William Henry Smith School
Boothroyd, Brighouse, West Yorkshire HD6 3JW
Tel: 01484 710123
Principal: B J Heneghan BA, PGCE, DipSpEd
Age range: B8–19
No. of pupils: 64
Fees: Day £57,810 FB £70,435
Special needs catered for: ADD, ADHD, ASD, BESD, CLD, GLD, SCD, SEBD, SPLD
(symbols)

Northern Ireland

County Down

Camphill Community Glencraig
Craigavad, Holywood,
County Down BT18 0DB
Tel: 028 9042 3396
School Co-ordinator: Vincent Reynolds
Age range: 7–19
No. of pupils: 32
Fees: FB £66,500
Special needs catered for: ADHD, ASP, AUT, CP, DYSP, EBD, EPI, HI, MLD, PH, PMLD, SLD, SP&LD, SPLD, VIS
16+ 🛌 16+

Scotland

Edinburgh

Harmeny Education Trust Ltd
Harmeny School, Balerno,
Edinburgh EH14 7JY
Tel: 0131 449 3938
Chief Executive: Peter Doran BA(Hons)Econ, CQSW, MA Social Work, AdvCert SW
Age range: 6–13
No. of pupils: 36
Special needs catered for: ADD, ADHD, ASP, DYS, EBD, SPLD
🛌

Fife

Falkland House School
Falkland Estate, Cupar,
Fife KY15 7AE
Tel: 01337 857268
Head: Mr Stuart Jacob
Age range: B5–18
No. of pupils: 30
Fees: FB £70,000
Special needs catered for: ADD, ADHD, ASP, BESD, DYS, EBD, EPI, SCD, SPLD
🚹 🛌 ✎ 16+

Hillside School
Hillside, Aberdour, Fife KY3 0RH
Tel: 01383 860731
Principal: Mrs Anne Smith
Age range: B10–16
No. of pupils: 39
Fees: Day £10,830
FB £26,594–£58,959
Special needs catered for: DYS, EBD, SPLD
🚹 🛌

Starley Hall School
Aberdour Road, Burntisland,
Fife KY3 0AG
Tel: 01383 860314
Head: Philip Barton BA
Age range: 10–16
No. of pupils: 48
Special needs catered for: EBD, MLD
🛌

North Ayrshire

Geilsland School
Beith, North Ayrshire KA15 1HD
Tel: 01505 504044
Head of School: Mr Paul Gilroy
Age range: B14–18
No. of pupils: 26
Special needs catered for: EBD, MLD, SEBD
🚹 🛌

North Lanarkshire

St Philip's School
10 Main Street, Plains, Airdrie,
North Lanarkshire ML6 7SF
Tel: 01236 765407
Head: Mr P Hanrahan
Age range: B12–16
No. of pupils: 61
Special needs catered for: EBD
🚹 🛌

Perth & Kinross

Balnacraig School
Fairmount Terrace, Perth,
Perth & Kinross PH2 7AR
Tel: 01738 636456
Head: Charles Kiddie
Age range: 12–16
No. of pupils: 24
Special needs catered for: BESD, EBD

Seamab House School
Rumbling Bridge, Kinross,
Perth & Kinross KY13 0PT
Tel: 01577 840307
Chief Executive: Ms Joanna McCreadie
Age range: 5–12
No. of pupils: 15
Special needs catered for: EBD
🛌

Renfrewshire

Kibble Education and Care Centre
Goudie Street, Paisley,
Renfrewshire PA3 2LG
Tel: 0141 889 0044
Head: Graham Bell
Age range: 12–16
No. of pupils: 93
Special needs catered for: EBD, MLD, SCD, SLD, SPLD
🛌

Spark of Genius
Trojan House, Phoenix Business Park, Paisley, Renfrewshire PA1 2BH
Tel: 0141 587 2710
Director: Mr Tom McGhee
Age range: 5–18
No. of pupils: 106
Special needs catered for: ASD, EBD
🛌

The Good Shepherd Secure/Close Support Unit
Greenock Road, Bishopton,
Renfrewshire PA7 5PW
Tel: 01505 864500
Head: Mr Sand Cunningham
Age range: G12–17
Special needs catered for: EBD, MLD
🚹 🛌

Stirling

Ballikinrain Residential School
Fintry Road, Balfron, Stirling G63 0LL
Tel: 01360 440244
Manager: Mr Paul Gilroy
Age range: B8–14
No. of pupils: 40
Special needs catered for: BESD
🚹 🛌

Snowdon School
31 Spittal Street, Stirling FK8 1DU
Tel: 01786 464746
Headteacher: Annette P Davison
Age range: G13–17
Special needs catered for: BESD
🚹 🛌

West Lothian

Moore House School
21 Edinburgh Road, Bathgate,
West Lothian EH48 1EX
Tel: 01506 652312
Age range: 8–16
No. of pupils: 37
Special needs catered for: ADHD, EBD
🛌

Wales

Denbighshire

The Branas School
Branas Isaf, Llandrillo, Corwen,
Denbighshire LL21 0TA
Tel: 01490 440545
Age range: B12–17
No. of pupils: 12
Special needs catered for: EBD

Monmouthshire

Talocher School
Talocher Farm, Wonastow
Road, Monmouth,
Monmouthshire NP25 4DN
Tel: 01600 740777
Principal: Mr Mike Borland
Age range: 11–18
No. of pupils: 25
Special needs catered for:
BESD, SEBD

Neath Port Talbot

Blackwood School
Ferryboat House, Ellwood
Jersey Marine, Neath, Neath
Port Talbot SA10 6NG
Headteacher: Nicky Jones
Age range: B11–18
No. of pupils: 4
Special needs catered for:
EBD, SPLD

Pembrokeshire

St David's Education Unit
Pembroke House, Brawdy
Business Park, Haverfordwest,
Pembrokeshire SA62 6NP
Tel: 01437 721234
Head: Mrs Alison Wilkinson
Age range: 8–17
No. of pupils: 7
Special needs catered for: EBD

Wrexham

Woodlands Children's Development Centre
27 Pentrefelyn Road,
Wrexham LL13 7NB
Tel: 01978 262777
Head of School: Ms Baljit
Gandhi-Johnson
Age range: B11–18
No. of pupils: 14
Special needs catered for:
ADD, ADHD, ASD, ASP, AUT,
BESD, DYS, DYSP, EBD, GLD,
HA, HI, LD, MLD, SCD, SLD

Schools and colleges specialising in learning difficulties (including dyslexia/SPLD)

Abbreviations

ACLD	Autism, Communication and Associated Learning Difficulties
ADD	Attention Deficit Disorder
ADHD	Attention Deficit and Hyperactive Disorder (Hyperkinetic Disorder)
ASD	Autistic Spectrum Disorder
ASP	Asperger Syndrome
AUT	Autism
BESD	Behavioural, Emotional and Social Difficulties
CCD	Complex Communication Difficulties
CLD	Complex Learning Difficulties
CP	Cerebral Palsy
D	Deaf
DEL	Delicate
DYS	Dyslexia
DYSP	Dyspraxia
EBD	Emotional and Behavioural Difficulties
EBSD	Emotional, Behavioural and/or Social Difficulties
EPI	Epilepsy
GLD	General Learning Difficulties
HA	High Ability
HI	Hearing Impairment
HS	Hospital School
LD	Learning Difficulties
MLD	Moderate Learning Difficulties
MSI	Multi-sensory Impairment
OCD	Obsessive Compulsive Disorder
PD	Physical Difficulties
PH	Physical Impairment
Phe	Partially Hearing
PMLD	Profound and Multiple Learning Difficulties
PNI	Physical Neurological Impairment
PRU	Pupil Referral Unit
SCD	Social and Communication Difficulties
SCLD	Severe and Complex Learning Difficulties
SEBD	Severe Emotional and Behavioural Disorders
SEBN	Social, Emotional and Behavioural Needs
SLD	Severe Learning Difficulties
SLI	Specific Language Impairment
SPLD	Specific Learning Difficulties
SP&LD	Speech and Language Difficulties
SLCN	Speech Language & Communication Needs
VIS	Visually Impaired

Key to Symbols

Type of school:

(symbol)	Boys' school
(symbol)	Girls' school
(symbol)	International school

School offers:

(A)	A levels
(symbol)	Boarding accommodation
(16+)	Entrance at 16+
(symbol)	Vocational qualifications
(symbol)	Learning support
(✓)	This is a DfE approved independent or non-maintained school under section 342 or 347(1) of the 1996 Education Act

Please note: Unless otherwise indicated, all schools are coeducational day schools. Single-sex and boarding schools will be indicated by the relevant icon.

Central & West

Bristol

Belgrave School
10 Upper Belgrave Road,
Clifton, Bristol BS8 2XH
Tel: 0117 974 3133
Head Teacher: Mr Jonathan Skinner
Age range: 5–13
Fees: Day £6,000
Special needs catered for: ADD,
DEL, DYS, DYSP, SP&LD, SLI
✔

Bristol Dyslexia Centre
10 Upper Belgrave Road,
Clifton, Bristol BS8 2XH
Tel: 0117 973 9405
Headmistress: Mrs Pat
Jones BEd(Hons), SEN, SpLD,
CertEd, IrSc, CMBDA
Special needs catered for:
DYS, DYSP, SLD

Sheiling School, Thornbury
Thornbury Park, Thornbury,
Bristol BS35 1HP
Tel: 01454 412194
Age range: 6–19
No. of pupils: 22
Fees: Day £66,419–£83,428
WB £125,931–£172,096
FB £140,578–£197,157
Special needs catered for: ADD,
ADHD, ASD, ASP, AUT, BESD, CLD,
CP, DEL, DYS, DYSP, EBD, EPI, GLD,
HA, HI, LD, MLD, MSI, PD, Phe, SCD,
SCLD, SEBD, SLD, SP&LD, SPLD, SLI
♿ 16 ✔

St Christopher's School
Carisbrooke Lodge, Westbury
Park, , Bristol BS6 7JE
Tel: 0117 973 6875
Principal: Ms Orna Matz
BEd, MEd(Autism)
Age range: 5–19
No. of pupils: 42
Special needs catered for:
ASD, AUT, CLD, CP, EPI, PD, PH,
PMLD, SCLD, SLD, SP&LD
♿ 16 ✔

Buckinghamshire

MacIntyre Wingrave School
Leighton Road, Wingrave,
Buckinghamshire HP22 4PA
Tel: 01296 681274
Principal: Ms Annemari Ottridge
Age range: 10–19
No. of pupils: 38
Fees: FB £182,000
Special needs catered for:
ASD, SCD, SLD
♿ 16 ✔

Gloucestershire

Cambian Southwick Park School
Gloucester Road, Tewkesbury,
Gloucestershire GL20 7DG
Tel: 01684853250
Head: Louise Tully-Middleton
Age range: 7–19
Special needs catered for: ASD,
AUT, CLD, DYSP, GLD, LD, MLD,
SCD, SCLD, SEBD, SLD, SP&LD, SLI
♿ 16

William Morris House
William Morris Camphill
Community, Eastington,
Stonehouse, Gloucestershire
GL10 3SH
Tel: 01453 824025
Contact: Admissions Group
Age range: 16–25
No. of pupils: 30
Special needs catered for: ASP,
AUT, DYSP, EBD, EPI, MLD
♿

Oxfordshire

Action for Children Penhurst School
New Street, Chipping Norton,
Oxfordshire OX7 5LN
Tel: 01608 642559
Principal: Derek Lyseight-Jones
Age range: 5–19
No. of pupils: 21
Special needs catered for: CP,
EPI, HI, PH, PMLD, SLD, SP&LD, VIS
♿ 16

Bruern Abbey School
Chesterton, Bicester,
Oxfordshire OX26 1UY
Tel: 01869 242448
Principal: Mr P Fawkes MBA, CertEd
Age range: B7–13
No. of pupils: 44
Fees: Day £5,703 WB £7,791
Special needs catered for:
DYS, DYSP
♟ ♟ ♿

Wiltshire

Calder House School
Thickwood Lane, Colerne,
Wiltshire SN14 8BN
Tel: 01225 743566
Head: Mrs Karen Parsons
Age range: 6–13
No. of pupils: 48
Fees: Day £16,200
Special needs catered for: DEL,
DYS, DYSP, SP&LD, SPLD, SLI
✔

Fairfield Farm College
Dilton Marsh, Westbury,
Wiltshire BA13 4DL
Tel: 01373 866066
Principal: Ms Janet Kenward
Age range: 16–25
Special needs catered for: MLD
16 ♿

Tumblewood Project School
The Laurels, 4 Hawkeridge
Road, Heywood, Westbury,
Wiltshire BA13 4LF
Tel: 01373 824 466
Head of School: Jennifer Lewis
Age range: G11–18
No. of pupils: 12
Special needs catered for:
ADHD, DYS, DYSP, LD
♟ ♿ 16 ✔

East

Cambridgeshire

Holme Court School
Abington Woods, Church
Lane, Little Abington,
Cambridgeshire CB21 6BQ
Tel: 01223 778030
Headteacher: Ms Anita Laws
Age range: 5–16
No. of pupils: 27
Special needs catered for: ADD,
ADHD, ASP, CLD, DYS, DYSP, GLD,
HA, LD, MLD, SCD, SP&LD, SPLD, VIS
✔

Essex

Doucecroft School
Abbots Lane, Eight Ash Green,
Colchester, Essex CO6 3QL
Tel: 01206 771234
Head Teacher: Miss
Kathy Cranmer BEd
Age range: 3–19
No. of pupils: 46
Fees: Day £52,779–£54,291
WB £86,211–£88,211
Special needs catered for:
ASD, ASP, AUT
♿ 16 ✔

Woodcroft School
Whitakers Way, Loughton,
Essex IG10 1SQ
Tel: 020 8508 1369
Headteacher: Mrs
Margaret Newton
Age range: 2–11
No. of pupils: 36
Special needs catered for:
ADD, ADHD, ASD, ASP, AUT,
CLD, CP, DEL, DYSP, EBD, EPI,
LD, MLD, MSI, PH, PMLD, SCLD,
SLD, SP&LD, SPLD, SLI, VIS
✔

Hertfordshire

Egerton Rothesay School
Durrants Lane, Berkhamsted,
Hertfordshire HP4 3UJ
Tel: 01442 865275
Headteacher: Mr Colin Parker
BSc(Hons), Dip.Ed (Oxon),
PGCE, C.Math MIMA
Age range: 6–19
No. of pupils: 143
Fees: Day £14,310–£20,370
Special needs catered for:
DYS, DYSP, MLD, SP&LD
♟ ✎

Learning difficulties (including dyslexia/SPLD)

Lincolnshire

Kisimul Upper School
Acacia Hall, Shortwood Lane, Friesthorpe, Lincoln, Lincolnshire LN3 5AL
Tel: 01673 880022
Head of School: Paul Routledge
Special needs catered for:
🏫

Norfolk

Copperfield School
22 Euston Road, Great Yarmouth, Norfolk NR30 1DX
Tel: 01493 849 499
Headteacher: Sally Alden
Age range: 11–16
No. of pupils: 12
Special needs catered for: ADD, ADHD, ASP, BESD, CLD, DYS, DYSP, EBD, GLD, LD, MLD, SCD, SCLD, SEBD, SPLD
✓

The Beehive
Stubbs House, Stubbs Green, Loddon, Norfolk NR14 6EA
Tel: 01508 521190
Headteacher: Mrs Valerie Freear
Age range: 5–14
No. of pupils: 4
Special needs catered for: ASD, BESD, MLD, SPLD
✓

Suffolk

Centre Academy East Anglia
Church Road, Brettenham, Ipswich, Suffolk IP7 7QR
Tel: 01449 736404
Principal: Dr. Duncan Rollo BA, MA, PhD
Age range: 4–19
Fees: Day £18,000–£25,875 WB £24,999–£36,225
Special needs catered for: ADHD, ASP, CLD, DYS, DYSP, GLD, HA, LD, SP&LD, SPLD
🏫 £ ✓

East Midlands

Derbyshire

Alderwasley Hall School & Sixth Form Centre
Alderwasley, Belper, Derbyshire DE56 2SR
Tel: 01629 822586
Head Teacher: Ms Angela Findlay MEd, NPQH, CertEd
Age range: 5–19
Special needs catered for: ASD, ASP, AUT, DYSP, GLD, HA, LD, SCD, SP&LD, SPLD, SLI
🏫 16+ ✓

Pegasus School
Caldwell Hall, Main Street, Caldwell, Derbyshire DE12 6RS
Tel: 01283 761352
Head Teacher: Ms Suzanne Pennington
Age range: 8–19
Special needs catered for: ADHD, ASD, AUT, CLD, EPI, HI, LD, PMLD, SCLD, SLD, SP&LD, SPLD, SLI, VIS
🏫 16+ ✓

Lincolnshire

KISIMUL SCHOOL
For further details see p. 88
The Old Vicarage, 61 High Street, Swinderby, Lincoln, Lincolnshire LN6 9LU
Tel: 01522 868279
Email: admissions@kisimul.co.uk
Website: www.kisimul.co.uk
Director of Education: Mr Danny Carter BA(Hons), MA, MEd
Age range: 8–19
No. of pupils: 60
Special needs catered for: ASD, AUT, CLD, EPI, LD, MSI, PMLD, SCLD, SLD, SP&LD, SPLD
🏫 16+ ✓

Linkage College - Toynton Campus
Toynton All Saints, Spilsby, Lincolnshire PE23 5AE
Tel: 01790 752499
Age range: 16–25
Special needs catered for: ADD, ADHD, ASD, ASP, AUT, CLD, CP, D, DEL, DYS, DYSP, EPI, GLD, HI, LD, MLD, PD, Phe, PH, SCD, SCLD, SLD, SP&LD, SPLD, VIS
16+ 🏫

Nottinghamshire

I CAN'S DAWN HOUSE SCHOOL
For further details see p. 90
Helmsley Road, Rainworth, Mansfield, Nottinghamshire NG21 0DQ
Tel: 01623 795361
Email: dawnhouse@ican.notts.sch.uk
Website: www.dawnhouseschool.org.uk
Principal: Angela Child
Age range: 5–19
No. of pupils: 79
Special needs catered for: CLD, DYS, DYSP, SCD, SLD, SP&LD, SPL
🏫 16+ ✓

Sutherland House - Continuing Education Centre
8 Clinton Avenue, Nottingham, Nottinghamshire NG5 1AW
Tel: 0115 9693373
Principal: Maria Allen
Age range: 11–19
Special needs catered for: ASD, AUT
16+

Sutherland House School
Sutherland Road, Nottingham, Nottinghamshire NG3 7AP
Tel: 0115 9873375
Executive Principal: Ian Thorsteinsson
Age range: 3–19
No. of pupils: 84
Fees: Day £41,525–£45,473
Special needs catered for: ASD, ASP, AUT
16+ ✓

Greater London

Essex

St John's RC Special School
Turpins Lane, Woodford Bridge, Essex IG8 8AX
Tel: 020 8504 1818
Principal: Mrs Susan Burnside
Age range: 5–19
Special needs catered for: MLD, SLD
✓

London

Middlesex

Hillingdon Manor School
Moorcroft Complex, Harlington Road, Hillingdon, Middlesex UB8 3HD
Tel: 01895 813679
Principal: Ms Angela Austin
Age range: 3–19
No. of pupils: 70
Fees: Day £32,646
Special needs catered for: ASD, CLD
16+ ✓

PIELD HEATH HOUSE SCHOOL
For further details see p. 92
Pield Heath Road, Uxbridge, Middlesex UB8 3NW
Tel: 01895 258507
Email: admin@pieldheathschool.org.uk
Website: pieldheathschool.org.uk
Executive Principal: Sister Julie Rose
Age range: 7–19
No. of pupils: 83
Special needs catered for: MLD, SLD, SP&LD
🏫 16+ ✓

Surrey

BLOSSOM LOWER SCHOOL AND UPPER HOUSE
For further details see p. 91
Station Road, Motspur Park,
New Malden, London KT3 6JJ
Tel: 020 8946 7348
Email: admin@
blossomhouseschool.co.uk
Website: www.blossomhouse
school.co.uk
Principal: Joanna Burgess
DipCST,MRCSLT,DipRS
A,SpLD,PGCE,HPC
Age range: 3–19
No. of pupils: 214
Special needs catered for:
ADD, ADHD, ASP, DYS,
DYSP, SCD, SP&LD, SPLD
16 ✔

Rutherford School
1A Melville Avenue, South
Croydon, Surrey CR2 7HZ
Tel: 020 8688 7560
Interim Head of School: Dr
Carole Nicolson
Age range: 3–19
No. of pupils: 26
Fees: Day £50,400
Special needs catered for:
CP, D, EPI, HI, MSI, PD, Phe, PH,
PMLD, PNI, SLD, SP&LD, VIS
16 ✔

THE LINK PRIMARY SCHOOL
For further details see p. 93
138 Croydon Road, Beddington,
Croydon, Surrey CR0 4PG
Tel: 020 8688 5239
Email: office@linkprim.co.uk
Website: www.linkprim.co.uk
Head Teacher: Mrs Beverley
Dixon CertEd, ASE, NPQH
Age range: 4–11
No. of pupils: 45
Special needs catered for:
ASD, ASP, DYSP, GLD, LD,
MLD, SCD, SP&LD, SLI
✔

London

East London

Side by Side Kids School
9 Big Hill, London E5 9HH
Tel: 020 88808300
Headteacher: Ms R Atkins
Age range: 2–16
No. of pupils: 60
Special needs catered for:
MLD, SLD, SP&LD
✔

North London

LIMESPRING SCHOOL
For further details see p. 95
Park House, 16 High Road,
East Finchley, London N2 9PJ
Tel: 020 8444 1387
Email: info@
limespringschool.co.uk
Website:
www.limespringschool.co.uk
Principal: Denise Drinkwater
Age range: 7–11
Special needs catered for:
DYS, DYSP
✔

North-West London

Abingdon House School
Broadley Terrace, London NW1 6LG
Tel: 0845 2300426
Head: Ms Julie Fardell
Age range: 5–13
No. of pupils: 55
Fees: Day £26,665
Special needs catered for: ADD,
ADHD, ASP, DYS, DYSP, SP&LD, SPLD
🌍 🖉 ✔

Kisharon School
1011 Finchley Road,
London NW11 7HB
Tel: 020 8455 7483
Age range: 4–19
No. of pupils: 35
Fees: Day £27,000–£42,000
Special needs catered for: ADD,
ADHD, ASD, ASP, AUT, BESD, CLD,
CP, D, DEL, DYS, DYSP, EBD, EPI,
GLD, HA, HI, LD, MLD, MSI, PD,
Phe, PH, PMLD, PNI, SCD, SCLD,
SEBD, SLD, SP&LD, SPLD, SLI, VIS
✔

South-West London

Centre Academy London
92 St John's Hill, Battersea,
London SW11 1SH
Tel: 020 7738 2344
Principal: Dr. Duncan
Rollo BA, MA, PhD
Age range: 9–19
Fees: Day £27,600–£40,100
Special needs catered for:
ADD, ADHD, ASD, ASP, AUT,
CLD, DYS, DYSP, HA, SP&LD
£ 🖉 16 ✔

Fairley House School
30 Causton Street,
London SW1P 4AU
Tel: 020 7976 5456
Headmaster: Michael Taylor
Age range: 5–16
No. of pupils: 195
Fees: Day £29,922
Special needs catered for:
DYS, DYSP, HA, SPLD
🌍 ✔

FREDERICK HUGH HOUSE
For further details see p. 94
48 Old Church Street,
London SW3 5BY
Tel: 0207 349 8833
Email: info@
frederickhughhouse.com
Website:
www.frederickhughhouse.com
Headteacher: Miss Tanya Jamil
Age range: 10–16
Special needs catered for:
ADHD, ASD, AUT, CLD, CP,
DEL, DYSP, EPI, GLD, LD, MLD,
MSI, PD, SCD, SP&LD, SPLD
✔

PARAYHOUSE SCHOOL
For further details see p. 96
New Kings School Annex,
New Kings Road, Fulham,
London SW6 4LY
Tel: 020 7751 0914
Email: a.sullivan@
parayhouse.com
Website: www.parayhouse.com
Head: Mrs Sarah Jackson
CertEd, DipEd(Complex
Learning Handicap)
Age range: 7–16
No. of pupils: 46
Fees: Day £27,540
Special needs catered for:
ADD, BESD, CLD, CP, DEL,
EBD, EPI, MLD, Phe, SCD,
SCLD, SLD, SP&LD
✔

The Dominie
55 Warriner Gardens,
Battersea, London SW11 4DX
Tel: 020 7720 8783
Principal: Miss Anne O'Doherty
Age range: 6–13
No. of pupils: 30
Special needs catered for:
DYS, DYSP, SP&LD
✔

THE MOAT SCHOOL
For further details see p. 98
Bishops Avenue, Fulham,
London SW6 6EG
Tel: 020 7610 9018
Email: office@
moatschool.org.uk
Website:
www.moatschool.org.uk
Head: Ms Clare King
Age range: 9–16
Fees: Day £28,800
Special needs catered for: SPLD
🌍 🖉 ✔

West London

THE INDEPENDENT SCHOOL (TIS)
For further details see p. 97
23-31 Beavor Lane, Ravenscourt
Park, Hammersmith,
London W6 9AR
Tel: 0203 086 8687
Email: admin@tis-london.org
Website: www.tis-london.org
Principal: Ms Tanya Moran
Age range: 11–16
Special needs catered for:
DYS, DYSP

Learning difficulties (including dyslexia/SPLD)

North-East

Northumberland

Cambian Dilston College
Dilston Hall, Corbridge,
Northumberland NE45 5RJ
Tel: 0800 138 1184
Vice Principal: Nicola Moxon
Age range: 16–25
Special needs catered for: ADD,
ADHD, ASD, ASP, AUT, BESD, CP,
DEL, EBD, EPI, GLD, LD, MLD,
SCD, SCLD, SLD, SP&LD, SPLD
(symbols)

**Nunnykirk Centre
for Dyslexia**
Netherwitton, Morpeth,
Northumberland NE61 4PB
Tel: 01670 772685
Headteacher: B Frost NPQH,
MSc, MEd, BA(QTS), PGDip
Age range: 9–18
No. of pupils: 24 VIth7
Fees: Day £12,960–£13,935
WB £21,555–£23,520
Special needs catered for:
DYS, DYSP, SPLD
(symbols) 16+ (✓)

North-West

Cheshire

The David Lewis School
Mill Lane, Warford, Alderley
Edge, Cheshire SK9 7UD
Tel: 01565 640066
Headteacher: Mrs Pauline
Greenall BA, MEd
Age range: 14–19
No. of pupils: 20
Special needs catered for:
AUT, CP, EPI, HI, PD, PMLD,
SCD, SLD, SP&LD, SPLD, VIS
(symbols) 16+ (✓)

Greater Manchester

Birtenshaw School
Bromley Cross, Bolton, Greater
Manchester BL7 9AB
Tel: 01204 306043
Head Teacher: Mrs Julie Barnes
Age range: 3–19
No. of pupils: 35 VIth25
Fees: Day £49,757–£71,084
Special needs catered for: ADD,
ADHD, ASD, ASP, AUT, CLD, CP,
DEL, EPI, GLD, HI, LD, MLD, MSI,
PD, Phe, PH, PMLD, PNI, SCD,
SCLD, SLD, SP&LD, SLI, VIS
(symbols) 16+ (✓)

Bridge College
Curzon Road, Offerton, Stockport,
Greater Manchester SK2 5DG
Tel: 0161 487 4293
Principal: Maggie Thompson
Age range: 16–23
No. of pupils: 75
Special needs catered for:
AUT, CLD, PH

**Inscape Centre for
Autism (INCA)**
Schools Hill, Cheadle, Greater
Manchester SK8 1JE
Tel: 0161 283 4761
Head: Susan Allison
Special needs catered for: AUT

Inscape House Salford
Walkden Road, Worsley,
Manchester, Greater
Manchester M28 7FG
Tel: 0161 975 2340
Headteacher: Keith Cox
Age range: 5–19
No. of pupils: 65
Special needs catered for: AUT
16+

Langdon College
9 Leicester Avenue, Salford,
Greater Manchester M7 4HA
Tel: 0161 740 5900
Principal: Mr Christopher Mayho
Age range: 16–25
Special needs catered for:
ASD, ASP, AUT, BESD, DYS, DYSP,
EBD, GLD, HI, LD, MLD, Phe, PH,
SCD, SP&LD, SPLD, SLI, VIS

Lancashire

Pontville
Black Moss Lane, Ormskirk,
Lancashire L39 4TW
Tel: 01695 578734
Head Teacher: Ms Elaine Riley
Age range: 5–19
No. of pupils: 59
Special needs catered for:
ASD, ASP, CLD, MLD, SCD,
SP&LD, SPLD, SLI
(symbols) 16+ (✓)

Progress School
Gough Lane, Bamber Bridge,
Preston, Lancashire PR26 7TZ
Tel: 01772 334832
Principal: Mrs Lyn Lewis
Age range: 7–19
No. of pupils: 17
Fees: WB £3,269 FB £170,000
Special needs catered for:
AUT, PMLD, SCLD, SLD
(symbols) 16+ (✓)

Merseyside

**Liverpool Progressive
School**
Rice Lane, Liverpool,
Merseyside L9 1NR
Tel: 0151 525 4004
Headteacher: Ms Linda Butcher
Age range: 8–19
No. of pupils: 20
Special needs catered for: AUT, SLD
16+ (✓)

Wargrave House School
449 Wargrave Road, Newton-le-
Willows, Merseyside WA12 8RS
Tel: 01925 224899
Principal: Mrs Wendy Mann
BSc, PGCE, DipSpLD, NPQH
Age range: 5–19
No. of pupils: 70
Special needs catered for: ASP, AUT
(symbols) 16+ (✓)

South-East

East Sussex

Frewen College
Brickwall, Rye Road, Northiam,
Rye, East Sussex TN31 6NL
Tel: 01797 252494
Principal: Mrs Linda Smith
BA(Hons), PGCE
Age range: 7–19
No. of pupils: 103
Fees: Day £13,686–£21,801
WB £21,078–£30,264
FB £21,078–£30,264
Special needs catered for:
DYS, DYSP, SP&LD, SPLD
(symbols)

Northease Manor School
Rodmell, Lewes, East Sussex BN7 3EY
Tel: 01273 472915
Headteacher: Carmen Harvey-
Browne BA(Hons), PGCE, NPQH
Age range: 10–17
No. of pupils: 95
Special needs catered for:
ADD, ADHD, ASD, ASP, DYS,
DYSP, SCD, SP&LD, SPLD
(symbols) (✓)

Owlswick School
Newhaven Road, Kingston,
Lewes, East Sussex BN7 3NF
Tel: 01273 473078
Headteacher: Michael Mayne
Age range: 10–17
Special needs catered for: ADD,
ADHD, ASD, ASP, BESD, DYS,
DYSP, EBD, GLD, LD, MLD, SCD
(symbols) 16+ (✓)

ST JOHN'S SCHOOL & COLLEGE
For further details see p. 103
Business Centre, 17
Walpole Road, Brighton,
East Sussex BN2 0AF
Tel: 01273 244000
Email: admissions@st-johns.co.uk
Website: www.st-johns.co.uk
Principal & Chief Executive: Mr Mark Hughes
Age range: 7–25
No. of pupils: 97
Fees: Day £50,000 FB £95,000
Special needs catered for:
ADD, ADHD, ASD, ASP, AUT, BESD, CLD, CP, D, DEL, DYS, DYSP, EBD, EPI, GLD, HA, LD, MLD, PD, PNI, SCD, SCLD, SEBD, SLD, SP&LD, SPLD, SLI

Hampshire

Chiltern Tutorial School
Otterbourne New Hall,
Cranbourne Drive, Otterbourne,
Winchester, Hampshire SO21 2ET
Tel: 01962 717696
Headmistress: Mrs Jane Gaudie BA, CertEd, AMBDA
Age range: 7–12
No. of pupils: 20
Fees: Day £8,850
Special needs catered for:
DYS, DYSP

Clay Hill School
Clay Hill, Lyndhurst,
Hampshire SO43 7DE
Tel: 023 8028 3633
Head of School: Mrs. Helen Sharpe
Age range: 5–19
Special needs catered for: ASD, LD

Minstead Training Project
Minstead Lodge, Minstead,
Lyndhurst, Hampshire SO43 7FT
Tel: 023 80812254
Principal: Mr Martin Lenaerts
Age range: 18+
No. of pupils: 14
Special needs catered for:
GLD, LD, MLD

Sheiling College
Horton Road, Ashley, Ringwood,
Hampshire BH24 2EB
Tel: 01425 477488
Principal: Ms Corine van Barneveld
Age range: 19–25
No. of pupils: 32
Special needs catered for: ASD, AUT, CLD, EPI, GLD, LD, MLD, SCD, SCLD, SLD, SP&LD, SPLD

Sheiling School
Horton Road, Ashley, Ringwood,
Hampshire BH24 2EB
Tel: 01425 477488
Head of School: Ms Corine van Barneveld
Age range: 6–19
No. of pupils: 31
Fees: Day £39,070
WB £88,260 FB £106,008
Special needs catered for: ASD, AUT, CLD, EBD, EPI, GLD, LD, MLD, SCD, SCLD, SLD, SP&LD, SPLD

The Loddon School
Wildmoor Lane, Sherfield-on-Loddon, Hook,
Hampshire RG27 0JD
Tel: 01256 884600
Principal: Gill Barrett MEd,BA(Hons),NPQH,PCGE
Age range: 8–19
No. of pupils: 26
Fees: FB £229,000
Special needs catered for:
ADD, ADHD, ASD, AUT, CLD, EPI, SCLD, SLD, SP&LD

Isle of Wight

ST CATHERINE'S SCHOOL
For further details see p. 102
Grove Road, Ventnor,
Isle of Wight PO38 1TT
Tel: 01983 852722
Email: general@stcatherines.org.uk
Website: www.stcatherines.org.uk
Principal: Mrs R Weldon
Age range: 7–19
No. of pupils: 55 VIth28
Special needs catered for:
ADD, ADHD, ASD, ASP, AUT, DYS, DYSP, SCD, SLD, SP&LD, SLI

Kent

Great Oaks Small School
Ebbsfleet Farmhouse,
Ebbsfleet Lane, Minster,
Ramsgate, Kent CT12 5DL
Tel: 01843 822 022
Head of School: Mrs Liz Baker
Age range: 10–18
No. of pupils: 18 VIth3
Special needs catered for: SPLD

Trinity School
13 New Road, Rochester,
Medway, Kent ME1 1BG
Tel: 01634 812233
Principal: Mrs C Dunn BA(Hons), RSA(Dip), SpLD(NHCSS)
Age range: 6–16
No. of pupils: 43
Fees: Day £9,270–£9,750
Special needs catered for: ASD, ASP, DYS, DYSP, SLD, SP&LD

Surrey

I CAN'S MEATH SCHOOL
For further details see p. 99
Brox Road, Ottershaw,
Surrey KT16 0LF
Tel: 01932 872302
Email: meath@meath-ican.org.uk
Website: www.meathschool.org.uk
Headteacher: Janet Dunn OBE, MA, AdvDipSpecEduc
No. of pupils: 56
Special needs catered for:
SP&LD

KISIMUL SCHOOL - WOODSTOCK HOUSE
For further details see p. 100
Woodstock Lane North, Long Ditton, Surbiton, Surrey KT6 5HN
Tel: 020 8335 2570
Email: admissions@kisimul.co.uk
Website: www.kisimul.co.uk
Director of Education: Mr Danny Carter BA(Hons), MA, MEd
Age range: 8–19
No. of pupils: 40
Special needs catered for:
ASD, AUT, CLD, EPI, LD, MSI, PMLD, SCLD, SLD, SP&LD, SPLD

Moon Hall College
Burys Court, Flanchford Road,
Leigh, Reigate, Surrey RH2 8RE
Tel: 01306 611372
Principal: Mrs Berry Baker BA(Hons)Hist,PGCE,BSc(Hons)Psych,BDA Diploma,AMBDA
Age range: 3–16
Fees: Day £6,630–£17,220
Special needs catered for:
DYS, LD, SPLD

Moon Hall School
Pasturewood Road, Holmbury St Mary, Dorking, Surrey RH5 6LQ
Tel: 01306 731464
Head: Mrs Pamela Lore BA(Hons) (Psych), MA(Ed), Dip RSA SpLD, PGCE
Age range: 7–13
Fees: Day £14,400–£16,470
WB £16,015–£18,085
Special needs catered for:
DYS, SPLD

More House School
Moons Hill, Frensham,
Farnham, Surrey GU10 3AP
Tel: 01252 792303
Headmaster: Jonathan Hetherington BA(Hons), MSc(ed), QTS
Age range: B8–18
No. of pupils: 452
Fees: Day £12,234–£17,145
WB £19,071–£24,636
FB £21,066–£26,685
Special needs catered for: SPLD

Orchard Hill College and Academy Trust
BedZED, 20 Sandmartin Way,
Hackbridge, Surrey SM6 7DF
Tel: 0345 402 0453
Principal: Ms Caroline Allen OBE, BEd(Hons), MBA(Ed)
Age range: 16+
Special needs catered for: ADD, ADHD, ASD, ASP, AUT, BESD, CLD, CP, DEL, DYS, DYSP, EBD, EPI, GLD, HA, HI, LD, MLD, MSI, PD, Phe, PH, PMLD, PNI, SCD, SCLD, SEBD, SLD, SP&LD, SPLD, SLI, VIS

St Dominic's School
Hambledon, Godalming,
Surrey GU8 4DX
Tel: 01428 684693/682741
Principal: Mrs Angela Drayton
Age range: 7–19
No. of pupils: 77 VIth19
Special needs catered for:
ADD, ADHD, ASD, ASP, BESD, CLD, DEL, DYS, DYSP, EPI, HA, SCD, SP&LD, SPLD

ST JOSEPH'S SPECIALIST SCHOOL & COLLEGE
For further details see p. 104
Amlets Lane, Cranleigh,
Surrey GU6 7DH
Tel: 01483 272449
Email: admissions@st-josephscranleigh.surrey.sch.uk
Website: www.st-josephs cranleigh.surrey.sch.uk
Principal: Mrs Annie Sutton
Age range: 5–19
No. of pupils: 75
Fees: Day £57,905 FB £83,898
Special needs catered for:
ADHD, ASD, CLD, DYS, DYSP, EPI, LD, MLD, SCLD, SLD, SP&LD

The Knowl Hill School
School Lane, Pirbright,
Woking, Surrey GU24 0JN
Tel: 01483 797032
Principal: Dr. Ruth Bailey D.Ed,MA,MSc,MSc(FPC),BA(Hons),MBPSS,PGCE,NPQH
Age range: 7–16
No. of pupils: 57
Fees: Day £15,606
Special needs catered for:
DYS, DYSP, SPLD

Wiltshire

Appleford School
Shrewton, Salisbury,
Wiltshire SP3 4HL
Tel: 01980 621020
Headmaster: Mr. David King
Age range: 7–18
No. of pupils: 126
Fees: Day £16,608 FB £25,491
Special needs catered for:
ADD, ADHD, ASP, DYS, DYSP, HA, MLD, SP&LD, SPLD

South-West

Devon

Devon Progressive School
, Devon
Tel: 01822 616627
Age range: 9–18
(16+)

Kingsley School
Northdown Road, Bideford,
Devon EX39 3LY
Tel: 01237 426200
Headmaster: Mr Simon
Woolcott BSc ARCS
Age range: 0–18
No. of pupils: 395
Fees: Day £1,870–£3,180
WB £5,410 FB £6,870
Special needs catered for:
DYS, DYSP
(symbols) (A) (symbols) (£) (symbols) (16+)

Dorset

Boveridge House School (formerly Philip Green Memorial School)
Boveridge House, Cranborne,
Wimborne, Dorset BH21 5RU
Tel: 01725 517218
Headmistress: Mrs L Water
Age range: 8–19
No. of pupils: 38
Special needs catered for:
MLD, SCD, SLD
(symbols) (16+) (✓)

Somerset

Cambian Lufton College
Lufton, Yeovil, Somerset BA22 8ST
Tel: 0800 288 9779
Principal: Jonathan James
Age range: 16–25
No. of pupils: 72
Special needs catered for:
HI, MLD, PH, PMLD, SLD
(symbol)

Foxes Academy
The Esplanade, Minehead,
Somerset TA24 5QP
Tel: 01643 708529
Principal: Sharon Bowden
Age range: 18–25
No. of pupils: 80
Special needs catered for: ASD,
ASP, AUT, MLD, Phe, SCD, SP&LD
(symbol)

Foxes Fields
Foxes Academy, The Esplanade,
Minehead, Somerset TA24 5QP
Tel: 01643 708529
Principal: Sharon Bowden
Age range: 11–19
No. of pupils: 20
Special needs catered for:
ADD, ADHD, ASD, ASP, AUT,
BESD, CLD, DEL, DYS, DYSP, EBD,
GLD, HA, HI, LD, MLD, MSI, PD,
Phe, SCD, SCLD, SLD, SPLD
(symbol)

Mark College
Mark, Highbridge,
Somerset TA9 4NP
Tel: 01278 641632
Principal: Mr Chris Sweeney
Age range: 10–19
No. of pupils: 75
Fees: Day £19,829
WB £26,956 FB £28,019
Special needs catered for:
DYS, DYSP, SLD, SPLD
(symbols) (symbols) (16+) (✓)

Shapwick Prep
Mark Road, Burtle, Bridgwater,
Somerset TA7 8NJ
Tel: 01278 722012
Headmaster: Mr M Lee
BA (Hons); PGCE
Age range: 8–18
No. of pupils: 142
Fees: Day £11,220–£13,533
WB £16,995 FB £16,473–£19,515
Special needs catered for: DYS
(symbols) (symbols) (✓)

West Midlands

Herefordshire

Rowden House School
Rowden, Bromyard,
Herefordshire HR7 4LS
Tel: 01885 488096
Principal: Mr Martin Carter
NPQH, BEd(Hons), Adv Diploma
(Behaviour Support)
Age range: 11–19
Special needs catered for: ADD,
ADHD, ASD, AUT, CLD, EPI, GLD,
LD, MLD, PMLD, SCLD, SLD, SPLD
(symbols) (16+) (✓)

Shropshire

Access School
Holbrook Villa Farm, Harmer
Hill, Broughton, Shrewsbury,
Shropshire SY4 3EW
Tel: 01939 220797
Headteacher: Miss Verity White
Age range: 5–16
No. of pupils: 10
Special needs catered for:
EBD, GLD, MLD
(✓)

Jigsaw School
Queensway, Hadley, Telford,
Shropshire TF1 6AJ
Tel: 01952 388555
Headteacher: Nigel Griffiths
Age range: 11–16
Special needs catered for:
EBD, SPLD
(✓)

Staffordshire

Bladon House School
Newton Solney, Burton upon
Trent, Staffordshire DE15 0TA
Tel: 01283 563787
Head Teacher: Mrs Kate Britt
CEd, MA(Educ Management)
Age range: 5–19
Special needs catered for: ADD,
ADHD, ASD, AUT, CLD, EPI, HI, LD,
MLD, SLD, SP&LD, SPLD, SLI, VIS
(symbols) (16+) (✓)

Maple Hayes Dyslexia School
Abnalls Lane, Lichfield,
Staffordshire WS13 8BL
Tel: 01543 264387
Principal: Dr E N Brown MSc,
BA, MINS, MSCMe, AFBPsS,
CPsychol, FRSA, CSci
Age range: 7–17
No. of pupils: 118
Fees: Day £14,190–£18,975
Special needs catered for:
DYS, DYSP, SPLD
(symbols) (£) (✓)

Regent College
77 Shelton New Road, Shelton,
Stoke-on-Trent, Staffordshire ST4 7AA
Tel: 01782 263326
Principal: Ms Wendy Williams
Age range: 16–25
No. of pupils: 30
Special needs catered for:
CLD, EPI, PD, SLD, SP&LD

West Midlands

ARGENT COLLEGE
For further details see p. 106
New Standard Works, 43–47
Vittoria Street, Birmingham,
West Midlands B1 3PE
Tel: 01384 399400
Email: enquiries@argent.rmt.org
Website: www.rmt.org
Executive Principal: Oliver
Cheney
Age range: 16–25
(16+)

GLASSHOUSE COLLEGE
For further details see p. 107
Wollaston Road,
Amblecote, Stourbridge,
West Midlands DY8 4HF
Tel: 01384 399400
Email: enquiries@ghc.rmt.org
Website: www.rmt.org
Executive Principal: Oliver
Cheney
Age range: 16–25
Special needs catered for:
ADHD, ASD, ASP, BESD, CLD,
EBD, GLD, LD, PMLD, SCD,
SCLD, SEBD, SLD, SPLD
(16+) (symbol)

OVERLEY HALL SCHOOL
For further details see p. 108
Overley, Wellington, Telford,
West Midlands TF6 5HE
Tel: 01952 740262
Email: info@overleyhall.com
Website: www.overleyhall.com
Headteacher: Mrs
Beverley Doran
Age range: 8–19
No. of pupils: 20
Special needs catered for:
ADD, ADHD, ASD, ASP, AUT,
CLD, DYSP, EPI, GLD, LD, PMLD,
SCD, SCLD, SLD, SP&LD
(symbols) (16+) (✓)

Sunfield School
Clent Grove, Woodman Lane,
Stourbridge, West Midlands DY9 9PB
Tel: 01562 882253
Principal: Caroline Bell
Age range: 6–19
Special needs catered for: ADD,
ADHD, ASD, AUT, BESD, CLD, DYS,
EPI, GLD, LD, MLD, MSI, PMLD,
SCD, SCLD, SEBD, SLD, SP&LD, SLI
(symbols) (16+) (✓)

Worcestershire

Our Place School
The Orchard, Bransford,
Worcestershire WR6 5JE
Tel: 01886 833378
Head of School: Paula McElearney
Special needs catered for:
ASD, MLD, PMLD, SLD

Yorkshire & Humberside

North-East Lincolnshire

Linkage College - Weelsby Campus
Weelsby Road, Grimsby, North-East Lincolnshire DN32 9RU
Tel: 01472 241044
Director of Education: Hugh Williams
Age range: 16–25
No. of pupils: 220
Special needs catered for:
ADD, ADHD, ASD, ASP, AUT, CLD, CP, D, DEL, DYS, DYSP, EPI, GLD, HI, LD, MLD, Phe, PH, SCD, SCLD, SLD, SP&LD, SPLD, VIS
(16) (♿)

South Yorkshire

FREEMAN COLLEGE
For further details see p. 109
Sterling Works, 88 Arundel Street, Sheffield, South Yorkshire S1 2NG
Tel: 0114 252 5940
Email: enquiries@fmc.rmt.org
Website: www.rmt.org
Principal: Perdita Mousley
Age range: 16–25
Special needs catered for:
ADHD, ASD, ASP, BESD, CLD, EBD, GLD, LD, MLD, PMLD, SCD, SCLD, SEBD, SLD
(16) (♿)

FULLERTON HOUSE COLLEGE
For further details see p. 110
Tickhill Square, Denaby, Doncaster, South Yorkshire DN12 4AR
Tel: 01709 861663
Email: enquiries@hesleygroup.co.uk
Website: www.hesleygroup.co.uk
Head: Richard Webster
Age range: 18–25
Special needs catered for:
ASD, ASP, AUT, CLD, DYS, DYSP, GLD, LD, MLD, SCLD, SLD, SPLD
(♿)

FULLERTON HOUSE SCHOOL
For further details see p. 111
Tickhill Square, Denaby, Doncaster, South Yorkshire DN12 4AR
Tel: 01709 861663
Email: enquiries@hesleygroup.co.uk
Website: www.fullertonhouseschool.co.uk
General Manager: Michael Cavan
Age range: 8–19
Special needs catered for:
ASD, ASP, AUT, CLD, DYS, DYSP, GLD, LD, MLD, SCLD, SLD, SPLD
(♿) (16) (✔)

WILSIC HALL COLLEGE
For further details see p. 110
Wadworth, Doncaster, South Yorkshire DN11 9AG
Tel: 01302 856382
Head: Geoff Turner
Age range: 19–25
No. of pupils: 3
Special needs catered for:
ASD, ASP, AUT, CLD, DYS, DYSP, GLD, LD, MLD, SCLD, SLD, SPLD
(♿)

WILSIC HALL SCHOOL
For further details see p. 112
Wadworth, Doncaster, South Yorkshire DN11 9AG
Tel: 01302 856382
Email: enquiries@hesleygroup.co.uk
Website: www.wilsichallschool.co.uk
Head: Geoff Turner
Age range: 11–19
Special needs catered for:
ASD, ASP, AUT, CLD, DYS, DYSP, GLD, LD, MLD, SCLD, SLD, SPLD
(♿) (16) (✔)

West Yorkshire

Hall Cliffe School
Dovecote Lane, Horbury, Wakefield, West Yorkshire WF4 6BB
Tel: 01924 663 420
Head of School: Dr. Chris Lingard
Age range: 8–16
Special needs catered for:
ADHD, AUT, BESD, MLD, SLD
(16)

Pennine Camphill Community
Wood Lane, Chapelthorpe, Wakefield, West Yorkshire WF4 3JL
Tel: 01924 255281
Principal: S Hopewell
Age range: 16–25
No. of pupils: 56
Fees: Day £14,000–£45,000
FB £26,000–£69,000
Special needs catered for: ADHD, ASD, ASP, AUT, CLD, DYSP, EBD, EPI, LD, MLD, SCLD, SLD, SPLD
(♿) (✏)

Northern Ireland

County Tyrone

Parkanaur College
57 Parkanaur Road, Dungannon, County Tyrone BT70 3AA
Tel: 028 87761272
Principal: Mr Wilfred Mitchell
Age range: 18–65
Special needs catered for: ADD, ADHD, ASP, AUT, BESD, CLD, CP, DYS, DYSP, EBD, EPI, GLD, HA, HI, LD, MLD, PD, Phe, PH, PMLD, PNI, SCD, SCLD, SLD, SPLD, VIS

Scotland

Aberdeen

VSA Linn Moor Campus
Peterculter, Aberdeen AB14 0PJ
Tel: 01224 732246
Head Teacher: Victoria Oumarou
Age range: 5–18
No. of pupils: 25
Fees: Day £38,326
FB £76,650–£239,114
Special needs catered for:
ASD, AUT, CLD, GLD, LD, MLD, SCD, SCLD, SPLD
(♿) (16)

Clackmannanshire

Struan House
Bradbury Campus, 100 Smithfield Loan, Alloa, Clackmannanshire FK10 1NP
Tel: 01259 222000
Director of Education & Support Services: Jim Taylor
Age range: 5–17
Special needs catered for: ASD, AUT
(♿)

Glasgow

East Park
1092 Maryhill Road, Glasgow G20 9TD
Tel: 0141 946 2050
Principal: Mrs L Gray
Age range: 0–25
Fees: Day £12,298 FB £22,958
Special needs catered for:
AUT, CP, DEL, EPI, HI, MLD, PH, PMLD, SLD, SP&LD, VIS
(♿) (16)

Learning difficulties (including dyslexia/SPLD)

Perth & Kinross

Ochil Tower
140 High Street, Auchterarder,
Perth, Perth & Kinross PH3 1AD
Tel: 01764 662416
Co-ordinators: Mr Ueli Ruprecht
& Ms Hilary Ruprecht
Age range: 5–18
No. of pupils: 35
Fees: Day £23,500 FB £41,100
Special needs catered for: ADD,
ADHD, ASD, BESD, CLD, EBD, EPI, LD,
MLD, MSI, PMLD, SCD, SCLD, SP&LD

THE NEW SCHOOL
For further details see p. 113
Butterstone, Dunkeld,
Perth & Kinross PH8 0HA
Tel: 01350 724216
Email: info@thenewschool.co.uk
Website:
www.thenewschool.co.uk
Head of School: Mr Scott Gordon
Age range: 11–19
No. of pupils: 25
Special needs catered for:
ADD, ADHD, ASD, ASP, AUT, BESD,
CLD, DEL, DYS, DYSP, EBD, GLD,
HA, LD, MLD, SCD, SEBD, SPLD

Wales

Denbighshire

Cambian Pengwern College
Sarn Lane, Rhuddlan, Rhyl,
Denbighshire LL18 5UH
Tel: 0800 288 9779
Principal: Tina Ruane
Age range: 16–25
Special needs catered for: ADD,
ADHD, ASD, ASP, AUT, BESD, CLD,
CP, DYSP, EBD, EPI, GLD, HI, LD,
MLD, MSI, PD, Phe, PH, PMLD, SCD,
SCLD, SEBD, SLD, SP&LD, SLI, VIS

Gwynedd

Aran Hall School
Rhydymain, Dolgellau,
Gwynedd LL40 2AR
Tel: 01341 450641
Head Teacher: Mr Duncan
Pritchard CertEd, DipAppSS,
BSc(Hons), MSc(psych)
Age range: 11–19
Special needs catered for:
ADHD, ASD, ASP, AUT, CLD,
EPI, GLD, LD, MLD, PMLD, SCD,
SCLD, SLD, SP&LD, SPLD, SLI

Pembrokeshire

COLEG PLAS DWBL
For further details see p. 114
Mynachlog-ddu, Clunderwen,
Pembrokeshire SA66 7SE
Tel: 01994 419420
Email: enquiries@
plasdwbl.rmt.org
Website: www.rmt.org
Principal: Paul Garnault
Age range: 16–25
Special needs catered for:
ASD, ASP, CLD, EBD

Vale of Glamorgan

Action for Children Headlands School
2 St Augustine's Road, Penarth,
Vale of Glamorgan CF64 1YY
Tel: 02920 709771
Principal: Matthew Burns
Age range: 8–19
Special needs catered for: ADD,
ADHD, ASD, ASP, AUT, BESD,
DYS, EBD, MLD, SP&LD, SPLD

Wrexham

Prospects for Young People
12 Grosvenor Road,
Wrexham LL11 1BU
Tel: 01978 313777
Head Teacher: Tony Clifford
Age range: 11–16
No. of pupils: 21
Special needs catered for: MLD, SPLD

Schools and colleges specialising in sensory or physical impairment

Abbreviations

ACLD	Autism, Communication and Associated Learning Difficulties
ADD	Attention Deficit Disorder
ADHD	Attention Deficit and Hyperactive Disorder (Hyperkinetic Disorder)
ASD	Autistic Spectrum Disorder
ASP	Asperger Syndrome
AUT	Autism
BESD	Behavioural, Emotional and Social Difficulties
CCD	Complex Communication Difficulties
CLD	Complex Learning Difficulties
CP	Cerebral Palsy
D	Deaf
DEL	Delicate
DYS	Dyslexia
DYSP	Dyspraxia
EBD	Emotional and Behavioural Difficulties
EBSD	Emotional, Behavioural and/or Social Difficulties
EPI	Epilepsy
GLD	General Learning Difficulties
HA	High Ability
HI	Hearing Impairment
HS	Hospital School
LD	Learning Difficulties
MLD	Moderate Learning Difficulties
MSI	Multi-sensory Impairment
OCD	Obsessive Compulsive Disorder
PD	Physical Difficulties
PH	Physical Impairment
Phe	Partially Hearing
PMLD	Profound and Multiple Learning Difficulties
PNI	Physical Neurological Impairment
PRU	Pupil Referral Unit
SCD	Social and Communication Difficulties
SCLD	Severe and Complex Learning Difficulties
SEBD	Severe Emotional and Behavioural Disorders
SEBN	Social, Emotional and Behavioural Needs
SLD	Severe Learning Difficulties
SLI	Specific Language Impairment
SPLD	Specific Learning Difficulties
SP&LD	Speech and Language Difficulties
SLCN	Speech Language & Communication Needs
VIS	Visually Impaired

Key to Symbols

Type of school:

⚊	Boys' school
⚊	Girls' school
🌐	International school

School offers:

(A)	A levels
🛏	Boarding accommodation
(16+)	Entrance at 16+
⚙	Vocational qualifications
✎	Learning support
✓	This is a DfE approved independent or non-maintained school under section 342 or 347(1) of the 1996 Education Act

Please note: Unless otherwise indicated, all schools are coeducational day schools. Single-sex and boarding schools will be indicated by the relevant icon.

Central & West

Buckinghamshire

Penn School
Church Road, Penn,
High Wycombe,
Buckinghamshire HP10 8LZ
Tel: 01494 812139
Headteacher: Mary-Nest Richardson
Age range: 11–18
No. of pupils: 29
Special needs catered for: HI, SP&LD

The PACE Centre
Philip Green House,
Coventon Road, Aylesbury,
Buckinghamshire HP19 9JL
Tel: 01296 392739
Head Teacher: Mr David O'Connor
Age range: 0–12
Special needs catered for: CLD, CP, DYSP, HI, LD, MLD, MSI, PD, PNI, SCLD, SLD, SP&LD, VIS

Gloucestershire

National Star College
Ullenwood, Cheltenham,
Gloucestershire GL53 9QU
Tel: 01242 527631
Principal & Chief Executive Officer: Ms Kathryn Rudd OBE
Age range: 16–25
No. of pupils: 178
Special needs catered for: ASD, ASP, AUT, CLD, CP, DYS, DYSP, EPI, GLD, HI, LD, MLD, MSI, PD, Phe, PH, PMLD, PNI, SCD, SCLD, SLD, SP&LD, SPLD, VIS

St Rose's School
Stratford Lawn, Stroud,
Gloucestershire GL5 4AP
Tel: 01453 763793
Headteacher: Mr Jan Daines
Age range: 2–25
No. of pupils: 54
Special needs catered for: CLD, CP, D, DEL, DYS, DYSP, EPI, GLD, HI, LD, MLD, MSI, PD, Phe, PH, PMLD, PNI, SCD, SCLD, SLD, SP&LD, SLI, VIS

West Berkshire

Mary Hare Primary School for the Deaf
Mill Hall, Pigeons Farm Road,
Thatcham, Newbury, West
Berkshire RG19 8XA
Tel: 01635 573800
Head Teacher: Mrs P Robinson
Age range: 5–12
No. of pupils: 27
Fees: Day £25,590 FB £35,844
Special needs catered for: HI, SP&LD, SLI

Mary Hare School
Arlington Manor, Snelsmore
Common, Newbury, West
Berkshire RG14 3BQ
Tel: 01635 244200
Principal: Mr D A J Shaw BTech, MEd(Aud), NPQH
Age range: 11–19
No. of pupils: 205 VIth68
Fees: Day £28,372 FB £31,676
Special needs catered for: D, HI

East

Hertfordshire

Meldreth Manor School
Fenny Lane, Meldreth, Royston,
Hertfordshire SG8 6LG
Tel: 01763 268000
Principal: Roger Gale MSc(Ed)
Age range: 9–19+
No. of pupils: 30
Special needs catered for: CP, D, EPI, GLD, HI, LD, MLD, MSI, PD, Phe, PH, PMLD, SP&LD, VIS

St Elizabeth's School
South End, Much Hadham,
Hertfordshire SG10 6EW
Tel: 01279 844270
Principal: Ms. Sharon Wallin
Age range: 5–19
Special needs catered for: AUT, CP, DYS, DYSP, EBD, EPI, MLD, SLD, SP&LD, SPLD

East Midlands

Derbyshire

ROYAL SCHOOL FOR THE DEAF DERBY
For further details see p. 117
Ashbourne Road, Derby,
Derbyshire DE22 3BH
Tel: 01332 362512
Email: enquiries@rsdd.org.uk
Website: www.rsd-derby.org
Headteacher: Helen Shepherd
Age range: 3–19
No. of pupils: 125
Fees: Day £21,912 WB £33,807
Special needs catered for: D

Leicestershire

Homefield College
42 St Mary's Road,
Sileby, Loughborough,
Leicestershire LE12 7TL
Tel: 01509 815696
Principal: Mr Gerry Short
Age range: 16–25
No. of pupils: 54 VIth54
Special needs catered for: ASD, BESD, LD, SCD

RNIB COLLEGE LOUGHBOROUGH
For further details see p. 116
Radmoor Road, Loughborough,
Leicestershire LE11 3BS
Tel: 01509 611077
Email: enquiries@rnibcollege.ac.uk
Website: www.rnibcollege.ac.uk
Principal: June Murray
Age range: 16–65
No. of pupils: 109
Special needs catered for: ASP, AUT, MLD, VIS

Northamptonshire

Hinwick Hall College of Further Education
Hinwick, Wellingborough,
Northamptonshire NN29 7JD
Tel: 01933 312470
Principal: Mr Martyn Hays
Age range: 19–25
No. of pupils: 58
Special needs catered for: CP, DYSP, EPI, PH, SCD, SLD, SP&LD

Sensory or physical impairment

Nottinghamshire

Portland College
Nottingham Road,
Mansfield, Nottingham,
Nottinghamshire NG18 4TJ
Tel: 01623 499111
Principal: Dr Mark Dale
Age range: 16–59
No. of pupils: 230
Special needs catered for:
ASD, ASP, AUT, CP, D, DYS,
DYSP, EBD, EPI, GLD, HI, MLD,
MSI, PD, Phe, PH, PMLD, PNI,
SCLD, SP&LD, SPLD, SLI, VIS

Rutland

The Shires School
Great North Road, Stretton,
Rutland LE15 7QT
Tel: 01780 411944
Director of Care &
Education: Gail Pilling
Age range: 11–19
Special needs catered for: AUT, SLD

Greater London

Kent

Nash College
Croydon Road, Bromley,
Kent BR2 7AG
Tel: 020 8315 4844
Principal: Ms Claire Howley-
Mummery BEd (Hons)
Age range: 18–25
Special needs catered for: AUT,
CP, EPI, MLD, PH, PMLD, PNI, SCD,
SCLD, SLD, SP&LD, SPLD, VIS

Middlesex

RNIB SUNSHINE HOUSE SCHOOL AND RESIDENCE
For further details see p. 118
33 Dene Road, Northwood,
Middlesex HA6 2DD
Tel: 01923 822538
Email: sunshinehouse@
rnib.org.uk
Website:
www.rnib.org.uk/sunshinehouse
Head: Jackie Seaman
Age range: 2–14
Special needs catered for: VIS

London

North London

The London Centre for Children with Cerebral Palsy
143 Coppetts Road,
London N10 1JP
Tel: 020 8444 7242
Headteacher: Ms. Gabriella Czifra
Age range: 5–11
Special needs catered for: CP, PD

North-East

Tyne & Wear

Percy Hedley College
Station Road, Forest Hall, Newcastle
upon Tyne, Tyne & Wear NE12 8YY
Tel: 0191 266 5491
Headteacher: Mr N O
Stromsoy MA, DipSE
Age range: 14–19
No. of pupils: 170
Fees: Day £19,944 FB £42,134
Special needs catered for: HI

Percy Hedley School - Newcastle
Great North Road, Newcastle
upon Tyne, Tyne & Wear NE2 3BB
Tel: 0191 281 5821
Headteacher: Mrs Frances Taylor
Age range: 3–19
Fees: Day £13,767–£29,772
FB £19,134–£33,162
Special needs catered for:
AUT, HI, PMLD, SLD, VIS

Percy Hedley School - North Tyneside
Forest Hall, Newcastle upon
Tyne, Tyne & Wear NE12 8YY
Head Teacher: Ms Lynn Watson
Age range: 3–14
Special needs catered for: CP, SCD

North-West

Greater Manchester

Seashell Trust
Stanley Road, Cheadle
Hulme, Cheadle, Greater
Manchester SK8 6RQ
Tel: 0161 610 0100
Age range: 2–22
No. of pupils: 83
Fees: Day £37,280–£59,354
FB £61,866–£178,658
Special needs catered for:
ASD, AUT, CLD, CP, D, HI,
MSI, PD, PH, PMLD, PNI, SCD,
SCLD, SLD, SP&LD, VIS

Lancashire

Beaumont College
Slyne Road, Lancaster,
Lancashire LA2 6AP
Tel: 01524 541400
Principal: Mr Graeme Pyle
Age range: 16–25
No. of pupils: 77
Special needs catered for:
ASD, AUT, BESD, CLD, CP, DYS,
DYSP, EBD, EPI, GLD, HI, MSI,
PD, PH, PMLD, PNI, SCD, SCLD,
SEBD, SLD, SP&LD, SLI, VIS

Merseyside

Royal School for the Blind
Church Road North, Wavertree,
Liverpool, Merseyside L15 6TQ
Tel: 0151 733 1012
Principal: J Byrne
Age range: 2–19
Fees: Day £35,721–£40,418
FB £47,185–£55,649
Special needs catered for:
BESD, CLD, CP, EBD, EPI, HI,
MLD, MSI, PD, PH, PMLD, PNI,
SCLD, SLD, SPLD, SLI, VIS

St Vincent's School for the Visually Handicapped
Yew Tree Lane, West Derby,
Liverpool, Merseyside L12 9HN
Tel: 0151 228 9968
Headmaster: Mr A Macquarrie
Age range: 3–17
Fees: Day £19,566 FB £27,363
Special needs catered for:
MLD, VIS

South-East

East Sussex

CHAILEY HERITAGE SCHOOL
For further details see p. 119
Haywards Heath Road,
North Chailey, Lewes,
East Sussex BN8 4EF
Tel: 01825 724444
Email: office@chf.org.uk
Website: www.chf.org.uk
Charity Chief Executive: Helen Hewitt
Age range: 3–19
No. of pupils: 73
Special needs catered for:
ASD, AUT, CLD, CP, D, EBD, EPI,
HI, MLD, MSI, PD, PH, PMLD,
PNI, SCLD, SLD, SP&LD, VIS

Hamilton Lodge School
9 Walpole Road, Brighton,
East Sussex BN2 0LS
Tel: 01273 682362
Principal: Mrs A K Duffy MEd
Age range: 5–18
No. of pupils: 72
Fees: Day £23,008–£24,846
FB £30,766–£32,799
Special needs catered for: HI

ST MARY'S SCHOOL & 6TH FORM COLLEGE
For further details see p. 122
Wrestwood Road, Bexhill-on-
Sea, East Sussex TN40 2LU
Tel: 01424 730740
Email: admin@
stmarysbexhill.org
Website: www.stmarysbexhill.org
Principal: Amanda Clugston
Age range: 7–19
No. of pupils: 73
Special needs catered for:
ASD, ASP, AUT, CLD, CP, D,
DEL, DYS, DYSP, EPI, GLD, HI,
LD, MLD, MSI, PD, Phe, PH,
SCD, SP&LD, SPLD, SLI, VIS

Hampshire

TRELOAR SCHOOL
For further details see p. 124
Holybourne, Alton,
Hampshire GU34 4GL
Tel: 01420 547400
Email: admissions@treloar.org.uk
Website: www.treloar.org.uk
Head: Jo McSherrie
Age range: 2–19 yrs
No. of pupils: 95 VIth31
Special needs catered for:
CLD, CP, DEL, DYSP, EPI, HA,
HI, MLD, MSI, PD, Phe, PH, PNI,
SCLD, SP&LD, SPLD, SLI, VIS

Kent

Dorton College of Further Education
Seal Drive, Seal, Sevenoaks,
Kent TN15 0AH
Tel: 01732 592600
Director of Education: Dorothea
Hackman
Age range: 16–19
No. of pupils: 60
Special needs catered for: VIS

Surrey

MOOR HOUSE SCHOOL & COLLEGE
For further details see p. 120
Mill Lane, Hurst Green,
Oxted. Surrey RH8 9AQ
Tel: 01883 712271
Email: admissionsteam@
moorhouseschool.co.uk; info@
moorhouseschool.co.uk
Website:
www.moorhouseschool.co.uk
Principal: Mrs H A Middleton
Age range: 7–19
No. of pupils: 121
Special needs catered for:
ASP, DYS, DYSP, SLD, SP&LD, SLI

Queen Elizabeth's Training College
Leatherhead Court,
Leatherhead, Surrey KT22 0BN
Tel: 01372 841100
Principal: Garry Billing
Age range: 18–63
No. of pupils: 171
Special needs catered for: ADD,
ADHD, ASD, ASP, AUT, CP, DYS,
DYSP, EPI, GLD, LD, MLD, PD, PH

St Piers School and College
St Piers Lane, Lingfield,
Surrey RH7 6PW
Tel: 01342 832243
Chief Executive: Ms Carol
Long BSc(hons),MSc,CQSW
Age range: 5–25
No. of pupils: 181
Special needs catered for: ADD,
ADHD, ASP, AUT, CP, EPI, MLD,
PMLD, PNI, SCD, SCLD, SLD, SP&LD

Stepping Stones School
Tower Road, Hindhead,
Surrey GU26 6SU
Tel: 01428 609083
Headteacher: Melissa Farnham
NPQH,BAQTS(Hon)
Age range: 8–19
No. of pupils: 40
Fees: Day £11,000–£14,800
Special needs catered for: ASD,
ASP, AUT, MLD, PD, SP&LD

THE CHILDREN'S TRUST SCHOOL
For further details see p. 123
Tadworth Court, Tadworth,
Surrey KT20 5RU
Tel: 01737 365810
Email: school@
thechildrenstrust.org.uk
Website: www.thechildrens
trust.org.uk/school
Head Teacher: Samantha
Newton
Age range: 3–19
No. of pupils: 51
Special needs catered for:
CLD, CP, EPI, HI, MSI, PD, PH,
PMLD, PNI, SLD, SP&LD, VIS

West Sussex

Ingfield Manor School
Five Oaks, Billingshurst,
West Sussex RH14 9AX
Tel: 01403 782294/784241
Age range: 3–16
Special needs catered for: CP

South-West

Devon

Dame Hannah Rogers School
Woodland Road, Ivybridge,
Devon PL21 9HQ
Tel: 01752 892461
Head: Mr Brian Carlyon
Age range: 5–19
Special needs catered for:
CP, PH, PMLD

Exeter Royal Academy for Deaf Education
50 Topsham Road, Exeter,
Devon EX2 4NF
Tel: 01392 267023
Chief Executive: Jonathan Farnhill
Age range: 5–25
No. of pupils: VIth68
Fees: Day £23,007–£39,195
WB £31,779–£46,800
FB £36,360–£48,990
Special needs catered for: AUT, CP,
D, EPI, HI, MLD, MSI, Phe, SP&LD, VIS

On Track Training Centre
Unit 8, Paragon Buildings, Ford
Road, Totnes, Devon TQ9 5LQ
Tel: 01803 866462
Head Teacher: Mrs J Cox
Age range: 11–18
No. of pupils: 24
Special needs catered for:
ADD, ADHD, ASD, ASP, AUT,
BESD, DEL, DYS, DYSP, EBD,
GLD, MLD, MSI, SCD, SPLD

Vranch House
Pinhoe Road, Exeter,
Devon EX4 8AD
Tel: 01392 468333
Head Teacher: Miss Viktoria
Pavlics MEd(SEN)
Age range: 2–12
Fees: Day £19,425
Special needs catered for: CP,
EPI, MLD, PD, PH, PMLD, SP&LD

WESC FOUNDATION - THE SPECIALIST COLLEGE FOR VISUAL IMPAIRMENT
For further details see p. 125
Countess Wear, Exeter,
Devon EX2 6HA
Tel: 01392 454200
Email: info@
wescfoundation.ac.uk
Website:
www.wescfoundation.ac.uk
Principal: Mrs Tracy de
Bernhardt-Dunkin
Age range: 16+
Special needs catered for:
EPI, PH, PMLD, VIS

WESC FOUNDATION - THE SPECIALIST SCHOOL FOR VISUAL IMPAIRMENT
For further details see p. 126
Countess Wear, Exeter,
Devon EX2 6HA
Tel: 01392 454200
Email: info@
wescfoundation.ac.uk
Website:
www.wescfoundation.ac.uk
Chief Executive: Mrs Tracy
de Bernhardt-Dunkin
Age range: 5–16
Special needs catered for:
EPI, PH, PMLD, VIS

Dorset

Langside School
Langside Avenue, Parkstone,
Poole, Dorset BH12 5BN
Tel: 01202 518635
Principal: J. Seaward BEd
(Hons) Oxon NPQH
Age range: 2–19
No. of pupils: 23
Special needs catered for: CLD, CI
EPI, MSI, PD, PMLD, SCD, SCLD, SLD

The Fortune Centre of Riding Therapy
Avon Tyrrell, Bransgore,
Christchurch, Dorset BH23 8EE
Tel: 01425 673297
Director: Mrs J Dixon-Clegg SRN
Age range: 16–25
No. of pupils: 47
Special needs catered for: AUT,
CP, DEL, DYS, EBD, EPI, HI, MLD,
PH, PMLD, SLD, SP&LD, SPLD, VIS

Victoria Education Centre
12 Lindsay Road, Branksome
Park, Poole, Dorset BH13 6AS
Tel: 01202 763697
Head: Mrs Christina Davies
Age range: 3–19
No. of pupils: 90
Special needs catered for:
DEL, EPI, PH, SP&LD

West Midlands

Herefordshire

THE ROYAL NATIONAL COLLEGE FOR THE BLIND (RNC)
For further details see p. 128
Venns Lane, Hereford,
Herefordshire HR1 1DT
Tel: 01432 376621
Email: info@rnc.ac.uk
Website: www.rnc.ac.uk
Principal: Mr Mark Fisher
Age range: 16–65
Special needs catered for: ASP,
AUT, DYS, HA, MLD, PD, Phe, VIS

Shropshire

Derwen College
Oswestry, Shropshire SY11 3JA
Tel: 01691 661234
Director: D J Kendall
BEng, FCA, MEd
Age range: 16–25
No. of pupils: 160
Fees: FB £17,928
Special needs catered for:
CP, DEL, DYS, EPI, HI, MLD, PH,
PMLD, SLD, SP&LD, SPLD, VIS

West Midlands

Hereward College of Further Education
Bramston Crescent, Tile Hill Lane,
Coventry, West Midlands CV4 9SW
Tel: 024 7646 1231
Principal: Sheila Fleming
Age range: 16+
No. of pupils: 400
Special needs catered for: ASP,
AUT, CP, DEL, DYS, DYSP, EBD,
EPI, HA, HI, MLD, PH, SPLD, VIS

National Institute for Conductive Education
Cannon Hill House, Russell
Road, Moseley, Birmingham,
West Midlands B13 8RD
Tel: 0121 449 1569
Director of Services: Dr
Melanie R Brown
Age range: 0–11
No. of pupils: 18
Fees: Day £25,000
Special needs catered for:
CP, DYSP, PNI

Queen Alexandra College (QAC)
Court Oak Road, Harborne,
Birmingham, West Midlands B17 9TG
Tel: 0121 428 5050
Principal: Hugh J Williams
Age range: 16–25
No. of pupils: 190
Special needs catered for: ADD,
ADHD, ASD, ASP, AUT, BESD, CLD,
CP, D, DEL, DYS, DYSP, EBD, EPI,
GLD, HA, HI, LD, MLD, MSI, PD,
Phe, PH, PMLD, PNI, SCD, SCLD,
SLD, SP&LD, SPLD, SLI, VIS

RNIB PEARS CENTRE FOR SPECIALIST LEARNING
For further details see p. 127
Wheelwright Lane, Ash Green,
Coventry, West Midlands CV7 9RA
Tel: 024 7636 9500
Email: pearscentre@rnib.org.uk
Website:
www.rnib.org.uk/pearscentre
Headteacher: Emily Hopkins-Hayes
Age range: 2–19
No. of pupils: 29
Special needs catered for:
ASD, AUT, CLD, CP, D, EPI,
HI, LD, MSI, PD, PH, PMLD,
SCLD, SLD, SPLD, VIS

Worcestershire

New College Worcester
Whittington Road, Worcester,
Worcestershire WR5 2JX
Tel: 01905 763933
Principal: Mardy Smith
Age range: usually 11–19
No. of pupils: 88
Fees: Day £30,049–£32,485
WB £40,076–£42,268
FB £44,366–£46,813
Special needs catered for: VIS

Yorkshire & Humberside

North Yorkshire

Henshaws College
Bogs Lane, Harrogate,
North Yorkshire HG1 4ED
Tel: 01423 886451
Head of Education: Mr Robert Jones
Age range: 16–25
Special needs catered for: CLD,
CP, D, EPI, HI, LD, MLD, MSI, PD,
Phe, SCD, SLD, SP&LD, VIS
16+

South Yorkshire

Doncaster College for the Deaf
Leger Way, Doncaster,
South Yorkshire DN2 6AY
Tel: 01302 386720
Executive Principal: Alan
W Robinson
Age range: 16–59
No. of pupils: 185
Special needs catered for: HI

DONCASTER SCHOOL FOR THE DEAF
For further details see p. 129
Leger Way, Doncaster,
South Yorkshire DN2 6AY
Tel: 01302 386733
Email: principal@ddt-deaf.org.uk or secretary@ddt-deaf.org.uk
Website: www.deaf-trust.co.uk
Executive Principal: Mr Alan W Robinson
Age range: 4–19
No. of pupils: 29
Special needs catered for: BESD, CP, D, DYS, GLD, HI, MLD, PH, PMLD, SLD, SP&LD, SPLD, VIS

Paces High Green School for Conductive Education
Paces High Green Centre, Pack
Horse Lane, High Green, Sheffield,
South Yorkshire S35 3HY
Tel: 0114 284 5298
Headteacher: Gabor Fellner
Age range: 0–18
No. of pupils: 30
Fees: Day £27,452
Special needs catered for: CP, PD
16+

West Yorkshire

Holly Bank School
Roe Head, Far Common Road,
Mirfield, West Yorkshire WF14 0DQ
Tel: 01924 490833
Headteacher: Ms Lyn Pollard
Age range: 5–19
No. of pupils: 20 VIth10
Fees: Day £35,000–£45,000
WB £70,000–£75,000
FB £99,000–£105,000
Special needs catered for: CLD, CP, MSI, PD, PH, PMLD, PNI, SCLD, SLD
16+

ST JOHN'S CATHOLIC SCHOOL FOR THE DEAF
For further details see p. 130
Church Street, Boston
Spa, Wetherby, West
Yorkshire LS23 6DF
Tel: 01937 842144
Email: info@stjohns.org.uk
Website: www.stjohns.org.uk
Headteacher: Mrs A Bradbury BA(Hons), MSc, NPQH
Age range: 4–19
No. of pupils: 68
Special needs catered for: ADD, ADHD, ASD, ASP, AUT, BESD, CP, D, DEL, DYS, DYSP, EBD, EPI, HI, LD, MLD, MSI, PD, Phe, PH, PMLD, SCD, SLD, SP&LD, SLI, VIS

Northern Ireland

County Antrim

Jordanstown Schools
85 Jordanstown Road,
Newtownabbey, County
Antrim BT37 0QE
Tel: 028 9086 3541
Principal: Mrs A P Magee
MEd, DipSpEd(VI), PQH(NI)
Age range: 4–19
No. of pupils: 67
Special needs catered for:
ASD, D, EBD, GLD, HI, LD,
MSI, PD, SP&LD, VIS
16+

County Tyrone

Buddy Bear Trust Conductive Education School
Killyman Road, Dungannon,
County Tyrone BT71 6DE
Tel: 02887 752 025
Special needs catered for: CP

Scotland

Aberdeen

Camphill School Aberdeen
Murtle House, Bieldside,
Aberdeen AB15 9EP
Tel: 01224 867935
Administrator: Mr Piet Hogenboom
Age range: 3–19
Fees: Day £25,198–£50,397
FB £50,397–£100,794
Special needs catered for: ADD, ADHD, ASD, ASP, AUT, BESD, CLD, CP, D, DEL, DYS, DYSP, EBD, EPI, GLD, HA, HI, LD, MLD, MSI, PD, Phe, PH, PMLD, PNI, SCD, SCLD, SEBD, SLD, SP&LD, SPLD, SLI, VIS
16+

Edinburgh

THE ROYAL BLIND SCHOOL
For further details see p. 132
43-45 Canaan Lane,
Edinburgh EH10 4SG
Tel: 0131 446 3120
Email: office@royalblindschool.org.uk
Website: www.royalblind.org/education
Head Teacher: Elaine Brackenridge (BEd)
Age range: 5–19
No. of pupils: 39
Special needs catered for: AUT, CP, DEL, EPI, MLD, PH, PMLD, SLD, SP&LD, SPLD, VIS

Renfrewshire

Corseford School
Milliken Park, Johnstone,
Renfrewshire PA10 2NT
Tel: 01505 702141
Headteacher: Mrs M Boyle
Age range: 3–18
No. of pupils: 50
Special needs catered for:
CP, DEL, DYSP, EPI, HI, MLD,
PH, SP&LD, SPLD, VIS
16+

South Lanarkshire

Stanmore House School
Lanark, South Lanarkshire ML11 7RR
Tel: 01555 665041
Head Teacher: Hazel Aitken
Age range: 0–18
No. of pupils: 47
Special needs catered for:
CP, PH, SCLD, SP&LD, VIS
16+

West Lothian

Donaldson's School
Preston Road, Linlithgow,
West Lothian EH49 6HZ
Tel: 01506 841900
Principal: Ms Laura Battles
Age range: 2–19
No. of pupils: 43
Special needs catered for:
ASP, AUT, D, HI, Phe, PMLD,
SCD, SLD, SP&LD, SLI

Wales

Glamorgan

Craig-y-Parc School
Pentyrch, Cardiff,
Glamorgan CF15 9NB
Tel: 029 2089 0397/2089 0361
Principal: Anthony Mulcamy
Age range: 3–19
Special needs catered for: CP,
EPI, HI, LD, MLD, MSI, PD, Phe, PH,
PMLD, SCLD, SLD, SP&LD, VIS

Special Educational Needs and the independent and non-maintained schools and colleges that cater for them

Attention Deficit Disorder (ADD)

Attention Deficit and Hyperactive Disorder (ADHD)

Autistic Spectrum Disorder(s) (ASD)

Schools and colleges by category

Asperger Syndrome (ASP)

Autism (AUT)

Schools and colleges by category

Behaviour, Emotional and Social Difficulties (BESD) – see also EBSD and SEBD

Complex Learning Difficulties (CLD)

Cerebral Palsy (CP)

Deaf (D) – see also Hearing Impairment (HI)

Delicate (DEL)

Dyslexia (DYSL) – see also SPLD

Dyspraxia (DYSP)

Emotional, Behavioural Difficulties (EBD) – see also BESD and SEBD

Epilepsy (EPI)

General Learning Difficulties (GLD)

Access School, Shropshire..........................D166
Alderwasley Hall School & Sixth Form Centre, Derbyshire D162
Appletree School, Cumbria.............................82, D150
Aran Hall School, Gwynedd D168
Barton School, Lincolnshire D142
Beaumont College, Lancashire D173
Birtenshaw School, Greater Manchester D164
Brantwood Specialist School, South Yorkshire..........................84, D155
Brewood Middle School, Kent D152
Brewood Secondary School, Kent..........................D152
Cambian Dilston College, Northumberland D164
Cambian Pengwern College, Denbighshire D168
Cambian Southwick Park School, Gloucestershire D161
Camphill School Aberdeen, Aberdeen D175
Cedar House School, Lancashire D151
Centre Academy East Anglia, Suffolk..........................D162
Chaigeley, Warrington..........................D151
Chelfham Mill School, Devon D153
Chelfham Senior School, Devon D141
Chilworth House Upper School, Oxfordshire D147
Coleg Elidyr, Carmarthenshire D143
Copperfield School, Norfolk..........................D162
Doncaster School for the Deaf, South Yorkshire 129, D175
Foxes Fields, Somerset..........................D166
Frederick Hugh House, London 94, D163
Freeman School, South Yorkshire..........................109, D164
Fullerton House College, South Yorkshire 110, D167
Fullerton House School, South Yorkshire 111, D167
Glasshouse College, West Midlands..........................107, D164
Higford School, Shropshire..........................D141
Hillcrest Oaklands College, Staffordshire..........................D154
Hillcrest Park School, Oxfordshire D147
Hillcrest Slinfold School, West Sussex..........................D153
Holme Court School, Cambridgeshire D161
Horton House School, East Riding of Yorkshire D155
Insights Independent School, London D149
Jordanstown Schools, County Antrim..........................D175
Kinsale School, Flintshire D143

Kisharon School, London D163
Langdon College, Greater Manchester D164
Learn 4 Life, Lancashire D151
Linkage College – Toynton Campus, Lincolnshire D162
Linkage College – Weelsby Campus, North-East Lincolnshire..........................D167
Meldreth Manor School, Hertfordshire D171
Minstead Training Project, Hampshire D165
National Star College, Gloucestershire D171
On Track Training Centre, Devon D174
Orchard Hill College and Academy Trust, Surrey D165
Overley Hall School, West Midlands 108, D166
Owlswick School, East Sussex D164
Parkanaur College, County Tyrone D167
Philpots Manor School, West Sussex 83, D153
Portland College, Nottinghamshire D172
Queen Alexandra College (QAC), West Midlands..........................D174
Queen Elizabeth's Training College, Surrey D173
Ripplevale School, Kent..........................D153
Rowden House School, Herefordshire D166
Ruskin Mill College, Gloucestershire 86, D161
Sheiling College, Hampshire D165
Sheiling School, Hampshire D165
Sheiling School, Thornbury, Bristol D161
St John's School & College, East Sussex 103, D165
St Mary's School & 6th Form College, East Sussex..........................122, D173
St Rose's School, Gloucestershire..........................D171
Strathmore College, Staffordshire D141
Sunfield School, West Midlands D166
The Link Primary School, Surrey 93, D163
The Linnet Independent Learning Centre, Derbyshire D148
The Mount Camphill Community, East Sussex D152
The New School, Perth & Kinross 113, D168
VSA Linn Moor Campus, Aberdeen D167
William Henry Smith School, West Yorkshire D155
Wilsic Hall College, South Yorkshire 110, D167
Wilsic Hall School, South Yorkshire 112, D167
Woodlands Children's Development Centre, Wrexham D157
Young Options Pathway College Stoke, Staffordshire D154

High Ability (HA)

Alderwasley Hall School & Sixth Form Centre, Derbyshire D162
Appleford School, Wiltshire D165
Appletree School, Cumbria..........................82, D150
Barton School, Lincolnshire D142
Breckenbrough School, North Yorkshire D155
Brewood Middle School, Kent D152
Brewood Secondary School, Kent..........................D152
Camphill School Aberdeen, Aberdeen D175
Centre Academy East Anglia, Suffolk..........................D162
Centre Academy London, London D163
Chaigeley, Warrington..........................D151
Eastwood Grange School, Derbyshire..........................D148
Fairley House School, London D163
Foxes Fields, Somerset..........................D166
Hereward College of Further Education, West Midlands..........................D174
Higford School, Shropshire D141

Holme Court School, Cambridgeshire D161
Kisharon School, London D163
Lakeside School, Merseyside D140
Orchard Hill College and Academy Trust, Surrey D165
Parkanaur College, County Tyrone D167
Queen Alexandra College (QAC), West Midlands..........................D174
Ripplevale School, Kent D153
Rossendale School, Lancashire D139
Sheiling School, Thornbury, Bristol D161
St Dominic's School, Surrey D165
St John's School & College, East Sussex..........................103, D165
The New School, Perth & Kinross 113, D168
The Royal National College for the Blind (RNC), Herefordshire...128, D174
Treloar School, Hampshire..........................124, D173
Woodlands Children's Development Centre, Wrexham D157
Young Options Pathway College Stoke, Staffordshire D154

Hearing Impairment (HI)

Action for Children Penhurst School, Oxfordshire..........................D161
Advanced Education – Somerset School, Somerset..........................D154
Beaumont College, Lancashire D173
Birtenshaw School, Greater Manchester D164
Bladon House School, Staffordshire D166
Brewood Middle School, Kent D152
Brewood Secondary School, Kent..........................D152
Cambian Lufton College, Somerset..........................D166
Cambian Pengwern College, Denbighshire D168
Camphill Community Glencraig, County Down D156
Camphill School Aberdeen, Aberdeen D175
Chailey Heritage School, East Sussex..........................119, D173

Chilworth House Upper School, Oxfordshire D147
Corseford School, Renfrewshire D175
Craig-y-Parc School, Glamorgan D176
Derwen College, Shropshire D174
Donaldson's School, West Lothian D176
Doncaster College for the Deaf, South Yorkshire D175
Doncaster School for the Deaf, South Yorkshire 129, D175
East Park, Glasgow D167
Exeter Royal Academy for Deaf Education, Devon D174
Foxes Fields, Somerset..........................D166
Hamilton Lodge School, East Sussex D173
Henshaws College, North Yorkshire D175

Learning Difficulties (LD)

Moderate Learning Difficulties (MLD)

Multi-sensory Impairment (MSI)

Partially Hearing (Phe)

Physical Difficulties (PD)

Physical Impairment (PH)

Profound and Multiple Learning Difficulties (PMLD)

Physical Neurological Impairment (PNI)

Social and Communication Difficulties (SCD)

Severe and Complex Learning Difficulties (SCLD)

Severe Emotional and Behavioural Difficulties (SEBD) – see also BESD and EBD

Severe Learning Difficulties (SLD)

Schools and colleges by category

Speech and Language Difficulties (SP&LD)

Specific Learning Difficulties (SPLD)

Specific Language Impairment (SLI)

Visually Impaired (VIS)

Maintained special schools and colleges

ENGLAND – BEDFORD BOROUGH COUNCIL
Education Authority

Bedford SEND Team, 5th Floor, Borough Hall, Cauldwell Street, Bedford, MK42 9AP
Tel: 01234 228375 Email: statass@bedford.gov.uk Website: www.bedford.gov.uk

BEDFORD

Ridgeway Special School

Hill Rise, Kempston,
BEDFORD MK42 7EB
Tel: 01234 402402
Head: Mr G Allard
Category: PD (Coed 2-19)

St Johns Special School & College

Austin Cannons, Kempston,
BEDFORD MK42 8AA
Tel: 01234 345565
Interim Head: Ms A Rizzo
Category: SLD PMLD (Coed 2-19)

CENTRAL BEDFORDSHIRE COUNCIL
Children & Young People Service

Central Bedfordshire SEND Team, Priory House, Monks Walk, Chicksands Shefford, SG17 5TQ
Tel: 0300 300 4768 Email: send.feedback@centralbedfordshire.gov.uk Website: www.centralbedfordshire.gov.uk

BIGGLESWADE

Ivel Valley Primary School

The Baulk, BIGGLESWADE,
Bedfordshire SG18 0PT
Tel: 01767 601010
Head: Miss Julie Mudd
Category: SLD PMLD (Coed 3-10)

Ivel Valley Secondary School

Hitchmead Road, BIGGLESWADE,
Bedfordshire SG18 0NL
Tel: 01767 601010
Head: Miss Julie Mudd
Category: SLD PMLD (Coed 11-19)

DUNSTABLE

The Chiltern Primary School

Beech Road, DUNSTABLE,
Bedfordshire LU6 3LY
Tel: 01582 667106
Head: Mrs Shirley Crosbie
Category: SLD PMLD (Coed 3-10)

HOUGHTON REGIS

The Chiltern Secondary School

Kingsland Campus, Parkside
Drive, HOUGHTON REGIS,
Bedfordshire LU5 5PX
Tel: 01582 667106
Head: Mrs Shirley Crosbie
Category: SLD PMLD (Coed 11-19)

LEIGHTON BUZZARD

Oak Bank School

Sandy Lane, LEIGHTON BUZZARD,
Bedfordshire LU7 3BE
Tel: 01525 374550
Head: Mr Peter Cohen
Category: BESD (Coed 9-16)

WEST BERKSHIRE
Council

West Berkshire FIS, The SEN Team, West Street House, West Street Newbury, Berkshire, RG14 1BZ
Tel: 01635 503100 Email: fis@westberks.gov.uk Website: www.westberks.gov.uk

NEWBURY

The Castle School
Love Lane, Donnington,
NEWBURY, Berkshire RG14 2JG
Tel: 01635 42976
Heads: Mr Jon Hewitt
Category: ASD SLD SPLD
GLD PH (Coed 2-19)

READING

Brookfields Special School
Sage Road, Tilehurst, READING,
Berkshire RG31 6SW
Tel: 01189 421382
Head: Mrs Jane Headland
Category: AUT MSI Complex Needs

BLACKBURN WITH DARWEN
Borough Council

Blackburn SEND Team, 10 Duke Street, Floor 5, Blackburn, Lancashire, BB2 1DH
Tel: 01254 666739 Email: sendss@blackburn.gov.uk Website: www.blackburn.gov.uk

BLACKBURN

Crosshill School
Haslingden Road, BLACKBURN,
Lancashire BB2 3HJ
Tel: 01254 667713
Head: Mr Ian Maddison
Category: MLD (Coed Day 11-16)

Newfield School
Old Bank Lane, Off Shadsworth
Road, BLACKBURN,
Lancashire BB1 2PW
Tel: 01254 588600
Head: Mr Geoff Fitzpatrick
Category: Complex
(Coed Day 2-19)

St. Thomas' Centre
Lambeth Street, BLACKBURN,
Lancashire BB1 1NA
Tel: 01254 680523
Head: Ms Joanne Siddle
Category: Pupil Referral
Unit (Coed Day 5-16)

DARWEN

Sunnyhurst Centre
Salisbury Road, DARWEN,
Lancashire BB3 1HZ
Tel: 01254 702317
Head: Mrs Shazia Sarwar
Category: Pupil Referral
Unit (Coed Day 5-11)

BLACKPOOL
Children and Young People's Department

Blackpool SEN Team, PO Box 4, Town Hall, Municipal Buildings Blackpool, FY1 1NA
Tel: 01253 477100 Email: local.offer@blackpool.gov.uk Website: www.blackpool.gov.uk

BLACKPOOL

Highfurlong School
Blackpool Old Road, BLACKPOOL,
Lancashire FY3 7LR
Tel: 01253 392188
Acting Head: Ms Rosie Sycamore
Category: PH

Woodlands School
Whitegate Drive, BLACKPOOL,
Lancashire FY3 9HF
Tel: 01253 316722
Head: Mr Cole Andrew
Category: SLD PMLD
MSI (Coed 2-19)

BOURNEMOUTH
Children and Families Services

Bournemouth SEN Team, Bournemouth Council, St Stephen's Road, Bournemouth, Dorset, BH2 6DY
Tel: 01202 451451 Email: cs@bournemouth.gov.uk Website: www.bournemouth.gov.uk

BOURNEMOUTH

Linwood School
Alma Road, BOURNEMOUTH,
Dorset BH9 1AJ
Tel: 01202 525107
Head: Mr S Brown
Category: ASD MLD SLD
PMLD (Coed 3-19)

Tregonwell Academy
Petersfield Road, BOURNEMOUTH,
Dorset BH7 6QP
Tel: 01202 424361
Associate Principal: Mr
Adam Coshan
Category: BESD (Coed 7-16)

BRACKNELL FOREST
Children, Young People and Learning

Bracknell SEN Team, Time Square, Market Street, Bracknell, Berkshire, RG12 1JD
Tel: 01344 352000 Email: cypl@bracknell-forest.gov.uk Website: www.bracknell-forest.gov.uk

BRACKNELL

Kennel Lane School
Kennel Lane, BRACKNELL,
Berkshire RG42 2EX
Tel: 01344 483872
Head: Ms Andrea de Bunsen
Category: MLD SLD AUT PMLD

BRADFORD
Families Information Service

Bradford FIS, The SEND Team, Channing Way, Bradford, West Yorkshire, BD1 1HY
Tel: 01274 437503 Email: fis@bradford.gov.uk

BRADFORD

Chellow Heights School
Thorn Lane, Bingley Road,
BRADFORD, West Yorkshire BD9 6AL
Tel: 01274 484242
Head: Mrs Susan Haithwaite
Category: SLD PMLD ADS (Primary)

Delius School
Barkerend Road, BRADFORD,
West Yorkshire BD3 8QX
Tel: 01274 666472
Head: Miss Sally Joy
Category: SLD PMLD ASD (Primary)

Hazelbeck School
Wagon Lane, Bingley, BRADFORD,
West Yorkshire BD16 1EE
Tel: 01274 771444
Head: Mrs Sue Pierce
Category: SLD PMLD
ASD (Secondary)

High Park School
Thorn lane, BRADFORD,
West Yorkshire BD9 6RY
Tel: 01274 696740
Head: Mrs Ann Andrew
Category: ASD (Primary
& Secondary)

Oastler's School
Flockton Road, BRADFORD,
West Yorkshire BD4 7RH
Tel: 01274 307456
Head: Mrs Lyndsey Brown
Category: (Coed Day 11-19)

Southfield School
Haycliffe Lane, BRADFORD,
West Yorkshire BD5 9ET
Tel: 01274 779662
Head: Mr Dominic Wall
Category: SLD PMLD
ASD (Secondary)

KEIGHLEY

Beechcliffe School

Green Head Road, KEIGHLEY,
West Yorkshire BD20 6ED
Tel: 01535 603041
Head: Mrs Patricia Pearson
Category: SLD PMLD
ASD (Secondary)

Phoenix School

Braithwaite Avenue, KEIGHLEY,
West Yorkshire BD22 6HZ
Tel: 01535 607038
Head: Mrs Rachel Stirland
Category: SLD PMLD ASD (Primary)

BRIGHTON & HOVE
City Council

Brighton & Hove SEN Team, Kings House, Grand Avenue, Hove, East Sussex, BN3 2LS
Tel: 01273 293552 Fax: 01273 293547 Email: sen.team@brighton-hove.gov.uk Website: www.brighton-hove.gov.uk

BRIGHTON

Cedar Centre

Lynchet Close, Hollingdean,
BRIGHTON, East Sussex BN1 7FP
Tel: 01273 558622
Head: Ms Lalli Howell
Category: MLD

Downs Park School

Foredown Road, Portslade,
BRIGHTON, East Sussex BN41 2FU
Tel: 01273 417448
Head: Ms Jackie Brooks
Category: ASD (Coed 5-16)

Downs View School

Warren Road, BRIGHTON,
East Sussex BN2 6BB
Tel: 01273 601680
Head: Mr Adrian Carver
Category: SLD ASD HI VIS (4-19)

Hillside Special School

Foredown Road, Portslade,
BRIGHTON, East Sussex BN41 2FU
Tel: 01273 416979
Head: Ms Rachel Burstow
Category: SLD

Homewood College

Queensdown School Road,
off Lewes Road, BRIGHTON,
East Sussex BN1 7LA
Tel: 01273 604472
Head: Mr Mark Helstrip
Category: SEBD (Coed 5-16)

Patcham House School

Old London Road, Patcham,
BRIGHTON, East Sussex BN1 8XR
Tel: 01273 551028
Head: Ms Gayle Adam
Category: PD Del ASP
MLD SPLD (11-16)

BRISTOL
Children and Young People's Services

Bristol SEN Team, City Hall, College Green, Bristol, BS99 7EB
Tel: 0117 922 3700 Email: sen@bristol.gov.uk Website: www.bristol.gov.uk

BRISTOL

Briarwood School

Briar Way, Fishponds,
BRISTOL BS16 4EA
Tel: 01173 532651
Head: Mr David Hussey
Category: SLD PMLD
AUT (Coed 3-19)

Bristol Gateway School

Long Cross, Lawrence
Weston, BRISTOL BS11 0QA
Tel: 01173 772275
Head: Ms Kaye Palmer-Green
Category: SEBD (Coed 10-16)

Claremont School

Henleaze Park, Westbury-
on-Trym, BRISTOL BS9 4LR
Tel: 01173 533622
Head: Ms Alison Ewins
Category: PD SLD PMLD (Coed 3-19)

Elmfield School for Deaf Children

Greystoke Avenue, Westbury-
on-Trym, BRISTOL BS10 6AY
Tel: 01179 030366
Head: Mrs Babs Day
Category: D HI (Coed 5-16)

Kingsweston School

Napier Miles Road, Kingsweston,
BRISTOL BS11 0UT
Tel: 01179 030400
Head: Mr Neil Galloway
Category: MLD SLD AUT (Coed 3-19)

Knowle DGE

Leinster Avenue, Knowle,
BRISTOL BS4 1NN
Tel: 01173 532011
Head: Mr Peter Evans
Category: CLD SEBD MLD
Complex Needs (Coed 5-16)

New Fosseway School

Teyfant Road, Hartcliffe,
BRISTOL BS13 0RL
Tel: 01179 030220
Head: Mrs Shan Wynne-Jones
Category: SLD PMLD
AUT (Coed 6-19)

Notton House School

28 Notton, Lacock,
BRISTOL SN15 2NF
Tel: 01249 730407
Head: Mr Peter Evans
Category: SEBD (Boys 9-16)

Woodstock School

Rectory Gardens, Henbury,
BRISTOL BS10 7AH
Tel: 01173 772175
Head: Mr Les Haines
Category: SEBD (Primary)

BUCKINGHAMSHIRE
SEND Information, Advice & Support Service

Buckinghamshire SENDIASS, County Hall, Walton Street, Aylesbury, Buckinghamshire, HP20 1UA
Tel: 01296 383754 Email: sendias@buckscc.gov.uk Website: www.buckscc.gov.uk

AMERSHAM

Stony Dean School
Orchard End Avenue, Off Pineapple Road, AMERSHAM, Buckinghamshire HP7 9JW
Tel: 01494 762538
Head: Mr Neil Strain
Category: MLD Language & Communication (Coed 11-18)

AYLESBURY

Booker Park School
Stoke Leys Close, AYLESBURY, Buckinghamshire HP21 9ET
Tel: 01296 427221
Head: Ms Marianne Murphy
Category: MLD SLD ASD (Coed 3-11)

Chiltern Way Federation - Wendover House School
Church Lane, Wendover, AYLESBURY, Buckinghamshire HP22 6NL
Tel: 01296 622157
Head of Campus: Mr Gary Regan
Category: BESD (Boys Day/boarding 11-16)

Pebble Brook School
Churchill Avenue, AYLESBURY, Buckinghamshire HP21 8LZ
Tel: 01296 415761
Head: Mr David Miller
Category: MLD SLC (Coed Day/boarding 11-19)

Stocklake Park Community School
Stocklake, AYLESBURY, Buckinghamshire HP20 1DP
Tel: 01296 423507
Head: Ms Gill Mullis
Category: SLD (Coed 11-19)

BEACONSFIELD

Alfriston School
Penn Road, Knotty Green, BEACONSFIELD, Buckinghamshire HP9 2TS
Tel: 01494 673740
Head: Mrs Jinna Male
Category: MLD (Girls Day/boarding 11-19)

CHESHAM

Heritage House School
Cameron Road, CHESHAM, Buckinghamshire HP5 3BP
Tel: 01494 771445
Head: Mr James Boylan
Category: SLD (Coed 2-19)

GREAT MISSENDEN

Chiltern Way Federation - Prestwood Campus
Nairdwood Lane, Prestwood, GREAT MISSENDEN, Buckinghamshire HP16 0QQ
Tel: 01494 863514
Head of Campus: Mr James Sisk
Category: BESD (Boys Day/boarding 11-16)

HIGH WYCOMBE

Chiltern Gate School
Verney Avenue, HIGH WYCOMBE, Buckinghamshire HP12 3NE
Tel: 01494 532621
Head: Mr Bradley Taylor
Category: MLD EBD ASD SLD Communication difficulties (Coed Day/boarding 4-11)

Maplewood School
Faulkner Way, Downley, HIGH WYCOMBE, Buckinghamshire HP13 5HB
Tel: 01494 525728
Head: Mr Bradley Taylor
Category: SLD (Coed 2-19)

Westfield School
Highfield Road, Bourne End, HIGH WYCOMBE, Buckinghamshire SL8 5BE
Tel: 01628 533125
Head: Mr Geoff Allen
Category: BESD (Coed 4-11)

WINSLOW

Furze Down School
Verney Road, WINSLOW, Buckinghamshire MK18 3BL
Tel: 01296 711380
Head: Ms Alison Rooney
Category: A Range Of Needs (Coed 2-19)

CAMBRIDGESHIRE
SEND Information, Advice & Support Service

Cambridgeshire SEN Team, Box No. CC1101, Castle Court, Cambridge, CB3 0AP
Tel: 01223 699214 Email: pps@cambridgeshire.gov.uk Website: www.cambridgeshire.gov.uk

CAMBRIDGE

Castle School
Courtney Way, CAMBRIDGE CB4 2EE
Tel: 01223 442400
Head: Ms Carol McCarthy
Category: PMLD SLD MLD (Coed 2-19)

Granta School
Cambridge Road, Linton, CAMBRIDGE CB21 4NN
Tel: 01223 896890
Head: Mrs Lucie-Claire Calow
Category: ASD PMLD SLD MLD (Coed 2-19)

Trinity School
8 Station Road, Foxton, CAMBRIDGE, Cambridgeshire CB22 6SA
Tel: 01223 712995
Head: Ms Diane Stygal

COTTENHAM

The Centre School
Cottenham Village College, High Street, COTTENHAM, Cambridgeshire CB24 8UA
Tel: 01954 288789
Head: Mrs Susan Raven
Category: (Coed 11-16)

ELY

Highfield Special School

Downham Road, ELY,
Cambridgeshire CB6 1BD
Tel: 01353 662085
Head: Mr Simon Bainbridge
Category: PMLD SLD MLD
ASD PD VIS (Coed 2-19)

The Harbour School

Station Road, Wilburton, ELY,
Cambridgeshire CB6 3RR
Tel: 01353 740229
Head: Ms Julie Potter
Category: ADD EBD MLD
SEBN (Coed 5-17)

EYNESBURY

Samuel Pepys School

Cromwell Road, EYNESBURY,
Cambridgeshire PE19 2EZ
Tel: 01480 375012
Head: Ms Joanne Hardwick
Category: ASD PMLD SLD
Complex needs (Coed 2-19)

HUNTINGDON

Spring Common School

American Lane, HUNTINGDON,
Cambridgeshire PE29 1TQ
Tel: 01480 377403
Head: Mrs Kim Taylor
Category: PMLD SLD MLD
ASD EBD (Coed 2-19)

WISBECH

Meadowgate School

Meadowgate Lane, WISBECH,
Cambridgeshire PE13 2JH
Tel: 01945 461836
Head: Mrs Jackie McPherson
Category: SLD MLD (Coed 2-19)

CHESHIRE EAST
Borough Council

Cheshire East SEN Team, Westfields, Middlewich Road, Sandbach, CW11 1HZ
Tel: 03001 235500 **Email:** sen.reforms@cheshireeast.gov.uk **Website:** www.cheshireeast.gov.uk

CREWE

Springfield School

Crewe Green Road, CREWE,
Cheshire CW1 5HS
Tel: 01270 685446
Headteacher: Mr Mark Swaine
Category: SLD (Coed 2-19)

KNUTSFORD

St John's Wood Community School

Longridge, KNUTSFORD,
Cheshire WA16 8PA
Tel: 01625 383045
Headteacher: Mr
Anthony Armstrong
Category: BESD (Coed Day 11-16)

MACCLESFIELD

Park Lane School

Park Lane, MACCLESFIELD,
Cheshire SK11 8JR
Tel: 01625 384040
Headteacher: Mrs Lorraine Warmer
Category: SLD (Coed Day 2-19)

CHESHIRE WEST & CHESTER
Council

Chester SEN Assessment, Monitoring & Support Team, 4 Civic Way, Ellesmere Port, CH65 0BE
Tel: 03001 238123 **Email:** senteam@cheshirewestandchester.gov.uk **Website:** www.cheshirewestandchester.gov.uk

CHESTER

Dee Banks School

Dee Banks, Sandy Lane,
CHESTER, Cheshire CH3 5UX
Tel: 01244 981030
Head: Mr Ray Elliott
Category: ASD SLD PMLD
(Coed Day 2-19)

Dorin Park School & Specialist SEN College

Wealstone Lane, Upton,
CHESTER, Cheshire CH2 1HD
Tel: 01244 981191
Head: Ms Jane Hughes
Category: PD Complex
needs (Coed Day 2-19)

ELLESMERE PORT

Capenhurst Grange School

Chester Road, Great
Sutton, ELLESMERE PORT,
Cheshire CH66 2NA
Tel: 01513 382141
Head: Mr Graham Stothard
Category: BESD (Coed 11-16)

Hinderton School

Capenhurst Lane,
Whitby, ELLESMERE PORT,
Cheshire CH65 7AQ
Tel: 01513 382200
Head: Mr Liam Dowling
Category: ASD with complex
learning needs (Coed Day 3-11)

NORTHWICH

Greenbank School

Greenbank Lane, Hartford,
NORTHWICH, Cheshire CW8 1LD
Tel: 01606 288028
Head: Mr Mike McCann
Category: ASD MLD
(Coed Day 6-18)

Rosebank School

Townfield Lane, Barnton,
NORTHWICH, Cheshire CW8 4QP
Tel: 01606 74975
Head: Mrs Judith McGuiness
Category: ASD with complex
learning needs (Coed Day 3-11)

The Russett School

Middlehurst Avenue, Weaverham,
NORTHWICH, Cheshire CW8 3BW
Tel: 01606 853005
Head: Mrs Catherine Lewis
Category: SLD PMLD MSI
(Coed Day 2-19)

WINSFORD

**Hebden Green
Community School**

Woodford Lane West,
WINSFORD, Cheshire CW7 4EJ
Tel: 01606 594221
Head: Ms Alison Ashley
Category: PD Complex needs
(Coed Day/Residential 2-19)

Oaklands School

Montgomery Way, WINSFORD,
Cheshire CW7 1NU
Tel: 01606 551048
Head: Mr Kevin Boyle
Category: HI MLD SP&LD
(Coed Day 11-16)

CORNWALL
Children, Schools and Families

Cornwall SEN Team, County Hall, Treyew Road, Truro, Cornwall, TR1 3AY
Tel: 03001 234101 Email: children@cornwall.gov.uk Website: www.cornwall.gov.uk

PENZANCE

Nancealverne School

Madron Road, PENZANCE,
Cornwall TR20 8TP
Tel: 01736 365039
Head: Miss Sarah Moseley
Category: SLD PMLD (Coed 2-19)

REDRUTH

Curnow School

Drump Road, REDRUTH,
Cornwall TR15 1LU
Tel: 01209 215432
Head: Ms Gina Briggs
Category: PMLD SLD (Coed 2-19)

ST AUSTELL

Doubletrees School

St Blazey Gate, St Blazey, Par, ST
AUSTELL, Cornwall PL24 2DS
Tel: 01726 812757
Head: Ms Kim Robertson
Category: SLD PMLD (Coed 2-19)

CUMBRIA
Children's Services

Cumbria SEN Team, The Courts, Lower Gaol Yard, Carlisle, Cumbria, CA3 8NA
Tel: 07824 541499 Email: localoffer@cumbria.gov.uk Website: www.cumbria.gov.uk

BARROW IN FURNESS

George Hastwell School

Moor Tarn Lane, Walney, BARROW
IN FURNESS, Cumbria LA14 3LW
Tel: 01229 475253
Head: Mrs Karen Baxter
Category: SLD PMLD

CARLISLE

James Rennie School

California Road, Kingstown,
CARLISLE, Cumbria CA3 0BX
Tel: 01228 554280
Head: Mrs Kris Williams
Category: SLD PMLD

KENDAL

Sandgate School

Sandylands Road, KENDAL,
Cumbria LA9 6JG
Tel: 01539 792100
Head: Ms Joyce Fletcher
Category: SLD PMLD

ULVERSTON

Sandside Lodge School

Sandside Road, ULVERSTON,
Cumbria LA12 9EF
Tel: 01229 588825
Head: Ms Susan Gill
Category: SLD PMLD

WHITEHAVEN

Mayfield School

Moresby Road, Hensingham,
WHITEHAVEN, Cumbria CA28 8TU
Tel: 01946 691253
Head: Ms Gillian Temple
Category: SLD PMLD

DERBYSHIRE
Children & Younger Adults

Derbyshire Special Needs Section, County Hall, Matlock, Derbyshire, DE4 3AG
Tel: 01629 536539 Email: sen.admin@derbyshire.gov.uk Website: www.derbyshire.gov.uk

ALFRETON

Alfreton Park Community Special School
Alfreton Park, ALFRETON, Derbyshire DE55 7AL
Tel: 01773 832019
Head: Mrs Cheryl Smart
Category: SLD (2-19)

Swanwick School and Sports College
Hayes Lane, Swanwick, ALFRETON, Derbyshire DE55 1AR
Tel: 01773 602198
Head: Mr Christopher Greenhough
Category: MLD (5-16)

BELPER

Holbrook School for Autism
Port Way, Holbrook, BELPER, Derbyshire DE56 0TE
Tel: 01332 880208
Head: Mr Julian Scholefield
Category: AUT (5-19)

BUXTON

Peak School
Buxton Road, Chinley, High Peak, BUXTON, Derbyshire SK23 6ES
Tel: 01663 750324
Head: Mr John McPherson
Category: SLD (2-19)

CHESTERFIELD

Ashgate Croft School
Ashgate Road, CHESTERFIELD, Derbyshire S40 4BN
Tel: 01246 275111
Head: Mrs Claire Jones
Category: MLD SLD (2-19)

Holly House School
Church Street North, Old Whittington, CHESTERFIELD, Derbyshire S41 9QR
Tel: 01246 450530
Head: Mr Peter Brandt
Category: EBD (7-14)

ILKESTON

Bennerley Fields Specialist Speech & Language College
Stratford Street, ILKESTON, Derbyshire DE7 8QZ
Tel: 01159 326374
Acting Head: Ms Anne Harrison
Category: MLD (2-16)

LONG EATON

Brackenfield School
Bracken Road, LONG EATON NG10 4DA
Tel: 01159 733710
Head: Mrs Sarah Gilraine
Category: MLD (5-16)

Stanton Vale Special School
Thoresby Road, LONG EATON NG10 3NP
Tel: 01159 72 9769
Head: Mr Christopher White
Category: PMLD SLD (2-19)

SHIREBROOK

Stubbin Wood School
Common Lane, SHIREBROOK, Derbyshire NG20 8QF
Tel: 01623 742795
Head: Mr Lee Floyd
Category: MLD SLD (2-19)

DERBY CITY
Information & Advice Service

Derby SENDIASS, The Council House, Corporation Street, Derby, Derbyshire, DE1 2FS
Tel: 01332 641414 Email: sendiass@derby.gov.uk Website: www.derby.gov.uk

DERBY

Ivy House School
Moorway Lane, Littleover, DERBY DE23 2FS
Tel: 01332 777920
Head: Ms Susan Allen
Category: SLD PMLD (Coed 2-19)

Kingsmead School
Bridge Street, DERBY DE1 3LB
Tel: 01332 715970
Head: Mrs Sue Bradley
Category: EBD (Coed 11-16)

St Andrew's School
St Andrew's View, Breadsall Hilltop, DERBY DE21 4EW
Tel: 01332 832746
Head: Ms Heather Flockton
Category: SLD (Coed 11-19)

St Clare's School
Rough Heanor Road, Mickleover, DERBY DE3 9AZ
Tel: 01332 511757
Head: Ms Megan Stratton
Category: MLD SP&LD AUT PD SLD (Coed 11-16)

St Giles' School
Hampshire Road, Chaddesden, DERBY DE21 6BT
Tel: 01332 343039
Head: Mr Clive Lawrence
Category: SLD AUT (Coed 4-11)

St Martin's School
Bracknell Drive, Alvaston, DERBY DE24 0BR
Tel: 01332 571151
Head: Ms Debbie Gerring
Category: MLD AUT EBD SLD (Coed 11-16)

DEVON
Children & Young People's Services

Devon 0-25 SEN Team, County Hall, Topsham Road, Exeter, Devon, EX2 4QD
Tel: 01392 383913 Email: specialeducation0-25-mailbox@devon.gov.uk Website: www.devon.gov.uk

BARNSTAPLE

Pathfield School
Abbey Road, Pilton,
BARNSTAPLE, Devon EX31 1JU
Tel: 01271 342423
Head: Mrs Claire May
Category: SLD PMLD (3-19)

The Lampard Community School
St John's Lane, BARNSTAPLE,
Devon EX32 9DD
Tel: 01271 345416
Head: Mrs Karen Rogers
Category: Complex and difficulties with communication and interaction (including SLCN and/or ASC) (7-16)

BUDLEIGH SALTERTON

Mill Water Community School
Bicton, East Budleigh, BUDLEIGH
SALTERTON, Devon EX9 7BJ
Tel: 01395 568890
Head: Mrs Sarah Pickering
Category: SLD PMLD (3-19)

DAWLISH

Oaklands Park School
John Nash Drive, DAWLISH,
Devon EX7 9SF
Tel: 01626 862363
Acting Head: Mrs Cherie White
Category: SLD ASC PMLD
(Day/boarding 3-19)

Ratcliffe School
John Nash Drive, DAWLISH,
Devon EX7 9RZ
Tel: 01626 862939
Head: Mrs Cherie White
Category: ASC and Associated
Social Development Needs (5-16)

EXETER

Barley Lane School
Barley Lane, St Thomas,
EXETER, Devon EX4 1TA
Tel: 01392 430774
Head: Mr Michael MacCourt
Category: BESD (7-16)

Ellen Tinkham School
Hollow Lane, EXETER,
Devon EX1 3RW
Tel: 01392 467168
Head: Mrs Jacqueline Warne
Category: SLD PMLD (3-19)

Southbrook School
Bishop Westall Road,
EXETER, Devon EX2 6JB
Tel: 01392 258373
Head: Mrs Bronwen Caschere
Category: MLD ASC (11-16)

TORRINGTON

Marland School
Petersmarland, TORRINGTON,
Devon EX38 8QQ
Tel: 01805 601324
Head: Mr Keith Bennett
Category: SEBD (10-16)

TOTNES

Bidwell Brook School
Shinner's Bridge, Dartington,
TOTNES, Devon TQ9 6JU
Tel: 01803 864120
Head: Mrs Jacqueline Warne
Category: SLD PMLD (3-19)

DORSET
County Council

Dorset SEN Team, County Hall, Dorchester, DT1 1XJ
Tel: 01305 224888 Fax: 01305 224547 Email: dorsetdirect@dorsetcc.gov.uk Website: www.dorsetcc.gov.uk

BEAMINSTER

Mountjoy School
Tunnel Road, BEAMINSTER,
Dorset DT8 3HB
Tel: 01308 861155
Head: Ms J Shanks
Category: ASD SLD PMLD
Complex (2-19)

STURMINSTER NEWTON

Yewstock School
Honeymead Lane, STURMINSTER
NEWTON, Dorset DT10 1EW
Tel: 01258 472796
Head: Mr S Kretz
Category: ASD MLD/
Comlex PMLD SLD (2-19)

WEYMOUTH

Westfield Arts College
Littlemoor Road, Preston,
WEYMOUTH, Dorset DT3 6AA
Tel: 01305 833518
Head: Mr A Penman
Category: MLD/Complex ASD (3-16)

Wyvern School
Dorchester Road, WEYMOUTH,
Dorset DT3 5AL
Tel: 01305 817917
Head: Mr B Douglas
Category: ASD PMLD
SLD Complex (2-19)

WIMBORNE

Beaucroft Foundation School
Wimborne Road, Colehill,
WIMBORNE, Dorset BH21 2SS
Tel: 01202 886083
Head: Mr P McGill
Category: MLD/Complex ASD (4-16)

DURHAM
County Council

Durham SEN Team, Children and Adult Services, County Hall, Durham, County Durham, DH1 5UJ
Tel: 03000 265878 Website: www.durham.gov.uk

BISHOP AUCKLAND

Evergreen School
Warwick Road, BISHOP AUCKLAND, Durham DL14 6LS
Tel: 01388 459721
Head: Mrs Andrea E English
Category: MLD SLD PMLD AUT (2-11)

CONSETT

Villa Real School
Villa Real Road, CONSETT, Durham DH8 6BH
Tel: 01207 503651
Head: Mrs Sharon Common
Category: SLD PMLD AUT (2-19)

DURHAM

Durham Trinity School and Sports College
Aykley Heads, DURHAM DH1 5TS
Tel: 01913 864612
Head: Mrs Julie Anne Rutherford
Category: MLD SLD PMLD AUT (2-19)

FERRYHILL

Windlestone School
Chilton, FERRYHILL, Durham DL17 0HP
Tel: 01388 720337
Head: Mr Tim Bennett
Category: SEBD (11-16)

NEWTON AYCLIFFE

Walworth School
Bluebell Way, NEWTON AYCLIFFE, Durham DL5 7LP
Tel: 01325 300194
Head: Mr Peter Wallbanks
Category: SEBD (4-11)

SHERBURN

Elemore Hall School
Littletown, SHERBURN, Durham DH6 1QD
Tel: 01913 720275
Head: Mr Richard J Royle
Category: SEBD (11-16)

SPENNYMOOR

The Meadows School
Whitworth Lane, SPENNYMOOR, Durham DL16 7QW
Tel: 01388 811178
Head: Mrs Sarah Took
Category: SEBD (11-16)

The Oaks School
Rock Road, SPENNYMOOR, Durham DL16 7DB
Tel: 01388 827380
Head: Mrs Andrea E English
Category: MLD SLD PMLD AUT (11-19)

STANLEY

Croft Community School
Annfield Plain, STANLEY, Durham DH9 8PR
Tel: 01207 234547
Head: Mr Simon Adams
Category: MLD SLD AUT (5-16)

ESSEX
Essex Parent Partnership Service

Essex SENDIASS, County Hall, Market Road, Chelmsford, Essex, CM1 1QH
Tel: 03330 138913 Email: send.iass@essex.gov.uk Website: www.essex.gov.uk

BASILDON

Castledon School
Bromfords Drive, Wickford, BASILDON, Essex SS12 0PW
Tel: 01268 761252
Head: Mrs Philippa Holiday
Category: ASD MLD (5-16)

The Pioneer School
Ghyllgrove, BASILDON, Essex SS14 2LA
Tel: 01268 243300
Head: Mr Steve Horsted
Category: CLD (3-19)

BENFLEET

Cedar Hall School
Hart Road, Thundersley, BENFLEET, Essex SS7 3UQ
Tel: 01268 774723
Head: Mr Nic Maxwell
Category: MLD (4-16)

Glenwood School
Rushbottom Lane, New Thundersley, BENFLEET, Essex SS7 4LW
Tel: 01268 792575
Head: Mrs Judith Salter
Category: SLD (3-19)

BILLERICAY

Ramsden Hall School
Heath Road, Ramsden Heath, BILLERICAY, Essex CM11 1HN
Tel: 01277 624580
Head: Mr Garry Walker
Category: BESD (Boys 11-16)

BRAINTREE

The Edith Borthwick School
Springwood Drive, BRAINTREE, Essex CM7 2YN
Tel: 01376 529300
Head: Mr Ian Boatman
Category: ASD MLD SLD (3-19)

BRENTWOOD

Grove House School
Sawyers Hall Lane, BRENTWOOD, Essex CM15 9DA
Tel: 01277 361498
Head: Ms Lisa Christodoulides
Category: SP&LD Communication Difficulties (9-19)

The Endeavour School
Hogarth Avenue, BRENTWOOD, Essex CM15 8BE
Tel: 01277 217330
Head: Mr John Chadwick
Category: MLD (5-16)

Maintained special schools and colleges

CHELMSFORD

The Columbus School
Oliver Way, CHELMSFORD,
Essex CM1 4ZB
Tel: 01245 491492
Head: Mrs Ginny Bellard

Thriftwood School
Slades Lane, Galleywood,
CHELMSFORD, Essex CM2 8RW
Tel: 01245 266880
Head: Mrs Georgina Pryke
Category: LD (5-13)

CHIGWELL

Wells Park School
School Lane, Lambourne Road,
CHIGWELL, Essex IG7 6NN
Tel: 02085 026442
Acting Head: Ms Carol Mitchell
Category: BESD (5-12)

CLACTON ON SEA

Shorefields School
114 Holland Road, CLACTON
ON SEA, Essex CO15 6HF
Tel: 01255 424412
Head: Mrs Jo Hodges
Category: ASD MLD SLD (3-19)

COLCHESTER

Kingswode Hoe School
Sussex Road, COLCHESTER,
Essex CO3 3QJ
Tel: 01206 576408
Head: Mrs Elizabeth Drake
Category: MLD (5-16)

Langham Oaks School
School Road, Langham,
COLCHESTER, Essex CO4 5PA
Tel: 01206 271571
Head: Ms Emma Paramor
Category: SEMH (Boys 10-16)

Lexden Springs School
Halstead Road, Lexden,
COLCHESTER, Essex CO3 9AB
Tel: 01206 563321
Head: Mr Simon Wall
Category: SLD (3-19)

Market Field School
School Road, Elmstead Market,
COLCHESTER, Essex CO7 7ET
Tel: 01206 825195
Head: Mr Gary Smith
Category: ASD MLD SLD (4-16)

HARLOW

Harlow Fields School & College
Tendring Road, HARLOW,
Essex CM18 6RN
Tel: 01279 423670
Head: Mrs Kathleen Wall
Category: ASD MLD SLD (3-19)

LOUGHTON

Oak View School
Whitehills Road, LOUGHTON,
Essex IG10 1TS
Tel: 02085 084293
Head: Ms Dianne Ryan
Category: MLD SLD (3-19)

WITHAM

Southview School
Conrad Road, WITHAM,
Essex CM8 2TA
Tel: 01376 503505
Head: Mr Julian Cochrane
Category: PD (3-19)

GLOUCESTERSHIRE
Information Advice & Support Service

Gloucestershire SENDIASS, Messenger House (2nd Floor), 35 St. Michael's Square, Gloucester, GL1 1HX
Tel: 0800 158 3603 Email: sendiass@carersgloucestershire.org.uk Website: www.gloucestershire.gov.uk/learning

CHELTENHAM

Battledown Centre for Children and Families
Harp Hill, Battledown,
CHELTENHAM,
Gloucestershire GL52 6PZ
Tel: 01242 525472
Head: Ms Jane Cummins
Category: VI SLCN ASD
SEMH PD MLD SLD (2-7)

Belmont School
Warden Hill Road, CHELTENHAM,
Gloucestershire GL51 3AT
Tel: 01242 216180
Head: Mr Kevin Day
Category: MLD (Coed 4-16)

Bettridge School
Warden Hill Road, CHELTENHAM,
Gloucestershire GL51 3AT
Tel: 01242 514934
Head: Mrs Amanda Roberts
Category: VI SLCN ASD SLD (2-19)

CIRENCESTER

Paternoster School
Watermoor Road, CIRENCESTER,
Gloucestershire GL7 1JR
Tel: 01285 652480
Head: Ms Julie Mantell
Category: SLD (2-17)

COLEFORD

Heart of the Forest Community School
Speech House, Coalway,
COLEFORD, Gloucestershire
GL16 7EJ
Tel: 01594 822175
Head: Mrs Melissa Bradshaw
Category: SLD PMLD (Coed 3-19)

FAIRFORD

Coln House School
Horcott Road, FAIRFORD,
Gloucestershire GL7 4DB
Tel: 01285 712308
Head: Mrs Debra Henderson
Category: SEMH (Coed
Day/boarding 9-16)

GLOUCESTER

The Milestone School
Longford Lane, GLOUCESTER,
Gloucestershire GL2 9EU
Tel: 01452 500499
Head: Mrs Lyn Dance
Category: VI SLCN ASD SEMH
PD MLD SLD (Coed 2-16)

STONEHOUSE

The Shrubberies School
Oldends Lane, STONEHOUSE,
Gloucestershire GL10 2DG
Tel: 01453 822155
Head: Ms Jane Jones
Category: SLD (Coed 2-19)

TEWKESBURY

Alderman Knight School
Ashchurch Road, TEWKESBURY,
Gloucestershire GL20 8JJ
Tel: 01684 295639
Head: Mrs Clare Steel
Category: MLD (4-16)

SOUTH GLOUCESTERSHIRE
Council

0-25 Service, Department for Children, Adults & Health, PO Box 298, Civic Centre, High Street Bristol, South Gloucestershire, BS15 0DQ
Tel: 01454 863301 or 01454 863173 Website: www.southglos.gov.uk

KINGSWOOD

New Horizons Learning Centre
Mulberry Drive, KINGSWOOD,
South Gloucestershire BS15 4ED
Tel: 01454 865340
Head: Mrs T Craig
Category: BESD

THORNBURY

New Siblands School
Easton Hill Road, THORNBURY,
South Gloucestershire BS35 2JU
Tel: 01454 866754
Head: Mr A Buckton
Category: SLD

WARMLEY

Warmley Park School
Tower Road North, WARMLEY,
South Gloucestershire BS30 8XL
Tel: 01454 867272
Head: Miss L Parker
Category: SLD (Day 3-19)

YATE

Culverhill School
Kelston Close, YATE, South
Gloucestershire BS37 8SZ
Tel: 01454 866930
Head: Ms N Jones
Category: CLD (Day 7-16)

HALTON
Borough Council

Halton SEND Partnership, Rutland House, Halton Lea, Runcorn, Cheshire, WA7 2GW
Tel: 01515 117733 Email: sendpartnership@halton.gov.uk Website: www3.halton.gov.uk

WIDNES

Ashley School
Cawfield Avenue, WIDNES,
Cheshire WA8 7HG
Tel: 01514 244892
Head: Mrs Linda King
Category: MLD Complex
emotional needs (11-16)

Brookfields School
Moorfield Road, WIDNES,
Cheshire WA8 0JA
Tel: 01514 244329
Head: Mrs Sara Ainsworth
Category: SLD (2-11)

Chesnut Lodge School & Specialist SEN College
Green Lane, WIDNES,
Cheshire WA8 7HF
Tel: 01514 240679
Head: Mrs Heather Austin
Category: PH (2-16)

HAMPSHIRE
County Council

Children's Services Department, Elizabeth II Court, The Castle, Winchester, Hampshire, SO23 8UG
Tel: 03005 551384 Email: childrens.services@hants.gov.uk Website: www.hants.gov.uk

ANDOVER

Icknield School
River Way, ANDOVER,
Hampshire SP11 6LT
Tel: 01264 365297
Head: Ms Sharon Salmon
Category: SLD (Coed 2-19)

Norman Gate School
Vigo Road, ANDOVER,
Hampshire SP10 1JZ
Tel: 01264 323423
Head: Ms Christine Gayler
Category: MLD ASD (Coed 2-11)

The Mark Way School
Batchelors Barn Road, ANDOVER,
Hampshire SP10 1HR
Tel: 01264 351835
Head: Ms Sonia Longstaff-Bishop
Category: MLD ASD (Coed 11-16)

Wolverdene Special School
22 Love Lane, ANDOVER,
Hampshire SP10 2AF
Tel: 01264 362350
Head: Mr Paul Van Walwyk
Category: BESD (Coed 5-11)

BASINGSTOKE

Coppice Spring School
Pack Lane, BASINGSTOKE,
Hampshire RG22 5TH
Tel: 01256 336601
Head: Mr Matthew McLoughlin-Parker
Category: BESD (Coed 11-16)

Maintained special schools and colleges

Dove House School
Sutton Road, BASINGSTOKE,
Hampshire RG21 5SU
Tel: 01256 351555
Head: Mr Tom Pegler
Category: MLD ASD (Coed 11-16)

Limington House School
St Andrews Road, BASINGSTOKE,
Hampshire RG22 6PS
Tel: 01256 322148
Head: Mr Justin Innes
Category: SLD (Coed 2-19)

Maple Ridge School
Maple Crescent, BASINGSTOKE,
Hampshire RG21 5SX
Tel: 01256 323639
Head: Mrs Debby Gooderham
Category: MLD ASD (Coed 4-11)

Saxon Wood School
Rooksdown, Barron
Place, BASINGSTOKE,
Hampshire RG24 9NH
Tel: 01256 356635
Head: Mr Richard Parratt
Category: PD (Coed 2-11)

BORDON

Hollywater School
Mill Chase Road, BORDON,
Hampshire GU35 0HA
Tel: 01420 474396
Head: Ms Steph Clancy
Category: LD (Coed 2-19)

CHANDLERS FORD

Lakeside School
Winchester Road, CHANDLERS
FORD, Hampshire SO53 2DW
Tel: 02380 266633
Head: Mr Gareth Evans
Category: BESD (Boys 11-16)

FAREHAM

Baycroft School
Gosport Road, Stubbington,
FAREHAM, Hampshire PO14 2AE
Tel: 01329 664151
Head: Mr Chris Toner
Category: MLD ASD (Coed 11-16)

Heathfield School
Oldbury Way, FAREHAM,
Hampshire PO14 3BN
Tel: 01329 845150
Head: Mrs Nicola Cunningham
Category: MLD ASD PD (Coed 2-11)

St Francis Special School
Patchway Drive, Oldbury Way,
FAREHAM, Hampshire PO14 3BN
Tel: 01329 845730
Head: Mr Steve Hollinghurst
Category: SLD (Coed 2-19)

FARNBOROUGH

Henry Tyndale School
Ship Lane, FARNBOROUGH,
Hampshire GU14 8BX
Tel: 01252 544577
Head: Mr Rob Thompson
Category: LD ASD (Coed 2-19)

Samuel Cody Specialist Sports College
Ballantyne Road,
Cove, FARNBOROUGH,
Hampshire GU14 6SS
Tel: 01252 514194
Head: Mrs Anna Dawson
Category: MLD ASD (Coed 11-16)

HAVANT

Prospect School
Freeley Road, HAVANT,
Hampshire PO9 4AQ
Tel: 02392 485150
Head: Ms Marijke Miles
Category: BESD (Boys 11-16)

PORTSMOUTH

Glenwood School
Washington Road,
Emsworth, PORTSMOUTH,
Hampshire PO10 7NN
Tel: 01243 373120
Head: Ms Ruth Witton
Category: MLD ASD (Coed 11-16)

SOUTHAMPTON

Forest Park Primary School
Ringwood Road,
Totton, SOUTHAMPTON,
Hampshire SO40 8EB
Tel: 02380 864949
Head: Mr Robert Hatherley
Category: LD (Coed 2-11)

Forest Park Secondary School
Commercial Road,
Totton, SOUTHAMPTON,
Hampshire SO40 3AF
Tel: 02380 864211
Head: Mr Robert Hatherley
Category: LD (Coed 11-19)

Lord Wilson School
Montiefiore Drive, Sarisbury
Green, SOUTHAMPTON,
Hampshire SO31 7NL
Tel: 01489 582684
Head: Mr Stuart Parker-Tyreman
Category: BESD (Male 11-16)

Oak Lodge School
Roman Road, Dibden
Purlieu, SOUTHAMPTON,
Hampshire SO45 4RQ
Tel: 02380 847213
Head: Ms Tessa Care
Category: MLD ASD (Coed 11-16)

WATERLOOVILLE

Rachel Madocks School
Eagle Avenue, Cowplain,
WATERLOOVILLE,
Hampshire PO8 9XP
Tel: 02392 241818
Head: Ms Jacqueline Sumner
Category: SLD (Coed 2-19)

Riverside Community Special School
Scratchface Lane,
Purbrook, WATERLOOVILLE,
Hampshire PO7 5QD
Tel: 02392 250138
Head: Ms Catherine Marsh
Category: MLD ASD (Coed 3-11)

The Waterloo School
Warfield Avenue, WATERLOOVILLE,
Hampshire PO7 7JJ
Tel: 02392 255956
Head: Ms Kirsty Roman
Category: BESD (Boys 4-11)

WINCHESTER

Osborne School
Athelstan Road, WINCHESTER,
Hampshire SO23 7GA
Tel: 01962 854537
Head: Ms Sonia O'Donnell
Category: LD ASD (Coed 11-19)

Shepherds Down Special School
Shepherds Lane, Compton,
WINCHESTER, Hampshire SO21 2AJ
Tel: 01962 713445
Head: Ms Jane Sansome
Category: LD ASD (Coed 4-11)

HARTLEPOOL
Borough Council

Hartlepool SEN Team, IASS, Civic Centre, Victoria Road, Hartlepool, TS24 8AY
Tel: 01429 284876 Email: hartlepooliass@hartlepool.gov.uk Website: www.hartlepool.gov.uk

HARTLEPOOL

Springwell School
Wiltshire Way, HARTLEPOOL TS26 0TB
Tel: 01429 280600
Headteacher: Mr Karl Telfer
Category: MLD SLD PMLD ASD BESD

HEREFORDSHIRE
The Children, Young People and Families Directorate

Herefordshire SEN Team, Herefordshire Council, Plough Lane, Hereford, Herefordshire, HR4 0LE
Tel: 01432 260088 or 01432 260089 Email: senteam@herefordshire.gov.uk Website: www.herefordshire.gov.uk

HEREFORD

Barrs Court School

Barrs Court Road,
HEREFORD HR1 1EQ
Tel: 01432 265035
Head: Ms Lisa Appleton
Category: CLD PMLD MSI PD ADHD
ASD OCD SP&LD SLD (Coed 11-19)

Blackmarston School

Honddu Close, HEREFORD HR2 7NX
Tel: 01432 272376
Head: Mrs Sian Bailey
Category: SLD ASD
PMLD(Coed 3-11)

LEOMINSTER

Westfield School

Rylands Road, LEOMINSTER HR6 8NZ
Tel: 01568 613147
Head: Mrs Nicki Gilbert
Category: SLD ASD
PMLD (Coed 2-19)

HERTFORDSHIRE
Children's Services

Hertfordshire SEN Team, County Hall, Pegs Lane, Hertford, SG13 8DQ
Tel: 03001 234043 Email: hertsdirect@hertscc.gov.uk Website: www.hertsdirect.org

BALDOCK

Brandles School

Weston Way, BALDOCK,
Hertfordshire SG7 6EY
Tel: 01462 892189
Head: Mr David Vickery
Category: EBD (Boys 11-16)

BUSHEY

Meadow Wood School

Cold Harbour Lane, BUSHEY,
Hertfordshire WD23 4NN
Tel: 02084 204720
Head: Mr Nathan Taylor
Category: PI (Coed Day 3-12)

HATFIELD

Southfield School

Woods Avenue, HATFIELD,
Hertfordshire AL10 8NN
Tel: 01707 276504
Head: Ms Libby Duggan
Category: MLD (Coed Day 3-11)

HEMEL HEMPSTEAD

Haywood Grove School

St Agnells Lane, HEMEL HEMPSTEAD,
Hertfordshire HP2 7BG
Tel: 01442 250077
Head Teacher: C Smith
Category: EBD (Coed Day 5-11)

The Collett School

Lockers Park Lane, HEMEL
HEMPSTEAD, Hertfordshire HP1 1TQ
Tel: 01442 398988
Head: Mr Stephen Hoult-Allen
Category: MLD AUT (Coed 4-16)

Woodfield School

Malmes Croft, Leverstock
Green, HEMEL HEMPSTEAD,
Hertfordshire HP3 8RL
Tel: 01442 253406
Head: Mrs Gill Waceba
Category: SLD AUT (Coed Day 3-19)

HERTFORD

Hailey Hall School

Hailey Lane, HERTFORD,
Hertfordshire SG13 7PB
Tel: 01992 465208
Head: Ms Heather Boardman
Category: EBD (Boys 11-16)

LETCHWORTH GARDEN CITY

Woolgrove School Special Needs Academy

Pryor Way, LETCHWORTH GARDEN
CITY, Hertfordshire SG6 2PT
Tel: 01462 622422
Head: Mrs Susan Selley
Category: MLD AUT
(Coed Day 5-11)

REDBOURN

St Luke's School

Crouch Hall Lane, REDBOURN,
Hertfordshire AL3 7ET
Tel: 01582 626727
Head: Mr P Johnson
Category: MLD (Coed Day 9-16)

ST ALBANS

Batchwood School

Townsend Drive, ST ALBANS,
Hertfordshire AL3 5RP
Tel: 01727 868021
Acting Head: Mrs Anne Spencer
Category: EBD (Coed 11-16)

Heathlands School

Heathlands Drive, ST ALBANS,
Hertfordshire AL3 5AY
Tel: 01727 807807
Head: Ms Deborah Jones-Stevens
Category: HI (Coed Day
& boarding 3-16)

Watling View School

Watling View, ST ALBANS,
Hertfordshire AL1 2NU
Tel: 01727 850560
Head: Ms Pauline Atkins
Category: SLD (Coed Day 2-19)

STEVENAGE

Greenside School

Shephall Green, STEVENAGE,
Hertfordshire SG2 9XS
Tel: 01438 315356
Head: Mr David Victor
Category: SLD AUT (Coed Day 2-19)

Larwood School

Webb Rise, STEVENAGE,
Hertfordshire SG1 5QU
Tel: 01438 236333
Head: Mr Sean Trimble
Category: EBD (Coed
Day & boarding 5-11)

Maintained special schools and colleges

Lonsdale School

Brittain Way, STEVENAGE,
Hertfordshire SG2 8BL
Tel: 01438 726999
Head Teacher: Ms
Annemarie Ottridge
Category: PH (Coed Day
& boarding 5-19)

The Valley School

Valley Way, STEVENAGE,
Hertfordshire SG2 9AB
Tel: 01438 747274
Head: Mrs Corina Foster
Category: MLD (Coed Day 11-19)

WARE

Amwell View School & Specialist Sports College

Stanstead Abbotts, WARE,
Hertfordshire SG12 8EH
Tel: 01920 870027
Head: Mrs Janet Liversage
Category: SLD AUT (Coed Day 2-19)

Middleton School

Walnut Tree Walk, WARE,
Hertfordshire SG12 9PD
Tel: 01920 485152
Head: Ms Donna Jolly
Category: MLD AUT
(Coed Day 5-11)

Pinewood School

Hoe Lane, WARE,
Hertfordshire SG12 9PB
Tel: 01920 412211
Acting Head: Mr Dave McGachen
Category: MLD (Coed
Residential 11-16)

WATFORD

Breakspeare School

Gallows Hill Lane, Abbots Langley,
WATFORD, Hertfordshire WD5 0BU
Tel: 01923 263645
Head Teacher: M Paakkonen
Category: SLD (Coed Day 3-19)

Colnbrook School

Hayling Road, WATFORD,
Hertfordshire WD19 7UY
Tel: 02084 281281
Head: Ms Kerry Harris
Category: MLD AUT
(Coed Day 4-11)

Falconer School

Falconer Road, Bushey, WATFORD,
Hertfordshire WD23 3AT
Tel: 02089 502505
Head Teacher: Mr Jonathan Kemp
Category: EBD (Boys Day/
boarding 10-19)

Garston Manor School

Horseshoe Lane, Garston,
WATFORD, Hertfordshire WD25 7HR
Tel: 01923 673757
Head: Miss Christine
deGraft-Hanson
Category: MLD (Coed Day 11-16)

WELWYN GARDEN CITY

Knightsfield School

Knightsfield, WELWYN GARDEN
CITY, Hertfordshire AL8 7LW
Tel: 01707 376874
Head: Mrs Lucy Leith
Category: HI (Coed Day
& boarding 10-19)

Lakeside School

Stanfield, Lemsford Lane,
WELWYN GARDEN CITY,
Hertfordshire AL8 6YN
Tel: 01707 327410
Head: Mrs Judith Chamberlain
Category: SLD PD (Coed Day 2-19)

FORTROSE

Black Isle Education Centre

Raddery, FORTROSE IV10 8SN
Tel: 01381 621600
Head: Mr Ross Waldie
Category: BESD (Boys Day 9-16)

ISLE OF WIGHT
Children's Services Directorate

Isle of Wight SEN Service, Thompson House, Sandy Lane, Newport, Isle of Wight, PO30 3NA
Tel: 01983 821000 (Ext: 8421) Website: www.iwight.com; www.iwight.com/localoffer

NEWPORT

Medina House Special School

School Lane, NEWPORT,
Isle of Wight PO30 2HS
Tel: 01983 522917
Head: Ms Julie Stewart
Category: Severe & complex
needs (Coed 2-11)

St George's School

Watergate Road, NEWPORT,
Isle of Wight PO30 1XW
Tel: 01983 524634
Head: Mrs Sue Holman
Category: Severe complex
needs (Coed 11-19)

KENT
Information, Advice & Support Service

Kent SENDIASS, Shepway Centre, Oxford Road, Maidstone, Kent, ME15 8AW
Tel: 03000 412412 Fax: 01622 671198 Email: iask@kent.gov.uk Website: www.kent.gov.uk

ASHFORD

Goldwyn Community Special School
Godinton Lane, Great Chart, ASHFORD, Kent TN23 3BT
Tel: 01233 622958
Head: Mr Robert Law
Category: BESD (Coed 11-16)

The Wyvern School
Great Chart Bypass, ASHFORD, Kent TN23 4ER
Tel: 01233 621468
Head: Mr David Spencer
Category: PMLD SLD CLD PD (Coed 3-19)

BROADSTAIRS

Stone Bay School
70 Stone Road, BROADSTAIRS, Kent CT10 1EB
Tel: 01843 863421
Head: Mr Billy McInally
Category: SLD AUT SLCN MLD C&I (Coed Day & residential 11-19)

The Foreland School
Lanthorne Road, BROADSTAIRS, Kent CT10 3NX
Tel: 01843 863891
Head Teacher: Mr Adrian Mount
Category: ASD PMLD SLD PSCN (Coed 2-19)

CANTERBURY

St Nicholas' School
Holme Oak Close, Nunnery Fields, CANTERBURY, Kent CT1 3JJ
Tel: 01227 464316
Headteacher: Mr Daniel Lewis
Category: PMLD SLD CLD PSCN (Coed 3-19)

The Orchard School
Cambridge Road, CANTERBURY, Kent CT1 3QQ
Tel: 01227 769220
Headteacher: Ms Annabel Lilley
Category: MLD CLD B&L (Coed 11-16)

DARTFORD

Rowhill School
Main Road, Longfield, DARTFORD, Kent DA3 7PW
Tel: 01474 705377
Head: Mr Timothy South
Category: B&L AUT LD Complex needs Behavioural difficulties (Coed Day 4-16)

DOVER

Harbour School
Elms Vale Road, DOVER, Kent CT17 9PS
Tel: 01304 201964
Head Teacher: Mr Warren Deane
Category: BESD ASD MLD B&L (Coed 4-16)

Portal House School
Sea Street, St Margarets-at-Cliffe, DOVER, Kent CT15 6SS
Tel: 01304 853033
Head: Mrs Rose Bradley
Category: BESD (Coed 11-16)

FOLKESTONE

Highview School
Moat Farm Road, FOLKESTONE, Kent CT19 5DJ
Tel: 01303 258755
Executive Headteacher: Mr Neil Birch
Category: MLD CLD Complex needs (Coed 4-17)

GRAVESEND

The Ifield School
Cedar Avenue, GRAVESEND, Kent DA12 5JT
Tel: 01474 365485
Headteacher: Mrs Pamela Jones
Category: CLD PMLD SLD MLD PSCN (Coed 4-18)

HYTHE

Foxwood School
Seabrook Road, HYTHE, Kent CT21 5QJ
Tel: 01303 261155
Executive Headteacher: Mr Neil Birch
Category: AUT SLD (Coed 2-19)

MAIDSTONE

Bower Grove School
Fant Lane, MAIDSTONE, Kent ME16 8NL
Tel: 01622 726773
Headteacher: Mrs Lynn Salter
Category: BESD MLD ASD B&L (Coed Day 5-16)

Five Acre Wood School
Boughton Lane, Loose Valley, MAIDSTONE, Kent ME15 9QF
Tel: 01622 743925
Head: Ms Peggy Murphy
Category: ASD PMLD SLD PD CLD PSCN (Coed 4-19)

MARGATE

St Anthony's School
St Anthony's Way, MARGATE, Kent CT9 3RA
Tel: 01843 292015
Headteacher: Mr Robert Page
Category: MLD ASD LD SEBD SLCN B&L (Coed 3-11)

RAMSGATE

Laleham Gap School
Ozengell Place, RAMSGATE, Kent CT12 6FH
Tel: 01843 570598
Deputy Head: Ms Katie Reeves
Category: AUT ABD PD SLCN C&I (Coed 3-16)

SEVENOAKS

Grange Park School
Borough Green Road, Wrotham, SEVENOAKS, Kent TN15 7RD
Tel: 01732 882111
Head Teacher: Mr Robert Wyatt
Category: AUT C&I (Coed 11-19)

SITTINGBOURNE

Meadowfield School
Swanstree Avenue, SITTINGBOURNE, Kent ME10 4NL
Tel: 01795 477788
Head: Ms Jill Palmer
Category: CLD PMLD SLD ASD SP&LD PSCN (Coed 4-19)

SWANLEY

Broomhill Bank School (North)
Rowhill Road, Hextable, SWANLEY, Kent BR8 7RP
Tel: 01322 662937
Acting Head: Mrs R Cottage

TONBRIDGE

Ridge View School
Cage Green Road, TONBRIDGE, Kent TN10 4PT
Tel: 01732 771384
Head Teacher: Ms Jacqui Tovey
Category: PMLD SLD CLD PSCN (Coed 2-19)

TUNBRIDGE WELLS

Broomhill Bank School (West)
Broomhill Road, Rusthall, TUNBRIDGE WELLS, Kent TN3 0TB
Tel: 01892 510440
Executive Headteacher: Ms Emma Leitch
Category: MLD SP&LD CLD AUT C&I (Girls Boarding & day 8-19)

Oakley School
Pembury Road, TUNBRIDGE WELLS, Kent TN2 4NE
Tel: 01892 823096
Headteacher: Mr Gordon Tillman
Category: PMLD ASD MLD PSCN (Coed 3-19)

Maintained special schools and colleges

WESTERHAM

Valence School
Westerham Road, WESTERHAM,
Kent TN16 1QN
Tel: 01959 562156
Head: Mr Roland Gooding
Category: PD Sensory Medical
(Coed Day/boarding 4-19)

KINGSTON UPON HULL
City Council

Kingston Upon Hull 0-25 Integrated SEN Team, The Helmsley Centre, 64 Helmsley Grove, Hull, HU5 5ED
Tel: 01482 300300 Email: send@hullcc.gov.uk Website: www.hullcc.gov.uk

KINGSTON UPON HULL

Bridgeview School
262a Pickering Road, KINGSTON
UPON HULL HU4 7AB
Tel: 01482 303300
Head: Mrs C Patton
Category: BESD

Frederick Holmes School
Inglemire Lane, KINGSTON
UPON HULL HU6 8JJ
Tel: 01482 804766
Head: Mrs B Ribey
Category: PH

Ganton Primary School
The Compass, 1 Burnham Road,
KINGSTON UPON HULL HU4 7EB
Tel: 01482 564 646
Head: Mrs S Jones
Category: SLD

Ganton Secondary School
294 Anlaby Park Road South,
KINGSTON UPON HULL HU4 7JB
Tel: 01482 564646
Head: Mrs S Jones
Category: SLD

Northcott School
Dulverton Close, Bransholme,
KINGSTON UPON HULL HU7 4EL
Tel: 01482 825311
Head: Mrs K Coxall
Category: Vulnerable ASD

Oakfield School
Hopewell Road, KINGSTON
UPON HULL HU9 4HD
Tel: 01482 854588
Head: Mrs R Davies
Category: BESD

Tweendykes School
Midmere Avenue, Leads Road,
KINGSTON UPON HULL HU7 4PW
Tel: 01482 826508
Head: Mrs B Moorcroft
Category: SLD

LANCASHIRE
Information, Advice & Support Service

Lancashire SENDIASS, PO Box 78, County Hall, Fishergate Preston, Lancashire, PR1 8XJ
Tel: 03001 236706 Email: information.lineteam@lancashire.gov.uk Website: www.lancashire.gov.uk

ACCRINGTON

Broadfield Specialist School for SEN
Fielding Lane, Oswaldtwistle,
ACCRINGTON, Lancashire BB5 3BE
Tel: 01254 381782
Head: Mrs Angela Wilson
Category: MLD SLD
ASD (Coed 4-16)

White Ash School
Thwaites Road, Oswaldtwistle,
ACCRINGTON, Lancashire BB5 4QG
Tel: 01254 235772
Head: Mr Mark Montgomery
Category: SLD ASD
PMLD (Coed 3-19)

BURNLEY

Holly Grove School
Burnley Campus, Barden Lane,
BURNLEY, Lancashire BB10 1JD
Tel: 01282 682278
Head: Ms Sue Kitto
Category: SLD MLD PMLD ASD
Medical needs (Coed 2-11)

Ridgewood Community High School
Eastern Avenue, BURNLEY,
Lancashire BB10 2AT
Tel: 01282 682316
Head: Mrs Frances Entwhistle
Category: MSI PD LD (Coed 11-16)

The Rose School
Greenock Street, BURNLEY,
Lancashire BB11 4DT
Tel: 01282 683050
Head: Mr Russell Bridge
Category: BESD (Coed 11-16)

CARNFORTH

Bleasdale House School
27 Emesgate Lane, Silverdale,
CARNFORTH, Lancashire LA5 0RG
Tel: 01524 701217
Head: Ms Kairen Dexter
Category: PMLD PH (Coed 2-19)

CHORLEY

Astley Park School
Harrington Road, CHORLEY,
Lancashire PR7 1JZ
Tel: 01257 262227
Head: Mr Kieran Welsh
Category: MLD SLD ASD
EBD(Coed 4-17)

Mayfield Specialist School
Gloucester Road, CHORLEY,
Lancashire PR7 3HN
Tel: 01257 263063
Head: Ms Rachel Kay
Category: CLD ASD
EBD (Coed 2-19)

COLNE

Pendle View Primary School

Gibfield Road, COLNE, Lancashire BB8 8JT
Tel: 01282 865011
Head: Ms Debbie Morris
Category: LD PD SLD PMLD ASD MSI (Coed 2-11)

HASLINGDEN

Tor View Community Special School

Clod Lane, HASLINGDEN, Lancashire BB4 6LR
Tel: 01706 214640
Head: Mr Andrew Squire
Category: AUT MLD SLD PMLD MSI (Coed 4-19)

KIRKHAM

Pear Tree School

29 Station Road, KIRKHAM, Lancashire PR4 2HA
Tel: 01772 683609
Head: Ms Lesley Sullivan
Category: SLD PMLD ASD (Coed 2-19)

LANCASTER

The Loyne Specialist School

Sefton Drive, LANCASTER, Lancashire LA1 2PZ
Tel: 01524 64543
Head: Ms Susan Campbell
Category: MSI LD CLD PD AUT EPI (2-19)

Wennington Hall School

Lodge Lane, Wennington, LANCASTER, Lancashire LA2 8NS
Tel: 01524 221333
Head: Mr Joseph Prendergast
Category: SEBD (Boys Day or resident 11-16)

MORECAMBE

Morecambe Road School

Morecambe Road, MORECAMBE, Lancashire LA3 3AB
Tel: 01524 414384
Head: Mr Paul Edmondson
Category: LD ASD BESD (Coed 3-16)

NELSON

Pendle Community High School and College

Oxford Road, NELSON, Lancashire BB9 8LF
Tel: 01282 682240
Head: Mr Paul Wright
Category: MLD BESD ASD (Coed 11-19)

POULTON-LE-FYLDE

Brookfield School

Fouldrey Avenue, POULTON-LE-FYLDE, Lancashire FY6 7HE
Tel: 01253 886895
Head: Mrs Jane Fallon
Category: SEBD ADHD ASD SPLD (Coed 11-16)

PRESTON

Acorns Primary School

Blackpool Road, Moor Park, PRESTON, Lancashire PR1 6AU
Tel: 01772 792681
Head: Ms Gail Beaton
Category: AUT SLD PMLD (Coed 2-19)

Hillside Specialist School and College

Ribchester Road, Longridge, PRESTON, Lancashire PR3 3XB
Tel: 01772 782205
Head: Mrs Alison Foster
Category: ASD (Coed 2-16)

Moor Hey School

Far Croft, off Leyland Road, Lostock Hall, PRESTON, Lancashire PR5 5SS
Tel: 01772 336976
Head: Mrs Helen-Ruth McLenahan
Category: MLD CLD EBD (4-16)

Moorbrook School

Ainslie Road, Fulwood, PRESTON, Lancashire PR2 3DB
Tel: 01772 774752
Head: Mrs Claire Thompson
Category: SEBN (11-16)

Royal Cross Primary School

Elswick Road, Ashton-on-Ribble, PRESTON, Lancashire PR2 1NT
Tel: 01772 729705
Head: Ms Ruth Bonney
Category: SLCN D ASD (Coed 4-11)

Sir Tom Finney Community High School

Ribbleton Hall Drive, PRESTON, Lancashire PR2 6EE
Tel: 01772 795749
Head: Mr Shaun Jukes
Category: PD PMLD BESD MLD (Coed 2-19)

The Coppice School

Ash Grove, Bamber Bridge, PRESTON, Lancashire PR5 6GY
Tel: 01772 336342
Head: Mrs Liz Davies
Category: SLD PMLD CLD Medical needs (Coed 2-19)

RAWTENSTALL

Cribden House Community Special School

Haslingden Road, RAWTENSTALL, Lancashire BB4 6RX
Tel: 01706 213048
Head: Ms Siobhan Halligan
Category: SEBD (Coed 5-11)

SKELMERSDALE

Elm Tree Community Primary School

Elmers Wood Road, SKELMERSDALE, Lancashire WN8 6SA
Tel: 01695 50924
Head: Mr David Lamb
Category: BESD (Coed)

Hope High School

Clay Brow, SKELMERSDALE, Lancashire WN8 9DP
Tel: 01695 721066
Head: Ms Helen Dunbavin
Category: EBD (Coed 11-16)

Kingsbury Primary School

School Lane, Chapel House, SKELMERSDALE, Lancashire WN8 8EH
Tel: 01695 722991
Head: Ms Fiona Grieveson
Category: SLD PMLD LD ASD MLD (Coed 2-11)

West Lancashire Community High School

School Lane, Chapel House, SKELMERSDALE, Lancashire WN8 8EH
Tel: 01695 721487
Head: Mrs Austin
Category: MLD SLD PMLD AUT (Coed 11-19)

THORNTON-CLEVELEYS

Great Arley School

Holly Road, THORNTON-CLEVELEYS, Lancashire FY5 4HH
Tel: 01253 821072
Head: Mrs Anne Marshfield
Category: MLD ASD SLD BESD (Coed Day 4-16)

Red Marsh School

Holly Road, THORNTON-CLEVELEYS, Lancashire FY5 4HH
Tel: 01253 868451
Head: Ms Catherine Dellow
Category: SLD PMLD CLD (Coed 2-19)

LEICESTER CITY COUNCIL
Education Authority

Leicester SEN Team, City Hall, 115 Charles Street, Leicester, LE1 1FZ
Tel: 01164 541000 Website: www.leicester.gov.uk

LEICESTER

Children's Hospital School

University Hospitals of Leicester
NHS Trust, Infirmary Square,
LEICESTER LE1 5WW
Tel: 01162 585330
Head: Mr Stephen
Corsie-Deadman
Category: HS

Ellesmere College

40 Braunstone Lane East,
LEICESTER LE3 2FD
Tel: 01162 894242
Heads: Ms Lisa Pittwood &
Ms Linda Richardson

Keyham Lodge School

Keyham Lane, LEICESTER LE5 1FG
Tel: 01162 41 6852
Head: Mr Chris Bruce
Category: EBD (Boys Secondary)

Millgate School

18A Scott Street, LEICESTER LE2 6DW
Tel: 01162 704922
Head: Mr Chris Bruce

Nether Hall School

Keyham Lane West,
LEICESTER LE5 1RT
Tel: 01162 417258
Head: Ms Erica Dennies

Oaklands School

Whitehall Road, LEICESTER LE5 6GJ
Tel: 01162 415921
Head: Mrs E Shaw
Category: MLD (Primary)

On-Trak Inclusion Service (linked to PRU)

495 Welford Road,
LEICESTER LE2 6BN
Tel: 01162 706016
Head: Mr Shaun Whittingham
Category: PRU

Phoenix (PRU)

c/o Thurnby Lodge Primary School,
Dudley Avenue, LEICESTER LE5 2EG
Tel: 01162 419538
Team Leader: Ms Allison Benson
Category: Primary PRU

The ARC (PRU)

c/o Holy Cross Primary School,
Stonesby Avenue, LEICESTER LE2 6TY
Tel: 01162 832185
Team Leader: Mrs C H Pay
Category: Primary PRU

West Gate School

Glenfield Road, LEICESTER LE3 6DN
Tel: 01162 856181
Head: Ms Virginia Ursell
Category: SLD MLD

Wigston Lane Educational Unit (PRU)

126 Wigston Lane, Aylestone,
LEICESTER LE2 8TN
Tel: 01162 836139
Head: Mr Shaun Whittingham
Category: Children Centre, PRU

LEICESTERSHIRE
Information Advice & Support Service

Leicestershire SENDIASS, Abington House, 85 Station Road, Wigston, Leicestershire, LE18 2DP
Tel: 0116 305 6545 Email: sendqueries@leics.gov.uk Website: www.leics.gov.uk

HINCKLEY

Sketchley Hill Menphys Nursery

Sketchley Road, Burbage,
HINCKLEY, Leicestershire LE10 2DY
Tel: 01455 890684
Head: Miss Laura Jeffs

LOUGHBOROUGH

Ashmount School

Thorpe Hill, LOUGHBOROUGH,
Leicestershire LE11 4SQ
Tel: 01509 268506
Head: Mr Dave Thomas
Category: SLD PMLD (2-18)

Maplewell Hall School

Maplewell Road, Woodhouse
Eaves, LOUGHBOROUGH,
Leicestershire LE12 8QY
Tel: 01509 890237
Head: Mr Jason Brooks
Category: MLD AUT (10-15)

MELTON MOWBRAY

Birch Wood (Melton Area Special School)

Grange Drive, MELTON MOWBRAY,
Leicestershire LE13 1HA
Tel: 01664 483340
Head: Ms Nina Watts
Category: MLD SLD AUT (5-19)

WIGSTON

Wigston Birkett House Community Special School

Launceston Road, WIGSTON,
Leicestershire LE18 2FZ
Tel: 01162 885802
Head: Mrs Susan Horn
Category: SLD PMLD (2-18)

Wigston Menphys Centre

Launceston Road, WIGSTON,
Leicestershire LE18 2FZ
Tel: 01162 889977
Head: Mrs Helen Johnston

LINCOLNSHIRE
Information, Advice & Support Service

Lincolnshire SENDIASS, County Offices, Newland, Lincoln, Lincolnshire, LN1 1YL
Tel: 0800 195 1635 Email: iass@lincolnshire.gov.uk Website: www.lincolnshire.gov.uk

BOSTON

John Fielding School
Ashlawn Drive, BOSTON,
Lincolnshire PE21 9PX
Tel: 01205 363395
Executive Head Teacher: Mr
Daran Bland
Category: SLD (2-19)

BOURNE

Willoughby School
South Road, BOURNE,
Lincolnshire PE10 9JD
Tel: 01778 425203
Head: Mr James Husbands
Category: SLD (2-19)

GOSBERTON

Gosberton House School
11 Westhorpe Road, GOSBERTON,
Lincolnshire PE11 4EW
Tel: 01775 840250
Head: Ms Louise Stanton
Category: MLD (3-11)

GRANTHAM

Sandon School
Sandon Close, GRANTHAM,
Lincolnshire NG31 9AX
Tel: 01476 564994
Principal: Ms Sara Ellis
Category: SLD (2-19)

The Ambergate Sports College Specialist Education Centre
Dysart Road, GRANTHAM,
Lincolnshire NG31 7LP
Tel: 01476 564957
Principal: Mr James Ellis
Category: MLD (5-16)

HORNCASTLE

St Lawrence School
Bowl Alley Lane, HORNCASTLE,
Lincolnshire LN9 5EJ
Tel: 01507 522563
Head: Ms Michelle Hockham
Category: MLD (5-16)

LINCOLN

St Christopher's School
Hykeham Road, LINCOLN,
Lincolnshire LN6 8AR
Tel: 01522 528378
Head: Mr Allan Lacey
Category: MLD (3-16)

St Francis School
Wickenby Crescent, Ermine Estate,
LINCOLN, Lincolnshire LN1 3TJ
Tel: 01522 526498
Head: Mrs Ann Hoffmann
Category: PD Sensory (2-19)

The Fortuna Primary School
Kingsdown Road, Doddington
Park, LINCOLN, Lincolnshire LN6 0FB
Tel: 01522 705561
Head: Ms Hanna Jones
Category: EBD (4-11)

The Pilgrim School
Carrington Drive, LINCOLN,
Lincolnshire LN6 0DE
Tel: 01522 682319
Head: Mr Steve Barnes
Category: HS (4-16)

The Sincil Sports College
South Park Avenue, LINCOLN,
Lincolnshire LN5 8EL
Tel: 01522 534559
Interim Head: Ms Bridget Robson
Category: EBD (11-16)

LOUTH

St Bernard's School
Wood Lane, LOUTH,
Lincolnshire LN11 8RS
Tel: 01507 603776
Head: Ms Ann Stebbings
Category: SLD (2-19)

SLEAFORD

The Ash Villa School
Willoughby Road, Greylees,
SLEAFORD, Lincolnshire NG34 8QA
Tel: 01529 488066
Head: Mr Leigh Bentley
Category: HS (8-16)

SPALDING

The Garth School
Pinchbeck Road, SPALDING,
Lincolnshire PE11 1QF
Tel: 01775 725566
Head of Site: Dr Richard Gamman
Category: SLD (2-19)

The Priory School
Neville Avenue, SPALDING,
Lincolnshire PE11 2EH
Tel: 01775 724080
Head of Site: Mr Barrie Taylor
Category: MLD (11-16)

SPILSBY

The Eresby School
Eresby Avenue, SPILSBY,
Lincolnshire PE23 5HU
Tel: 01790 752441
Head: Ms Michele Holiday
Category: SLD (2-19)

The Lady Jane Franklin School
Partney Road, SPILSBY,
Lincolnshire PE23 5EJ
Tel: 01790 753902
Head: Mr Chris Armond
Category: EBD (11-16)

NORTH LINCOLNSHIRE
People Directorate

North Lincolnshire SEND Team, Hewson House, PO Box 35, Station Road Brigg, North Lincolnshire, DN20 8XJ
Tel: 01724 297148 Email: special.needssection@northlincs.gov.uk Website: www.northlincs.gov.uk

SCUNTHORPE

**St Hugh's Communication
& Interaction
Specialist College**
Bushfield Road, SCUNTHORPE,
North Lincolnshire DN16 1NB
Tel: 01724 842960
Head: Mrs Tracy Millard
Category: MLD SLD
PMLD (Coed 11-19)

St Luke's Primary School
Grange Lane North, SCUNTHORPE,
North Lincolnshire DN16 1BN
Tel: 01724 844560
Head: Mr Alastair Sutherland
Category: PMLD SLD
MLD (Coed 3-11)

NORTH EAST LINCOLNSHIRE
Family Information Service

NE Lincolnshire SEN Team, Riverside Children's Centre, Central Parade, Grimsby, DN34 4HE
Tel: 01472 326293 Email: fis@nelincs.gov.uk Website: www.nelincs.gov.uk

London
BARKING & DAGENHAM
Education, Health and Care Team

Barking & Dagenham Education Inclusion Team, 5th Floor, Roycraft House, 15 Linton Road, Barking, Essex, IG11 8HE
Tel: 020 8227 2636 Email: joseph.wilson@lbbd.gov.uk

DAGENHAM

Trinity School
Heathway, DAGENHAM,
Essex RM10 7SJ
Tel: 02082 701601
Head: Mr Peter McPartland
Category: SLD ASD
PMLD (Coed 3-19)

London

BARNET

Council

Barnet SEN Referral & Assessment Team, North London Business Park, Oakleigh Road South, London, N11 1NP
Tel: 02083 597007 Email: senadmin@barnet.gov.uk Website: www.barnet.gov.uk

LONDON

Mapledown School

Claremont Road, Golders
Green, LONDON NW2 1TR
Tel: 02084 554111
Head: Mr S Caroll
Category: SLD CLD (Mixed 11-19)

Northway School

The Fairway, Mill Hill,
LONDON NW7 3HS
Tel: 02083 595450
Head: Ms L Burgess
Category: CLD AUT (Mixed 5-11)

Oak Lodge School

Heath View, Off East End
Road, LONDON N2 0QY
Tel: 02084 446711
Head: Mrs L Walker
Category: MLD ASD SCLN
EBD (Mixed 11-19)

Oakleigh School

Oakleigh Road North,
Whetstone, LONDON N20 0DH
Tel: 02083 685336
Head: Ms J Gridley
Category: SLD AUT
PMLD (Mixed 3-11)

London

LONDON BOROUGH OF BEXLEY

Directorate of Education and Social Care

Bexley SEN Team, Civic Offices, 2 Watling Street, Bexleyheath, Kent, DA6 7AT
Tel: 02083 037777 Email: specialneeds.els@bexley.gov.uk Website: www.bexley.gov.uk

BELVEDERE

Woodside School

Halt Robin Road, BELVEDERE,
Kent DA17 6DW
Tel: 01322 433494
Executive Head Teacher: Ms
Madelaine Caplin
Category: MLD (Primary/
Secondary)

BEXLEY HEATH

Oakwood School

Woodside Road, BEXLEY
HEATH, Kent DA7 6LB
Tel: 01322 553787
Head: Mrs Beverley Evans
Category: BESD (Coed 11-16)

CRAYFORD

Shenstone School

94 Old Road, CRAYFORD,
Kent DA1 4DZ
Tel: 01322 524145
Head Teacher: Ms Lori Mackey
Category: SLD (2-11)

SIDCUP

Marlborough School

Marlborough Park Avenue,
SIDCUP, Kent DA15 9DP
Tel: 02083 006896
Headteacher: Ms Linda Lee
Category: SLD (11-19)

WELLING

Westbrooke School

Gypsy Road South,
WELLING, Kent DA16 1JB
Tel: 02083 041320
Head: Mr Phill Collins
Category: BESD (5-11)

London

BRENT

Children & Families Department

Brent SENDIASS, Brent Civic Centre, Engineers Way, Wembley, Middlesex, HA9 0FJ
Tel: 020 8937 3434 Email: sendias@brent.gov.uk Website: www.brent.gov.uk

KENSALE RISE

Manor School
Chamberlayne Road, KENSALE
RISE, London NW10 3NT
Tel: 02089 683160
Head: Ms Jayne Jardine
Category: MLD SLD CLD
ASD (Coed 4-11)

KINGSBURY

The Village School
Grove Park, KINGSBURY,
London NW9 0JY
Tel: 02082 045396
Head: Ms Kay Charles
Category: LD DD VIS Medical
needs (Coed 2-19)

Woodfield School
Glenwood Avenue, KINGSBURY,
London NW9 7LY
Tel: 02082 051977
Head: Ms Desi Lodge-Patch
Category: MLD BESD
ASD (Coed 11-16)

NEASDEN

Phoenix Arch School
Drury Way, NEASDEN,
London NW10 0NQ
Tel: 02084 516961
Head: Ms Jude Towell
Category: BESD LD ADHD
ASD (Coed 5-11)

London

BROMLEY

Information, Advice & Support Service

Bromley SENDIASS, Blenheim Children & Family Centre, Blenheim Road, Orpington, Kent, BR6 9BH
Tel: 01689 881024 Email: iass@bromley.gov.uk Website: www.bromley.gov.uk

BECKENHAM

Woodbrook School
2 Hayne Road, BECKENHAM,
Kent BR3 4HY
Tel: 02086 507205
Head: Mr Steve Gillow
Category: ASD (Coed 4-19)

CHISLEHURST

Marjorie McClure School
Hawkwood Lane,
CHISLEHURST, Kent BR7 5PS
Tel: 02084 670174
Head: Mrs Denise James-Mason
Category: PD SLD Medical
needs (Coed 3-18)

ORPINGTON

Burwood School
Avalon Road, ORPINGTON,
Kent BR6 9BD
Tel: 01689 821205
Head: Mr Neil Miller
Category: EBD (Boys 7-16)

Riverside School
Main Road, St Paul's Cray,
ORPINGTON, Kent BR5 3HS
Tel: 01689 870519
Head: Mr Steve Solomons
Category: (Coed 4-19)

WEST WICKHAM

Glebe School
Hawes Lane, WEST
WICKHAM, Kent BR4 9AE
Tel: 02087 774540
Head: Mr Keith Seed
Category: Complex needs
SCD ASD SLD (Coed 11-16)

London Borough

CAMDEN

Information, Advice and Support Service

Camden SENDIASS, 10th Floor, 5 Pancras Square, c/o Town Hall, Judd Street London, WC1H 9JE
Tel: 020 7974 6264 Email: sendiass@camden.gov.uk Website: www.camden.gov.uk

LONDON

Chalcot School
Harmood Street, LONDON NW1 8DP
Tel: 02074 852147
Head: Ms Jeanette Lowe
Category: BESD (Coed 11-16)

Community Children's
Nursing Service
Royal Free Hospital, Pond
Street, LONDON NW3 2QG
Tel: 02077 940500
Head: Mr Alex Yates
Category: HS (5-16)

Frank Barnes Primary
School for Deaf Children
4 Wollstonecraft Street,
LONDON N1C 4BT
Tel: 02073 917040
Head: Ms Karen Simpson
Category: HI (Coed 2-11)

Great Ormond Street
Hospital School
Great Ormond Street,
LONDON WC1N 3JH
Tel: 02078 138269
Head: Ms Jayne Franklin
Category: HS (Coed 0-19)

Swiss Cottage School Development and Research Centre
80 Avenue Road,
LONDON NW8 6HX
Tel: 02076 818080
Head: Ms Kay Bedford
Category: LD (2-16)

London
CROYDON
Children, Young People & Learners

Croydon SEN Team, 4th Floor, Zone A, Weatherill House, 8 Mint Walk Croydon, Surrey, CR0 1EA
Tel: 0208 604 7263 Email: senenquiries@croydon.gov.uk Website: www.croydon.gov.uk

BECKENHAM

Beckmead School
Monks Orchard Road,
BECKENHAM, Kent BR3 3BZ
Tel: 020 8777 9311
Executive Head Teacher: Mr Jonty Clark
Category: BESD (Boys 7-16)

CROYDON

Bramley Bank Short Stay School
170 Sanderstead Road,
CROYDON, Surrey CR2 0LY
Tel: 020 8686 0393
Head: Ms Alison Page
Category: Behaviour Support (Coed 5-11)

Chaffinch Brook School
32 Moorland Road, CROYDON,
Surrey CR0 6NA
Tel: 020 8325 4612
Head: Ms Judith Azzopardi
Category: AUT (Coed 5-11)

Red Gates
Farnborough Avenue,
CROYDON, Surrey CR2 8HD
Tel: 020 8651 6540
Head Teacher: Mrs Susan Beaman
Category: SLD AUT (Coed 4-12)

St Giles School
207 Pampisford Road,
CROYDON, Surrey CR2 6DF
Tel: 020 8680 2141
Head Teacher: Ms Virginia Marshall
Category: PD PMLD MLD (Coed 4-19)

PURLEY

St Nicholas School
Old Lodge Lane, PURLEY,
Surrey CR8 4DN
Tel: 020 8660 4861
Headteacher: Mr Nick Dry
Category: MLD AUT (Coed 4-11)

THORNTON HEATH

Bensham Manor School
Ecclesbourne Road, THORNTON
HEATH, Surrey CR7 7BN
Tel: 020 8684 0116
Head Teacher: Mr Philip Poulton
Category: MLD AUT (Coed 11-16)

UPPER NORWOOD

Priory School
Hermitage Road, UPPER
NORWOOD, Surrey SE19 3QN
Tel: 020 8653 7879
Headteacher: Mr Simon Vines
Category: SLD AUT (Coed 11-19)

London
EALING
Education Department

Ealing SEN Team, 2nd Floor NE, Perceval House, 14-16 Uxbridge Road London, W5 2HL
Tel: 02088 255533 Email: education@ealing.gov.uk Website: www.ealing.gov.uk

EALING

Castlebar School
Hathaway Gardens, EALING,
London W13 0DH
Tel: 02089 983135
Head: Mr Paul Adair
Category: MLD SLD ASD (Coed Day 4-11)

Springhallow School
Compton Close, Cavendish
Ave, EALING, London W13 0JG
Tel: 02089 982700
Head: Mr Andy Balmer
Category: ASD (Coed Day 4-16/17)

GREENFORD

Mandeville School
Horsenden Lane North,
GREENFORD, Middlesex UB6 0PA
Tel: 02088 644921/0911
Head: Ms Denise Feasey
Category: SLD ASD PMLD (Coed Day 2-12)

HANWELL

St Ann's School
Springfield Road, HANWELL,
London W7 3JP
Tel: 02085 676291
Head: Ms Gillian Carver
Category: SLD MSI PNLD SLCN Complex medical conditions (Coed Day 11-19)

NORTHOLT

Belvue School
Rowdell Road, NORTHOLT,
London UB5 6AG
Tel: 02088 455766
Head: Mrs Shelagh O'Shea
Category: MLD SLD ASD
(Coed Day 11-18)

John Chilton School
Compton Crescent, NORTHOLT,
London UB5 5LD
Tel: 02088 421329
Head: Mr Simon Rosenberg
Category: PH/Medical
(Coed Day 2-18)

London

ENFIELD
Education & Learning

Enfield SEN Team, Civic Centre, Silver Street, Enfield, Middlesex, EN1 3XY
Tel: 020 8379 3203 Email: sen@enfield.gov.uk Website: www.enfield.gov.uk

EDMONTON

West Lea School
Haselbury Road, EDMONTON,
London N9 9TU
Tel: 02088 072656
Head: Mrs Susan Tripp
Category: HA ASD PD
LD (Coed 4-18)

ENFIELD

Aylands School
Keswick Drive, ENFIELD,
London EN3 6NY
Tel: 01992 761229
Head: Ms Sashikala Sivaloganathan
Category: EBD (Coed 7-16)

Durants School
4 Pitfield Way, ENFIELD,
London EN3 5BY
Tel: 02088 041980
Head: Mr Peter De Rosa
Category: CLD ASD (Coed 4-19)

Russet House School
11 Autumn Close, ENFIELD,
London EN1 4JA
Tel: 02083 500650
Head: Mrs Julie Foster
Category: AUT (Coed 3-11)

Waverley School
105 The Ride, ENFIELD,
London EN2 7DL
Tel: 02088 051858
Head: Ms Gail Weir
Category: PMLD SLD (Coed 3-19)

SOUTHGATE

Oaktree School
Chase Side, SOUTHGATE,
London N14 4HN
Tel: 02084 403100
Head: Mr Richard Yarwood
Category: Complex
needs (Coed 7-19)

London

ROYAL BOROUGH OF GREENWICH
Children's Services

Greenwich SEN Team, 1st Floor, The Woolwich Centre, 35 Wellington Street, Woolwich London, SE18 6HQ
Tel: 02089 218945 Website: www.royalgreenwich.gov.uk

LONDON

Moatbridge School
Eltham Palace Road,
LONDON SE9 5LX
Tel: 02088 508081
Head: Mr Mike Byron
Category: BESD (Boys 11-19)

Waterside School
Robert Street, Plumstead,
LONDON SE18 7NB
Tel: 02083 177659
Head: Meic Griffiths
Category: BESD (Coed 5-11)

Willow Dene School
Swingate Lane, Plumstead,
LONDON SE18 2JD
Tel: 02088 549841
Executive Head: Mr John Camp
Category: SCLD CLD PMLD
PD ASD (Coed 3-11)

London

HACKNEY

Hackney Learning Trust

Hackney SEN Team, Hackney Family Information Service, 1 Reading Lane, London, E8 1GQ
Tel: 02088 207000 Fax: 02088 207001 Email: localoffer@learningtrust.co.uk Website: www.hackney.gov.uk

LONDON

Ickburgh School
Kenworthy Road, LONDON E9 5RB
Tel: 02088 064638
Head: Ms Sue Davis
Category: SLD PMLD (2-19)

New Regents College
Ickburgh Road, LONDON E5 8AD
Tel: 02089 856833
Head: Mr Shane Foley

Stormont House School
Downs Park Road, LONDON E5 8NP
Tel: 02089 854245
Head: Mr Kevin McDonnell
Category: Complex
needs (Secondary)

The Garden School
Wordsworth Road,
LONDON N16 8BZ
Tel: 02072 548096
Head: Ms Pat Quigley
Category: MLD ASD (Secondary)

London

HAMMERSMITH & FULHAM

Council

Hammersmith & Fulham SEN Team, Kensington Town Hall, 2nd Floor, Green Zone, Hammersmith London, W8 7NX
Tel: 020 7361 3311 Email: sen@rbkc.gov.uk Website: www.lbhf.gov.uk

LONDON

Cambridge School
61 Bryony Road, Hammersmith,
LONDON W12 0SP
Tel: 02087 350980
Head: Mr Anthony Rawdin
Category: MLD (11-16)

Jack Tizard School
South Africa Road,
LONDON W12 7PA
Tel: 02087 353590
Head: Ms Cathy Welsh
Category: SLD PMLD
(Coed Day 3-19)

Queensmill School
1 Askham Road, Shepherds
Bush, LONDON W12 0NW
Tel: 02073 842330
Head: Ms Jude Ragan
Category: ASD (Coed 3-19)

**The Courtyard at
Langford Primary**
The Courtyard, Langford Primary,
Gilstead Road, LONDON SW6 2LG
Tel: 02076 108075
Head: Ms Janet Packer
Category: BESD (5-11)

Woodlane High School
Du Cane Road, LONDON W12 0TN
Tel: 02087 435668
Head: Mr Peter Harwood
Category: SCLN SPLD SEBD MSI
Medical difficulties (Coed 11-16)

London

HARINGEY

Children & Young People's Service

Haringey Additional Needs & Disabilities, 40 Cumberland Road, London, N22 7SG
Tel: 020 8489 1913 Email: sen@haringey.gov.uk Website: www.haringey.gov.uk

MUSWELL HILL

**Blanche Nevile
Secondary School**
Burlington Road, MUSWELL
HILL, London N10 1NJ
Tel: 02084 422750
Head: Ms Veronica Held
Category: HI (Coed Day 11-18)

NORTH HILL

**Blanche Nevile
Primary School**
Storey Road, NORTH HILL,
London N6 4ED
Tel: 02083 473760
Head: Ms Veronica Held
Category: HI (Coed Day 3-10)

TOTTENHAM

Riverside School
Wood Green Inclusive Learning
Campus, White Hart Lane,
TOTTENHAM, London N22 5QJ
Tel: 02088 897814
Head: Mr Martin Doyle

The Brook on Broadwaters
Adams Road, TOTTENHAM,
London N17 6HW
Tel: 02088 087120
Head: Ms Margaret Sumner
Category: (Coed Day 4-11)

Maintained special schools and colleges

WEST GREEN

The Vale School
Northumberland Park Community
School, Trulock Road, WEST
GREEN, London N17 0PG
Tel: 02088 016111
Head: Ms Sarah McLay
Category: PD (Coed Day 2-16)

London
BOROUGH OF HARROW
Childrens Service

Harrow SEN Team, Alexandra Avenue Health & Social Care Centre, 275
Alexandra Avenue, South Harrow, Middlesex, HA2 9DX

Tel: 020 8966 6483 Fax: 020 8966 6489 Email: senassessment.reviewservice@
harrow.gov.uk Website: www.harrow.gov.uk

EDGWARE

Woodlands School
Bransgrove Road, EDGWARE,
Middlesex HA8 6JP
Tel: 02083 812188
Head: Ms Anna Smakowska
Category: SLD PMLD
ASD (Coed 3-11)

HARROW

Alexandra School
Alexandra Avenue, HARROW,
Middlesex HA2 9DX
Tel: 02088 642739
Head: Ms Perdy Buchanan-Barrow
Category: MLD EBD
ASD (Coed 4-11)

Kingsley High School
Whittlesea Road, HARROW,
Middlesex HA3 6ND
Tel: 02084 213676
Head: Mrs Hazel Paterson
Category: SLD PMLD (Coed 11-19)

Shaftesbury High School
Headstone Lane, HARROW,
Middlesex HA3 6LE
Tel: 02084 282482
Head: Mr Paul Williams
Category: MLD EBD
ASD (Coed 11-19)

London Borough of
HAVERING
Education Authority

Havering Early Education Inclusion Team, 9th Floor, Mercury House, Mercury Gardens, Romford, Essex, RM1 3DW
Tel: 01708 431783 Email: localoffer@havering.gov.uk Website: www.havering.gov.uk

ROMFORD

Dycorts School
Settle Road, Harold Hill,
ROMFORD, Essex RM3 9YA
Tel: 01708 343649
Executive Head: Mr Gary Pocock
Category: MLD

Ravensbourne School
Neave Cres, Faringdon Ave, Harold
Hill, ROMFORD, Essex RM3 8HN
Tel: 01708 341800
Head: Ms Joanna Cliffe
Category: SLD PMLD

UPMINSTER

Corbets Tey School
Harwood Hall Lane, Corbets Tey,
UPMINSTER, Essex RM14 2YQ
Tel: 01708 225888
Head: Mrs Emma Allen
Category: MLD/SLD/
Complex Needs

London
HILLINGDON
Education

Hillingdon SEN Team, 4E/05, Civic Centre, High Street, Uxbridge, Middlesex, UB8 1UW
Tel: 01895 250244 Fax: 01895 250878 Email: cmoses@hillingdon.gov.uk Website: www.hillingdon.gov.uk

HAYES

Hedgewood Special School
Weymouth Road, HAYES, Middlesex UB4 8NF
Tel: 02088 456756
Head: Mr John Goddard
Category: MLD ASD Complex moderate learning needs (Coed 5-11)

ICKENHAM

Pentland Field School
Pentland Way, ICKENHAM, Middlesex UB10 8TS
Tel: 01895 609120
Head: Audrey Pantelis
Category: MLD SLD (Coed 4-19)

PINNER

Grangewood School
Fore Street, Eastcote, PINNER, Middlesex HA5 2JQ
Tel: 01895 676401
Head: Ms Karen Clark
Category: SLD PMLD AUT (Coed 3-11)

UXBRIDGE

Meadow High School
Royal Lane, Hillingdon, UXBRIDGE, Middlesex UB8 3QU
Tel: 01895 443310
Head: Mr Ross McDonald
Category: CLD ASD Complex moderate learning needs (Coed 11-19)

London
HOUNSLOW
Children's Services and Lifelong Learning

Hounslow SEN Team, Civic Centre, Lampton Road, Hounslow, TW3 4DN
Tel: 02085 832672 Email: sen@hounslow.gov.uk Website: www.hounslow.gov.uk

BEDFONT

Marjory Kinnon School
Hatton Road, BEDFONT, London TW14 9QZ
Tel: 02088 902032
Head: Ms Denise Morton
Category: MLD AUT (5-16)

CRANFORD

The Cedars Primary School
High Street, CRANFORD, London TW5 9RU
Tel: 02082 300015
Head: Mrs Lesley Julian
Category: EBD (Primary)

HANWORTH

The Lindon Bennett School
Main Street, HANWORTH, London TW13 6ST
Tel: 02088 980479
Head: Ms Clare Longhurst
Category: SLD (Primary)

ISLEWORTH

Oaklands School
Woodlands Road, ISLEWORTH, London TW7 6JZ
Tel: 02085 603569
Head: Ms Anne Clinton
Category: SLD (Secondary)

London
ISLINGTON
Special Educational Needs team

Islington SEN Team, First Floor, 222 Upper Street, London, N1 1XR
Tel: 0-13: 020 7527 5518; 14-25: 020 7527 4860 Email: sen@islington.gov.uk Website: www.islington.gov.uk

LONDON

Richard Cloudesley Primary School
Golden Lane Campus, 101 Whitecross Street, LONDON EC1Y 8JA
Tel: 020 7786 4800
Head: Mr Sean McDonald
Category: PD (Coed 2-11)

Richard Cloudesley Secondary School
Tudor Rose Building, 1 Prebend Street, LONDON N1 8RE
Tel: 020 7704 8127
Head: Mr Sean McDonald
Category: PD (Coed 11-19)

Samuel Rhodes Primary School
Montem Community Campus, Hornsey Road, LONDON N7 7QT
Tel: 020 7281 5114
Head: Ms Julie Keylock
Category: MLD ASD BESD (Coed 5-11)

Samuel Rhodes Secondary School
11 Highbury New Park, LONDON N5 2EG
Tel: 020 7704 7490
Head: Ms Julie Keylock
Category: MLD ASD BESD (Coed 11-18)

The Bridge Primary School
251 Hungerford Road,
LONDON N7 9LD
Tel: 020 7619 1000
Head: Ms Penny Barratt
Category: ASD SLD
PMLD (Coed 2-11)

The Bridge Secondary School
28 Carleton Road, LONDON N7 0EQ
Tel: 020 7715 0320
Head: Ms Penny Barratt
Category: ASD SLD
PMLD (Coed 11-19)

London

ROYAL BOROUGH OF KINGSTON UPON THAMES

Education Authority

Richmond & Kingston SENDIASS, Moor Lane Centre, Chessington Kingston upon Thames, Surrey, KT9 2AA
Tel: 020 8831 6179 Email: richmondkingston@kids.org.uk Website: www.kingston.gov.uk

CHESSINGTON

St Philip's School & Post 16
Harrow Close, Leatherhead Road,
CHESSINGTON, Surrey KT9 2HR
Tel: 02083 972672
Head: Mrs Jude Bowen
Category: MLD SLD ASD (11-19)

KINGSTON UPON THAMES

Bedelsford School
Grange Road, KINGSTON UPON
THAMES, Surrey KT1 2QZ
Tel: 02085 469838
Head: Ms Julia James
Category: PD PMLD MSI CLD (2-19)

SURBITON

Dysart School
190 Ewell Road, SURBITON,
Surrey KT6 6HL
Tel: 02084 122600
Head: Ms Leigh Edser
Category: SLD ASD PMLD (5-19)

London

LAMBETH

Children & Young People's Service

Lambeth SEN Team, 10th Floor, International House, Canterbury Crescent, Brixton London, SW9 7QE
Email: sendsupport@lambeth.gov.uk Website: www.lambeth.gov.uk

RUSKIN PARK

The Michael Tippet School
Heron Road, RUSKIN PARK,
London SE24 0HZ
Tel: 02073 265898
Head: Ms Marilyn Ross
Category: CLD AUT PD
SLD PMLD (Coed 11-18)

STREATHAM

The Livity School
Adare walk, STREATHAM,
London SW16 2PW
Tel: 02087 691009
Acting Head: Ms Carol Argent
Category: SLD PMLD
ASD (Coed 2-11)

WEST NORWOOD

Elm Court School
96 Elm Park, WEST NORWOOD,
London SW2 2EF
Tel: 02086 743412
Head: Ms Joanna Tarrant
Category: SEBN SLCN (Coed 6-16)

STOCKWELL

Lansdowne School
Argyll Close, Dalyell Road,
STOCKWELL, London SW9 9QL
Tel: 02077 373713
Head: Ms Linda Adams
Category: MLD SEBD ASD
CLD SLD (Coed 11-15)

WEST DULWICH

Turney School
Turney Road, WEST DULWICH,
London SE21 8LX
Tel: 02086 707220
Head: Ms Linda Adams
Category: MLD SLD CLD
ASD (Coed 5-10)

London

LEWISHAM

Children & Young People

Lewisham SEN Team, Kaleidoscope Child Development Centre, 32 Rushey Green, London, SE6 4JF
Tel: 02030 491475 Email: sen@lewisham.gov.uk Website: www.lewisham.gov.uk

BROMLEY

Drumbeat School
Roundtable Road, Downham,
BROMLEY, Kent BR1 5LE
Tel: 02086 989738
Head: Dr Vivan Hinchcliffe
Category: ASD (5-19)

DOWNHAM

New Woodlands School
49 Shroffold Road,
DOWNHAM, Kent BR1 5PD
Tel: 02086 952380
Head: Mr Duncan Harper
Category: BESD (Coed 5-14)

LONDON

Abbey Manor College
40 Falmouth Close, Lee,
LONDON SE12 8PJ
Tel: 02082 977060
Head: Dr Liz Jones
Category: BESD (Coed 11-19)

Brent Knoll School
Mayow Road, Forest Hill,
LONDON SE23 2XH
Tel: 02086 991047
Head: Mr Jonathan Sharpe
Category: AUT ASP SLCN
Emotionally Vulnerable (Coed 4-16)

Greenvale School
Waters Road, LONDON SE6 1UF
Tel: 02084 650740
Head: Ms Lynne Haines
Category: SLD PMLD (Coed 11-19)

Watergate School
Lushington Road, Bellingham,
LONDON SE6 3WG
Tel: 02086 956555
Head: ¡ine Nì Ruairc
Category: SLD PMLD (Coed 3-11)

London

MERTON

Department of Children, Schools and Families

Merton SENDIS, 1st Floor, Civic Centre, London Road, Morden, Surrey, SM4 5DX
Tel: 02085 454810 Email: sen@merton.gov.uk Website: www.merton.gov.uk

MITCHAM

Cricket Green School
Lower Green West, MITCHAM,
Surrey CR4 3AF
Tel: 02086 401177
Head: Mrs Celia Dawson
Category: CLD (Coed 5-19)

Melrose School
Church Road, MITCHAM,
Surrey CR4 3BE
Tel: 02086 462620
Head: Mr Steve Childs
Category: SEBD (Coed 11-16)

MORDEN

Perseid School
Bordesley Road, MORDEN,
Surrey SM4 5LT
Tel: 02086 489737
Head: Mrs Tina Harvey
Category: PMLD (Coed 3-19)

London

NEWHAM

Local Authority

Newham SEN Team, Newham Dockside, 1st Floor, East Wing, 1000 Dockside Road London, E16 2QU
Tel: 02084 302000 Website: www.newham.gov.uk

Maintained special schools and colleges

BECKTON

Eleanor Smith KS3 Annexe (Secondary)
90a Lawson Close, BECKTON, London E16 3LU
Tel: 020 7511 3222
Head Teacher: Mr Graham Smith
Category: SEBD (11-16)

PLAISTOW

Eleanor Smith School (Primary)
North Street, PLAISTOW, London E13 9HN
Tel: 020 8471 0018
Head Teacher: Mr Graham Smith
Category: SEBD (5-10)

STRATFORD

John F Kennedy School
Pitchford Street, STRATFORD, London E15 4RZ
Tel: 020 8534 8544
Executive Head Teacher: Ms Diane Rochford
Category: SLD PMLD ASD Complex medical needs (Coed 2-19)

London
REDBRIDGE
Education Authority

Redbridge SEN Team, Lynton House, 255-259 High Road, Ilford, Essex, IG1 1NN
Tel: 02085 545000 Email: customer.cc@redbridge.gov.uk Website: www.redbridge.gov.uk

GOODMAYES

Newbridge School - Barley Lane Campus
258 Barley Lane, GOODMAYES, Essex IG3 8XS
Tel: 02085 991768
Head: Mrs L Parr
Category: SLD PMLD ASD Complex medical needs (11-19)

HAINAULT

New Rush Hall School
Fencepiece Road, HAINAULT, Essex IG6 2LB
Tel: 02085 013951
Head: Mr J V d'Abbro OBE
Category: SEMH (5-15)

ROMFORD

Little Heath Foundation School
Hainault Road, Little Heath, ROMFORD, Essex RM6 5RX
Tel: 02085 994864
Head: Mr J Brownlie
Category: MLD Learning difficulties & complex needs (11-19)

Newbridge School - Gresham Drive Campus
161 Gresham Drive, Chadwell Heath, ROMFORD, Essex RM6 4TR
Tel: 02085 907272
Head: Mrs L Parr
Category: SLD PMLD ASD Complex medical needs (2-11)

WOODFORD GREEN

Hatton School
Roding Lane South, WOODFORD GREEN, Essex IG8 8EU
Tel: 02085 514131
Head: Mrs Sue Blows
Category: AUT SP&LD (3-11)

London
RICHMOND UPON THAMES
Parent Partnership Service

Richmond SEN Team, Parent Partnership Service, Croft Centre, Windham Road, Richmond, Middlesex, TW9 2HP
Tel: 020 8891 7541 Website: www.richmond.gov.uk

HAMPTON

Clarendon School
Hanworth Road, HAMPTON, Surrey TW12 3DH
Tel: 02089 791165
Head: Mr John Kipps
Category: MLD (7-16) (offsite EBD 7-11)

RICHMOND

Strathmore School
Meadlands Drive, Petersham, RICHMOND, Surrey TW10 7ED
Tel: 02089 480047
Head: Mr Ivan Pryce
Category: SLD PMLD (7-19)

London
SOUTHWARK
Council

Southwark SEN Team, PO Box 64529, London, SE1P 5LX
Tel: 02075 254278 Email: sen@southwark.gov.uk Website: www.southwark.gov.uk

BERMONDSEY

Beormund Primary School
Crosby Row, Long Lane,
BERMONDSEY SE1 3PS
Tel: 02075 259027
Head: Mr Andrew Henderson
Category: EBD (Boys 5-11)

Cherry Garden School
Macks Road, BERMONDSEY
SE16 3XU
Tel: 02072 374050
Head: Ms Teresa Neary
Category: SCLD (Coed 2-11)

Spa School
Monnow Road,
BERMONDSEY SE1 5RN
Tel: 02072 373714
Head: Mr Simon Eccles
Category: MLD AUT ASP
SLD SCD (Coed 11-19)

PECKHAM

Highshore Secondary School
Bellenden Road,
PECKHAM SE15 5BB
Tel: 02076 397211
Head: Ms Christine Wood
Category: DYS PD SLCN EBD
Complex needs (Coed 11-16)

Newlands School
Stuart Road, PECKHAM SE15 3AZ
Tel: 02076 392541
Head: Ms Debbie Lipkin
Category: SEBD (Boys 11-16)

Tuke Secondary School
Daniels Gardens,
PECKHAM SE15 6ER
Tel: 02076 395584
Head: Ms Heidi Tully
Category: SLD PMLD
ASD (Coed 11-19)

London
SUTTON
Local Offer

Sutton SEN Team, Civic Offices, St Nicholas Way, Sutton, Surrey, SM5 3AL
Tel: 02087 706000 Email: familyinfo@sutton.gov.uk Website: www.sutton.gov.uk

WALLINGTON

Sherwood Park School
Streeters Lane, WALLINGTON,
Surrey SM6 7NP
Tel: 02087 739930
Head: Mrs Ann Nanasi
Category: SLD PMLD (Coed 2-19)

London
TOWER HAMLETS
Education Authority

Tower Hamlets SEN Team, 5th Floor, Mulberry Place, 5 Clove Crescent, London, E14 2BG
Tel: 02073 644880 Email: sen@towerhamlets.gov.uk Website: www.towerhamlets.gov.uk

BOW

Cherry Trees School
3 Campbell Road, BOW,
London E3 4EA
Tel: 02089 834344
Head: Mr Stuart Walker
Category: SEBD (Boys Day 5-11)

Phoenix School
49 Bow Road, BOW, London E3 2AD
Tel: 02089 804740
Head: Mr Stewart Harris
Category: ASD (Coed Day 3-19)

BROMLEY-BY-BOW

Ian Mikardo High School
60 William Guy Gardens,
Talwin Street, BROMLEY-BY-
BOW, London E3 3LF
Tel: 02089 812413
Head: Ms Claire Lillis
Category: SEBD (Boys Day 11-16)

LIMEHOUSE

Stephen Hawking School
2 Brunton Place, LIMEHOUSE,
London E14 7LL
Tel: 02074 239848
Head: Dr Matthew Rayner
Category: PMLD (Coed Day 2-11)

MILE END

Beatrice Tate School
41 Southern Grove, MILE
END, London E3 4PX
Tel: 02089 833760
Head: Mr Alan Black
Category: PMLD SLD
(Coed Day 11-19)

SEAFORD (East Sussex)

Bowden House School
Firle Road, SEAFORD (East
Sussex) BN25 2JB
Tel: 01323 893138
Head: Mr Gerry Crook
Category: BESD (Boys
Boarding 9-16)

London
WALTHAM FOREST
Children and Young People Services

Waltham Forest SEN Team, Wood Street Health Centre, 6 Linford Road, Walthamstow London, E17 3LA
Tel: 020 8496 6503/6505 Email: senteam@walthamforest.gov.uk Website: www.walthamforest.gov.uk

HALE END

Joseph Clarke School
Vincent Road, Highams Park,
HALE END, London E4 9PP
Tel: 02085 234833
Head: Ms Maureen Duncan
Category: VIS Complex
needs (Coed 2-18)

LEYTON

Belmont Park School
101 Leyton Green Road,
LEYTON, London E10 6DB
Tel: 02085 560006
Head: Mr Bruce Roberts
Category: Challenging
behaviour (Coed 11-16)

WALTHAM FOREST

Whitefield School & Centre
Macdonald Road, WALTHAM
FOREST, London E17 4AZ
Tel: 02085 313426
Executive Principal: Ms
Elaine Colquhoun
Category: LD MSI SP&LD
(Coed 2-19)

London
WANDSWORTH
Children's Services

Wandsworth SEN Team, The Town Hall, High Street, Wandsworth London, SW18 3LL
Tel: 02088 718061 Email: cssnas@wandsworth.gov.uk Website: www.wandsworth.gov.uk

BALHAM

Oak Lodge School
101 Nightingale Lane, BALHAM,
London SW12 8NA
Tel: 02086 733453
Head: Ms Shanee Buxton
Category: D (Coed, Day/
boarding 11-19)

BROADSTAIRS

Bradstow School
Dumpton Park Drive,
BROADSTAIRS, Kent CT10 1BY
Tel: 01843 862123
Head: Ms Sarah Dunn
Category: PD AUT Challenging
behaviour (Coed 5-19)

EARLSFIELD

Garratt Park School
Waldron Road, EARLSFIELD,
London SW18 3BT
Tel: 02089 465769
Head: Mrs Irene Parks
Category: MLD SP&LD (Coed 11-18)

PUTNEY

Paddock Primary School
St Margaret's Crescent,
PUTNEY, London SW15 6HL
Tel: 02087 885648
Head: Ms Sarah Santos
Category: ASD MLD
SLD (Coed 3-11)

ROEHAMPTON

Greenmead School
St Margaret's Crescent,
ROEHAMPTON, London SW15 6HL
Tel: 02087 891466
Head: Mrs Lucy Wijsveld
Category: PD PMLD (Coed 3-11)

Paddock Secondary School
Priory Lane, ROEHAMPTON,
London SW15 5RT
Tel: 02088 781521
Head: Ms Peggy Walpole
Category: SCLD ASD with
SLD (Coed 11-19)

SOUTHFIELDS

Linden Lodge School
61 Princes Way, SOUTHFIELDS,
London SW19 6JB
Tel: 02087 880107
Head: Mr Roger Legate
Category: VIS PMLD MSI (Coed 3-1

TOOTING

Nightingale School
Beechcroft Road, TOOTING,
London SW17 7DF
Tel: 02088 749096
Head: Ms Alina Page
Category: BESD (Boys 11-19)

London

CITY OF WESTMINSTER
Children's Service Authority

Westminster SEN Team, The Town Hall, 2nd Floor, Green Zone, Hornton Street London, W8 7NX
Tel: 02073 613311 Website: www.westminster.gov.uk

LONDON

College Park School
Garway Road, LONDON W2 4PH
Tel: 020 7221 3454
Head: Ms Olivia Meyrick
Category: MLD (Coed 5-19)

Queen Elizabeth II Jubilee School
Kennet Road, LONDON W9 3LG
Tel: 020 7641 5825
Head: Mr Scott Pickard
Category: SLD (Coed 5-19)

LUTON
Information, Advice & Support Service

Luton SENDIAS, Futures House, The Moakes, Luton, LU3 3QB
Tel: 01525 719754 Email: parentpartnership@luton.gov.uk Website: www.luton.gov.uk

LUTON

Lady Zia Werner School
Ashcroft Road, LUTON,
Bedfordshire LU2 9AY
Tel: 01582 728705
Head: Mrs Diane May
Category: SLD PMLD (Yr 1-6 & Early Years)

Richmond Hill School
Sunridge Avenue, LUTON,
Bedfordshire LU2 7JL
Tel: 01582 721019
Head: Mrs Jill Miller
Category: SLD PMLD (Primary Yr 1-6)

Woodlands Secondary School
Northwell Drive, LUTON,
Bedfordshire LU3 3SP
Tel: 01582 572880
Head: Mrs Debbie Foolkes
Category: SLD PMLD (11-19)

Greater Manchester

BOLTON
Children's Services Offices

Bolton Inclusion & Statutory Assessment, Paderborn House, 16 Howell Croft North, Bolton, BL1 1AU
Tel: 01204 338612 Email: ea.sen@bolton.gov.uk Website: www.bolton.gov.uk

BOLTON

Firwood School
Stitch Mi Lane, BOLTON BL2 4HU
Tel: 01204 333044
Head: Mrs Sally McFarlane
Category: SLD PMLD ASD (Coed 11-19)

Ladywood School
Masefield Road, Little
Lever, BOLTON BL3 1NG
Tel: 01204 333400
Head: Mrs Sally McFarlane
Category: MLD with Complex
needs incl ASD PD MSI (Coed 4-11)

Rumworth School
Armadale Road, Ladybridge,
BOLTON BL3 4TP
Tel: 01204 333600
Head: Mr Gary Johnson
Category: MLD with Complex
needs incl ASD PD MSI (Coed 11-19)

Thomasson Memorial School
Devonshire Road, BOLTON BL1 4PJ
Tel: 01204 333118
Head: Mr Bill Wilson
Category: D HI (Coed 4-11)

FARNWORTH

Green Fold School
Highfield Road,
FARNWORTH BL4 0RA
Tel: 01204 335883
Head: Mr Andrew Feeley
Category: SLD ASD
PMLD (Coed 4-11)

Maintained special schools and colleges

HORWICH

Lever Park School
Stocks Park Drive,
HORWICH BL6 6DE
Tel: 01204 332666
Head: Mr Colin Roscoe
Category: SEBD (Coed 11-16)

Greater Manchester

BURY

Children's Services

Bury SEN Team, Seedfield Centre, Parkinson Street, Bury, Lancashire, BL9 6NY
Tel: 01612 535969 Email: senteam@bury.gov.uk Website: www.bury.gov.uk

BURY

Elms Bank Specialist Arts College
Ripon Avenue, Whitefield,
BURY M45 8PJ
Tel: 01617 661597
Head: Mrs Elaine Parkinson
Category: LD (Coed 11-19)

Millwood Primary School
School Street, Radcliffe,
BURY M26 3BW
Tel: 01617 242266
Head: Ms Helen Chadwick
Category: SLD PMLD ASD AUT
Complex needs (Coed 2-11)

Primary PRU - The Ark
The Pupil Learning Centre,
Whitefield, BURY M45 8NH
Tel: 01617 963259
Head: Ms Julie Hart
Category: (Coed 5-11)

PRESTWICH

Cloughside College (Hospital Special School)
Bury New Road,
PRESTWICH M25 3BL
Tel: 01617 724625
Head: Ms Farzana Shah
Category: HS (Coed 11-19)

RAMSBOTTOM

Secondary PRU - Pupil Learning Centre (BSPRU)
New Summerseat House,
Summerseat Lane,
RAMSBOTTOM BL0 9UD
Tel: 01204 885275
Head: Mr Thomas Gledhill
Category: (Coed 9-16)

Greater Manchester

MANCHESTER

City Council

Manchester SEN Team, Children's Services, 1st Floor, Universal Square,
Devonshire Street North Manchester, Lancashire, M12 6JH
Tel: 01612 457459 Fax: 01612 747084 Email: sen@manchester.gov.uk Website: www.manchester.gov.uk

CONGLETON

Buglawton Hall
Buxton Road, CONGLETON,
Cheshire CW12 3PQ
Tel: 01260 274492
Head of Centre: Mr Jonathan Gillie
Category: SEBD
(Residential Boys 8-16)

MANCHESTER

Ashgate School
Crossacres Road, Peel
Hall, Wythenshawe,
MANCHESTER M22 5DR
Tel: 01612 196642
Headteacher: Ms Dianne
Wolstenholme
Category: SLD (5-11)

Camberwell Park
Bank House Road, Blackley,
MANCHESTER M9 8LT
Tel: 01617 401897
Headteacher: Mrs Mary Isherwood
Category: SLD (5-11)

Grange School
Matthews Lane, Longsight,
MANCHESTER M12 4GR
Tel: 01612 312590
Headteacher: Mr Keith Cox
Category: ASD CLD (4-19)

Lancasterian School
Elizabeth Springer Road, West
Didsbury, MANCHESTER M20 2XA
Tel: 01614 450123
Headteacher: Mrs Katie Cass
Category: PD (2-16)

Manchester Hospital Schools & Home Teaching Service
Third Floor School, Royal
Manchester Children's
Hospital, Oxford Road,
MANCHESTER M13 9WL
Tel: 01617 010684
Head of Centre: Mrs Sandra Hibbert
Category: HS

Meade Hill School
Chain Road, Higher Blackley,
MANCHESTER M9 6GN
Tel: 01612 343925
Head of Centre: Mr
George Campbell
Category: SEBD (11-16)

Melland High School
Gorton Education Village,
50 Wembley Road, Gorton,
MANCHESTER M18 7DT
Tel: 01612 239915
Headteacher: Ms Sue Warner
Category: SLD (11-19)

North Ridge High School
Higher Blackley Education
Village, Alworth Road,
MANCHESTER M9 0RP
Tel: 01612 343588
Headteacher: Mrs Bernice Kostick
Category: MLD (11-19)

Piper Hill High School
Firbank Road, Newall Green,
MANCHESTER M23 2YS
Tel: 01614 363009
Headteacher: Ms Linda Jones
Category: SLD (11-19)

Rodney House School
Barrass Street, Openshaw,
MANCHESTER M11 1WP
Tel: 0161 230 6854
Headteacher: Ms Nuala Finegan
Category: ASD (2-7)

Southern Cross School
Barlow Hall Road, Chorlton,
MANCHESTER M21 7JJ
Tel: 01618 812695
Head of Centre: Ms Kate Scott
Category: SEBD (11-16)

The Birches
Newholme Road, West Didsbury,
MANCHESTER M20 2XZ
Tel: 01614 488895
Headteacher: Mr Andrew Pitts
Category: SLD (5-11)

Greater Manchester

OLDHAM

Parent Partnership Service

Oldham SENDIASS, Italia House, Pass Street, Oldham, Greater Manchester, OL9 6HZ
Tel: 01616 672055 Email: iass@pointoldham.co.uk Website: www.oldham.gov.uk

CHADDERTON

**The Kingfisher Community
Special School**
Foxdenton Lane,
CHADDERTON OL9 9QR
Tel: 01617 705910
Head: Mrs Anne Redmond
Category: PMLD SLD
ASD (Coed 4-11)

OLDHAM

**New Bridge
Learning Centre**
St Martin's Road, Fitton
Hill, OLDHAM OL8 2PZ
Tel: 01618 832402
Head: Mrs Jean Warner
Category: (Coed 16-19)

New Bridge School
Roman Road, Hollinwood,
OLDHAM, Greater
Manchester OL8 3PH
Tel: 01618 832401
Head: Mrs Jane Hilldrup
Category: PMLD SLD MLD
ASD PD (Coed 11-19)

Spring Brook School
Heron Street, OLDHAM, Greater
Manchester OL8 4JD
Tel: 01617 705007
Head: Ms Rebeckah Hollingsworth
Category: BESD (Coed 4-16)

Greater Manchester

ROCHDALE

Metropolitan Borough Council

Rochdale SEN Assessment Team, Number One Riverside, Smith Street, Rochdale, OL16 1XU
Tel: 01706 925981 Email: sen@rochdale.gov.uk Website: www.rochdale.gov.uk

MIDDLETON

Newlands School
Waverley Road,
MIDDLETON M24 6JG
Tel: 01616 550220
Head: Mrs Deborah Rogers
Category: Generic Primary
Special School (Coed 3-11)

ROCHDALE

Brownhill School
Heights Lane, ROCHDALE OL12 0PZ
Tel: 03003 038384
Head: Mrs Kate Connolly
Category: EBD (Coed 7-16)

Redwood School
Hudson's Walk, ROCHDALE OL11 5EF
Tel: 01706 750815
Head: Mr Stuart Pidgeon
Category: Generic Secondary
Special School (Coed 11-19)

Springside School
Albert Royds Street,
ROCHDALE OL16 2SU
Tel: 01706 764451
Head: Ms Clare John
Category: Generic Primary
Special School (Coed 3-11)

Greater Manchester

SALFORD

Information, Advice & Support Services

Salford SENDIASS, Salford Civic Centre, Chorley Road, Swinton Salford, M27 5AW
Tel: 0161 778 0335 Email: siass@salford.gov.uk Website: www.salford.gov.uk

ECCLES

Chatsworth High School

Chatsworth Road, Ellesmere
Park, ECCLES M30 9DY
Tel: 01619 211405
Head: Mr Martin Hanbury
Category: SLD PMLD
ASD (Coed 11-19)

New Park High School

Green Lane, ECCLES M30 0RW
Tel: 01619 212000
Head: Ms Almut Bever-Warren
Category: SEBD LD (Coed 8-16)

SWINTON

Springwood Primary School

Barton Road, SWINTON M27 5LP
Tel: 01617 780022
Head: Ms Jacqui Wennington
Category: ASD MLD SLD
PMLD (Coed 2-11)

Greater Manchester

STOCKPORT

Metropolitan Borough Council

Stockport SEN Team, Town Hall, Edward Street, Stockport, SK1 3XE

Tel: 0161 474 2525 Email: sen@stockport.gov.uk Website: www.stockport.gov.uk

STOCKPORT

Castle Hill High School

The Fairway, Offerton,
STOCKPORT SK2 5DS
Tel: 01612 853925
Head: Mr John Law
Category: EBD GLD
CLD (Coed 11-16)

Heaton School

St James Road, Heaton Moor,
STOCKPORT SK4 4RE
Tel: 01614 321931
Head: Ms Jo Chambers-Shirley
Category: SLD PMLD (Coed 10-19)

Lisburne School

Half Moon Lane, Offerton,
STOCKPORT SK2 5LB
Tel: 01614 835045
Head: Ms Samantha Benson
Category: CLD (Coed 4-11)

Oakgrove School

Matlock Road, Heald Green,
STOCKPORT SK8 3BU
Tel: 01614 374956
Head: Mr Rob Metcalfe
Category: SEBD (Coed 5-11)

Valley School

Whitehaven Road, Bramhall,
STOCKPORT SK7 1EN
Tel: 01614 397343
Head: Ms Debbie Thompson
Category: PMLD ASD
SLD (Coed 2-11)

Windlehurst School

Windlehurst Road, Hawk Green,
Marple, STOCKPORT SK6 7HZ
Tel: 01614 274788
Head: Ms Lesley Abercromby
Category: EBD (Coed 11-16)

Greater Manchester

TAMESIDE

Services for Children and Young People

Tameside SENDIASS, Jubilee Gardens, Gardenfold Way, Droylsden, Tameside, M43 7XU

Tel: 0161 342 3383 Website: www.tameside.gov.uk

ASHTON-UNDER LYNE

Samuel Laycock School

Broadoak Road, ASHTON-UNDER
LYNE, Tameside OL6 8RF
Tel: 01613 441992
Head: Mrs Carol Lund
Category: MLD (Secondary)

AUDENSHAW

Hawthorns School

Sunnyside Moss Campus,
Lumb Lane, AUDENSHAW,
Tameside M34 5SF
Tel: 01613 701312
Head: Mrs Moira Thompson
Category: MLD (Primary)

DUKINFIELD

Cromwell School

Yew Tree Lane, DUKINFIELD,
Tameside SK16 5BJ
Tel: 01613 389730
Head: Mr Andrew Foord
Category: SLD PMLD
MLD (Secondary)

Oakdale School

Cheetham Hill Road, DUKINFIELD,
Tameside SK16 5LD
Tel: 01613 679299
Head: Ms Linda Lester
Category: SLD PMLD (Primary)

HATTERSLEY

Tameside E.B.D. Outreach Team

The Jet Centre, Fields Farm Road,
HATTERSLEY, Tameside SK14 3NP
Tel: 0161 367 7299
Head: Mrs H Hobday
Category: EBD

HYDE

Thomas Ashton School

Bennett Street, HYDE,
Tameside SK14 4SS
Tel: 01613 686208
Head: Mr Robin Elms
Category: BESD (Primary)

Greater Manchester
TRAFFORD
Family Information Service

Trafford SEN Team, 2nd Floor, Waterside House, Sale, Manchester, M33 72F
Tel: 01619 121053 Email: fis@trafford.gov.uk Website: www.trafford.gov.uk/localoffer

ALTRINCHAM

Brentwood School
Brentwood Avenue, Timperley, ALTRINCHAM, Cheshire WA14 1SR
Tel: 08448 429060
Head: Mrs Hilary Moon
Category: ASD SLD (Coed 11-19)

Pictor School
Grove Lane, Timperley, ALTRINCHAM, Cheshire WA15 6PH
Tel: 01619 123082
Head: Mrs Beverley Owens
Category: SLCN SPLD ASD PD MLD (Coed 2-11)

FLIXTON

Delamere School
Irlam Road, FLIXTON, Greater Manchester M41 6AP
Tel: 01617 475893
Head: Mrs Sally Burston
Category: ASD SLD (Coed 2-11)

Nexus Education Centre (Pupil Referral Unit)
Lydney Road, FLIXTON, Manchester M41 8RN
Tel: 01619 121479
Category: (Coed 5-16)

Trafford Medical Education Service (Pupil Referral Unit)
The Flixton Centre, 350 Flixton Road, FLIXTON, Manchester M41 5GW
Tel: 01619 124766

SALE

Manor High School
Manor Avenue, SALE, Cheshire M33 5JX
Tel: 01619 761553
Head: Mrs Helen Wilson
Category: ASD SEMH MLD (Coed 11-18)

STRETFORD

Longford Park School
74 Cromwell Road, STRETFORD, Greater Manchester M32 8QJ
Tel: 01619 121895
Head: Mr Andrew Taylor
Category: SEMH MLD ASD (Coed 5-11)

URMSTON

Egerton High School
Kingsway Park, URMSTON, Greater Manchester M41 7FF
Tel: 01617 497094
Head: Mr Burgess
Category: SEMH (Coed 5-16)

Greater Manchester
WIGAN
Children and Young People's Services

Wigan Access & Inclusion Team, Progress House, Westwood Park Drive, Wigan, Greater Manchester, WN3 4HH
Tel: 01942 486145 Website: www.wigan.gov.uk

ATHERTON

Rowan Tree Primary School
Green Hall Close, ATHERTON, Greater Manchester M46 9HP
Tel: 01942 883928
Head: Ms E Loftus
Category: PD CLD AUT (Coed 2-11)

WIGAN

Landgate School
Landgate Lane, Bryn, WIGAN WN4 0EP
Tel: 01942 776688
Head: Ms J Sharps
Category: AUT SP&LD (Coed 4-19)

Newbridge Learning Community School
Moss Lane, Platt Bridge, WIGAN WN2 3TL
Tel: 01942 776020
Head: Mrs E Kucharski

Oakfield High School
Long Lane, Hindley Green, WIGAN WN2 4XA
Tel: 01942 776142
Head: Mrs C Taylor
Category: MLD SLD PD SEBD (Coed 11-19)

Wigan Hope School
Kelvin Grove, Marus Bridge, WIGAN WN3 6SP
Tel: 01942 824150
Head: Mr J P R Dahlstrom
Category: ASD SLD PMLD (Coed 2-19)

Willow Grove Primary School
Willow Grove, Ashton-in-Makerfield, WIGAN WN4 8XF
Tel: 01942 727717
Head: Ms V Pearson
Category: SEBD (Coed 5-11)

MEDWAY
Children's Services

Medway SEN Team, Gun Wharf, Dock Road, Chatham, ME4 4TR
Tel: 01634 306000 Email: childrens.services@medway.gov.uk Website: www.medway.gov.uk

CHATHAM

Inspire Free School
Churchill Avenue, CHATHAM,
Kent ME5 0LB
Tel: 01634 827372
Head: Ms S McDermott
Category: SEMH (Coed 11-19)

GILLINGHAM

Danecourt School
Hotel Road, Watling Street,
GILLINGHAM, Kent ME8 6AA
Tel: 01634 232589
Head: Mr John Somers
Category: ASD SLD (Coed 4-11)

Rivermead School
Forge Lane, GILLINGHAM,
Kent ME7 1UG
Tel: 01634 338348
Head: Ms T Lovey
Category: ASD Complex
emotional needs (Coed 11-19)

STROOD

Abbey Court
Rede Court Road,
STROOD, Kent ME2 3SP
Tel: 01634 338220
Head: Ms Karen Joy
Category: SLD PMLD (Coed 4-19)

Merseyside
KNOWSLEY
Children & Family Services

Knowsley SEN Team, The Cordingley Building, Scotchbarn Lane, Prescot, Merseyside, L35 7JD
Tel: 01514 435145 Email: sen@knowsley.gov.uk Website: www.knowsley.gov.uk

HALEWOOD

Finch Woods Academy
Baileys Lane, HALEWOOD,
Merseyside L26 0TY
Tel: 01512 888930
Head: Ms Pam Kilham
Category: SEBD (Coed 6-16)

HUYTON

**Alt Bridge Secondary
Support Centre**
Wellcroft Road, HUYTON,
Merseyside L36 7TA
Tel: 01514 778310
Head: Mr Barry Kerwin
Category: MLD SPLD CLD
ASD SLD PD (Coed 11-16)

**Knowsley Central
Primary Support Centre**
Mossbrow Road, HUYTON,
Merseyside L36 7SY
Tel: 01514 778450
Head: Mrs Patricia Thomas
Category: CLD SEBD (Coed 2-11)

KIRKBY

Bluebell Park School
Cawthorne Walk, Southdene,
KIRKBY, Merseyside L32 3XP
Tel: 01514 778350
Head: Mr John Parkes
Category: PD PMLD SLD
MLD (Coed 2-19)

STOCKBRIDGE VILLAGE

Meadow Park School
Haswell Drive, STOCKBRIDGE
VILLAGE, Merseyside L28 1RX
Tel: 01514 778100
Head: Mr Mike Marshall

Merseyside

LIVERPOOL

City Council

Liverpool Children's Services (Education), Municipal Buildings, Dale Street, Liverpool, L2 2DH
Tel: 01512 333000 Email: liverpool.direct@liverpool.gov.uk Website: www.liverpool.gov.uk

LIVERPOOL

Abbot's Lea School
Beaconsfield Road, Woolton, LIVERPOOL, Merseyside L25 6EE
Tel: 01514 281161
Head: Mrs Margaret Lucas
Category: AUT (Coed 5-19)

Aigburth High School
Minehead Road, Aigburth, LIVERPOOL, Merseyside L17 6AX
Tel: 0151 4271863
Head: Mrs C Piercy
Category: CLD ASD

Bank View High School
Sherwoods Lane, Fazakerley, LIVERPOOL, Merseyside L10 1LW
Tel: 01515 253451
Head: Mr Jim Pearce
Category: CLD (Coed 11-18)

Clifford Holroyde School
Thingwall Lane, LIVERPOOL, Merseyside L14 7NX
Tel: 01512 289500
Head: Ms Elaine Dwyer
Category: EBD (Coed 7-16)

Ernest Cookson School
54 Bankfield Road, West Derby, LIVERPOOL, Merseyside L13 0BQ
Tel: 01512 201874
Head: Mr S Roberts
Category: EBD (Boys 5-16)

Hope School
Naylorsfield Drive, LIVERPOOL, Merseyside L27 0YD
Tel: 01514 984055
Head: Mr Rohit Naik
Category: EBD (Boys 5-16)

Millstead Special Needs Primary
Old Mill Lane, Wavertree, LIVERPOOL, Merseyside L15 8LW
Tel: 01517 220974
Head: Ms Michelle Beard
Category: SLD (Coed 2-11)

Palmerston School
Beaconsfield Road, Woolton, LIVERPOOL, Merseyside L25 6EE
Tel: 01514 282128
Head: Mrs Alison Burbage
Category: SLD (Coed 11-19)

Princes Primary School
Selborne Street, LIVERPOOL, Merseyside L8 1YQ
Tel: 01517 092602
Head: Mrs Kathy Brent
Category: SLD (Coed 2-11)

Redbridge High School
Sherwoods Lane, Fazakerley, LIVERPOOL, Merseyside L10 1LW
Tel: 01515 255733
Head: Mr Paul Cronin
Category: SLD (Coed 11-19)

Sandfield Park School
Sandfield Walk, West Derby, LIVERPOOL, Merseyside L12 1LH
Tel: 01512 280324
Head: Mr J M Hudson
Category: PD HS (Coed 11-19)

Woolton High School
Woolton Hill Road, Woolton, LIVERPOOL, Merseyside L25 6JA
Tel: 01514 284071
Head: Mr M Christian
Category: (Coed 11-16)

Merseyside

SEFTON

Children, Schools & Families

Sefton SEN Team, Town Hall, Bootle, Merseyside, L20 7AE
Tel: 01519 343250 Email: special.needs@sefton.gov.uk Website: www.sefton.gov.uk

BOOTLE

Rowan Park School
Sterrix Lane, BOOTLE, Merseyside L21 0DB
Tel: 01512 224894
Head: Ms K Lynskey
Category: SLD (Coed 3-18)

CROSBY

Crosby High School
De Villiers Avenue, CROSBY, Merseyside L23 2TH
Tel: 01519 243671
Head: Ms T Oxton-Grant
Category: MLD (Coed 11-16)

Newfield School
Edge Lane, CROSBY, Merseyside L23 4TG
Tel: 01519 342991
Head: Mrs J Starkey
Category: BESD (Coed 5-17)

SOUTHPORT

Merefield School
Westminster Drive, SOUTHPORT, Merseyside PR8 2QZ
Tel: 01704 577163
Head: Mrs S Clare
Category: SLD (Coed 3-16)

Presfield High School and Specialist College
Preston New Road, SOUTHPORT, Merseyside PR9 8PA
Tel: 01704 227831
Head: Ms N Zielonka
Category: ASD (Coed 11-16)

Merseyside

ST HELENS

Community, Education & Leisure Services Department

St Helens Additional Needs Team, Atlas House, Corporation Street, St Helens, Merseyside, WA9 1LD
Tel: 01744 671104 Website: www.sthelens.gov.uk

NEWTON-LE-WILLOWS

Penkford School
Wharf Road, NEWTON-LE-WILLOWS, Merseyside WA12 9XZ
Tel: 01744 678745
Head: Ms Julie Johnson
Category: SEBD (9-16)

ST HELENS

Lansbury Bridge School
Lansbury Avenue, Parr, ST HELENS, Merseyside WA9 1TB
Tel: 01744 678579
Head: Mrs Jane Grecic
Category: CLD PD MLD ASD (Coed 3-16)

Mill Green School
Lansbury Avenue, Parr, ST HELENS, Merseyside WA9 1BU
Tel: 01744 678760
Head: Mr Colin Myers
Category: SLD CLD PMLD ASD (Coed 14-19)

Merseyside

WIRRAL

Local Offer

Wirral SEN Team, Community Action Wirral, St James Centre, 344 Laird Street, Birkenhead Wirral, CH41 7AL
Tel: 0151 353 9700 (Ext:8) Email: info@localofferwirral.org Website: www.wirral.gov.uk

BIRKENHEAD

Kilgarth School
Cavendish Street, BIRKENHEAD, Merseyside CH41 8BA
Tel: 01516 528071
Head: Mr Steven Baker
Category: EBD ADHD (Boys 11-16)

PRENTON

The Observatory School
Bidston Village Road, Bidston, PRENTON, Merseyside CH43 7QT
Tel: 01516 527093
Head: Mrs Elaine Idris
Category: SEBD LD (Coed 11-16)

THINGWALL

Stanley School
Greenbank Drive, Pensby, THINGWALL, Merseyside CH61 5UE
Tel: 01513 426741
Head: Mr Anthony Roberts
Category: SLD AUT CLD (Coed 2-11)

WALLASEY

Clare Mount Specialist Sports College
Fender Lane, Moreton, WALLASEY, Merseyside CH46 9PA
Tel: 01516 069440
Head: Mrs Kim Webster
Category: MLD (Coed 11-19)

Elleray Park School
Elleray Park Road, WALLASEY, Merseyside CH45 0LH
Tel: 01516 393594
Acting Head: Mr Col Hughes
Category: CLD SLD PD AUT PMLD (Coed 2-11)

Foxfield School
Douglas Drive, Moreton, WALLASEY, Merseyside CH46 6BT
Tel: 01516 778555
Head: Mr Andre Baird
Category: ADHD SLD ASD PD (Coed 11-19)

Orrets Meadow School
Chapelhill Road, Moreton, WALLASEY, Merseyside CH46 9QQ
Tel: 01516 788070
Head: Mrs Carolyn Duncan
Category: SPLD SP&LD LD AUT ASD EBD (Coed 7-11)

WIRRAL

Gilbrook School
Glebe Hey Road, Woodchurch, WIRRAL, Merseyside CH49 8HE
Tel: 01515 223900
Head: Mrs Kirsten Brown
Category: EBD DYS (Coed 4-12)

Hayfield School
Manor Drive, Upton, WIRRAL, Merseyside CH49 4LN
Tel: 01516 779303
Head: Mr Lee Comber
Category: MLD CLD ASD (Coed 4-11)

Meadowside School
Pool Lane, Woodchurch, WIRRAL, Merseyside CH49 5LA
Tel: 01516 787711
Head: Ms Paula Wareing
Category: CLD SLD (Coed 11-19)

The Lyndale School
Lyndale Avenue, Eastham, WIRRAL, Merseyside CH62 8DE
Tel: 01513 273682
Head: Mrs Kim Owen
Category: CLD SLD MLD PMLD (Coed 2-11)

Wirral Hospitals School
Joseph Paxton Campus, 157 Park Road North, Claughton, WIRRAL, Merseyside CH41 0EZ
Tel: 01514 887680
Head: Mr Derek Kitchin
Category: HS (Coed 2-19)

MIDDLESBROUGH
Education and Learning

Middlesbrough SEN Team, Civic Centre, P.O. Box 505, Middlesbrough, TS1 9FZ
Tel: 01642 728677 Email: sen@middlesbrough.gov.uk Website: www.middlesbrough.gov.uk

MIDDLESBROUGH

Beverley School

Saltersgill Avenue,
MIDDLESBROUGH,
Cleveland TS4 3JS
Tel: 01642 811350
Head: Ms Joanne Smith
Category: AUT (Coed 3-19)

Holmwood School

Saltersgill Avenue, Easterside,
MIDDLESBROUGH,
Cleveland TS4 3PT
Tel: 01642 819157
Head: Mrs Jan Mather
Category: EBD (Coed 4-11)

Priory Woods School

Tothill Avenue, Netherfields,
MIDDLESBROUGH,
Cleveland TS3 0RH
Tel: 01642 770540
Head: Ms Janis French
Category: SLD PMLD (Coed 4-19)

MILTON KEYNES
Children and Families Service

Milton Keynes SEND Team, Saxon Court, 502 Avebury Boulevard, Milton Keynes, MK9 3HS
Tel: 01908 253414 Email: sen@milton-keynes.gov.uk Website: www.milton-keynes.gov.uk

MILTON KEYNES

Romans Field School

Shenley Road, Bletchley, MILTON
KEYNES, Buckinghamshire MK3 7AW
Tel: 01908 376011
Head: Dr Diane Elleman
Category: SEBD (Coed
Day/boarding 5-12)

Slated Row School

Old Wolverton Road,
Wolverton, MILTON KEYNES,
Buckinghamshire MK12 5NJ
Tel: 01908 316017
Head: Mr Jonathan Budd
Category: MLD Complex
needs (Coed Day 4-19)

The Redway School

Farmborough, Netherfield, MILTON
KEYNES, Buckinghamshire MK6 4HG
Tel: 01908 206400
Head: Ms Ruth Sylvester
Category: PMLD CLD
SCD (Coed Day 2-19)

The Walnuts School

Admiral Drive, Hazeley, MILTON
KEYNES, Buckinghamshire MK8 0PU
Tel: 01908 563885
Head: Ms Jo Yates
Category: ASD SCD (Coed
Day/boarding 4-19)

White Spire School

Rickley Lane, Bletchley, MILTON
KEYNES, Buckinghamshire MK3 6EW
Tel: 01908 373266
Head: Mr Finlay Douglas
Category: MLD (Coed
Day & boarding 5-19)

NORFOLK
Children's Services

Norfolk SEN Team, County Hall, Martineau Lane, Norwich, Norfolk, NR1 2DH
Tel: 03448 008020 Email: send@norfolk.gov.uk Website: www.norfolk.gov.uk

ATTLEBOROUGH

Chapel Road School
Chapel Road, ATTLEBOROUGH,
Norfolk NR17 2DS
Tel: 01953 453116
Head: Mrs Karin Heap
Category: SLD ASD
PMLD (Coed 3-19)

CROMER

Sidestrand Hall School
Cromer Road, Sidestrand,
CROMER, Norfolk NR27 0NH
Tel: 01263 578144
Head: Mrs Sarah Young
Category: MLD (Coed 3-19)

DEREHAM

Fred Nicholson School
Westfield Road, DEREHAM,
Norfolk NR19 1JB
Tel: 01362 693915
Head: Mrs Alison Kahn
Category: MLD SEBD SLD
ASD (Coed 3-19)

GREAT YARMOUTH

John Grant School
St George's Drive, Caister-
on-Sea, GREAT YARMOUTH,
Norfolk NR30 5QW
Tel: 01493 720158
Head: Mrs Pamela Ashworth
Category: SLD ASD
PMLD (Coed 3-19)

KING'S LYNN

Churchill Park School
Winston Churchill Drive, KING'S
LYNN, Norfolk PE30 4RP
Tel: 01553 763679
Head: Mr Paul Donkersloot
Category: Complex
Needs (Day 2-19)

NORWICH

Hall School
St Faith's Road, Old Catton,
NORWICH, Norfolk NR6 7AD
Tel: 01603 466467
Head: Mr Keith McKenzie
Category: CLD (Coed 3-19)

Harford Manor School
43 Ipswich Road, NORWICH,
Norfolk NR2 2LN
Tel: 01603 451809
Head: Mr Paul Eteson
Category: ASD PMLD
SLD (Coed 3-19)

The Clare School
South Park Avenue, NORWICH,
Norfolk NR4 7AU
Tel: 01603 454199
Head: Mr Fyfe Johnston
Category: PH MSI LD Complex
medical needs (Coed 3-19)

The Parkside School
College Road, NORWICH,
Norfolk NR2 3JA
Tel: 01603 441126
Head: Ms Susan Booth
Category: SLD AUT EBD
MLD MSI PD (Coed 3-19)

SHERINGHAM

Woodfields School
Holt Road, SHERINGHAM,
Norfolk NR26 8ND
Tel: 01263 820520
Head: Mr James Stanbrook
Category: CLD (Coed 3-19)

NORTHAMPTONSHIRE
County Council

Northamptonshire CYPS, John Dryden House, 8-10 The Lakes, Northampton, NN4 7YD
Tel: 01001 261000 Email: education@northamptonshire.gov.uk Website: www.northamptonshire.gov.uk

KETTERING

Isebrook SEN Cognition & Learning College
Eastleigh Road, KETTERING,
Northamptonshire NN15 6PT
Tel: 01536 500030
Head: Mrs Denise Williams
Category: MLD ASD SLD
SP&LD PH (11-19)

Wren Spinney Community Special School
Westover Road, KETTERING,
Northamptonshire NN15 7LB
Tel: 01536 481939
Head: Mr Simon Bishop
Category: SLD PMLD ASD MSI (11-19)

NORTHAMPTON

Fairfields School
Trinity Avenue, NORTHAMPTON,
Northamptonshire NN2 6JN
Tel: 01604 714777
Head: Ms Karen Lewis
Category: PMLD PH
MSI SLD ASD (3-11)

Greenfields School and Sports College
Prentice Court, Lings Way,
Goldings, NORTHAMPTON,
Northamptonshire NN3 8XS
Tel: 01604 741960
Head: Mrs Lisa-Marie Atack
Category: PMLD SLD ASD MSI (11-19)

Kings Meadow School
Manning Road, Moulton
Leys, NORTHAMPTON,
Northamptonshire NN3 7AR
Tel: 01604 673730
Head: Ms Helen McCormack
Category: BESD (4-11)

Northgate School Arts College
Queens Park Parade,
NORTHAMPTON,
Northamptonshire NN2 6LR
Tel: 01604 714098
Head: Miss Sheralee Webb
& Mike Trundley
Category: MLD SLD ASD (11-19)

TIFFIELD

The Gateway School
St Johns Road, TIFFIELD,
Northamptonshire NN12 8AA
Tel: 01604 878977
Head: Mr Conor Renihan
Category: BESD (11-19)

WELLINGBOROUGH

Rowan Gate Primary School
Finedon Road, WELLINGBOROUGH
Northamptonshire NN8 4NS
Tel: 01933 304970
Head: Mrs Laura Clarke
Category: PMLD ASD (3-11)

NORTHUMBERLAND
County Council

Northumberland SENDIASS, County Hall, Morpeth, Northumberland, NE61 2EF
Tel: 01670 623555 Email: sen@northumberland.gov.uk Website: www.northumberland.gov.uk

ALNWICK

Barndale House School

Howling Lane, ALNWICK,
Northumberland NE66 1DQ
Tel: 01665 602541
Head: Mr Colin Bradshaw
Category: SLD

BERWICK UPON TWEED

The Grove Special School

Grove Gardens, Tweedmouth,
BERWICK UPON TWEED,
Northumberland TD15 2EN
Tel: 01289 306390
Head: Ms Penelope Derries
Category: SLD

BLYTH

The Dales School

Cowpen Road, BLYTH,
Northumberland NE24 4RE
Tel: 01670 352556
Head: Mr Hugh Steele
Category: MLD CLD PH EBD

CHOPPINGTON

Cleaswell Hill School

School Avenue, Guide
Post, CHOPPINGTON,
Northumberland NE62 5DJ
Tel: 01670 823182
Head: Mr Kevin Burdis
Category: MLD

CRAMLINGTON

Atkinson House School

North Terrace, Seghill,
CRAMLINGTON,
Northumberland NE23 7EB
Tel: 0191 2980838
Head: Mr Derek Cogle
Category: EBD

Cramlington Hillcrest School

East View Avenue, CRAMLINGTON,
Northumberland NE23 1DY
Tel: 01670 713632
Head: Mrs Andrea Mead
Category: MLD

HEXHAM

Hexham Priory School

Corbridge Road, HEXHAM,
Northumberland NE46 1UY
Tel: 01434 605021
Head: Mr Michael Thompson
Category: SLD

MORPETH

Collingwood School & Media Arts College

Stobhillgate, MORPETH,
Northumberland NE61 2HA
Tel: 01670 516374
Head: Mr Richard Jones
Category: MLD CLD AUT
SP&LD PH Emotionally fragile
Specific medical conditions

NOTTINGHAM
Children, Families and Cultural Services

Nottingham SEN Team, Glenbrook Management Centre, Wigman Road, Bilborough Nottingham, NG8 4PD
Tel: 01158 764300 Email: special.needs@nottinghamcity.gov.uk Website: www.nottinghamcity.gov.uk

NOTTINGHAM

Oak Field School and Specialist Sports College

Wigman Road, Bilborough,
NOTTINGHAM NG8 3HW
Tel: 01159 153265
Head: Mr David Stewart
Category: SCD ASD SPLI
(Coed Day 3-19)

Rosehill Special School

St Matthias Road, St Ann's,
NOTTINGHAM NG3 2FE
Tel: 01159 155815
Head: Mr Andy Sloane
Category: AUT (Coed Day 4-19)

Westbury School

Chingford Road, Bilborough,
NOTTINGHAM NG8 3BT
Tel: 01159 155858
Executive Head: Mr John Dyson
Category: EBD (Coed Day 7-16)

Woodlands Special School

Beechdale Road, Aspley,
NOTTINGHAM NG8 3EZ
Tel: 01159 155734
Executive Head: Mr John Dyson
Category: MLD (Coed Day 3-16)

NOTTINGHAMSHIRE
Children, Families and Cultural Services

The Personalisation Service, County Hall, Loughborough Road, West Bridgford Nottingham, Nottinghamshire, NG2 7QP
Tel: 01159 773779 Email: casework.teamleader@nottscc.gov.uk Website: www.nottinghamshire.sendlocaloffer.org.uk

ASHFIELD

Bracken Hill School
Chartwell Road, ASHFIELD,
Nottinghamshire NG17 7HZ
Tel: 01623 477268
Head: Mrs Catherine Askham
Category: (Coed Day 3-19)

GEDLING

Carlton Digby School
Digby Avenue, Mapperley,
GEDLING, Nottingham NG3 6DS
Tel: 01159 568289
Head: Ms Janet Spratt-Burch
Category: (Coed 3-19)

Derrymount School (Lower)
Churchmoor Lane, Arnold,
GEDLING, Nottingham NG5 8HN
Tel: 01159 534015
Head: Mrs Kathy McIntyre
Category: (Coed 3-13)

Derrymount School (Upper)
Sherbrook Road, Daybrook,
GEDLING, Nottingham NG5 6AT
Head: Mrs Kathy McIntyre
Category: (Coed 14-19)

MANSFIELD

Fountaindale School
Nottingham Road, MANSFIELD,
Nottinghamshire NG18 5BA
Tel: 01623 792671
Head: Mr Mark Dengel
Category: PD (Coed 3-19)

Redgate School
Somersall Street, MANSFIELD,
Nottinghamshire NG19 6EL
Tel: 01623 455944
**Acting Executive
Head:** Pauline Corfield
Category: (Coed Day 3-11)

Yeoman Park School
Park Hall Road, Mansfield
Woodhouse, MANSFIELD,
Nottinghamshire NG19 8PS
Tel: 01623 459540
**Acting Executive
Head:** Jane Cooper
Category: (Coed Day 3-19)

NEWARK

**The Newark Orchard
School (Lower)**
Appleton Gate, NEWARK,
Nottinghamshire NG24 1JR
Tel: 01636 682255
Head: Ms Margot Tyers
Category: (Coed 3-14)

**The Newark Orchard
School (Upper)**
London Road, New
Balderton, NEWARK,
Nottinghamshire NG24 3AL
Tel: 01636 682256
Head: Ms Margot Tyers
Category: (Coed 14-19)

RETFORD

St Giles Special School
North Road, RETFORD,
Nottinghamshire DN22 7XN
Tel: 01777 703683
Head: Mrs Hilary Short
Category: (Coed 3-19)

RUSHCLIFFE

Ash Lea School
Owthorpe Road, RUSHCLIFFE,
Nottinghamshire NG12 3PA
Tel: 01159 892744
Head: Mrs Dawn Wigley
Category: (Coed Day 3-19)

OXFORDSHIRE
Children, Education & Families

SEN Casework Team - Central, Knights Court, 21 Between Towns Road, Cowley Oxford, OX4 3LX
Tel: 01865 815275 Email: sen@oxfordshire.gov.uk Website: www.oxfordshire.gov.uk

BANBURY

Frank Wise School
Hornbeam Close, BANBURY,
Oxfordshire OX16 9RL
Tel: 01295 263520
Head: Mr Sean O'Sullivan
Category: SLD PMLD (Coed 2-19)

BICESTER

Bardwell School
Hendon Place, Sunderland Drive,
BICESTER, Oxfordshire OX26 4RZ
Tel: 01869 242182
Head: Mr John Riches
Category: SLD PMLD MSI
SP&LD CLD (Coed 2-19)

OXFORD

John Watson School
Littleworth Road, Wheatley,
OXFORD OX33 1NN
Tel: 01865 452725
Head: Mr Stephen Passey
Category: SLD PMLD (Coed 2-19)

Mabel Prichard School
Cuddesdon Way, OXFORD OX4 6SB
Tel: 01865 777878
Head: Mrs Jane Wallington
Category: SLD PMLD (Coed 2-19)

Northfield School
Knights Road, Blackbird
Leys, OXFORD OX4 6DQ
Tel: 01865 771703
Head: Mr Mark Blencowe
Category: BESD (Boys 11-18)

**Oxfordshire
Hospital School**
The Harlow Centre, Raymund Road,
Old Marston, OXFORD OX3 0SW
Tel: 01865 253177
Interim Headteacher: Mr
Gareth Lewis
Category: HS (Coed 3-18)

Woodeaton Manor School
Woodeaton, OXFORD OX3 9TS
Tel: 01865 558722
Head: Mrs Anne Pearce
Category: BESD (Day/residential
weekday boarding 7-18)

SONNING COMMON

**Bishopswood
Special School**
Grove Road, SONNING
COMMON, Oxfordshire RG4 9RH
Tel: 01189 724311
Head: Mrs Janet Kellett
Category: SLD PMLD (Coed 2-16)

WITNEY

Springfield School
Cedar Drive, WITNEY,
Oxfordshire OX28 1AR
Tel: 01993 703963
Head: Mrs Emma Lawley
Category: SLD (Coed 2-16)

PETERBOROUGH
SEND Partnership Service

Peterborough SEN Team, Town Hall, Bridge Street, Peterborough, PE1 1HF
Tel: 01733 863979 Email: pps@peterborough.gov.uk Website: www.peterborough.gov.uk

PETERBOROUGH

Heltwate School
North Bretton, PETERBOROUGH,
Cambridgeshire PE3 8RL
Tel: 01733 262878
Head: Mr Adam Brewster
Category: MLD SLD AUT
PD SCD (Coed 4-16)

Marshfields School
Eastern Close, Dogsthorpe,
PETERBOROUGH,
Cambridgeshire PE1 4PP
Tel: 01733 568058
Head: Mrs Janet James
Category: MLD SCD SEBD
SLD (Coed 11-19)

NeneGate School
Park Lane, Eastfield,
PETERBOROUGH,
Cambridgeshire PE1 5GZ
Tel: 01733 349438
Head: Ms Ruth O'Sullivan
Category: EBD (Coed 11-16)

Phoenix School
Clayton, Orton Goldhay,
PETERBOROUGH,
Cambridgeshire PE2 5SD
Tel: 01733 391666
Head: Mr Phil Pike
Category: SLD PMLD PD SCN
ASD MSI (Coed 2-19)

PLYMOUTH
City Council

Plymouth SEN Team, Ballard House, West Hoe Road, Plymouth, Devon, PL1 3BJ
Tel: 01752 307409 Email: senadmin@plymouth.gov.uk Website: www.plymouth.gov.uk

PLYMOUTH

**Brook Green Centre
for Learning**
Bodmin Road, Whitleigh,
PLYMOUTH, Devon PL5 4DZ
Tel: 01752 773875
Head: Ms Sara Jordan
Category: MLD BESD (11-16)

Cann Bridge School
Miller Way, Estover, PLYMOUTH,
Devon PL6 8UN
Tel: 01752 207909
Head: Mr Michael Loveman
Category: SLD (3-19)

Courtlands School
Widey Lane, Crownhill,
PLYMOUTH, Devon PL6 5JS
Tel: 01752 776848
Head: Mr Lee Earnshaw
Category: MLD BESD (4-11)

**Longcause Community
Special School**
Longcause, Plympton,
PLYMOUTH, Devon PL7 1JB
Tel: 01752 336881
Head: Mrs Anne Thorne
Category: MLD (5-17)

**Mill Ford Community
Special School**
Rochford Crescent, Ernesettle,
PLYMOUTH, Devon PL5 2PY
Tel: 01752 300270
Head: Mrs Claire Wills
Category: SLD PMLD (3-19)

Mount Tamar School
Row Lane, Higher St Budeaux,
PLYMOUTH, Devon PL5 2EF
Tel: 01752 365128
Head: Mr Brett Storry
Category: BESD (5-16)

Woodlands School
Picklecombe Drive, Off
Tamerton Foliot Road, Whitleigh,
PLYMOUTH, Devon PL6 5ES
Tel: 01752 300101
Head: Mrs Andrea Hemmens
Category: PD PMLD MSI (2-19)

BOROUGH OF POOLE
Children, Young People & Learning

Poole SEN Team, Dolphin Centre, Poole, Dorset, BH15 1SA
Tel: 01202 262277 Email: childrenyoungpeople&learning@poole.gov.uk Website: www.poole.gov.uk

POOLE

Winchelsea School
Guernsey Road, Parkstone,
POOLE, Dorset BH12 4LL
Tel: 01202 746240
Head: Ms Rachel Weldon
Category: ADHD ASD
ASP MLD (3-16)

PORTSMOUTH
Directorate of Children, Families and Learning

Portsmouth SEN Team, Floor 2 Core 1, Civic Offices, Guildhall Square Portsmouth, Hampshire, PO1 2EA
Tel: 02392 841238 Email: sen.education@portsmouthcc.gov.uk Website: www.portsmouth.gov.uk

PORTSMOUTH

Mary Rose School
Gisors Road, Southsea,
PORTSMOUTH, Hampshire PO4 8GT
Tel: 02392 852330
Executive Head: Ms Alison Beane
Category: SLDCLD PD
MLD (Coed 2-19)

Redwood Park School
Wembley Grove, Cosham,
PORTSMOUTH, Hampshire PO6 2RY
Tel: 02392 377500
Executive Head: Ms Alison Beane
Category: MLD SP&LD
ASD (Coed 11-16)

The Harbour School
Tipner Lane, PORTSMOUTH,
Hampshire PO2 8RA
Tel: 02392 665664
Head: Mr Krishna Purbhoo
Category: BESD

READING
Directorate of Education, Adult & Childrenís Services

Reading SEN Team, Civic Offices, Bridge Street, Reading, RG1 2LU
Tel: 01189 372674 Email: sen@reading.gov.uk Website: www.reading.gov.uk/servicesguide

READING

Phoenix College
40 Christchurch Road,
READING, Berkshire RG2 7AY
Tel: 01189 375524
Head: Mrs Ekie Lansdown-Bridge
Category: BESD ADHD (Coed 11-16)

**The Holy Brook
Special School**
145 Ashampstead Road,
Southcote, READING,
Berkshire RG30 3LJ
Tel: 01189 375489
Head: Mr Lee Smith

REDCAR & CLEVELAND
Information, Advice & Support Service

Redcar & Cleveland SENDIASS, Redcar Children's Centre, Kielder Close, Redcar, Middlesborough, TS10 4HS
Tel: 01642 759073 Email: sendiass@redcar-cleveland.gov.uk Website: www.redcar-cleveland.gov.uk

MIDDLESBROUGH

Pathways School

Tennyson Avenue, Grangetown,
MIDDLESBROUGH TS6 7NP
Tel: 01642 779292
Head: Mr Steve O'Gara
Category: SEBD (Coed Day 7-15)

REDCAR

Kirkleatham Hall School

Kirkleatham Village, REDCAR,
Cleveland TS10 4QR
Tel: 01642 483009
Head: Mrs Karen Robson
Category: SLD PMLD SLCN ASC
PD CLDD (Coed Day 4-19)

RUTLAND
Information Advice & Support Service

Rutland SENDIASS, Rutland Citizens Advice Bureau, 56 High Street, Oakham, Rutland, LE15 6AL
Tel: 01572 757420 Email: office@rutlandcab.org.uk Website: www.rutland.gov.uk

OAKHAM

The Parks School

Burley Road, OAKHAM,
Rutland LE15 6GY
Tel: 01572 722404
Head: Mr Steven Cox
Category: AUT MLD PMLD
SP&LD VIS SEBD (Coed 2-5)

SHROPSHIRE
Shropshire Council

Shropshire SEN Team, The Shirehall, Abbey Foregate, Shrewsbury, Shropshire, SY2 6ND
Tel: 01743 254366 Email: senteam@shropshire.gov.uk Website: www.shropshire.gov.uk

OSWESTRY

Acorns Centre

Middleton Road, OSWESTRY,
Shropshire SY11 2LF
Head: Mr Robin Wilson
Category: SEMH (Coed 9-11)

SHREWSBURY

Woodlands School

Tilley Green, Wem, SHREWSBURY,
Shropshire SY4 5PJ
Tel: 01939 232372
Head: Mr Robin Wilson
Category: SEMH (Coed 11-16)

SLOUGH
Slough Borough Council

Slough SEN Team, Slough Family Information Service (FIS), St Martins Place, 51 Bath Road Slough, Berkshire, SL1 3UF
Tel: 01753 476589 Email: fis@slough.gov.uk Website: www.slough.gov.uk

SLOUGH

Arbour Vale School

Farnham Road, SLOUGH,
Berkshire SL2 3AE
Tel: 01753 515560
Head: Mrs Debbie Richards
Category: SLD ASD
MLD (Coed 2-19)

Haybrook College/ Millside School

112 Burnham Lane, SLOUGH,
Berkshire SL1 6LZ
Tel: 01628 696077/696079
Executive Head: Ms Helen Huntley
Category: BESD (Coed 11-16)

Littledown School

Queen's Road, SLOUGH,
Berkshire SL1 3QW
Tel: 01753 521734
Head: Jo Matthews
Category: BESD (Coed 5-11)

SOMERSET
Children and Young People's Services

Somerset SEN Team, County Hall, Taunton, Somerset, TA1 4DY
Tel: 0300 123 2224 Email: somersetdirect@somerset.gov.uk Website: www.somerset.gov.uk

BRIDGWATER

Elmwood School

Hamp Avenue, BRIDGWATER,
Somerset TA6 6AW
Tel: 01278 456243
Head: Ms Elizabeth Hayward
Category: SLD MLD ASD
EBD (Coed Day 11-16)

Penrose School

Albert Street, Willow Brook,
BRIDGWATER, Somerset TA6 7ET
Tel: 01278 423660
Head: Mrs E Hayward
Category: CLD ASD SLD
(4-10 and Post-16)

FROME

Critchill School

Nunney Road, FROME,
Somerset BA11 4LB
Tel: 01373 464148
Head: Mr Mark Armstrong
Category: SLD MLD CLD
(Coed Day 4-16)

STREET

Avalon Special School

Brooks Road, STREET,
Somerset BA16 0PS
Tel: 01458 443081
Head: Mrs Alison Murkin
Category: SLD MLD PMLD
ASD (Coed Day 3-16)

TAUNTON

Selworthy School

Selworthy Road, TAUNTON,
Somerset TA2 8HD
Tel: 01823 284970
Head: Mr Mark Ruffett
Category: SLD PMLD MLD
ASD BESD (Coed Day 4-19)

Sky College (formerly The Priory School)

Pickeridge Close, TAUNTON,
Somerset TA2 7HW
Tel: 01823 275569
Executive Head: Mr Richard Berry
Category: EBD (Boys
Boarding 11-16)

YEOVIL

Fairmead School

Mudford Road, YEOVIL,
Somerset BA21 4NZ
Tel: 01935 421295
Head: Miss Diana Denman
Category: MLD SEBD AUT
SLD (Coed Day 4-16)

Fiveways Special School

Victoria Road, YEOVIL,
Somerset BA21 5AZ
Tel: 01935 476227
Head: Mr M Collis
Category: SLD PMLD ASD
(Coed Day 4-19)

NORTH SOMERSET
Children and Young People's Services

North Somerset SEN Team, Town Hall, Room 119, Weston-Super-Mare, North Somerset, BS23 1UJ
Tel: 01275 888297 Website: www.n-somerset.gov.uk

NAILSEA

Ravenswood School
Pound Lane, NAILSEA, North Somerset BS48 2NN
Tel: 01275 854134
Head: Mrs P Clark
Category: CLD SLD (3-19)

WESTON-SUPER-MARE

Baytree School
The Campus, Highlands Lane, WESTON-SUPER-MARE, North Somerset BS24 7DX
Tel: 01934 427555
Head: Mrs F Richings
Category: SLD (3-19)

Westhaven School
Ellesmere Road, Uphill, WESTON-SUPER-MARE, North Somerset BS23 4UT
Tel: 01934 632171
Acting Head: Mrs T Towler
Category: CLD (7-16)

SOUTHAMPTON
City Council

Southampton SEN Team, Civic Centre (North Block), Southampton, Hampshire, SO14 7LY
Tel: 02380 832248 Email: sen.team@southampton.gov.uk Website: www.southampton.gov.uk

SOUTHAMPTON

Great Oaks School
Vermont Close, SOUTHAMPTON, Hampshire SO16 7LT
Tel: 02380 767660
Head: Mr Andy Evans
Category: MLD AUT ASP SLD (11-18)

Springwell School
Hinkler Road, Thornhill, SOUTHAMPTON, Hampshire SO19 6DH
Tel: 02380 445981
Head: Ms Jackie Partridge
Category: CLD SP&LD AUT SLD Challenging behaviour (4-11)

The Cedar School
Redbridge Lane, Nursling, SOUTHAMPTON, Hampshire SO16 0NX
Tel: 02380 734205
Head: Mr Jonathan Howells
Category: PD (3-16)

The Polygon School
Handel Terrace, SOUTHAMPTON, Hampshire SO15 2FH
Tel: 02380 636776
Head: Mrs Anne Hendon-John
Category: EBD (Boys 11-16)

Vermont School
Vermont Close, Off Winchester Rd, SOUTHAMPTON, Hampshire SO16 7LT
Tel: 02380 767988
Head: Ms Maria Smyth
Category: EBD (Boys 5-11)

SOUTHEND-ON-SEA
Borough Council

Southend-on-Sea SEN Team, Civic Centre, Victoria Avenue, Southend-on-Sea, Essex, SS2 6ER
Tel: 01702 215007 Email: council@southend.gov.uk Website: www.southend.gov.uk

SOUTHEND-ON-SEA

Kingsdown School
Snakes Lane, SOUTHEND-ON-SEA, Essex SS2 6XT
Tel: 01702 527486
Head: Ms Margaret Rimmer
Category: PNI PD SLD PMLD (Coed Day 6-16)

Seabrook College
Burr Hill Chase, SOUTHEND-ON-SEA, Essex SS2 6PE
Tel: 01702 347490
Interim Principal: Ms Linda Burrage
Category: SEBD (Coed Day 15-16)

St Nicholas School
Philpott Avenue, SOUTHEND-ON-SEA, Essex SS2 4RL
Tel: 01702 462322
Head: Mrs June Mitchell
Category: SEBD AUT MLD (Coed Day 11-16)

WESTCLIFF-ON-SEA

Lancaster School
Prittlewell Chase, WESTCLIFF-ON-SEA, Essex SS0 0RT
Tel: 01702 342543
Head: Ms Melanie Hall
Category: PNI PD SLD PMLD (Coed Day 14-19)

STAFFORDSHIRE
Children & Lifelong Learning Directorate

The SEN Team, Tipping Street, Stafford, Staffordshire, ST16 2DH
Tel: 03001 118000 Email: education@staffordshire.gov.uk Website: www.staffordshire.gov.uk

BURNTWOOD

Chasetown Community School
Church Street, Chasetown, BURNTWOOD, Staffordshire WS7 3QL
Tel: 01543 686315
Head: Dr Linda James
Category: SEBD (Coed Day 4-11)

BURTON UPON TRENT

The Fountains High School
Bitham Lane, Stretton, BURTON UPON TRENT, Staffordshire DE13 0HB
Tel: 01283 239161
Head: Mrs Melsa Buxton
Category: Generic (Coed Day 11-19)

The Fountains Primary School
Bitham Lane, Stretton, BURTON UPON TRENT, Staffordshire DE13 0HB
Tel: 01283 239700
Head: Mrs Melsa Buxton
Category: Generic (Coed Day 2-11)

CANNOCK

Hednesford Valley High School
Stanley Road, Hednesford, CANNOCK, Staffordshire WS12 4JS
Tel: 01543 423714
Head: Mrs Anita Rattan
Category: Generic (Coed Day 11-19)

Sherbrook Primary School
Brunswick Road, CANNOCK, Staffordshire WS11 5SF
Tel: 01543 510216
Head: Ms Carol Shaw
Category: Generic (Coed Day 2-11)

LEEK

Horton Lodge Community Special School & Key Learning Centre
Reacliffe Road, Rudyard, LEEK, Staffordshire ST13 8RB
Tel: 01538 306214
Head: Ms Jane Dambach
Category: PD MSI SP&LD (Coed Day/Boarding 2-11)

Meadows Special School
Springfield Road, LEEK, Staffordshire ST13 6EU
Tel: 01538 225050
Head: Mr Christopher Best
Category: Generic (Coed Day 11-19)

Springfield Community Special School
Springfield Road, LEEK, Staffordshire ST13 6LQ
Tel: 01538 383558
Head: Ms Diane Finney
Category: Generic (Coed Day 2-11)

LICHFIELD

Queen's Croft High School
Birmingham Road, LICHFIELD, Staffordshire WS13 6PJ
Tel: 01543 510669
Head: Mr Peter Hawksworth
Category: Generic (Coed Day11-19)

Rocklands School
Purcell Avenue, LICHFIELD, Staffordshire WS13 7PH
Tel: 01543 510760
Head: Ms Sandra Swift
Category: ASD MLD PMLD SLD (Coed Day 2-11)

NEWCASTLE UNDER LYME

Merryfields School
Hoon Avenue, NEWCASTLE UNDER LYME, Staffordshire ST5 9NY
Tel: 01782 296076
Head: Mrs Sarah Poyner
Category: Generic (Coed Day 2-11)

STAFFORD

Greenhall Nursery
Second Avenue, Holmcroft, STAFFORD, Staffordshire ST16 1PS
Tel: 01785 246159
Head: Ms Joanne di Castiglione
Category: PD (Coed Day 2-5)

Marshlands Special School
Second Avenue, STAFFORD, Staffordshire ST16 1PS
Tel: 01785 356385
Head: Mrs Kim Ellis
Category: Generic (Coed Day 2-11)

TAMWORTH

Two Rivers High School

Deltic, off Silver Link Road,
Glascote, TAMWORTH,
Staffordshire B77 2HJ
Tel: 01827 475690
Head: Mr Anthony Dooley
Category: Generic
(Coed Day 11-19)

Two Rivers Primary School

Quince, Amington Heath,
TAMWORTH, Staffordshire B77 4EN
Tel: 01827 475740
Head: Mr Anthony Dooley
Category: Generic (Coed Day 2-11)

WOLVERHAMPTON

Cherry Trees School

Giggetty Lane, Wombourne,
WOLVERHAMPTON, West
Midlands WV5 0AX
Tel: 01902 894484
Head: Mr Paul Elliot
Category: Generic (Coed Day 2-11)

Wightwick Hall School

Tinacre Hill, Wightwick,
WOLVERHAMPTON, West
Midlands WV6 8DA
Tel: 01902 761889
Head: Mr Paul Elliot
Category: Generic
(Coed Day 11-19)

STOCKTON-ON-TEES
Borough Council

Stockton-on-Tees FIS, The SEN Team, 16 Church Road, Stockton-on-Tees, TS18 1XE
Tel: 01642 527225 Email: fis@stockton.gov.uk Website: www.stockton.gov.uk

STOCKTON-ON-TEES

Horizons Specialist Academy Trust, Abbey Hill Academy & Sixth Form

Ketton Road, Hardwick Green,
STOCKTON-ON-TEES TS19 8BU
Tel: 01642 677113
Principal: Ms Rebecca Whelan
Category: SLD PMLD
AUT (Coed 11-19)

Horizons Specialist Academy Trust, Westlands at Green Gates

Melton Road, STOCKTON-
ON-TEES TS19 0JD
Tel: 01642 570104
Principal: Mrs Anita Amos
Category: BESD (Coed
Residential 5-11)

STOKE-ON-TRENT
Local Offer

Stoke-on-Trent SEND Services, The Mount Education Centre, Mount
Avenue, Penkhull Stoke-on-Trent, Staffordshire, ST4 7JU
Tel: 01782 232538 Email: localoffer@stoke.gov.uk Website: www.stoke.gov.uk

BLURTON

Kemball Special School

Beaconsfield Drive, BLURTON,
Stoke-on-Trent ST4 3NR
Tel: 01782 883120
Acting Head: Ms Lisa Hughes
Category: PMLD SLD ASD
CLD (Coed Day 2-19)

BLYTHE BRIDGE

Portland School and Specialist College

Uttoxeter Road, BLYTHE BRIDGE,
Staffordshire ST11 9JG
Tel: 01782 392071
Head: Mr Rob Faulkner
Category: MLD SEBD
(Coed Day 3-16)

STOKE-ON-TRENT

Abbey Hill School and Performing Arts College

Box Lane, Meir, STOKE-ON-
TRENT, Staffordshire ST3 5PR
Tel: 01782 882882
Head: Mr Philip Kidman
Category: MLD AUT
(Coed Day 2-18)

TUNSTALL

Watermill Special School

Turnhurst Road, Packmoor,
TUNSTALL, Stoke-on-Trent ST6 6JZ
Tel: 01782 883737
Head: Mr Jonathon May
Category: MLD (Coed Day 5-16)

SUFFOLK
County Council

Suffolk SENDIASS, Endeavour House, 8 Russell Road, Ipswich, Suffolk, IP1 2BX
Tel: 01473 264702 Email: sendiass@suffolk.gov.uk Website: www.suffolk.gov.uk

BURY ST EDMUNDS

Riverwalk School
South Close, BURY ST
EDMUNDS, Suffolk IP33 3JZ
Tel: 01284 764280
Head: Mrs Jan Hatchell
Category: SLD (Coed Day 3-19)

IPSWICH

**The Bridge School
(Primary Campus)**
Sprites Lane, IPSWICH,
Suffolk IP8 3ND
Tel: 01473 556200
Head: Mr Odran Doran
Category: SLD PMLD
(Coed Day 3-11)

**The Bridge School
(Secondary Campus)**
Sprites Lane, Belstead,
IPSWICH, Suffolk IP8 3ND
Tel: 01473 556200
Head: Mr Odran Doran
Category: SLD PMLD
(Coed Day 11-16)

LOWESTOFT

Warren School
Clarkes Lane, LOWESTOFT,
Suffolk NR33 8HT
Tel: 01502 561893
Head: Mrs Janet Bird
Category: SLD PMLD
(Coed Day 3-19)

SUDBURY

Hillside School
Hitchcock Place, SUDBURY,
Suffolk CO10 1NN
Tel: 01787 372808
Head: Mrs Sue Upson
Category: SLD PMLD
(Coed day 3-19)

SURREY
City Council

The SEN Team, County Hall, Penrhyn Road, Kingston upon Thames, Surrey, KT1 2DN
Tel: 03456 009009 Email: localoffer@surreycc.gov.uk Website: www.surreycc.gov.uk

ADDLESTONE

Philip Southcote School
Addlestone Moor, ADDLESTONE,
Surrey KT15 2QH
Tel: 01932 562326
Head: Mr R W Horton
Category: HI LD (11-19)

CAMBERLEY

**Carwarden House
Community School**
118 Upper Chobham Road,
CAMBERLEY, Surrey GU15 1EJ
Tel: 01276 709080
Head: Mr Jarlath O'Brien
Category: LD (11-19)

Portesbery School
Newfoundland Road,
CAMBERLEY, Surrey GU15 3SZ
Tel: 01276 63078
Head: Mr M Sartin
Category: SLD (2-19)

CATERHAM

Clifton Hill School
Chaldon Road, CATERHAM,
Surrey CR3 5PH
Tel: 01883 347740
Executive Head: Mrs
Sharon Lawrence
Category: SLD (11-19)

Sunnydown School
Portley House, 152 Whyteleafe
Road, CATERHAM, Surrey CR3 5ED
Tel: 01883 342281
Head: Mr Paul Jensen
Category: ASD SLCN
(Boarding & day 11-16)

DORKING

Starhurst School
Chart Lane South, DORKING,
Surrey RH5 4DB
Tel: 01306 883763
Executive Head: Mr Craig Anderson
Category: BESD (Boarding
& day 11-16)

FARNHAM

The Abbey School
Menin Way, FARNHAM,
Surrey GU9 8DY
Tel: 01252 725059
Head: Mr Nathan Aspinall
Category: LD (11-16)

**The Ridgeway
Community School**
Frensham Road, FARNHAM,
Surrey GU9 8HB
Tel: 01252 724562
Head: Mr D Morgan
Category: SLD (2-19)

GUILDFORD

Gosden House School
Horsham Road, Bramley,
GUILDFORD, Surrey GU5 0AH
Tel: 01483 892008
Interim Head: Mr Darryl Morgan
Category: LD (Day 5-16)

Pond Meadow School
Larch Avenue, GUILDFORD,
Surrey GU1 1DR
Tel: 01483 532239
Head: Mr D J Monk
Category: SLD (2-19)

Wey House School
Horsham Road, Bramley,
GUILDFORD, Surrey GU5 0BJ
Tel: 01483 898130
Interim Head: Mr Simon Dawson
Category: BESD (Day only 7-11)

LEATHERHEAD

West Hill School
Kingston Road, LEATHERHEAD,
Surrey KT22 7PW
Tel: 01372 814714
Head: Mrs J V Nettleton
Category: LD (11-16)

Woodlands School

Fortyfoot Road, LEATHERHEAD,
Surrey KT22 8RY
Tel: 01372 273427
Head: Mrs Adrienne Knight
Category: SLD (Day 12-19)

OXTED

Limpsfield Grange School

89 Bluehouse Lane, Limpsfield,
OXTED, Surrey RH8 0RZ
Tel: 01883 713928
Head: Ms Sarah Wild
Category: ELD (Boarding
& day 11-16)

REDHILL

St Nicholas School

Taynton Drive, Merstham,
REDHILL, Surrey RH1 3PU
Tel: 01737 215488
Head: Mr Craig Anderson
Category: BESD (Boarding
& day 11-16)

Woodfield School

Sunstone Grove, Merstham,
REDHILL, Surrey RH1 3PR
Tel: 01737 642623
Head: Mrs S Lawrence
Category: LD (11-19)

REIGATE

Brooklands School

27 Wray Park Road,
REIGATE, Surrey RH2 0DF
Tel: 01737 249941
Head: Mr Mark Bryant
Category: SLD (2-11)

SHEPPERTON

Manor Mead School

Laleham Road, SHEPPERTON,
Middlesex TW17 8EL
Tel: 01932 241834
Executive Head: Ms Linda Mardell
Category: SLD (2-11)

WALTON-ON-THAMES

Walton Leigh School

Queens Road, WALTON-ON-
THAMES, Surrey KT12 5AB
Tel: 01932 223243
Executive Head: Ms Linda Mardell
Category: SLD (11-19)

WOKING

Freemantles School

Smarts Heath Road, Mayford
Green, WOKING, Surrey GU22 0AN
Tel: 01483 545680
Head: Mr Justin Price
Category: ASD (4-19)

The Park School

Onslow Crescent, WOKING,
Surrey GU22 7AT
Tel: 01483 772057
Co-Heads: Mrs K Eastwood
& Mr Paul Walsh
Category: LD (11-16)

WORCESTER PARK

Linden Bridge School

Grafton Road, WORCESTER
PARK, Surrey KT4 7JW
Tel: 02083 303009
Head: Ms Rachel Watt
Category: ASD (Residential
& day 4-19)

EAST SUSSEX

Children's Services Authority

East Sussex ISEND Assessment & Planning Team, PO Box 4, County Hall, St Anne's Crescent Lewes, East Sussex, BN7 1UE
Tel: 01273 336740 Fax: 01273 481599 Email: senteam@eastsussex.gov.uk Website: www.eastsussex.gov.uk

BEXHILL-ON-SEA

Glyne Gap School

Hastings Road, BEXHILL-ON-
SEA, East Sussex TN40 2PU
Tel: 01424 217720
Head: Ms Kirsty Prawanna
Category: CLD/ASD (Coed 2-19)

CROWBOROUGH

Grove Park School

Church Road, CROWBOROUGH,
East Sussex TN6 1BN
Tel: 01892 663018
Head: Ms Angela Wellman
Category: CLD/ASD (Coed 2-19)

EASTBOURNE

Hazel Court Special School

Larkspur Drive, EASTBOURNE,
East Sussex BN23 8EJ
Tel: 01323 465720
Head: Ms Sophie Gurney
Category: CLD/ASD (Coed 11-19)

The Lindfield School

Lindfield Road, EASTBOURNE,
East Sussex BN22 0BQ
Tel: 01323 502988
Head: Ms Kirsty McIlhargey
Category: ACLD (Coed 11-16)

**The South Downs
Community Special School**

(West Site), Beechy Avenue,
EASTBOURNE, East Sussex BN20 8NU
Tel: 01323 730302
Head: Ms Sharon James
Category: ACLD (Coed 3-11)

HASTINGS

Torfield School

Croft Road, HASTINGS,
East Sussex TN34 3JT
Tel: 01424 428228
Head: Ms Natalie Shuttleworth
Category: ACLD (Coed 3-11)

HEATHFIELD

St Mary's School Horam

Maynards Green, Horam,
HEATHFIELD, East Sussex TN21 0BT
Tel: 01435 812278
Head: Mr Paul Murphy
Category: LD EBSD (Boys 9-16)

SEAFORD

Cuckmere House School

Eastbourne Road, SEAFORD,
East Sussex BN25 4BA
Tel: 01323 893319
Head: Ms Lorraine Myles
Category: SEBD (Boys 6-16)

ST LEONARDS-ON-SEA

New Horizons School

Beauchamp Road, ST LEONARDS-
ON-SEA, East Sussex TN38 9JU
Tel: 01424 858020
Head: Ms Simone Hopkins
Category: SEBD (Coed 7-16)

Saxon Mount School

Edinburgh Road, ST LEONARDS-
ON-SEA, East Sussex TN38 8HH
Tel: 01424 426303
Head: Ms Elaine Gardner
Category: ACLD (Coed 11-16)

WEST SUSSEX
Parent Partnership Service

West Sussex SEN Team, County Hall, West Street, Chichester, West Sussex, PO19 1RQ
Tel: 01243 777100 Email: localoffer@westsussex.gov.uk Website: www.westsussex.gov.uk

BURGESS HILL

Woodlands Meed
Chanctonbury Road, BURGESS HILL, West Sussex RH15 9EY
Tel: 01444 244133
Head: Mr Adam Rowland
Category: LD (Coed 2-19)

CHICHESTER

Fordwater School
Summersdale Road, CHICHESTER, West Sussex PO19 6PP
Tel: 01243 782475
Head: Mrs Sue Meekings
Category: SLD (Coed 2-19)

Littlegreen School
Compton, CHICHESTER, West Sussex PO18 9NW
Tel: 02392 631259
Head: Ms Lynda Butt
Category: SEBD (Boys 7-16)

St Anthony's School
Woodlands Lane, CHICHESTER, West Sussex PO19 5PA
Tel: 01243 785965
Head: Ms Helen Ball
Category: MLD (Coed 4-16)

CRAWLEY

Manor Green College
Lady Margaret Road, Ifield, CRAWLEY, West Sussex RH11 0DX
Tel: 01293 520351
Head: Mr Grahame Robson
Category: LD (Coed 11-19)

Manor Green Primary School
Lady Margaret Road, Ifield, CRAWLEY, West Sussex RH11 0DU
Tel: 01293 526873
Head: Mr David Reid
Category: LD (Coed 2-11)

HORSHAM

Queen Elizabeth II Silver Jubilee School
Compton's Lane, HORSHAM, West Sussex RH13 5NW
Tel: 01403 266215
Head: Mrs Lesley Dyer
Category: SLD AUT PMLD (Coed 2-19)

LITTLEHAMPTON

Cornfield School
Cornfield Close, Wick, LITTLEHAMPTON, West Sussex BN17 6HY
Tel: 01903 731277
Head: Mrs Maria Davis
Category: SEBD (Coed 7-16)

SHOREHAM-BY-SEA

Herons Dale Primary School
Hawkins Crescent, SHOREHAM-BY-SEA, West Sussex BN43 6TN
Tel: 01273 596904
Head: Ms Trish Stepney
Category: LD (Coed 4-11)

WORTHING

Oak Grove College
The Boulevard, WORTHING, West Sussex BN13 1JX
Tel: 01903 708870
Head: Mr Phillip Potter
Category: LD (Coed 11-19)

Palatine Primary School
Palatine Road, Goring-By-Sea, WORTHING, West Sussex BN12 6JP
Tel: 01903 242835
Head: Mrs Catriona Goldsmith
Category: LD (Coed 3-11)

SWINDON
Borough Council

Swindon SEN Team, Civic Offices, Euclid Street, Swindon, Wiltshire, SN1 2JH
Email: sendproject@swindon.gov.uk Website: www.swindon.gov.uk

SWINDON

Brimble Hill School
Tadpole Lane, Redhouse, SWINDON, Wiltshire SN25 2NB
Tel: 01793 493900
Head: Mrs Alison Paul
Category: SLD (2-11)

Chalet School
Liden Drive, Liden, SWINDON, Wiltshire SN3 6EX
Tel: 01793 534537
Head: Ms Katherine Bryan
Category: CLD including ASD (2-11)

Crowdys Hill School
Jefferies Avenue, Cricklade Road, SWINDON, Wiltshire SN2 7HJ
Tel: 01793 332400
Head: Mrs Mags Clarke
Category: CLD & other difficulties (11-16)

Nyland Campus
Nyland Road, Nythe, SWINDON, Wiltshire SN3 3RD
Tel: 01793 535023
Head: Ms Becky O'Brien
Category: BESD (5-11)

St Luke's School
Cricklade Road, SWINDON, Wiltshire SN2 7AS
Tel: 01793 705566
Head: Mr Geoff Cherrill
Category: BESD (11-16)

Uplands School
The Learning Campus, Tadpole Lane, Redhouse, SWINDON, Wiltshire SN25 2NB
Tel: 01793 493910
Head: Mrs Jackie Smith
Category: SLD (11-19)

TELFORD & WREKIN
Information, Advice & Support Service

Telford & Wrekin SENDIASS, The Glebe Centre, Glebe Street, Wellington Telford, TF1 1JP
Tel: 01952 457176 Email: info@pps-shropshireandtelford.org.uk Website: www.telford.gov.uk

TELFORD

Haughton School
Queen Street, Madeley,
TELFORD, Shropshire TF7 4BW
Tel: 01952 387540
Head: Mrs Gill Knox
Category: MLD ASD SLD
SP&LD BESD (Coed 5-11)

Mount Gilbert School
Hinkshay Road, Dawley,
TELFORD, Shropshire TF4 3PP
Tel: 01952 387670
Head: Mrs Lisa Lyon
Category: SEBD SPLD
AUT (Coed 11-16)

Queensway HLC
Hadley, TELFORD, Shropshire TF1 6AJ
Tel: 01952 388555
Head: Mr Nigel Griffiths
Category: ASD (11-18)

Southall School
Off Rowan Avenue, Dawley,
TELFORD, Shropshire TF4 3PN
Tel: 01952 387600
Acting Head: Mr Chris Lloyd
Category: MLD ASD
SEBD (Coed 11-16)

The Bridge
HLC, Waterloo Road, Hadley,
TELFORD, Shropshire TF1 5NQ
Tel: 01952 387108
Head: Ms Heather Davies
Category: (3-16)

THURROCK
Council

Thurrock SEN Team, Children's Services, PO Box 118, Grays, Essex, RM17 6GF
Tel: 01375 652555 Email: sen@thurrock.gov.uk Website: www.thurrock.gov.uk

GRAYS

Beacon Hill Academy (Post 16 Provision)
Buxton Road, GRAYS,
Essex RM16 2WU
Tel: 01375 898656
Head: Mrs Sue Hewitt
Category: SLD PNI PMLD
(Coed 16-19)

Treetops School
Buxton Road, GRAYS,
Essex RM16 2WU
Tel: 01375 372723
Head: Mr Paul Smith
Category: MLD ASD (Coed 3-16)

Treetops School (6th Form)
Buxton Road, GRAYS,
Essex RM16 2WU
Tel: 01375 372723
Head: Mr Paul Smith

TORBAY
Council

Torbay SEN Team, Town Hall, Castle Circus, Torquay, Devon, TQ1 3DR
Tel: 01803 208274 Email: info@sendiasstorbay.org.uk Website: www.torbay.gov.uk

PAIGNTON

Torbay School
170b Torquay Road, Preston,
PAIGNTON, Devon TQ3 2AL
Tel: 01803 665522
Executive Head: Mr James Evans
Category: BESD (11-16)

TORQUAY

Mayfield School
Moor Lane, Watcombe,
TORQUAY, Devon TQ2 8NH
Tel: 01803 328375
Head: Mrs June Palmer
Category: SLD PMLD PH
AUT (3-19) BESD (5-11)

Tyne & Wear
GATESHEAD
Council

Gateshead SEND Team, Civic Centre, Regent Street, Gateshead, Tyne & Wear, NE8 1HH
Tel: 0191 433 3626 Email: senteam@gateshead.gov.uk Website: www.gateshead.gov.uk

GATESHEAD

Dryden School Business & Enterprise College
Shotley Gardens, Low Fell, GATESHEAD, Tyne & Wear NE9 5UR
Tel: 01914 203811
Executive Head: Ms Jayne Bryant
Category: SLD (Coed 11-19)

Eslington Primary School
Hazel Road, GATESHEAD, Tyne & Wear NE8 2EP
Tel: 01914 334131
Head: Ms Michelle Richards
Category: EBD (Coed 5-11)

Furrowfield School
Whitehills Drive, Felling, GATESHEAD, Tyne & Wear NE10 9RZ
Tel: 01914 954700
Head: Ms Michelle Richards
Category: EBD (Boys 11-16)

Hill Top Specialist Arts College
Wealcroft, Leam Lane Estate, GATESHEAD, Tyne & Wear NE10 8LT
Tel: 01914 692462
Executive Head: Ms Jayne Bryant
Category: MLD AUT (Coed 11-16)

NEWCASTLE UPON TYNE

Gibside School
Burnthouse Lane, Whickham, NEWCASTLE UPON TYNE, Tyne & Wear NE16 5AT
Tel: 01914 410123
Head: Ms Judith Donovan
Category: SLD MLD AUT (Coed 4-11)

NEWCASTLE UPON TYNE
City Council

Newcastle SEN Assessment Service, Room 213, Civic Centre, Newcastle upon Tyne, Tyne & Wear, NE1 8QH
Tel: 01912 774650 Email: localoffer@newcastle.gov.uk Website: www.newcastlechildrenservices.org.uk

NEWCASTLE UPON TYNE

Hadrian School
Bertram Crescent, Pendower, NEWCASTLE UPON TYNE, Tyne & Wear NE15 6PY
Tel: 01912 734440
Head: Mr Christopher Rollings
Category: PMLD SLD (Coed Day 2-11)

Linhope Pupil Referral Unit
Linhope Centre, Linhope Road, NEWCASTLE UPON TYNE, Tyne & Wear NE5 2NW
Tel: 01912 674447
Head: Mr Jeff Lough
Category: (Coed Day 5-16)

Newcastle Bridges School
c/o Kenton College, Drayton Road, Kenton, NEWCASTLE UPON TYNE, Tyne & Wear NE3 3RU
Tel: 01918 267086
Head: Mrs Margaret Dover
Category: HS (Coed 2-19)

Sir Charles Parson School
Westbourne Avenue, NEWCASTLE UPON TYNE, Tyne & Wear NE6 4ED
Tel: 01912 952280
Head: Mr Nick Sharing
Category: SLD PD PMLD (Coed Day 11-19)

Thomas Bewick School
Linhope Road, West Denton, NEWCASTLE UPON TYNE, Tyne & Wear NE5 2LW
Tel: 01912 296020
Head: Ms Diane Scott
Category: AUT (Coed Day/boarding 3-19)

Trinity School
Condercum Road, NEWCASTLE UPON TYNE, Tyne & Wear NE4 8XJ
Tel: 01912 986950
Head: Mr Bill Curley
Category: SEBD (Coed Day 7-16)

Tyne & Wear
SUNDERLAND
Children's Services

Sunderland SEN and Accessibility Team, Sunderland Customer Service Centre, Bunny Hill, Hylton Lane Sunderland, Tyne & Wear, SR5 4BW
Tel: 01915 205553 Email: sen@sunderland.gov.uk Website: www.sunderland.gov.uk

SUNDERLAND

Sunningdale School

Shaftoe Road, Springwell,
SUNDERLAND, Tyne & Wear SR3 4HA
Tel: 01915 535880
Head: Mrs C Wright
Category: PMLD SLD
(Coed Day 2-11)

WASHINGTON

Columbia Grange School

Oxclose Road, WASHINGTON,
Tyne & Wear NE38 7NY
Tel: 01912 193860
Head: Mrs L Mavin
Category: SLD ASD (Coed Day 3-11)

Tyne & Wear

NORTH TYNESIDE

Information, Advice & Support Service

North Tyneside SENDIASS, Quadrant East, Floor 2, Second Left, The Silverlink North,
Cobalt Business Park North Tyneside, Tyne & Wear, NE27 0BY

Tel: 0345 2000 109 Email: sendiass@northtyneside.gov.uk Website: www.northtyneside.gov.uk

LONGBENTON

Benton Dene School

Hailsham Avenue, LONGBENTON,
Tyne & Wear NE12 8FD
Tel: 01916 432730
Head: Mrs Alison McAllister-Williams
Category: MLD ASD (Coed 5-11+)

NORTH SHIELDS

Southlands School

Beach Road, Tynemouth, NORTH
SHIELDS, Tyne & Wear NE30 2QR
Tel: 01912 006348
Head: Mr Dave Erskine
Category: MLD BESD (Coed 11-16+)

WALLSEND

Beacon Hill School

Rising Sun Cottages, High Farm,
WALLSEND, Tyne & Wear NE28 9JW
Tel: 01916 433000
Head: Mrs Helen Jones
Category: ASD SLD
PMLD (Coed 2-16)

Silverdale School

Langdale Gardens, WALLSEND,
Tyne & Wear NE28 0HG
Tel: 01916 053230
Head: Mr Peter Gannon
Category: BESD (Coed 7-16)

WHITLEY BAY

Woodlawn School

Drumoyne Gardens, Monkseaton,
WHITLEY BAY, Tyne & Wear NE25 9DL
Tel: 01916 432590
Head: Mrs Gill Wilson
Category: PD MSI Medical
needs (Coed 2-16)

Tyne & Wear

SOUTH TYNESIDE

Pupil Services

South Tynesdie SEN Team, Children, Adults & Families, Level 0, Town Hall & Civic
Offices, Westoe Road South Shields, Tyne & Wear, NE33 2RL

Tel: 01914 247808 Email: tracey.wilson@southtyneside.gov.uk Website: www.southtyneside.info

HEBBURN

**Hebburn Lakes
Primary School**

Campbell Park Road, HEBBURN,
Tyne & Wear NE31 1QY
Tel: 01914 839122
Head: Mr A S Watson
Category: BESD LD Complex
medical needs

Keelman's Way School

Campbell Park Road, HEBBURN,
Tyne & Wear NE31 1QY
Tel: 01914 897480
Head: Mrs Paula Selby
Category: PMLD SLD
(Coed Day 2-19)

JARROW

**Epinay Business &
Enterprise School**

Clervaux Terrace, JARROW,
Tyne & Wear NE32 5UP
Tel: 01914 898949
Head: Mrs Hilary Harrison
Category: MLD EBD (Coed 5-17)

Fellgate Autistic Unit

Oxford Way, Fellgate Estate,
JARROW, Tyne & Wear NE32 4XA
Tel: 01914 894801
Head: Miss C Wilson
Category: AUT (Coed 3-11)

**Hedworthfield Language
Development Unit**

Linkway, Hedworth Estate,
JARROW, Tyne & Wear NE32 4QF
Tel: 01915 373373
Head: Ms G Jeynes
Category: SP&LD (Coed)

Jarrow School

Field Terrace, JARROW,
Tyne & Wear NE32 5PR
Tel: 01914 283200
Head: Miss J Gillies
Category: HI ASD

Maintained special schools and colleges

Simonside Primary School

Glasgow Road, JARROW,
Tyne & Wear NE32 4AU
Tel: 01914 898315
Head: Ms Bland
Category: HI

SOUTH SHIELDS

Ashley Child Development Centre

Temple Park Road, SOUTH
SHIELDS, Tyne & Wear NE34 0QA
Tel: 01914 564977
Head: Mrs D Todd
Category: Other Early Years

Bamburgh School

Horsley Hill Community
Campus, SOUTH SHIELDS,
Tyne & Wear NE34 7TD
Tel: 01914 274330
Head: Mr Peter Nord
Category: PD MED VIS HI
MLD (Coed Day 2-17)

Harton Speech and Language and ASD Resource Bases

c/o Harton Technology College,
Lisle Road, SOUTH SHIELDS,
Tyne & Wear NE34 6DL
Tel: 01914 274050
Head: Mr K A Gibson
Category: Speech and
language ASD

Park View School

Temple Park Road, SOUTH
SHIELDS, Tyne & Wear NE34 0QA
Tel: 01914 541568
Head: Mr Chris Rue
Category: BESD (Coed Day 11-16)

WARRINGTON
Children & Young People

Warrington Pupil Assessment Support Team, New Town House, Buttermarket Street, Warrington, WA1 2NH
Tel: 01925 443322 Email: contact@warrington.gov.uk Website: www.warrington.gov.uk

WARRINGTON

Fox Wood Special School

Woolston Learning Village, Holes
Lane, Woolston, WARRINGTON,
Cheshire WA1 4LS
Tel: 01925 818534
Headteacher: Mrs Lucinda Duffy
Category: SLD (Coed Day 4-19)

Green Lane Special School

Woolston Learning Village, Holes
Lane, Woolston, WARRINGTON,
Cheshire WA1 4LS
Tel: 01925 811617
Headteacher: Mr Paul King
Category: MLD CLD
(Coed Day 4-19)

Woolston Brook Special School

Green Lane, WARRINGTON,
Cheshire WA1 4JL
Tel: 01925 818549
Headteacher: Mr Michael Frost
Category: BESD (Coed Day 7-16)

WARWICKSHIRE
Information, Advice & Support Service

Warwickshire SENDIASS, Canterbury House, Exhall Grange Campus,
Easter Way, Ash Green Coventry, Warwickshire, CV7 9HP
Tel: 024 7636 6054 Email: dawn.rowley@family-action.org.uk Website: www.warwickshire.gov.uk

ASH GREEN

Exhall Grange School & Science College

Easter Way, ASH GREEN,
Warwickshire CV7 9HP
Tel: 02476 364200
Head: Mrs Christine Marshall
Category: VIS PD Med
(Coed Day 2-19)

COLESHILL

Woodlands School

Packington Lane, COLESHILL,
West Midlands B46 3JE
Tel: 01675 463590
Head: Mr Iain Paterson
Category: Generic SLD VIS HI AUT
MSI PD MLD PMLD (Coed Day 2-19)

HENLEY-IN-ARDEN

River House School

Stratford Road, HENLEY-IN-
ARDEN, West Midlands B95 6AD
Tel: 01564 792514
Head: Mr Tony Dickens
Category: SEBD (Boys Day 11-16)

NUNEATON

Oak Wood Primary School

Morris Drive, NUNEATON,
Warwickshire CV11 4QH
Tel: 02476 740907
Head: Mr Kevin Latham
Category: Generic SLD MLD VIS HI
AUT MSI PD PMLD (Coed Day 2-11)

Oak Wood Secondary School

Morris Drive, NUNEATON,
Warwickshire CV11 4QH
Tel: 02476 740901
Head: Mr Kevin Latham
Category: Generic SLD MLD VIS HI
AUT MSI PD PMLD (Coed Day 11-16)

RUGBY

Brooke School

Overslade Lane, RUGBY, Warwickshire CV22 6DY
Tel: 01788 812324
Head: Mr Christopher Pollitt
Category: Generic SLD VIS HI AUT MSI PD MLD PMLD (Coed Day 2-19)

STRATFORD-UPON-AVON

Welcombe Hills School

Blue Cap Road, STRATFORD-UPON-AVON, Warwickshire CV37 6TQ
Tel: 01789 266845
Head: Mrs Judith Humphry
Category: Generic SLD VIS HI AUT MSI PD MLD PMLD (Coed Day 2-19)

WARWICK

Ridgeway School

Deansway, WARWICK, Warwickshire CV34 5DF
Tel: 01926 491987
Head: Ms Debra Hewitt
Category: Generic SLD VIS HI AUT MSI PD MLD PMLD (Coed Day 2-11)

Round Oak School & Support Service & Sports College

Brittain Lane, off Myton Road, WARWICK, Warwickshire CV34 6DX
Tel: 01926 423311
Head: Mrs Jayne Naylor
Category: Generic SLD VIS HI AUT MSI PD MLD PMLD (Coed Day 11-19)

West Midlands

BIRMINGHAM

Children, Young People & Families

Birmingham SEN Team, Council House, Victoria Square, Birmingham, B1 1BB
Tel: 01213 031888 Email: senar@birmingham.gov.uk Website: www.birmingham.gov.uk

EDGBASTON

Baskerville School

Fellows Lane, Harborne, EDGBASTON, Birmingham B17 9TS
Tel: 01214 273191
Head: Mrs Rosemary Adams
Category: ASD (Coed boarding 11-19)

ERDINGTON

Bridge School

290 Reservoir Road, ERDINGTON, Birmingham B23 6DE
Tel: 01214 648265
Head: Mr Adrian Coleman
Category: ASD PMLD AUT (Coed Boarding 2-11)

Queensbury School

Wood End Road, ERDINGTON, Birmingham B24 8BL
Tel: 01213 735731
Head: Mrs Veronica Jenkins
Category: MLD AUT SLD (Coed Day 11-19)

HALL GREEN

Fox Hollies School

Highbury Campus, Queensbridge Road, Moseley, HALL GREEN, Birmingham B13 8QB
Tel: 01214 646566
Head: Mr Paul Roberts
Category: SLD PD CLD MSI (Coed Day 11-19)

Uffculme School

Queensbridge Road, Moseley, HALL GREEN, Birmingham B13 8QB
Tel: 01214 645250
Head: Mr Alex MacDonald
Category: ASD (Coed day 3-11)

HODGE HILL

Beaufort School

Stechford Road, HODGE HILL, Birmingham B34 6BJ
Tel: 01216 758500
Head: Ms Fiona Woolford
Category: SLD AUT PMLD (Coed Day 2-11)

Braidwood School

Bromford Road, HODGE HILL, Birmingham B36 8AF
Tel: 01214 645558
Head: Mrs Karen Saywood
Category: D HI ASD MLD (Coed Day 11-19)

Hallmoor School

Hallmoor Road, Kitts Green, HODGE HILL, Birmingham B33 9QY
Tel: 01217 833972
Head: Mrs Susan Charvis
Category: MLD MSI SP&LD (Coed Day 5-19)

The Pines Special School

Dreghorn Road, Castle Bromwich, HODGE HILL, Birmingham B36 8LL
Tel: 01214 646136
Head: Mrs Susan Brandwood
Category: SP&LD ASD (Coed Day 2-11)

LADYWOOD

Calthorpe School & Sports College

Darwin Street, Highgate, LADYWOOD, Birmingham B12 0TP
Tel: 01217 734637
Head: Mr Graham Hardy
Category: SLD MLD CLD PD MSI AUT (Coed Day 2-19)

NORTHFIELD

Longwill Primary School for Deaf Children

Bell Hill, NORTHFIELD, Birmingham B31 1LD
Tel: 01214 753923
Head: Ms Barbara Day
Category: HI D (Coed Day 2-12)

Victoria School and Specialist Arts College

Bell Hill, NORTHFIELD, Birmingham B31 1LD
Tel: 01214 769478
Head: Mrs Justine Sims
Category: PD (Coed Day 2-19)

PERRY BARR

Hamilton School

Hamilton Road, Handsworth, PERRY BARR, Birmingham B21 8AH
Tel: 01214 641676
Head: Mr Jonathan Harris
Category: ASD SP&LD (Coed Day 4-11)

Mayfield School

Heathfield Road, Handsworth, PERRY BARR, Birmingham B19 1HJ
Tel: 01214 643354
Head: Mr Paul Jenkins
Category: SLD PMLD (Coed Day 3-19)

Oscott Manor School

Old Oscott Hill, Kingstanding, PERRY BARR, Birmingham B44 9SP
Tel: 01213 608222
Head: Ms Joy Hardwick
Category: PMLD ASD MLD (Coed Day 11-19)

Priestley Smith School

Beeches Road, Great Barr, PERRY BARR, Birmingham B42 2PY
Tel: 01213 253900
Head: Mrs Helen Porter
Category: VIS (Coed Day 2-17)

REDDITCH

Skilts School

Gorcott Hill, REDDITCH, West Midlands B98 9ET
Tel: 01527 853851
Head: Mr Charles Herriotts
Category: EBD (Coed Boarding 5-12)

SELLY OAK

Cherry Oak School

60 Frederick Road, SELLY OAK, Birmingham B29 6PB
Tel: 01214 642037
Head: Mrs Justine Sims
Category: SLD PMLD (Coed Day 3-11)

Dame Ellen Pinsent School

Ardencote Road, SELLY OAK, Birmingham B13 0RW
Tel: 01216 752487
Head: Ms Debbie Allen
Category: ASD EBD SP&LD HI (Coed day 4-11)

Lindsworth School

Monyhull Hall Road, Kings Norton, SELLY OAK, Birmingham B30 3QA
Tel: 01216 935363
Head: Mr David McMahon
Category: SEBD (Coed Boarding 11-16)

Selly Oak Trust School

Oak Tree Lane, SELLY OAK,
Birmingham B29 6HZ
Tel: 01214 720876
Head: Mr Chris Field
Category: MLD (Coed Day 11-19)

SOLIHULL

Springfield House Community Special School

Kenilworth Road, Knowle,
SOLIHULL, West Midlands B93 0AJ
Tel: 01564 772772
Head: Mrs Janet Collins
Category: SEBD (Coed Boarding 5-11)

SUTTON COLDFIELD

Bridge School - Longmoor Campus

Coppice View Road, SUTTON
COLDFIELD, Birmingham B73 6UE
Tel: 01213 537833
Head: Mr Adrian Coleman
Category: PMLD AUT ASD (Coed 2-11)

Langley School

Trinity Road, SUTTON COLDFIELD,
West Midlands B75 6TJ
Tel: 01216 752929
Head: Mrs Fiona Woolford
Category: MLD ASD (Coed Day 3-11)

YARDLEY

Brays School

Brays Road, Sheldon, YARDLEY,
Birmingham B26 1NS
Tel: 01217 435730
Head: Mrs Jane Edgerton
Category: PD SLD EBD CLD MSI (Coed 2-11)

West Midlands
COVENTRY
Education Authority

Coventry SEN & Inclusion, Civic Centre 2.3, Earl Street, Coventry, West Midlands, CV1 5RS
Tel: 02476 831624 Website: www.coventry.gov.uk

COVENTRY

Baginton Fields Secondary School

Sedgemoor Road, COVENTRY,
West Midlands CV3 4EA
Tel: 02476 303854
Head: Mr Simon Grant
Category: SLD (Coed Day 11-19)

Castle Wood

Deedmore Road, COVENTRY,
West Midlands CV2 1EQ
Tel: 02476 709060
Head: Mrs Yvonne McCall
Category: (Coed Day 3-11)

Corley Centre

Church Lane, Fillongley, COVENTRY,
West Midlands CV7 8AZ
Tel: 01676 540218
Head: Ms Lisa Batch
Category: Complex SCD (Coed 11-19)

River Bank Academy

Ashington Grove, COVENTRY,
West Midlands CV3 4DE
Tel: 02476 303776
Head: Mr David Lisowski/ Mrs Jackie Smith
Category: (Coed Day 11-19)

Sherbourne Fields Primary & Secondary School

Rowington Close, Off
Kingsbury Road, COVENTRY,
West Midlands CV6 1PS
Tel: 02476 591501
Head: Ms Shivaun Moriaty
Category: PD (Coed Day 2-19)

Tiverton Primary

Rowington Close, Off
Kingsbury Road, COVENTRY,
West Midlands CV6 1PS
Tel: 02476 594954
Head: Mrs Carolyn Claridge
Category: SLD (Coed Day 3-11)

Woodfield School

Stoneleigh Road Primary Site,
COVENTRY, West Midlands CV4 7AB
Tel: 02476 418755
Head: Mr Steve Poole
Category: ESBD (Coed Day 5-11)

Woodfield School

Hawthorn Lane Secondary Site,
COVENTRY, West Midlands CV4 9PB
Tel: 02476 462335
Head: Mr Steve Poole
Category: EBD (Boys Day 11-16)

West Midlands
DUDLEY
Children's Services

Dudley SEN Team, Westox House, 1 Trinity Road, Dudley, West Midlands, DY1 1JQ
Tel: 01384 814214 Website: www.dudley.gov.uk

DUDLEY

Old Park School

Thorns Road, Brierley Hill, DUDLEY,
West Midlands DY5 2JY
Tel: 01384 818905
Head: Mrs G Cartwright
Category: SLD (3-19)

Rosewood School

Bell Street, Coseley, DUDLEY,
West Midlands WV14 8XJ
Tel: 01384 816800
Head: Mr D Kirk
Category: EBD (11-16)

The Brier School

Bromley Lane, Kingswinford,
DUDLEY, West Midlands DY6 8QN
Tel: 01384 816000
Head: Mr R Hinton
Category: MLD (5-16)

The Sutton School & Specialist College

Scotts Green Close, Russells
Hall Estate, DUDLEY, West
Midlands DY1 2DU
Tel: 01384 818670
Head: Mr D Charles
Category: MLD (11-16)

The Woodsetton School
Tipton Road, Woodsetton,
DUDLEY, West Midlands DY3 1BY
Tel: 01384 818265
Head: Mr P A Rhind-Tutt
Category: MLD (4-11)

HALESOWEN

Halesbury School
Feldon Lane, HALESOWEN,
West Midlands B62 9DR
Tel: 01384 818630
Acting Head: Mr J Kulyk
Category: MLD (4-16)

STOURBRIDGE

Pens Meadow School
Ridge Hill, Brierley Hill Road,
Wordsley, STOURBRIDGE,
West Midlands DY8 5ST
Tel: 01384 818945
Head: Mrs M Hunter
Category: SLD (3-19)

West Midlands
SANDWELL
Children & Families Services

Sandwell SEN Service, PO Box 16230, Sandwell Council House, Freeth Street Oldbury, West Midlands, B69 9EX
Tel: 01215 698240 Email: children_families@sandwell.gov.uk Website: www.sandwell.gov.uk

LICHFIELD

Shenstone Lodge School
Birmingham Road, Shenstone,
LICHFIELD, Staffordshire WS14 0LB
Tel: 01543 480369
Head: Mr N C Toplass
Category: EBD (Coed Day 4-16)

OLDBURY

**The Meadows
Sports College**
Dudley Road East, OLDBURY,
West Midlands B69 3BU
Tel: 01215 697080
Head: Mr G Phillips
Category: PMLD (Coed Day 11-19)

The Orchard School
Causeway Green Road, OLDBURY,
West Midlands B68 8LD
Tel: 01215 697040
Head: Mrs G Kew
Category: PMLD(Coed Day 2-11)

ROWLEY REGIS

The Westminster School
Curral Road, ROWLEY REGIS,
West Midlands B65 9AN
Tel: 01215 882421
Head: Mrs C Hill
Category: MLD (Coed Day 11-19)

West Midlands
SOLIHULL
Education Authority

Solihull SEN Team, Council House, Manor Square, Solihull, West Midlands, B91 3QB
Tel: 01217 046690 Email: sen@solihull.gov.uk Website: www.solihull.gov.uk

BIRMINGHAM

Forest Oak School
Windward Way, Smith's
Wood, BIRMINGHAM, West
Midlands B36 0UE
Tel: 01217 170088
Principal: Mrs A R Mordey
Category: MLD (Coed Day 4-18)

Merstone School
Windward Way, Smith's
Wood, BIRMINGHAM, West
Midlands B36 0UE
Tel: 01217 171040
Principal: Mrs A R Mordey
Category: SLD (Coed Day 2-19)

Northern House School
Lanchester Way, Castle
Bromwich, BIRMINGHAM,
West Midlands B36 9LF
Tel: 01217 489760
Head: Mr Trevor Scott
Category: EBD (Coed Day 11-16)

SOLIHULL

Hazel Oak School
Hazel Oak Road, Shirley, SOLIHULL,
West Midlands B90 2AZ
Tel: 01217 444162
Head: Ms Debbie Jenkins
Category: MLD (Coed Day 4-18)

Reynalds Cross School
Kineton Green Road, SOLIHULL,
West Midlands B92 7ER
Tel: 01217 073012
Head: Mrs Jane Davenport
Category: SLD (Coed Day 2-19)

West Midlands

WALSALL

Walsall Information, Advice & Support Service

Walsall SEN Team, Blakenhall Village Centre, Thames Road, Blakenhall Walsall, West Midlands, WS3 1LZ
Tel: 01922 650330 Email: iasssend@walsall.gov.uk Website: www.walsall.gov.uk

WALSALL

Castle Business & Enterprise College

Odell Road, Leamore, WALSALL,
West Midlands WS3 2ED
Tel: 01922 710129
Head: Mrs Christine Fraser
Category: MLD, Additional
Needs (Coed Day 7-19)

Elmwood School

King George Crescent, Rushall,
WALSALL, West Midlands WS4 1EG
Tel: 01922 721081
Head: Mr Simon Hubbard
Category: EBD (Coed Day 11-16)

Mary Elliot Special School

Leamore Lane, WALSALL,
West Midlands WS2 7NR
Tel: 01922 490190
Head: Mr Adrian Coleman
Category: SLD PMLD AUT
(Coed day 11-19)

Oakwood School

Druids Walk, Walsall Wood,
WALSALL, West Midlands WS9 9JS
Tel: 01543 452040
Head: Mrs Kay Mills
Category: SLD CLD PMLD
ASD Challenging behaviour
(Coed Day 3-11)

Old Hall Special School

Bentley Lane, WALSALL,
West Midlands WS2 7LU
Tel: 01902 368045
Head: Mrs Lynn Hill
Category: SLD PMLD AUT
(Coed day 3-11)

Phoenix Primary

Odell Road, Leamore, WALSALL,
West Midlands WS3 2ED
Tel: 01922 712834
Head: Mrs Jeanette Ashwin
Category: EBD (Coed Day 4-11)

The Jane Lane School - A College for Cognition and Learning

Churchill Road, Bentley, WALSALL,
West Midlands WS2 0JH
Tel: 01922 721161
Head: Mr Tony Milovsorov
Category: MLD, Additional
Needs (Coed Day 7-19)

West Midlands

WOLVERHAMPTON

Communities Directorate- Health, Wellbeing and Disabilities

Wolverhampton SEN Team, Civic Centre, St Peter's Square, Wolverhampton, West Midlands, WV1 1RT
Tel: 01902 555873 Email: city.direct@wolverhampton.gov.uk Website: www.wolverhampton.gov.uk

WOLVERHAMPTON

Broadmeadow Nursery School

Lansdowne Road,
WOLVERHAMPTON, West
Midlands WV1 4AL
Tel: 01902 558330
Head: Miss K Warrington
Category: SLD ASD PMLD
(Coed Day 2-6)

Green Park School

The Willows, Green Park Avenue,
Bilston, WOLVERHAMPTON,
West Midlands WV14 6EH
Tel: 01902 556429
Head: Mrs L Dawney
Category: PMLD SLD
(Coed Day 4-19)

Penn Fields School

Boundary Way, Penn,
WOLVERHAMPTON, West
Midlands WV4 4NT
Tel: 01902 558640
Head: Miss E Stanley
Category: MLD SLD ASD
(Coed Day 4-19)

Penn Hall School

Vicarage Road, Penn,
WOLVERHAMPTON, West
Midlands WV4 5HP
Tel: 01902 558355
Head: Mr D Parry
Category: PD SLD MLD
(Coed Day 3-19)

Tettenhall Wood School

Regis Road, Tettenhall,
WOLVERHAMPTON, West
Midlands WV6 8XG
Tel: 01902 556519
Head: Ms S Wewellyn
Category: ASD (Coed Day 5-19)

WILTSHIRE
Children & Education Department

Wiltshire SEN/Disability 0-25 Service, County Hall, Bythesea Road, Trowbridge, Wiltshire, BA14 8JN
Tel: 01225 757985 Email: Statutorysen.service@wiltshire.gov.uk Website: www.wiltshirelocaloffer.org.uk

CHIPPENHAM

St Nicholas School
Malmesbury Road, CHIPPENHAM,
Wiltshire SN15 1QF
Tel: 01249 650435
Head: Mr Bruce Douglas
Category: SLD PMLD
(Coed Day 3-19)

DEVIZES

Downland School
Downlands Road, DEVIZES,
Wiltshire SN10 5EF
Tel: 01380 724193
Head: Mr Phil Beaumont
Category: BESD SPLD
(Boys Boarding 11-16)

Rowdeford School
Rowde, DEVIZES, Wiltshire SN10 2QQ
Tel: 01380 850309
Head: Mrs Ingrid Sidmouth
Category: MLD (Coed
Boarding 11-16)

SALISBURY

Exeter House Special School
Somerset Road, SALISBURY,
Wiltshire SP1 3BL
Tel: 01722 334168
Head: Mr Richard Chapman
Category: SLD PMLD SPLD
Del (Coed Day 2-19)

TROWBRIDGE

Larkrise School
Ashton Street, TROWBRIDGE,
Wiltshire BA14 7EB
Tel: 01225 761434
Head: Mr Phil Cook
Category: SLD MLD
(Coed Day 3-19)

WINDSOR & MAIDENHEAD
Adult, Children and Health Services

Windsor & Maidenhead CYPDS, Town Hall, St Ives Road, Maidenhead, Berkshire, SL6 1RF
Tel: 01628 685878 Email: CYPDS@rbwm.gov.uk Website: www.rbwm.gov.uk

MAIDENHEAD

Manor Green School
Elizabeth Hawkes Way,
MAIDENHEAD, Berkshire SL6 3EQ
Tel: 01628 513800
Head: Ms Ania Hildrey
Category: SLD PMLD ASD
MLD (Coed 2-19)

WOKINGHAM
Children's Services

Wokingham SEN Team, Highwood Annexe, Fairwater Drive, Woodley Wokingham, Berkshire, RG5 3RU
Tel: 01189 746216 Email: sen@wokingham.gov.uk Website: www.wokingham.gov.uk

WOKINGHAM

Addington School
Woodlands Avenue, Woodley,
WOKINGHAM, Berkshire RG5 3EU
Tel: 01189 669073
Head: Mrs Liz Meek
Category: SLD PMLD ASD
MLD (Coed 4-18)

Southfield School
Gipsy Lane, WOKINGHAM,
Berkshire RG40 2HR
Tel: 01189 771293
Head: Mr Dominic Geraghty
Category: BESD (Coed 7-16)

WORCESTERSHIRE
Children's Services Directorate

Worcestershire SENDIASS, PO Box 73, Worcester, WR5 2YA
Tel: 01905 610858 Email: sendiass@worcestershire.gov.uk Website: www.worcestershire.gov.uk

BROMSGROVE

Chadsgrove School & Specialist Sports College
Meadow Road,
Catshill, BROMSGROVE,
Worcestershire B61 0JL
Tel: 01527 871511
Head: Mrs Debbie Rattley
Category: PD PMLD MSI LD (2-19)

Rigby Hall School
19 Rigby Lane, Astonfields,
BROMSGROVE,
Worcestershire B60 2EP
Tel: 01527 875475
Head: Mrs Sarah Radford
Category: SLD MLD ASD (3-19)

EVESHAM

Vale of Evesham School
Four Pools Lane, EVESHAM,
Worcestershire WR11 1BN
Tel: 01386 443367
Head: Mr Stephen Garside
Category: SLD MLD PMLD ASD (4-19)

KIDDERMINSTER

Wyre Forest School
Comberton Road, KIDDERMINSTER,
Worcestershire DY10 3DX
Tel: 01562 823156
Head: Mrs Susan Price
Category: MLD SLD ASD
BESD (Coed 7-16)

REDDITCH

Pitcheroak School
Willow Way, Brockhill, REDDITCH,
Worcestershire B97 6PQ
Tel: 01527 65576
Head: Ms Sheila Holden
Category: SLD MLD AUT (2-19)

The Kingfisher School
Clifton Close, Matchborough,
REDDITCH, Worcestershire B98 0HF
Tel: 01527 502486
Head: Mrs Jodie McCracken
Category: BESD (Coed 7-16)

WORCESTER

Fort Royal Community Primary School
Wylds Lane, WORCESTER WR5 1DR
Tel: 01905 355525
Head: Mrs Jane Long
Category: MLD PD SLD (2-11)

Regency High School
Carnforth Drive,
WORCESTER WR4 9JL
Tel: 01905 454828
Head: Mr Frank Steel
Category: PD MLD SLD (11-19)

Riversides School
Thorneloe Road,
WORCESTER WR1 3HZ
Tel: 01905 21261
Head: Mr Paul Yeomans
Category: BESD (Coed 7-16)

CITY OF YORK
Council

York SEN Team, West Offices, Station Rise, York, YO1 6GA
Tel: 01904 554302 Email: sendept@york.gov.uk Website: www.york.gov.uk

YORK

Applefields School
Bad Bargain Lane, YORK YO31 0LW
Tel: 01904 553900
Head: Mr Adam Booker
Category: MLD AUT SLD PMLD

Hob Moor Oaks & Hob Moor Community Primary School
Green Lane, Acomb,
YORK YO24 4PS
Tel: 01904 555000
Principal: Mrs Cath Hindmarch
Category: MLD AUT SLD PMLD

EAST RIDING OF YORKSHIRE
Council

E Riding of Yorkshire SENDIASS, Families Information Service Hub (FISH),
County Hall, Beverley, East Riding of Yorkshire, HU17 9BA
Tel: 01482 396469 Email: fish@eastriding.gov.uk Website: www.eastriding.gov.uk

BROUGH

St Anne's School & Sixth Form College
St Helen's Drive, Welton, BROUGH,
East Riding of Yorkshire HU15 1NR
Tel: 01482 667379
Headteacher: Mrs Lesley Davis
Category: SLD

DRIFFIELD

Kings Mill School & Nursery
Victoria Road, DRIFFIELD, East
Riding of Yorkshire YO25 6UG
Tel: 01377 253375
Headteacher: Mrs Gail Lawton
Category: SLD

GOOLE

Riverside Special School
Ainsty Street, GOOLE, East
Riding of Yorkshire DN14 5JS
Tel: 01405 763925
Acting Headteacher: Mr
Andrew Hall
Category: MLD and other
complex needs

NORTH YORKSHIRE
Education Authority

North Yorkshire SEN Team, County Hall, Northallerton, North Yorkshire, DL7 8AD
Email: send@northyorks.gov.uk Website: www.northyorks.gov.uk

BEDALE

Mowbray School
Masham Road, BEDALE,
North Yorkshire DL8 2SD
Tel: 01677 422446
Head: Mr Jonathan Tearle
Category: MLD SP&LD (2-16)

HARROGATE

Forest Moor School
Menwith Hill Road, HARROGATE,
North Yorkshire HG3 2RA
Tel: 01423 779232
Head: Mr Marc Peart
Category: BESD (Boys 11-16)

Springwater School
High Street, Starbeck, HARROGATE,
North Yorkshire HG2 7LW
Tel: 01423 883214
Head: Mrs Sarah Edwards
Category: SLD PMLD (2-19)

KIRKBYMOORSIDE

Welburn Hall School
KIRKBYMOORSIDE, York YO62 7HQ
Tel: 01751 431218
Head: Mrs Marianne Best
Category: PHLD (8-18)

KNARESBOROUGH

The Forest School
Park Lane, KNARESBOROUGH,
North Yorkshire HG5 0DG
Tel: 01423 864583
Head: Mr Peter Hewitt
Category: MLD (2-16)

NORTHALLERTON

The Dales School
Morton-on-Swale,
NORTHALLERTON, North
Yorkshire DL7 9QW
Tel: 01609 772932
Head: Mrs Hanne Barton
Category: SLD PMLD (2-19)

SCARBOROUGH

Brompton Hall School
Brompton-by-Sawdon,
SCARBOROUGH, North
Yorkshire YO13 9DB
Tel: 01723 859121
Head: Mr Mark Mihkelson
Category: BESD (Boys 8-16)

Springhead School
Barry's Lane, Seamer Road,
SCARBOROUGH, North
Yorkshire YO12 4HA
Tel: 01723 367829
Head: Mrs Debbie Wilson
Category: SLD PMLD (2-19)

SKIPTON

Brooklands School
Burnside Avenue, SKIPTON,
North Yorkshire BD23 2DB
Tel: 01756 794028
Head: Mrs Denise Sansom
Category: MLD SLD PMLD (2-19)

South Yorkshire

BARNSLEY

Families Information Service

Barnsley SEN Team, Families Information Service, Gateway Plaza, Sackville Street Barnsley, South Yorkshire, S70 2RD
Tel: 0800 0345 340 Email: infofis@barnsley.go.uk Website: www.barnsley.gov.uk

BARNSLEY

Greenacre School

Keresforth Hill Road, BARNSLEY,
South Yorkshire S70 6RG
Tel: 01226 287165
Head: Mrs Susan Hayter
Category: SLD CLD PMLD
MSI AUT (Coed Day 2-19)

Springwell Learning Community

St Helen's Boulevard, Carlton Road,
BARNSLEY, South Yorkshire S71 2AY
Tel: 01226 291133
Head: Mr David Whitaker

South Yorkshire

DONCASTER

Council

Doncaster SEN Team, Civic Office, Waterdale, Doncaster, DN1 3BU
Tel: 01302 737209 Email: sen@doncaster.gov.uk Website: www.doncaster.gov.uk

DONCASTER

Coppice School

Ash Hill Road, Hatfield,
DONCASTER, South
Yorkshire DN7 6JH
Tel: 01302 844883
Head: Mrs Lynne Jarred
Category: SLD ASD BESD
(Coed Day 3-19)

Heatherwood School

Leger Way, DONCASTER,
South Yorkshire DN2 6HQ
Tel: 01302 322044
Head: Mrs Lisa Suter
Category: SLD PD (Coed Day 3-19)

North Ridge Community School

Tenter Balk Lane, Adwick
le Street, DONCASTER,
South Yorkshire DN6 7EF
Tel: 01302 720790
Head: Mrs Christine Djezzar
Category: SLD (Coed Day 3-19)

Pennine View School

Old Road, Conisbrough,
DONCASTER, South
Yorkshire DN12 3LR
Tel: 01709 864978
Head: Ms Jo Barker-Carr
Category: MLD (Coed Day 7-16)

Stone Hill School

Barnsley Road, Scawsby,
DONCASTER, South
Yorkshire DN5 7UB
Tel: 01302 800090
Head: Mr Steve Leone
Category: MLD (Coed 6-16)

South Yorkshire

ROTHERHAM

Education, Health & Care Assessment Team

Wing C, 1st Floor, Riverside House, Main Street, Rotherham, South Yorkshire, S60 1AE
Tel: 01709 822660 Fax: 01709 371444 Email: parentpartnership@rotherham.gov.uk Website: www.rotherham.gov.uk

MEXBOROUGH

Milton School

Storey Street, Swinton,
MEXBOROUGH, South
Yorkshire S64 8QG
Tel: 01709 570246
Head: Ms Rebecca Hughes
Category: MLD (5-16) ASD (5-11)

ROTHERHAM

Abbey School

Little Common Lane,
Kimberworth, ROTHERHAM,
South Yorkshire S61 2RA
Tel: 01709 740074
Head: Ms Lucy Windle
Category: MLD

Hilltop School

Larch Road, Maltby, ROTHERHAM,
South Yorkshire S66 8AZ
Tel: 01709 813386
Heads: Mr Robert Mulvey
& Mr David Burdett
Category: SLD

Kelford School

Oakdale Road, Kimberworth,
ROTHERHAM, South
Yorkshire S61 2NU
Tel: 01709 512088
Head: Ms Jackie Tattershall
Category: SLD

Newman School

East Bawtry Road, Whiston,
ROTHERHAM, South
Yorkshire S60 3LX
Tel: 01709 828262
Head: Ms Julie Mott
Category: PH Medical needs

The Willows School

Locksley Drive, Thurcroft,
ROTHERHAM, South
Yorkshire S66 9NT
Tel: 01709 542539
Head: Mrs Anne Sanderson
Category: MLD

South Yorkshire

SHEFFIELD

Information, Advice & Support Service

Sheffield SENDIASS, Floor 6, North Wing, Moorfoot Building, Sheffield, S1 4PL
Tel: 0114 273 6009 Email: ed-parent.partnership@sheffield.gov.uk Website: www.sheffield.gov.uk

SHEFFIELD

Becton School

Beighton Community Hospital,
Sevenairs Road, SHEFFIELD,
South Yorkshire S20 1NZ
Tel: 01143 053121
Head: Mrs Sacha Schofield
Category: LD EBD SCD ADHD
Speech&LangD (Coed 5-18)

Bents Green School

Ringinglow Road, SHEFFIELD,
South Yorkshire S11 7TB
Tel: 01142 363545
Category: AUT ASD
SCD (Coed 11-19)

Heritage Park Foundation School

Norfolk Park Road, SHEFFIELD,
South Yorkshire S2 2RU
Tel: 01142 796850
Executive Head: Mr Tony Middleton
Category: BESD (KS 2/3/4)

Holgate Meadows Foundation School

Lindsay Road, SHEFFIELD,
South Yorkshire S5 7WE
Tel: 01142 456305
Head: Mr Tony Middleton
Category: BESD (KS 2/3/4)

Mossbrook Special School

Bochum Parkway, SHEFFIELD,
South Yorkshire S8 8JG
Tel: 01142 372768
Head: Mr Dean Linkhorn
Category: AUT SCD LD (Coed 4-11)

Norfolk Park School

Park Grange Road, SHEFFIELD,
South Yorkshire S2 3QF
Tel: 01142 726165
Interim Head: Ms Jan Kartawick
Category: PMLD LD (Coed 3-11)

Rowan School

4 Durvale Court, Furniss Avenue,
SHEFFIELD, South Yorkshire S17 3PT
Tel: 01142 350479
Category: AUT (Primary)

Seven Hills School

Granville Road, SHEFFIELD,
South Yorkshire S2 2RJ
Tel: 01142 743560
Heads: Ms Elaine Everett
& Mr Clive Rockliff
Category: SLD PMLD

Talbot Specialist School

Lees Hall Road, SHEFFIELD,
South Yorkshire S8 9JP
Tel: 01142 507394
Executive Head: Ms Judith Smith
Category: LD (Coed 11-19)

Woolley Wood Community Primary School

Chaucer Road, SHEFFIELD,
South Yorkshire S5 9QN
Tel: 01142 327160
Head: Mr David Whitehead
Category: SLD PMLD

West Yorkshire

CALDERDALE

Children & Young People's Services

Calderdale SEN Team, Town Hall, PO Box 51, Halifax, West Yorkshire, HX1 1TP
Tel: 01422 394141 Email: zena.taylor@calderdale.gov.uk Website: www.calderdale.gov.uk

BRIGHOUSE

Highbury School

Lower Edge Road, Rastrick,
BRIGHOUSE, West Yorkshire HD6 3LD
Tel: 01484 716319
Head: Ms Debbie Sweet
Category: All (3-11)

HALIFAX

Ravenscliffe High School

Skircoat Green, HALIFAX,
West Yorkshire HX3 0RZ
Tel: 01422 358621
Head: Mr Martin Moorman
Category: All (11-18)

Wood Bank School

Dene View, Luddendenfoot,
HALIFAX, West Yorkshire HX2 6PB
Tel: 01422 884170
Head: Mr Richard Pawson
Category: All (4-11)

Maintained special schools and colleges

West Yorkshire

KIRKLEES

Directorate for Children & Young People

Kirklees ASN Team, Civic Centre 1, High Street, Huddersfield, West Yorkshire, HD1 2NF
Tel: 01484 225057 Email: senact@kirklees.gov.uk Website: www.kirklees.gov.uk

BATLEY

Fairfield School

White Lee Road, BATLEY,
West Yorkshire WF17 8AS
Tel: 01924 326103
Head: Ms Anne Tierney
Category: SLD (Coed Day 3-19)

DEWSBURY

Ravenshall School

Ravensthorpe Road, Thornhill Lees,
DEWSBURY, West Yorkshire WF12 9EE
Tel: 01924 325234
Head: Mrs Jeanette Tate
Category: MLD (Coed Day 5-16)

HOLMFIRTH

Lydgate School

Kirkroyds Lane, New Mill,
HOLMFIRTH, West Yorkshire HD9 1LS
Tel: 01484 222484
Head: Mrs Nicola Rogers
Category: MLD (Coed Day 5-16)

HUDDERSFIELD

Castle Hill School

Newsome Road South,
Newsome, HUDDERSFIELD,
West Yorkshire HD4 6JL
Tel: 01484 226659
Head: Mrs Gill Robinson
Category: SLD AUT PMLD
(Coed Day 3-19)

Longley School

Dog Kennel Bank, HUDDERSFIELD,
West Yorkshire HD5 8JE
Tel: 01484 223937
Head: Ms Anne Lawton
Category: MLD AUT EBD
(Coed Day 5-16)

Nortonthorpe Hall School (Residential & Day)

Busker Lane, Scissett,
HUDDERSFIELD, West
Yorkshire HD8 9JU
Tel: 01484 222921
Head: Ms Sarah Wilson
Category: EBD (Coed
Residential & Day 7-16)

West Yorkshire

LEEDS

Inclusion Services

Leeds SENDIASS, Adams Court, Kildare Terrace, Leeds, West Yorkshire, LS12 1DB
Tel: 01133 951200 Website: www.educationleeds.co.uk

LEEDS

East SILC - John Jamieson (main site)

Hollin Hill Drive, Oakwood,
LEEDS, West Yorkshire LS8 2PW
Tel: 01132 930236
Head: Ms Diane Reynard
Category: Complex
physical, learning and care
needs (Coed 2-19)

North West SILC - Pennyfields (main site)

Tongue Lane, LEEDS, West
Yorkshire LS6 4QD
Tel: 01133 368270
Head: Mr Michael Purches
Category: Complex
physical, learning and care
needs (Coed 2-19)

South SILC - Broomfield (main site)

Broom Place, Belle Isle, LEEDS,
West Yorkshire LS10 3JP
Tel: 01132 771603
Head: Mr John Fryer
Category: Complex
physical, learning and care
needs (Coed 2-19)

West Oaks SEN Specialist School & College

Westwood Way, Boston
Spa, Wetherby, LEEDS, West
Yorkshire LS23 6DX
Tel: 01937 844772
Head: Mr Andrew Hodkinson
Category: Complex
physical, learning and care
needs (Coed 2-19)

West Yorkshire

WAKEFIELD
Social Care Direct

Wakefield SEN Team, Wakefield One, PO Box 700, Burton Street Wakefield, WF1 2EB
Tel: 08458 503503 Email: schoolsinformation@wakefield.gov.uk Website: www.wakefield.gov.uk

BARNSLEY

High Well School
Rook Hill Road, South Hiendley,
BARNSLEY, West Yorkshire WF8 2DD
Tel: 01924 572100
Head: Mr Will Carpenter
Category: EBD (Coed 11-16)

CASTLEFORD

Wakefield Pathways School
Poplar Avenue, Townville,
CASTLEFORD, West
Yorkshire WF10 3QJ
Tel: 01977 723085
Head: Ms Dawn Coombes
Category: SLD MLD (Coed 4-11)

OSSETT

Highfield School
Gawthorpe Lane, Gawthorpe,
OSSETT, West Yorkshire WF5 9BS
Tel: 01924 302980
Head: Mrs Pat Marshall
Category: MLD (Coed 11-16)

PONTEFRACT

Oakfield Park School
Barnsley Road, Ackworth,
PONTEFRACT, West
Yorkshire WF7 7DT
Tel: 01977 613423
Head: Mr Stephen Copley
Category: SLD PMLD (Coed 11-19)

WAKEFIELD

Kingsland School
Aberford Road, Stanley,
WAKEFIELD, West Yorkshire WF3 4BA
Tel: 01924 303100
Head: Miss Paula Trow
Category: SLD PMLD (Coed 2-11)

Pinderfields Hospital (Pupil Referral Unit)
Wrenthorpe Centre, Imperial
Avenue, WAKEFIELD, West
Yorkshire WF2 0LW
Tel: 01924 303695
Head: Mrs Helen Ferguson
Category: HS PMLD (Coed 2-19)

GUERNSEY
The Education Department

Guernsey SEN Team, PO Box 32, Grange Road, St Peter Port, Guernsey, GY1 3AU
Tel: 01481 733000 Email: office@education.gov.gg Website: www.education.gg

FOREST

Le Rondin School and Centre
Rue des Landes, FOREST,
Guernsey GY8 0DP
Tel: 01481 268300
Head: Mrs P Sullivan
Category: MLD SLD PMLD (3-11)

ST SAMPSON'S

Le Murier School
Rue de Dol, ST SAMPSON'S,
Guernsey GY2 4DA
Tel: 01481 246660
Head: Mr J Teehan
Category: MLD PMLD
SLD (Coed 11-16)

ST. PETER PORT

Les Voies School
Collings Road, ST. PETER
PORT, Guernsey GY1 1FW
Tel: 01481 710721
Head: Mr J Furley
Category: SEBD (Coed 4-16)

JERSEY
Education Support Team

Jersey SEN Team, PO Box 142, Highlands Campus, St. Saviour, Jersey, JE4 8QJ
Tel: 01534 449424 Email: education@gov.je Website: www.gov.je/esc

ST HELIER

Mont a l'Abbe School
La Grande Route de St
Jean, La Pouquelaye, ST
HELIER, Jersey JE2 3FN
Tel: 01534 875801
Head: Ms Sharon Eddie
Category: LD (3-19)

ST SAVIOUR

D'Hautree House
St Saviour's Hill, ST SAVIOUR,
Jersey JE2 7LF
Tel: 01534 618042
Head: Mr Robert Mathews
Category: SEBD (Coed 11-16)

The Alternative Curriculum
Oakside House, La Grande
Route de St Martin, Five Oaks,
ST SAVIOUR, Jersey JE2 7GS
Tel: 01534 872840
Head: Mr Kevin Mansell
Category: EBD

NORTHERN IRELAND – BELFAST
The Education Authority

Education Authority, SEN Team, Forestview, Purdys Lane, Belfast, Northern Ireland, BT8 7AR
Tel: 028 9069 4964 Email: info@eani.org.uk Website: www.eani.org.uk

BELFAST

Belfast Hospital School
Royal Belfast Hospital School
for Sick Children, Falls Road,
BELFAST, Co Antrim BT12 6BE
Tel: 02890 633498
Head: Mrs Michele Godfrey
Category: HS (Coed 4-19)

Cedar Lodge School
24 Lansdowne Park North,
BELFAST, Co Antrim BT15 4AE
Tel: 02890 777292
Head: Mrs Lois Little
Category: EPI ASD ADHD
Medical needs (Coed 4-16)

Clarawood School
Clarawood Park, BELFAST,
Co Antrim BT5 6FR
Tel: 02890 472736
Head: Ms Joanne White
Category: SEBD (Coed 8-12)

Fleming Fulton School
35 Upper Malone Road,
BELFAST, Co Antrim BT9 6TY
Tel: 02890 613877
Head: Ms Karen Hancock
Category: PH MLD (Coed 3-19)

Glenveagh School
Harberton Park, BELFAST,
Co Antrim BT9 6TX
Tel: 02890 669907
Head: Ms Anne Moore
Category: SLD (Coed 8-19)

**Greenwood House
Assessment Centre**
Greenwood Avenue, Upper
Newtownards Road, BELFAST,
Co Antrim BT4 3JJ
Tel: 02890 471000
Head: Mrs Katherine Calvert
Category: SP&LD MLD EBD SLD
Medical needs (Coed 4-7)

Harberton Special School
Haberton Park, BELFAST,
Co Antrim BT9 6TX
Tel: 02890 381525
Head: Mr Martin McGlade
Category: AUT ASP SP&LD EBD
Medical needs (Coed 4-11)

**Loughshore Educational
Resource Centre**
889 Shore Road, BELFAST,
Co Antrim BT36 7DH
Tel: 02890 773062
Teacher in Charge: Mrs G Cameron

Mitchell House School
Marmont Park, Holywood Road,
BELFAST, Co Antrim BT4 2GT
Tel: 02890 768407
Head: Miss Laura Matchett
Category: PD MSI (Coed 3-18)

**Oakwood Assessment
Centre**
Harberton Park, BELFAST,
Co Antrim BT9 6TX
Tel: 02890 605116
Head: Mrs P McCann
Category: SLD PMLD
ASD (Coed 3-8)

**Park Education
Resource Centre**
145 Ravenhill Road, BELFAST,
Co Antrim BT6 8GH
Tel: 02890 450513
Head: Ms R McCausland
Category: MLD (Coed 11-16)

**St Gerard's School &
Support Services**
Blacks Road, BELFAST,
Co Antrim BT10 0NB
Tel: 02890 600330
Head: Mrs Siobh·n McIntaggart
Category: MLD (Coed 4-16)

**St Teresa's Speech,
Language &
Communication Centre**
Glen Road, BELFAST, Co
Antrim BT11 8BL
Tel: 02890 611943
Co-ordinator: Miss N Campbell

St Vincent's Centre
6 Willowfield Drive, BELFAST,
Co Antrim BT6 8HN
Tel: 02890 461444
Teacher in Charge: Mr J McAuley

NORTH EASTERN
The Education Authority

Education Authority, SEN Team, Forestview, Purdys Lane, Belfast, Northern Ireland, BT8 7AR
Tel: 028 9069 4964 Email: info@eani.org.uk Website: www.eani.org.uk

ANTRIM

Riverside School
Fennel Road, ANTRIM,
Co Antrim BT41 4PB
Tel: 02894 428946
Head: Mr Colin Ward
Category: SLD

BALLYMENA

Castle Tower School
91 Fry's Road, BALLYMENA,
Co Antrim BT43 7EN
Tel: 02825 648264
Head: Mr Raymond McFeeters
Category: MLD SLD PD SEBD

COLERAINE

Sandelford Special School
4 Rugby Avenue, COLERAINE,
Co Londonderry BT52 1JL
Tel: 02870 343062
Category: SLD

MAGHERAFELT

Kilronan School
46 Ballyronan Road, MAGHERAFELT,
Co Londonderry BT45 6EN
Tel: 02879 632168
Head: Mrs Alison Millar
Category: SLD

NEWTOWNABBEY

Hillcroft Special School
Manse Way, NEWTOWNABBEY,
Co Antrim BT36 5UW
Tel: 02890 837488
Category: SLD

Jordanstown Special School
85 Jordanstown Road,
NEWTOWNABBEY, Co
Antrim BT37 0QE
Tel: 02890 863541
Head: Mrs Ann Magee
Category: HI VIS (Coed 4-19)

Rosstulla Special School
2 Jordanstown Road,
NEWTOWNABBEY, Co
Antrim BT37 0QS
Tel: 02890 862743
Head: Mrs Fiona Burke
Category: MLD (Coed 5-16)

SOUTH EASTERN
The Education Authority

Education Authority, SEN Team, Forestview, Purdys Lane, Belfast, Northern Ireland, BT8 7AR
Tel: 028 9069 4964 Email: info@eani.org.uk Website: www.eani.org.uk

BANGOR

Clifton Special School
292A Old Belfast Road,
BANGOR, Co Down BT19 1RH
Tel: 02891 270210
Head: Mrs Stephanie Anderson
Category: SLD

Lakewood Special School
96 Newtownards Road,
BANGOR, Co Down BT19 1GZ
Tel: 02891 456227
Head: Mr Jon Bleakney

BELFAST

Longstone Special School
Millar's Lane, Dundonald,
BELFAST, Co Down BT16 2DA
Tel: 02890 480071
Head: Mr Ioannis Skarmoutsos
Category: MLD

Tor Bank School
5 Dunlady Road, BELFAST,
Co Down BT16 1TT
Tel: 02890 484147
Head: Mr Colm Davis
Category: SLD

CRAIGAVON

Brookfield Special School
65 Halfpenny Gate Road, Moira,
CRAIGAVON, Co Armagh BT67 0HP
Tel: 02892 622978
Head: Mrs Barbara Spence
Category: MLD (Coed 5-11)

DONAGHADEE

Killard House
Cannyreagh Road, DONAGHADEE,
Co Down BT21 0AU
Tel: 02891 882361
Head: Mr Colin Millar
Category: MLD

DOWNPATRICK

Ardmore House
95A Saul Street, DOWNPATRICK,
Co Down BT30 6NJ
Tel: 02844 614881
Head: Mr Barry Fettes
Category: EBD

Knockevin Special School
33 Racecourse Hill, DOWNPATRICK,
Co Down BT30 6PU
Tel: 02844 612167
Head: Mrs Anne Cooper
Category: SLD

HILLSBOROUGH

Beechlawn Special School
3 Dromore Road, HILLSBOROUGH,
Co Down BT26 6PA
Tel: 02892 682302
Head: Mrs Barbara Green
Category: MLD

LISBURN

Parkview Special School
2 Brokerstown Road, LISBURN,
Co Antrim BT28 2EE
Tel: 02892 601197
Head: Mr James Curran
Category: SLD

SOUTHERN
The Education Authority

Education Authority, SEN Team, Forestview, The MallPurdys Lane, Belfast, Northern Ireland, BT8 7AR
Tel: 028 9069 4964 Email: info@eani.org.uk Website: www.eani.org.uk

ARMAGH

Lisanally School
85 Lisanally Lane, ARMAGH,
Co Armagh BT61 7HF
Tel: 02837 523563
Head: Ms Sandra Flynn
Category: SLD (Coed)

BANBRIDGE

Donard School
22A Castlewellan Road,
BANBRIDGE, Co Down BT32 4XY
Tel: 02840 662357
Head: Mrs Edel Lavery
Category: SLD (Coed)

CRAIGAVON

Ceara School
Sloan Street, Lurgan, CRAIGAVON,
Co Armagh BT66 8NY
Tel: 02838 323312
Head: Dr Peter Cunningham
Category: SLD (Coed)

NEWRY

Rathore School
23 Martin's Lane, Carnagat,
NEWRY, Co Down BT35 8PJ
Tel: 02830 261617
Head: Mr Raymond Cassidy
Category: SLD (Coed)

WESTERN
The Education Authority

Education Authority, SEN Team, Forestview, Purdys Lane, Belfast, Northern Ireland, BT8 7AR
Tel: 028 9069 4964 Email: info@eani.org.uk Website: www.eani.org.uk

ENNISKILLEN

Willowbridge School
8 Lough Shore Road,
Drumlyon, ENNISKILLEN, Co
Fermanagh BT74 7EY
Tel: 02866 329947
Principal: Mrs Julie Murphy
Category: SLD MLD (Coed)

LIMAVADY

Rossmar School
2 Ballyquin Road, LIMAVADY,
Co Londonderry BT49 9ET
Tel: 02877 762351
Head: Mr Brian McLaughlin
Category: MLD (Coed)

LONDONDERRY

**Ardnashee School and
College (Lower Campus)**
15 Racecourse Road,
LONDONDERRY, Co
Londonderry BT48 7RE
Tel: 02871 263270
Acting Principal: Mr Pell-Ilderton
Category: SLD (Coed)

**Ardnashee School and
College (Upper Campus)**
17 Racecourse Road,
LONDONDERRY, Co
Londonderry BT48 7RE
Tel: 02871 351266
Acting Principal: Mr Pell-Ilderton
Category: EBD MLD (Coed)

OMAGH

**Arvalee School &
Resource Centre**
17 Deverney Road, OMAGH,
Co Tyrone BT79 0ND
Tel: 02882 255710
Principal: Mr Jonathan Gray
Category: MLD SLD (Coed)

STRABANE

**Knockavoe School and
Resource Centre**
10A Melmount Gardens,
STRABANE, Co Tyrone BT82 9EB
Tel: 02871 883319
Head: Ms Martina McComish
Category: SLD MLD (Coed)

SCOTLAND – ABERDEEN
Education, Culture & Sport

Aberdeen ASN Team, Business Hub 13, Second Floor North, Marischal College, Broad Street Aberdeen, AB10 1AB
Tel: 01224 523449 Email: fis@aberdeencity.gov.uk Website: www.aberdeencity.gov.uk

ABERDEEN

**Aberdeen School
for the Deaf**
c/o Sunnybank School, Sunnybank
Road, ABERDEEN AB24 3NJ
Tel: 01224 261722
Head: Ms Alison Buchan
Category: HI

Cordyce School
Riverview Drive, Dyce,
ABERDEEN AB21 7NF
Tel: 01224 724215
Head: Ms Maureen Simmers
Category: EBD

Hazlewood School
Fernielea Road,
ABERDEEN AB15 6GU
Tel: 01224 321363
Head: Ms Jill Barry
Category: SLD MLD PMLD

**Hospital and Home
Tuition Service**
Royal Aberdeen Children's
Hospital, Lowit Unit, Westburn
Road, ABERDEEN AB25 2ZG
Tel: 01224 550317
Head: Ms Maureen Simmers
Category: HS

Woodlands School
Regent Walk, ABERDEEN AB24 1SX
Tel: 01224 524393
Head: Ms Caroline Stirton
Category: PMLD

ABERDEENSHIRE
Education & Children's Services

Aberdeenshire ASN Team, St Leonards, Sandyhill Road, Banff, AB45 1BH
Tel: 01261 813340 Email: education.development@aberdeenshire.gov.uk Website: www.aberdeenshire.gov.uk

FRASERBURGH

Westfield School
Argyll Road, FRASERBURGH,
Aberdeenshire AB43 9BL
Tel: 01346 518699
Head: Ms Kerri Dalton
Category: PMLD SCLD
(Coed 5-18, 0-3 Nursery)

INVERURIE

St Andrew's School
St Andrew's Garden, INVERURIE,
Aberdeenshire AB51 3XT
Tel: 01467 621215
Acting Head: Ms Susan Stewart
Category: PMLD SCLD (Coed 3-18)

PETERHEAD

Anna Ritchie School
Grange Gardens, PETERHEAD,
Aberdeenshire AB42 2AP
Tel: 01779 473293
Heads: Ms Catriona Creighton
& Ms Sharon Ferguson
Category: PMLD SCLD (Coed 3-18)

STONEHAVEN

Carronhill School
Mill of Forest Road, STONEHAVEN,
Kincardineshire AB39 2GZ
Tel: 01569 763886
Head: Mrs Glenda Fraser
Category: PMLD SCLD (Coed 3-18)

EAST AYRSHIRE
Education & Social Services

East Ayrshire ASN Team, Council Headquarters, London Road, Kilmarnock, KA3 7BU
Tel: 01563 576000 Website: www.east-ayrshire.gov.uk

CUMNOCK

Hillside School
Dalgleish Avenue, CUMNOCK,
East Ayrshire KA18 1QQ
Tel: 01290 423239
Head: Ms Debbie Skeoch
Category: SLD PMLD (Coed 6-17)

KILMARNOCK

Park School
Beech Avenue, KILMARNOCK,
East Ayrshire KA1 2EW
Tel: 01563 549988
Acting Head: Ms Carol Anne Burns
Category: LD PD (Coed 5-18)

Willowbank School
Grassyards Road, KILMARNOCK,
East Ayrshire KA3 7BB
Tel: 01563 526115
Head: Ms Tracy Smallwood
Category: SLD PMLD

SOUTH AYRSHIRE
Council

South Ayrshire ASN Team, County Buildings, Wellington Square, Ayr, KA7 1DR
Tel: 03001 230900 Website: www.south-ayrshire.gov.uk

AYR

Southcraig Campus
Belmont Avenue, AYR,
South Ayrshire KA7 2ND
Tel: 01292 612146
Head: Mrs Jane Gordon
Category: SLD CLD (Coed 1-5)

GIRVAN

Invergarven School
15 Henrietta Street, GIRVAN,
South Ayrshire KA26 9EB
Tel: 01465 716808
Head: Ms Kimberley Keenan
Category: SLD CLD PD
MSI (Coed 3-16)

CLACKMANNANSHIRE
Council

Clackmannanshire Educational Development Service, Kilncraigs,
Greenside Street, Alloa, Clackmannanshire, FK10 1EB
Tel: 01259 450000 Fax: 01259 452440 Email: education@clacks.gov.uk Website: www.clacksweb.org.uk

ALLOA

**Extended Additional
Support Needs Provision
within Alloa Academy**
Bowhouse Road, ALLOA,
Clackmannanshire FK10 1DN
Tel: 01259 214979
**Principal Teacher of
Provision:** Linda Brown
Category: CLD MSI PD PH PMLD SLD

**Primary School Support
Service located in
Park Primary School**
East Castle Street, ALLOA,
Clackmannanshire FK10 1AN
Tel: 01259 212151
Head Teacher: Julie Ann Miller
Category: SEBD EBSD BESD

**Secondary Support
Service within
South School**
Bedford Place, ALLOA,
Clackmannanshire FK10 1JK
Tel: 01259 724345
Head Teacher: Julie Ann Miller
Category: SEBD EBSD BESD

ALVA

**Primary ASD Provision
within Alva Primary
(from August 2014)**
Brook Street, ALVA,
Clackmannanshire FK12 5AN
**Principal Teacher of
Provision:** Tracey Howard
Category: ASD AUT ADHD ADD

**Secondary ASD Provision
within Alva Academy**
Academy Avenue, ALVA,
Clackmannanshire FK12 5FE
Tel: 01259 760342
**Principal Teacher of
Provision:** Laura Fowler
Category: ASD AUT ADHD ADD

SAUCHIE

Lochies School
Gartmorn Road, SAUCHIE,
Clackmannanshire FK10 3PB
Tel: 01259 216928
Head: Rhoda MacDougall
Category: CLD SLD (Coed 5-11)

TILLICOULTRY

**Inclusion Support Service
located in Tillicoultry
Primary School**
Fir Park, TILLICOULTRY,
Clackmannanshire FK13 6PL
Tel: 01259 452455
Acting Manager: Audrey
McCormick
Category: Supports all children
with ASN in mainstream schools

COMHAIRLE NAN EILEAN SIAR
Department of Education & Children's Services

Comhairle Nan Eilean Siar ASN Team, Sandwick Road, Stornoway, Isle of Lewis, HS1 2BW
Tel: 08456 007090 Email: enquiries@cne-siar.gov.uk Website: www.cne-siar.gov.uk

SANDWICK

**Sandwickhill
Learning Centre**
East Street, SANDWICK,
Isle of Lewis HS2 0AG
Tel: 01851 822680
Principal Teacher: Mrs A Campbell
Category: SLD PMLD (Coed 3-11)

EAST DUNBARTONSHIRE
Council

East Dunbartonshire ASN Team, 12 Strathkelvin Place, Kirkintilloch, Glasgow, Lanarkshire, G66 1TJ
Tel: 0300 123 4510 Email: education@eastdunbarton.gov.uk Website: www.eastdunbarton.gov.uk

KIRKINTILLOCH

Merkland School
Langmuir Road, KIRKINTILLOCH,
East Dunbartonshire G66 2QF
Tel: 01419 552336
Head: Ms Anne Mulvenna
Category: MLD PH

LENZIE

Campsie View School
Boghead Road, LENZIE, East
Dunbartonshire G66 4DP
Tel: 01419 552339
Head: Mrs Carole Bowie
Category: SCLD

WEST DUNBARTONSHIRE
Council

West Dunbartonshire ASN Team, Educational Services, Council Offices, Garshake Road Dunbarton, G82 3PU
Tel: 01389 737374 Email: contact.centre@west-dunbarton.gov.uk Website: www.west-dunbarton.gov.uk

CLYDEBANK

Cunard School
Cochno Street, Whitecrook,
CLYDEBANK, West
Dunbartonshire G81 1RQ
Tel: 01419 521621
Head: Jenni Curson
Category: SEBD (Primary)

Kilpatrick School
Mountblow Road,
Dalmuir, CLYDEBANK, West
Dunbartonshire G81 4SW
Tel: 01389 872171/872168
Head: Debbie Queen
Category: SCLD (Primary/
Secondary)

CITY OF EDINBURGH
Council

Edinburgh ASN Team, Waverley Court, 4 East Market Street, Edinburgh, Midlothian, EH8 8BG
Tel: 0131 200 2000 Website: www.edingburgh.gov.uk

EDINBURGH

Braidburn Special School

107 Oxgangs Road North,
EDINBURGH EH14 1ED
Tel: 01313 122320
Head: Ms Morna Phillips
Category: EPI PH (Coed 2-18)

Kaimes School

140 Lasswade Road,
EDINBURGH EH16 6RT
Tel: 01316 648241
Head: Mrs Ros Miller
Category: SP&LD ASD (Coed 5-18)

Oaklands School

750 Ferry Road,
EDINBURGH EH4 4PQ
Tel: 01313 158100
Category: SLD CLD PD MSI

Panmure St Ann's

6 South Grays Close,
EDINBURGH EH1 1TQ
Tel: 01315 568833

Pilrig Park Special School

12 Balfour Place,
EDINBURGH EH6 5DW
Tel: 01314 677960
Head: Ms Rebecca Chad
Category: MLD SLD (Coed 11-16)

Prospect Bank Special School

81 Restalrig Road,
EDINBURGH EH6 8BQ
Tel: 01315 532239
Head: Ms Susan McLaren
Category: LD SP&LD (Coed 5-12)

Redhall Special School

3c Redhall Grove,
EDINBURGH EH14 2DU
Tel: 01314 431256
Head: Ms Susan Shipway
Category: LD (Coed 4-11)

Rowanfield Special School

67c Groathill Road North,
EDINBURGH EH4 2SA
Tel: 01313 436116
Category: EBD

St Crispin's Special School

19 Watertoun Road,
EDINBURGH EH9 3HZ
Tel: 01316 674831
Head: Ms Ruth Hendery
Category: SLD AUT (Coed 5-16)

Woodlands Special School

36 Dolphin Avenue,
EDINBURGH EH14 5RD
Tel: 01314 493447

FALKIRK
Council

Falkirk Additional Support for Learning, Sealock House, 2 Inchyra Road, Grangemouth, FK3 9XB
Tel: 01324 506649 Email: additionalsupport@falkirk.gov.uk Website: www.falkirk.gov.uk

FALKIRK

Mariner Support Service

Weedingshall, Edinburgh Road,
Polmont, FALKIRK FK2 0XS
Tel: 01324 506770
Acting Head: Ms Gillian Macadam
Category: SEBD (Secondary)

Windsor Park School

Bantaskine Road, FALKIRK FK1 5HT
Tel: 01324 508640
Head: Mrs Catherine Finestone
Category: D (Coed 3-16)

GRANGEMOUTH

Oxgang School

c/o Moray Primary School, Moray
Place, GRANGEMOUTH FK3 9DL
Tel: 01324 501311
Acting Head: Mr David MacKay
Category: BESD (5-11)

LARBET

Carrongrange School

Carrongrange Avenue,
LARBET, Falkirk FK5 3BH
Tel: 01324 555266
Head: Ms Gillian Robertson
Category: CLD MLD (Secondary)

FIFE
Education Service

Fife ASN Team, Rothesay House, Rothesay Place, Glenrothes, Fife, KY7 5PQ
Tel: 03451 555555 (Ext 442126) Email: jennifer.allan@fife.gov.uk Website: www.fifedirect.org.uk/fifecouncil

CUPAR

Kilmaron School
Balgarvie Road, CUPAR,
Fife KY15 4PE
Tel: 01334 659480
Head: Ms Isla Lumsden
Category: CLD PD (Coed 3-18)

DUNFERMLINE

Calaiswood School
Nightingale Place,
DUNFERMLINE, Fife KY11 8LW
Tel: 01383 602481
Head: Ms Deborah Davidson
Category: CLD (Coed 3-18)

Woodmill High School ASN
Shields Road, DUNFERMLINE,
Fife KY11 4ER
Tel: 01383 602406
Category: SEBD

GLENROTHES

John Fergus School
Erskine Place, GLENROTHES,
Fife KY7 4JB
Tel: 01592 583489
Head: Ms Pamela Kirkum
Category: CD PD (Coed Day 3-18)

KIRKCALDY

Rosslyn School
Viewforth Terrace,
KIRKCALDY, Fife KY1 3BW
Tel: 01592 583482
Head: Mr Nick Caiger
Category: SLD PMLD PD (Coed 3-19)

LEVEN

Hyndhead School
Barncraig Street, Buckhaven,
LEVEN, Fife KY8 1JE
Tel: 01592 583480
Head: Ms Agnes Lindsay
Category: SLD (Coed 5-18)

GLASGOW
Education Services

Glasgow ASN Team, 40 John Street, Glasgow, G1 1JL
Tel: 01412 872000 Website: www.glasgow.gov.uk

GLASGOW

Abercorn Secondary School
195 Garscube Road,
GLASGOW G4 9QH
Tel: 01413 326212
Head: Ms Patricia McGowan
Category: MLD

Ashton Secondary School
100 Avenue End Road,
GLASGOW G33 3SW
Tel: 01417 743428
Head: Mr Danny McGrorry
Category: PH VIS CLD

Broomlea Primary School
Keppoch Campus, 65 Stonyhurst
Street, GLASGOW G22 5AX
Tel: 01413 368428
Head: Ms Fiona Shields
Category: CLD

Cardinal Winning Secondary School
30 Fullarton Avenue,
GLASGOW G32 8NJ
Tel: 01417 783714
Head: Mr Gerard McDonald
Category: MLD

Cartvale Secondary School
3 Burndyke Court,
GLASGOW G51 2BG
Tel: 01414 451767
Head: Ms Pauline Harte
Category: SEBN

Croftcroighn Primary School
290 Mossvale Road,
GLASGOW G33 5NY
Tel: 01417 743760
Head: Mrs Margaret McFadden
Category: CLD

Drummore Primary School
129 Drummore Road,
GLASGOW G15 7NH
Tel: 01419 441323
Head: Ms Fiona McLean
Category: MLD

Eastmuir Primary School
211 Hallhill Road,
GLASGOW G33 4QL
Tel: 01417 713464
Head: Mrs Lorraine Campbell
Category: MLD

Greenview Learning Centre
384 Drakemire Drive,
GLASGOW G45 9SR
Tel: 01416 341551
Head: Mrs Aisling Boyle
Category: SEBN

Hampden Primary School
18 Logan Gardens,
GLASGOW G5 0LJ
Tel: 01414 296095
Head: Ms Seana Moore
Category: CLD

Hazelwood School
50 Dumbreck Court,
GLASGOW G41 5DQ
Tel: 01442 79334
Head: Ms Andrea Haugh-Reid
Category: HI VIS CLD (2-19)

Howford Primary School
487 Crookston Road,
GLASGOW G53 7TX
Tel: 01418 822605
Head: Ms Karen Keith
Category: MLD

Kelbourne Park Primary School
109 Hotspur Street,
GLASGOW G20 8LH
Tel: 01419 461405
Head: Ms Andrea MacBeath
Category: PH CLD

Kirkriggs Primary School
500 Croftfoot Road,
GLASGOW G45 0NJ
Tel: 01416 347158
Acting Head: Ms Denise Laverty
Category: MLD

Maintained special schools and colleges

Langlands Primary School

Glenside Avenue,
GLASGOW G53 5FD
Tel: 01418 920952
Head: Mr Mark Beattie
Category: CLD

Middlefield School

80 Ardnahoe Avenue,
GLASGOW G42 0DL
Tel: 01413 340159
Head: Ms Catherine Gilius
Category: ASD (Day)

Newhills Secondary School

42 Newhills Road,
GLASGOW G33 4HJ
Tel: 01417 731296
Head: Ms Alison Lochrie
Category: CLD

Parkhill Secondary School

375 Cumbernauld Road,
GLASGOW G31 3LP
Tel: 01415 542765
Head: Ms Evelyn Hill
Category: MLD

St Kevin's Primary School

25 Fountainwell Road,
GLASGOW G21 1TN
Tel: 01415 573722
Head: Ms Lorna Ferguson
Category: MLD

St Oswald's Secondary School

9 Birgidale Road,
GLASGOW G45 9NJ
Tel: 01416 373952
Head: Ms Margaret MacLeay
Category: MLD

Westmuir High School

255 Rigby Street,
GLASGOW G32 6DJ
Tel: 01415 566276
Head: Ms Pauline Harte
Category: SEBN

HIGHLAND
Education, Culture & Sport Service

Highland ASN Team, Glenurquhart Road, Inverness, IV3 5NX
Tel: 01463 702801 Website: www.highland.gov.uk

INVERNESS

Drummond School

Drummond Road, Inverness,
INVERNESS, Highland IV2 4NZ
Tel: 01463 701050
Head: Mr Mark Elvines
Category: SLD PMLD
CLD (Coed 3-16)

The Bridge

12-14 Seafield Road, INVERNESS,
Highland IV1 1SG
Tel: 01463 256606
Head: Mr Raymond Hall

ROSS-SHIRE

St Clement's School

Tulloch Street, Dingwall, ROSS-
SHIRE, Highland IV15 9JZ
Tel: 01349 863284
Head: Ms Toni Macartney
Category: SP&LD VIS
HI PD (Coed 5-11)

St Duthus School

Academy Street, Tain, ROSS-
SHIRE, Highland IV19 1ED
Tel: 01862 894407
Head: Ms Clare Whiteford
Category: SLD PLD CLD (Coed 3-18)

INVERCLYDE
Council

Inverclyde ASN Team, Wallace Place, Greenock, PA15 1JB
Tel: 01475 717171 Email: admin.educationhq@inverclyde.gov.uk Website: www.inverclyde.gov.uk

GOUROCK

Garvel Deaf Centre

c/o Moorfoot Primary School,
GOUROCK, Inverclyde PA19 1ES
Tel: 01475 715642
Head: Ms Sylvia Gillen
Category: D

PORT GLASGOW

Craigmarloch School

Port Glasgow Community
Campus, Kilmacolm Road, PORT
GLASGOW, Inverclyde PA14 6PP
Tel: 01475 715345
Head: Ms Eileen Stewart

NORTH LANARKSHIRE
Council

North Lanarkshire ASN Team, Learning and Leisure Services, Municipal Buildings, Kildonan Street Coatbridge, ML5 3BT
Tel: 01236 812790 Website: www.northlan.gov.uk

AIRDRIE

Mavisbank School and Nursery
Mitchell Street, AIRDRIE, North Lanarkshire ML6 0EB
Tel: 01236 632108
Head: Mr John Lochrie
Category: PMLD (Coed 3-18)

COATBRIDGE

Buchanan High School
67 Townhead Road, COATBRIDGE, North Lanarkshire ML5 2HT
Tel: 01236 632052
Head: Mrs M Fannan
Category: (Coed Day 12-18)

Drumpark School
Albert Street, COATBRIDGE, North Lanarkshire ML5 3ET
Tel: 01236 794884
Category: MLD PH SP&LD (3-18)

Pentland School
Tay Street, COATBRIDGE, North Lanarkshire ML5 2NA
Tel: 01236 794833
Head: Ms Kathleen Cassidy
Category: SEBD (Coed 5-11)

Portland High School
31-33 Kildonan Street, COATBRIDGE, North Lanarkshire ML5 3LG
Tel: 01236 632060
Head: Mr McGovern
Category: SEBD (Coed 11-16)

Willowbank School
299 Bank Street, COATBRIDGE, North Lanarkshire ML5 1EG
Tel: 01236 632078
Category: SEBD (Coed 11-18)

CUMBERNAULD

Glencryan School
Greenfaulds Road, CUMBERNAULD, North Lanarkshire G67 2XJ
Tel: 01236 794866
Category: MLD PH ASD (Coed 5-18)

Redburn School and Nursery
Kildrum Ring Road, CUMBERNAULD, North Lanarkshire G67 2EL
Tel: 01236 736904
Category: SLD CLD PH (Coed 2-18)

MOTHERWELL

Bothwellpark High School
Annan Street, MOTHERWELL, North Lanarkshire ML1 2DL
Tel: 01698 274939
Category: SLD (Coed 11-18)

Clydeview School and Nursery
Magna Street, MOTHERWELL, North Lanarkshire ML1 3QZ
Tel: 01698 264843
Head: Ms Marie Jo McGurl
Category: SLD (Coed 5-11)

Firpark Primary School
177 Milton Street, MOTHERWELL, North Lanarkshire ML1 1DL
Tel: 01698 274933
Category: (Coed Day 3-10)

Firpark Secondary School
Firpark Street, MOTHERWELL, North Lanarkshire ML1 2PR
Tel: 01698 251313
Category: MLD PH (Coed 11-18)

UDDINGSTON

Fallside Secondary School
Sanderson Avenue, Viewpark, UDDINGSTON, North Lanarkshire G71 6JZ
Tel: 01698 274986
Category: EBD (Coed 11-16)

SOUTH LANARKSHIRE
Council

South Lanarkshire ASN Team, Council Offices, Almada Street, Hamilton, ML3 0AA
Tel: 03031 231015 Email: customer.services@southlanarkshire.gov.uk Website: www.southlanarkshire.gov.uk

CAMBUSLANG

Rutherglen High School
anglea Road, CAMBUSLANG, South Lanarkshire G72 8ES
el: 01416 433480
Head: Mrs Jan Allen

CARLUKE

Victoria Park School
Market Road, CARLUKE, South Lanarkshire ML8 4BE
el: 01555 750591
Head: Miss Anne Fisher
Category: PMLD SLD

EAST KILBRIDE

Greenburn School
Maxwellton Avenue, EAST KILBRIDE, South Lanarkshire G74 3DU
Tel: 01355 237278
Head: Mrs Helen Nicol
Category: PMLD

Sanderson High School
High Common Road, St Leonard's, EAST KILBRIDE, South Lanarkshire G74 2LP
Tel: 01355 588625
Head: Mrs Aisling Boyle

West Mains School
Logie Park, EAST KILBRIDE, South Lanarkshire G74 4BU
Tel: 01355 249938
Head: Mrs Rosemary Payne
Category: SLD

HAMILTON

Hamilton School for the Deaf
Anderson Street, HAMILTON, South Lanarkshire ML3 0QL
Tel: 01698 823377
Head: Ms Eileen Burns
Category: D

MIDLOTHIAN
Education, Communities & Economy

Midlothian ASN Team, Fairfield House, 8 Lothian Road, Dalkeith, Midlothian, EH22 3ZG
Tel: 01312 713689 Email: asn.officer@midlothian.gov.uk Website: www.midlothian.gov.uk

DALKEITH

Saltersgate School
3 Cousland Road, DALKEITH,
Midlothian EH22 2PS
Tel: 01316 544703
Head: Ms Fiona Hume
Category: GLD (Coed Secondary)

WEST LOTHIAN
Education & Learning

West Lothian ASN Team, West Lothian Civic Centre, Howden South Road, Livingston, West Lothian, EH54 6FF
Tel: 01506 282634 Email: alison.raeburn@westlothian.gov.uk Website: www.westlothian.gov.uk

BATHGATE

Pinewood Special School
Elm Grove, Blackburn, BATHGATE,
West Lothian EH47 7QX
Tel: 01506 656374
Head: Ms Pamela Greig
Category: MLD SLD

BLACKBURN

Connolly School Campus
Hopefield Road, BLACKBURN,
West Lothian EH47 7HZ
Tel: 01506 283888
Head: Mrs Laura Quilter
Category: SEBN (Primary)

LIVINGSTON

Beatlie School Campus
The Mall, Craigshill, LIVINGSTON,
West Lothian EH54 5EJ
Tel: 01506 777598
Head: Mrs Carol Robbie
Category: CLD MSI PD (Coed 3-16)

Cedarbank School
Cedarbank, Ladywell East,
LIVINGSTON, West Lothian EH54 6DR
Tel: 01506 442172
Acting Head: Ms Carol McDonald
Category: ASD LD (Coed 12-18)

Ogilvie School Campus
Ogilvie Way, Knightsridge,
LIVINGSTON, West Lothian EH54 8HL
Tel: 01506 777489
Head: Ms Liz Speirs
Category: EBD (Primary)

LIVINGSTONE

Willowgrove House
1/6 Willowgrove, Craigshill,
LIVINGSTONE, West
Lothian EH54 5LU
Tel: 01506 434274
Head: Mrs Laura Quilter

WHITBURN

Burnhouse School
The Avenue, WHITBURN,
West Lothian EH47 0BX
Tel: 01501 678100
Head: Mrs Laura Quilter
Category: EBD (Secondary)

PERTH & KINROSS
Education & Children's Services

Perth & Kinross SEN Team, Pullar House, 35 Kinnoull Street, Perth, PH1 5GD
Tel: 01738 476200 Email: enquiries@pkc.gov.uk Website: www.pkc.gov.uk

PERTH

Fairview School
Oakbank Crescent, PERTH,
Perthshire & Kinross PH1 1DF
Tel: 01738 473050
Head: Ms Fiona Gillespie
Category: SLD CLD (Coed 2-18)

RENFREWSHIRE
Education & Learning

Renfrewshire ASN Team, Renfrewshire House, Cotton Street, Paisley, PA1 1UJ
Tel: 03003 000170 Email: asn.els@renfrewshire.gov.uk Website: www.renfrewshire.gov.uk

LINWOOD

Clippens School
Brediland Road, LINWOOD,
Renfrewshire PA3 3RX
Tel: 01505 325333
Acting Head: Ms Teresa Brown
Category: ASD CLD PI
MSI (Coed 5-19)

PAISLEY

Kersland School
Ben Nevis Road, PAISLEY,
Renfrewshire PA2 7BU
Tel: 01418 898251
Head Teacher: Ms Michelle Welsh
Category: SLD (Coed 5-18)

Mary Russell School
Hawkhead Road, PAISLEY,
Renfrewshire PA2 7BE
Tel: 01418 897628
Head: Ms Julie McCallum
Category: MLD (Coed 5-18)

EAST RENFREWSHIRE
Education Department

East Renfrewshire ASN Team, Council Offices, 211 Main Street, Barrhead, East Renfrewshire, G78 1SY
Tel: 0141 577 3001 Email: customerservices@eastrenfrewshire.gov.uk Website: www.eastrenfrewshire.gov.uk

NEWTON MEARNS

The Isobel Mair School
58 Stewarton Road, NEWTON
MEARNS, East Renfrewshire G77 6NB
Tel: 0141 577 7600
Head: Mrs Sarah Clark
Category: CLD (Coed 5-18)

STIRLING
Council

Stirling ASN Team, Teith House, Kerse Road, Stirling, FK7 7QA
Tel: 08452 777000 Website: www.stirling.gov.uk

CALLANDER

Callander ASD Provision (at Callander Primary School)
Bridgend, CALLANDER FK17 8AG
Tel: 01877 331576
Head: Ms Audrey Ross
Category: ASD

FALLIN

SEBN Support Service (Primary)
Fallin Primary School, Lamont Crescent, FALLIN FK7 7EJ
Tel: 01786 272330
Acting Head: David McKellar
Category: SEBD EBSD BESD

STIRLING

ASN Outreach Service
Raploch Community Campus, Drip Road, STIRLING FK8 1SD
Tel: 01786 272333
Co-ordinator: Ms Christine Stones

Castleview School
Raploch Community Campus, Drip Road, STIRLING FK8 1SD
Tel: 01786 272326
Acting Head: Ms Janet Stirling
Category: PD PMLD

Ochil House (at Wallace High School)
Airthrey Road, STIRLING FK9 5HW
Tel: 01786 462166/7
Head: Mr Scott Pennock
Category: CLD SLD PD PH PMLD

Riverside ASD Provision (at Riverside Primary)
Forrest Road, STIRLING FK8 1UJ
Tel: 01786 474128
Head of Provision: Ms Sandra Croug
Category: ASD

SEBN Support Service (S1-S3)
Riverside Base, Forrest Road, STIRLING FK8 1UJ
Tel: 01786 448929
Acting Head: David McKellar
Category: SEBD EBSD BESD

SEBN Support Service (S3-S5)
Chartershall, Fairhill Road, Whins of Milton, STIRLING FK7 0LL
Tel: 01786 812667
Acting Head: David McKellar
Category: SEBD EBSD BESD

St Modan's ASD Provision (at St Modan's High School)
Royal Stuart Way, STIRLING FK7 7WS
Tel: 01786 470962
Head of Provision: Ms Bridget Raeside
Category: ASD

WALES – BLAENAU GWENT
County Borough Council

Blaenau Gwent SEN Team, Anvil Court, Church Street, Abertillery, NP13 1DB
Tel: 01495 311556 Email: education.department@blaenau-gwent.gov.uk Website: www.blaenau-gwent.gov.uk

EBBW VALE

Pen-y-Cwm Special School
Ebbw Fawr Learning Community, Strand Annealing Lane, EBBW VALE, Blaenau Gwent NP23 6AN
Tel: 01495 357755
Head: Ms Darya Brill-Williams
Category: SLD PMLD

BRIDGEND
County Borough Council

Bridgend Access & Inclusion Service, The SEN Team, Civic Offices, Angel Street Bridgend, CF31 4WB
Tel: 01656 815230 Email: ais@bridgend.gov.uk Website: www.bridgend.gov.uk

BRIDGEND

Heronsbridge Special School
Ewenny Road, BRIDGEND CF31 3HT
Tel: 01656 653974
Head: Mrs G James
Category: PMLD VIS AUT (Coed Day & boarding 3-18)

Ysgol Bryn Castell
Bryncethin Campus, Abergarw Road, Brynmenyn, BRIDGEND CF32 9NZ
Tel: 01656 815595
Head: Mrs H Ridout
Category: EBD LD HI ASD MLD SLD SP&LD (Coed 3-19)

CAERPHILLY
Family Information Service

Caerphilly FIS, The SEN Team, Penallta House, Tredomen Park Ystrad Mynach, Hengoed, CF82 7PG
Tel: 01443 863232 Website: www.caerphilly.gov.uk

CAERPHILLY

Trinity Fields Special School
Caerphilly Road, Ystrad Mynach, CAERPHILLY CF82 7XW
Tel: 01443 866000
Head: Mr Ian Elliott
Category: SLD VIS HI CLD SP&LD (Coed 3-19)

CARDIFF
Education Service

SNAP Cymru, County Hall, Atlantic Wharf, Cardiff, CF10 4UW
Tel: 08451 203730 Email: helpline@snapcymru.org Website: www.cardiff.gov.uk

CARDIFF

Greenhill School
Heol Brynglas, Rhiwbina, CARDIFF CF14 6UJ
Tel: 02920 693786
Head: Mrs Jane Counsell
Category: SEBD (Coed 11-16)

Meadowbank School
Colwill Road, Llandaff North, CARDIFF CF14 2QQ
Tel: 02920 616018
Head: Mrs Lorraine Felstead
Category: SLCD (Coed 4-11)

Riverbank School
Vincent Road, Caerau, CARDIFF CF5 5AQ
Tel: 02920 563860
Head: Mrs Amanda Gibson-Evans
Category: MLD SLD (Coed 4-11)

The Court School
Station Road, Llanishen, CARDIFF CF14 5UX
Tel: 02920 752713
Head: Mrs Beverley Smith
Category: SEBD (Coed 4-11)

The Hollies School
Brynheulog, CARDIFF CF23 7XG
Tel: 02920 734411
Head: Miss Kath Keely
Category: ASD PMED (Coed 4-11)

Ty Gwyn School
Vincent Road, Caerau, CARDIFF CF5 5AQ
Tel: 02920 838560
Head: Mr Kevin Tansley
Category: PMLD ASD (Coed 4-19)

Woodlands High School
Vincent Road, Caerau, CARDIFF CF5 5AQ
Tel: 02920 561279
Head: Mr Russell Webb
Category: MLD SLD (Coed 11-19)

CARMARTHENSHIRE
County Council

The Department for Education & Children, Building 2, St David's Park, Job's Well Road, Carmarthen, Carmarthenshire, SA31 3HB

Tel: 01267 246500 Email: ecs@carmarthenshire.gov.uk Website: www.carmarthenshire.gov.wales

CARMARTHEN

Rhydygors School & Support Services

Rhyd-y-gors, Johnstown, CARMARTHEN, Carmarthenshire SA31 3QU
Tel: 01267 231171
Head: Mrs K Corcoran
Category: EBD

LLANELLI

Ysgol Heol Goffa

Heol Goffa, LLANELLI, Carmarthenshire SA15 3LS
Tel: 01554 759465
Head: Mrs N Symmons
Category: SLD PMLD

CONWY
Education Services

Conwy SEN Team, Government Buildings, Dinerth Road, Colwyn Bay, LL28 4UL

Tel: 01492 575038 Email: education@conwy.gov.uk Website: www.conwy.gov.uk

LLANDUDNO

Ysgol Y Gogarth

Ffordd Nant y Gamar, Craig y Don, LLANDUDNO, Conwy LL30 1YE
Tel: 01492 860077
Head: Mr Jonathan Morgan
Category: General SEN (2-19)

DENBIGHSHIRE
County Council

Denbighshire SEN Team, Middle Lane, Denbigh, Denbighshire, LL16 3UW

Tel: 01745 351205 Email: jeremy.griffiths@denbighshire.gov.uk Website: www.denbighshire.gov.uk

DENBIGH

Ysgol Plas Brondyffryn

Park Street, DENBIGH, Denbighshire LL16 3DR
Tel: 01745 813914
Head: Dr I Barros-Curtis
Category: AUT SLD (Coed 4-19)

RHYL

Ysgol Tir Morfa

Derwen Road, RHYL, Denbighshire LL18 2RN
Tel: 01745 350388
Head: Mrs Carol Edwards
Category: MLD SLD (Coed 4-19)

FLINTSHIRE
County Council

Flintshire Education Department, County Hall, Mold, Flintshire, CH7 6ND
Website: www.flintshire.gov.uk

FLINT

Ysgol Maes Hyfryd

Fifth Avenue, FLINT,
Flintshire CH6 5QL
Tel: 01352 792720
Head: Mrs Helen Millard
Category: (Coed 11-16)

Ysgol Pen Coch

Prince of Wales Avenue,
FLINT, Flintshire CH6 5NF
Tel: 01352 792730
Head: Ms Ange Anderson
Category: (Coed 5-11)

GWYNEDD
Council

Gwynedd SEN Team, Council Offices, Penrallt, Caernarfon, Gwynedd, LL55 1BN
Tel: 01766 771000 Email: education@gwynedd.gov.uk Website: www.gwynedd.gov.uk

CAERNARFON

Ysgol Pendalar

Ffordd Bethel, CAERNARFON,
Gwynedd LL55 1DU
Tel: 01248 672141
Head: Mrs Donna Rees-Roberts
Category: SLD (3-18)

PWLLHELI

Ysgol Hafod Lon

Lon Caernarfon, Y Ffor,
PWLLHELI, Gwynedd LL53 6UP
Tel: 01766 810626
Head: Mrs Donna Rees-Roberts
Category: SLD (3-18)

MERTHYR TYDFIL
Integrated Children's Services

Merthyr Tydfil Additional Learning Needs Service, Unit 5, Triangle Business Park, Pentrebach, Merthyr Tydfil, CF48 4TQ
Tel: 01685 724616 Email: sen@merthyr.gov.uk Website: www.merthyr.gov.uk

MERTHYR TYDFIL

Greenfield Special School

Duffryn Road, Pentrebach,
MERTHYR TYDFIL CF48 4BJ
Tel: 01443 690468
Head: Mr Wayne Murphy
Category: SLD MLD PMLD ASD
EBD MSI SP&LD (Coed 3-19)

MONMOUTHSHIRE
County Council

Monmouthshire SEN Department, @Innovation House, Wales 1 Business Park, Magor, Monmouthshire, NP26 3DG
Tel: 01633 644528 Email: sen@monmouthshire.gov.uk Website: www.monmouthshire.gov.uk

CHEPSTOW

Mounton House School
Pwyllmeyric, CHEPSTOW,
Monmouthshire NP16 6LA
Tel: 01291 635050
Head: Mr P Absolom
Category: EBD (Boys Day/
Boarding 11-16)

NEATH PORT TALBOT
The Child Care (Disability) Team

Neath Port Talbot SEN Team, 2nd Floor, Neath Port Talbot CBC, Civic Centre, Neath, SA11 3QZ
Tel: 01639 685862 Email: education@npt.gov.uk Website: www.neath-porttalbot.gov.uk

NEATH

Ysgol Hendrefelin
Heol Hendre, Bryncoch,
NEATH SA10 7TY
Tel: 01639 642786
Head: Mr Jonathan Roberts
Category: GLD (Coed 2-19)

Ysgol Maes Y Coed
Hoel Hendre, Brynoch,
NEATH SA10 7TY
Tel: 01639 643648
Head: Mrs Helen Glover
Category: GLD (Coed 2-19)

NEWPORT
City Council

Newport Education Inclusion Department, Civic Centre, Newport, NP20 4UR
Tel: 01633 656656 Email: education@newport.gov.uk Website: www.newport.gov.uk

NEWPORT

Brynglas ASD Centre
St Johns Road, Maindee,
NEWPORT, Newport NP20 3DG
Tel: 01633 815480
Head: Ms Julie Nichols
Category: ASD AUT ASP

Maes Ebbw Bach
St Johns Road, Maindee,
NEWPORT, Newport NP19 8GR
Tel: 01633 815480
Head: Ms Julie Nichols

Maes Ebbw School
Maesglas Road, NEWPORT,
Newport NP20 3DG
Tel: 01633 815480
Head: Ms Julie Nichols
Category: SLD PMLD AUT PH

PEMBROKESHIRE
Education Department

Pembrokeshire Inclusion and SEN Service, County Hall, Haverfordwest, Pembrokeshire, SA61 1TP
Tel: 01437 775012 Email: nichola.jones@pembrokeshire.gov.uk Website: www.pembrokeshire.gov.uk

HAVERFORDWEST

Portfield School
off Portfield, HAVERFORDWEST,
Pembrokeshire SA61 1BS
Tel: 01437 762701
Head: Mrs S Painter
Category: SLD PMLD CLD
ASC (Coed 4-18+)

POWYS
County Council

Powys SEN Team, Powys County Hall, Spa Road East, Llandrindod Wells, Powys, LD1 5LG
Tel: 01597 826715 Email: pupil.inclusion@powys.gov.uk Website: www.powys.gov.uk

BRECON

Ysgol Penmaes
Canal Road, BRECON,
Powys LD3 7HL
Tel: 01874 623508
Head: Mrs Julie Kay
Category: SLD ASD PMLD
(Coed Day/Residential 3-19)

NEWTOWN

Brynllywarch Hall School
Kerry, NEWTOWN, Powys SY16 4PB
Tel: 01686 670276
Head: Mr Gavin Randell
Category: MLD EBD

Ysgol Cedewain
Maesyrhandir, NEWTOWN,
Powys SY16 1LH
Tel: 01686 627454
Head: Mrs Pippa Sillitoe
Category: SLD ASD PMLD
(Coed Day 3-19)

RHONDDA CYNON TAFF
County Borough Council

Rhondda Cynon Taff SEN Team, Ty Trevithick, Abercynon, Mountain Ash, CF45 4UQ
Tel: 01443 744000 Email: customerservices@rctcbc.gov.uk Website: www.rctcbc.gov.uk

ABERDARE

Maesgwyn Special School
Cwmdare Road, Cwmdare,
ABERDARE, Rhondda
Cynon Taf CF44 8RE
Tel: 01685 873933
Head: Mr S K Morgan
Category: MLD (Coed 11-18)

Park Lane Special School
Park Lane, Trecynon, ABERDARE,
Rhondda Cynon Taf CF44 8HN
Tel: 01685 874489
Head: Miss M C Hopkin
Category: SLD (3-19)

PENTRE

Ysgol Hen Felin
Gelligaled Park, Ystrad, PENTRE,
Rhondda Cynon Taf CF41 7SZ
Tel: 01443 431571
Head: Mr A Henderson
Category: SLD (3-19)

PONTYPRIDD

Ysgol Ty Coch
Lansdale Drive, Tonteg,
PONTYPRIDD, Rhondda
Cynon Taf CF38 1PG
Tel: 01443 203471
Head: Mr D Jenkins
Category: SLD (3-19)

**Ysgol Ty Coch -
Buarth y Capel**
Ynysybwl, PONTYPRIDD,
Rhondda Cynon Taf CF38 1PG

City and County of
SWANSEA
Education Directorate

Swansea SEN Team, Civic Centre, Oystermouth Road, Swansea, SA1 3SN
Tel: 01792 636000 Email: education.department@swansea.gov.uk Website: www.swansea.gov.uk

SWANSEA

Ysgol Crug Glas
Croft Street, SWANSEA SA1 1QA
Tel: 01792 652388
Head: Mrs Lisa Marshall
Category: SLD PMLD

Ysgol Pen-y-Bryn
Glasbury Road, Morriston,
SWANSEA SA6 7PA
Tel: 01792 799064
Head: Mr Gethin Sutton
Category: MLD SLD AUT

TORFAEN
County Borough Council

Torfaen SEN Team, Civic Centre, Pontypool, Torfaen, NP4 6YB
Tel: 01495 762200 Email: your.call@torfaen.gov.uk Website: www.torfaen.gov.uk

CWMBRAN

Crownbridge School
Turnpike Road, Croesyceiliog,
CWMBRAN, Torfaen NP44 2BJ
Tel: 01633 624201
Head: Mrs Lesley Bush
Category: SLD

VALE OF GLAMORGAN
Council

Vale of Glamorgan School Inclusion Service, Civic Offices, Holton Road, Barry, CF63 4RU
Tel: 01446 700111 Email: cajohns@valeofglamorgan.gov.uk Website: www.valeofglamorgan.gov.uk

PENARTH

Ysgol Y Deri
Sully Road, PENARTH, Vale
of Glamorgan CF64 2TP
Tel: 02920 352280
Head: Mr Chris Britten
Category: AUT PMLD MLD SLD
(Coed 5 Day/Residential 3-19)

WREXHAM
County Borough Council

Wrexham SEN Team, 16 Lord Street, Wrexham, LL11 1LG
Tel: 01978 292000 Email: education@wrexham.gov.uk Website: www.wrexham.gov.uk

WREXHAM

St Christopher's School
Brynycabanau Road,
WREXHAM LL13 7BW
Tel: 01978 346910
Head: Mrs Maxine Pittaway
Category: MLD SLD
PMLD (Coed 6-19)

ACADEMIES (in local authority area)

ENGLAND

BATH & NORTH EAST SOMERSET

– BATH

Aspire Academy
Frome Road, Odd Down,
BATH BA2 5RF
Tel: 01225 832212
Head: Mr Colin Cattanach
Category: EBD (Coed 4-16)

Fosse Way School
Longfellow Road, Midsomer
Norton, BATH BA3 3AL
Tel: 01761 412198
Head: Mr Justin Philcox
Category: PH SLD SPLD ASD
MLD MSI CLD (Coed 3-19)

Three Ways School
180 Frome Road, Odd
Down, BATH BA2 5RF
Tel: 01225 838070
Head: Mrs Julie Dyer
Category: PH SLD SPLD ASD
MLD MSI CLD (Coed 2-19)

BEDFORD

Grange Academy
Halsey Road, Kempston, BEDFORD,
Bedfordshire MK42 8AU
Tel: 01234 407100
Interim Head: Mr B Geen
Category: MLD with provision
for ASD (Coed 5-16)

CENTRAL BEDFORDSHIRE

– DUNSTABLE

Weatherfield Academy
Brewers Hill Road, DUNSTABLE,
Bedfordshire LU6 1AF
Tel: 01582 605632
Head: Mr Joe Selmes
Category: MLD (7-18)

BLACKPOOL

Park Community Academy
158 Whitegate Drive, BLACKPOOL,
Lancashire FY3 9HF
Tel: 01253 764130
Head: Mr Keith Berry
Category: MLD CLD
SEBD (Coed 4-16)

CHESHIRE EAST

– CREWE

Adelaide School
Adelaide Street, CREWE,
Cheshire CW1 3DT
Tel: 01270 685151
Executive Head: Mr Lloyd Willday
Category: BESD (Coed 11-16)

CORNWALL

– TRURO

Pencalenick School
St Clement, TRURO, Cornwall TR1 1TE
Tel: 01872 520385
Head: Mr A Barnett
Category: SCLD (Coed 11-16)

DURHAM

– PETERLEE

Hopewood Academy (Ascent Trust)
Crawlaw Road, Easington Colliery,
PETERLEE, Durham SR8 3LP
Tel: 01915 691420
Head: Mrs Carolyn Barker
Category: MLD SLD PMLD AUT (2-19)

HALTON

– RUNCORN

Cavendish Academy
Lincoln Close, RUNCORN,
Cheshire WA7 4YX
Tel: 01928 561706
Head: Mrs Elaine Haver
Category: SLD (11-19)

HARTLEPOOL

Catcote School
Catcote Road,
HARTLEPOOL TS25 4EZ
Tel: 01429 264036
Head: Mr Alan Chapman
Category: MLD SLD PMLD ASD BESD

HEREFORDSHIRE

– HEREFORD

The Brookfield School & Specialist College
Grandstand Road,
HEREFORD HR4 9NG
Tel: 01432 265153
Head: Dame Oremi Evans
Category: BESD MLD ASD
ADHD (Coed 7-16)

KENT

– DARTFORD

Milestone Academy
Ash Road, New Ash Green,
DARTFORD, Kent DA3 8JZ
Tel: 01474 709420
Head: Mr Nigel Jones
Category: PMLD SLD AUT
MLD PSCN (Coed 2-19)

LEICESTERSHIRE

– COALVILLE

Forest Way School

Warren Hills Road, COALVILLE,
Leicestershire LE67 4UU
Tel: 01530 831899
Head: Mrs Lynn Slinger
Category: SLD PMLD (2-18)

– HINCKLEY

Dorothy Goodman School Hinckley

Stoke Road, HINCKLEY,
Leicestershire LE10 0EA
Tel: 01455 634582
Head: Ms Janet Thompson
Category: (2-18)

– GRANTHAM

The Phoenix Academy Trust

Great North Road, GRANTHAM,
Lincolnshire NG31 7US
Tel: 01476 574112
Head: Mrs Diana Bush
Category: EBD (11-16)

NORTH-EAST LINCOLNSHIRE

– GRIMSBY

Humberston Park Special School

St Thomas Close, Humberston,
GRIMSBY, N E Lincolnshire DN36 4HS
Tel: 01472 590645
Head: Mr Andrew Zielinski
Category: SLD PMLD PD
CLD MSI (Coed 3-19)

The Cambridge Park Academy

Cambridge Road, GRIMSBY,
N E Lincolnshire DN34 5EB
Tel: 01472 230110
Head: Mr Mark Eames
Category: ASD SLCN MLD
SLD (Coed 3-19)

ROYAL BOROUGH OF GREENWICH

– LONDON

Charlton Park Academy

Charlton Park Road,
LONDON SE7 8HX
Tel: 02082 496844
Head: Mr Mark Dale-Emberton
Category: SCLD SCD PMLD
PD ASD (Coed 11-19)

HILLINGDON

– HAYES

The Willows School Academy Trust

Stipularis Drive, HAYES,
Middlesex UB4 9QB
Tel: 02088 417176
Head: Mr Malcolm Shaw
Category: SEBD ASD ADHD
Challenging behaviour (Coed 3-11)

– UXBRIDGE

Moorcroft (Eden Academy)

Bramble Close, Hillingdon,
UXBRIDGE, Middlesex UB8 3BF
Tel: 01895 437799
Head: Mr Andrew Sanders
Category: SLD PMLD
AUT (Coed 11-19)

– WEST DRAYTON

Young People's Academy

Falling Lane, Yiewsley, WEST
DRAYTON, Middlesex UB7 8AB
Tel: 01895 446747
Head: Ms Laurie Cornwell
Category: BESD AUT
ADHD (Coed 11-16)

SUTTON

– CARSHALTON

Wandle Valley School

Welbeck Road, CARSHALTON,
Surrey SM5 1LW
Tel: 02086 481365
Head: Mr Mal Fjord-Roberts
Category: SEBD (Coed 5-16)

– WALLINGTON

Carew Academy

Church Road, WALLINGTON,
Surrey SM6 7NH
Tel: 02086 478349
Head: Mr John Prior
Category: MLD ASD (Coed 7-16)

WALTHAM FOREST

– WALTHAMSTOW

Hornbeam Academy - William Morris School

Folly Lane, WALTHAMSTOW,
London E17 5NT
Tel: 02085 032225
Executive Principal: Mr
Gary Pocock
Category: MLD SLD
PMLD (Coed 11-16)

– WOODFORD GREEN

Hornbeam Academy - Brookfield House School

Alders Avenue, WOODFORD
GREEN, Essex IG8 9PY
Tel: 02085 272464
Executive Principal: Mr
Gary Pocock
Category: HI PD Complex
medical needs (Coed 2-16)

GREATER MANCHESTER (SALFORD)

– ECCLES

Oakwood Academy

Chatsworth Road, Ellesmere
Park, ECCLES M30 9DY
Tel: 01619 212880
Executive Principal: Ms
Amanda Nicolson
Category: MLD HI VIS SEBD
Complex needs (Coed 10-19)

MEDWAY

– CHATHAM

Bradfields Academy

Churchill Avenue, CHATHAM,
Kent ME5 0LB
Tel: 01634 683990
Head: Mr Kim Johnson
Category: MLD SLD
ASD (Coed 11-19)

MILTON KEYNES

Stephenson Academy

Crosslands, Stantonbury,
MILTON KEYNES,
Buckinghamshire MK14 6AX
Tel: 01908 889400
Head: Dr Neil Barrett
Category: EBD (Boys Day/
boarding 12-16)

NORFOLK

– NORWICH

Eaton Hall Specialist Academy

Pettus Road, NORWICH,
Norfolk NR4 7BU
Tel: 01603 457480
Head: Mr Keith Bates
Category: EBD (Coed 5-16)

NORTHANTS

– CORBY

Maplefields School

Tower Hill Road, CORBY,
Northamptonshire NN18 0TH
Tel: 01536 424090
Head: Ms Beverley Wright
Category: BESD (5-19)

– KETTERING

Kingsley Special Academy Trust

Churchill Way, KETTERING,
Northamptonshire NN15 5DP
Tel: 01536 316880
Head: Mr Tom O'Dwyer
Category: PMLD SLD ASD (3-11)

– NORTHAMPTON

Billing Brook Special Academy Trust School

Penistone Road, NORTHAMPTON,
Northamptonshire NN3 8EZ
Tel: 01604 773910
Head: Mrs Caroline Grant
Category: MLD ASD
SLD SPLD PH (3-19)

– WELLINGBOROUGH

Friars Academy

Friar's Close, WELLINGBOROUGH,
Northamptonshire NN8 2LA
Tel: 01933 304950
Head: Mrs Suzzanne Ijewsky
Category: MLD SLD ASD (11-19)

NOTTINGHAM

Nethergate School

Swansdowne Drive, Clifton,
NOTTINGHAM NG11 8HX
Tel: 01159 152959
Head: Mrs Tracey Ydlibi

NOTTINGHAMSHIRE

– BROXTOWE

Foxwood Academy
Off Derby Road, Bramcote Hills, Beeston, BROXTOWE, Nottingham NG9 3GF
Tel: 01159 177202
Head: Mr Chris Humphreys
Category: (Coed 3-19)

– MANSFIELD

The Beech Academy
Fairholme Drive, MANSFIELD, Nottinghamshire NG19 6DX
Tel: 01623 626008
Head: Mr Adrian O'Malley
Category: (Coed 11-19)

PETERBOROUGH

City of Peterborough Special School
Reeves Way, PETERBOROUGH, Cambridgeshire PE1 5LQ
Tel: 01733 821403
Head: Mrs Sue Bailey
Category: (Coed 4-18)

POOLE

Longspee Academy
Learoyd Road, Canford Heath, POOLE, Dorset BH17 8PJ
Tel: 01202 380266
Head: Ms Nicky Morton
Category: BESD (5-14)

Montacute School
3 Canford Heath Road, POOLE, Dorset BH17 9NG
Tel: 01202 693239
Head: Ms Jill Owen
Category: PMLD SLD CLD PH Medical needs (3-19)

PORTSMOUTH

Cliffdale Primary Academy
Battenburg Avenue, North End, PORTSMOUTH, Hampshire PO2 0SN
Tel: 02392 662601
Executive Head: Ms Alison Beane
Category: MLD PD SLCN (Coed 4-11)

READING

The Avenue Special School
Conwy Close, Tilehurst, READING, Berkshire RG30 4BZ
Tel: 0189 375554
Head: Mrs Sue Bourne
Category: CLD (Coed 2-19)

REDCAR & CLEVELAND

SALTBURN-BY-SEA

KTS Academy
Marshall Drive, Brotton, SALTBURN-BY-SEA, Cleveland TS12 2UW
Tel: 01287 677265
Head: Mr Kevin Thompson
Category: SLD PMLD SLCN ASC PD CLDD (Coed day 2-19)

SHROPSHIRE

– SHREWSBURY

Severndale Specialist Academy
Monkmoor Campus, Woodcote Way, Monkmoor, SHREWSBURY, Shropshire SY2 5SL
Tel: 01743 281600
Principal: Ms Sabrina Hobbs
Category: PMLD SLD MLD CLDD (Coed Day 2-19)

SOUTHEND-ON-SEA

– LEIGH-ON-SEA

The St Christopher School
Mountdale Gardens, LEIGH-ON-SEA, Essex SS9 4AW
Tel: 01702 524193
Head: Mrs Jackie Mullan
Category: SEBD AUT ADHD (Coed Day 3-11) ADHD AUT (Coed 11-16)

STAFFORDSHIRE

– LICHFIELD

Saxon Hill Academy & Physical Disability Support Service
Kings Hill Road, LICHFIELD, Staffordshire WS14 9DE
Tel: 01543 414892
Head: Mr Jon Thickett
Category: PD (Coed Day 2-19)

– STOKE ON TRENT

Cicely Haughton Community Special School
Westwood Manor, Wetley Rocks, STOKE ON TRENT, Staffordshire ST9 0BX
Tel: 01782 550202
Head: Mr Richard Redgate
Category: SEBD (Coed Boarding 5-11)

– UTTOXETER

Loxley Hall School
Stafford Road, Loxley, UTTOXETER, Staffordshire ST14 8RS
Tel: 01889 256390
Head: Mr Richard Redgate
Category: EBD (Boys Boarding 11-16)

STOCKTON-ON-TEES

– BILLINGHAM

Ash Trees Academy
Bowes Road, BILLINGHAM, Stockton-on-Tees TS23 2BU
Tel: 01642 563712
Headteacher: Ms Yvonne Limb
Category: SLD PMLD AUT (Coed 4-11)

– THORNABY-ON-TEES

Horizons Specialist Academy Trust, Westlands School
Eltham Crescent, THORNABY-ON-TEES TS17 9RA
Tel: 01642 883030
Principal: Mr Pete Ewart
Category: BESD (Coed Residential 11-16)

SUFFOLK

– BURY ST EDMUNDS

Priory School
Mount Road, BURY ST EDMUNDS, Suffolk IP32 7BH
Tel: 01284 761934
Head: Mr Lawrence Chapman
Category: MLD (Coed Day & boarding 8-16)

– HAVERHILL

Churchill Special Free School
Chalkstone Way, HAVERHILL, Suffolk CB9 0LD
Tel: 01440 760338
Head: Mrs Georgina Ellis

– IPSWICH

Stone Lodge Academy
Stone Lodge Lane West, IPSWICH, Suffolk IP2 9HW
Tel: 01473 601175
Head: Mr Rick Tracey
Category: MLD ASD (Coed Day 5-16)

Thomas Wolsey School
Defoe Road, IPSWICH, Suffolk IP1 6SG
Tel: 01473 467600
Head: Ms Rupinder Hosie
Category: PD/Comunication (Coed Day 3-16)

– LOWESTOFT

The Ashley School Academy Trust
Ashley Downs, LOWESTOFT, Suffolk NR32 4EU
Tel: 01502 565439
Head: Mrs Sally Garrett
Category: MLD (Coed Day & boarding 7-16)

SURREY

– CHOBHAM

Wishmore Cross School
Alpha Road, CHOBHAM, Surrey GU24 8NE
Tel: 01276 857555
Head: Mr J Donnelly
Category: BESD (Boarding & day 11-16)

THURROCK

– SOUTH OCKENDON

Beacon Hill Academy (Main Site)
Erriff Drive, SOUTH OCKENDON, Essex RM15 5AY
Tel: 01708 852006
Head: Mrs Sue Hewitt
Category: PNI PMLD SLD (Coed 3-16)

TORBAY

– TORQUAY

Combe Pafford School
Steps Lane, Watcombe, TORQUAY TQ2 8NL
Tel: 01803 327902
Head: Mr Michael Lock

GATESHEAD

The Cedars Academy
Ivy Lane, Low Fell, GATESHEAD, Tyne & Wear NE9 6QD
Tel: 01914 874595
Head: Mrs Jane M Fraser
Category: PD (Coed 2-16)

SUNDERLAND

Barbara Priestman Academy

Meadowside, SUNDERLAND,
Tyne & Wear SR2 7QN
Tel: 01915 536000
Head: Mrs C Barker
Category: ASD CLD
(Coed Day 11-19)

North View Academy

St Lukes Road, SUNDERLAND,
Tyne & Wear SR4 0HB
Tel: 01915 534580
Head: Mr G Mellefont
Category: EBD ASD (4-11)

Portland Academy

Weymouth Road,
Chapelgarth, SUNDERLAND,
Tyne & Wear SR3 2NQ
Tel: 01915 536050
Head: Mrs M Carson
Category: SLD (Coed Day 11-19)

The New Bridge Academy (Lower Site)

Swindon Road, SUNDERLAND,
Tyne & Wear SR3 4EE
Tel: 01915 536067
Head: Mr G Shillinglaw
Category: EBD (Coed Day 11-16)

The New Bridge Academy (Upper School)

Craigshaw Road, Hylton Castle,
SUNDERLAND, Tyne & Wear SR5 3NF
Tel: 01915 535335
Head: Mr G Shillinglaw
Category: SEBD (Coed Day 11-18)

WARWICKSHIRE

– NUNEATON

Discovery Academy

Vernons Lane, NUNEATON,
Warwickshire CV11 5HJ
Tel: 07494 457314
Head: Mr Matthew Pike
Category: (Coed 9-19)

BIRMINGHAM

– ERDINGTON

Wilson Stuart School

Perry Common Road, ERDINGTON,
Birmingham B23 7AT
Tel: 01213 734475
Head: Mr Stephen Hughes
Category: PD (Coed Day 2-19)

– LADYWOOD

James Brindley Hospital School

Bell Barn Road, Edgbaston,
LADYWOOD, Birmingham B15 2AF
Tel: 01216 666409
Head: Mrs Nicky Penny
Category: HS (Coed Day 2-19)

COVENTRY

RNIB Three Spires Academy

Kingsbury Road, COVENTRY,
West Midlands CV6 1PJ
Tel: 02476 594952
Head: Mr Robert Jones
Category: MLD (Coed Day 3-11)

WOLVERHAMPTON

Northern House School

Cromer Gardens, Whitmore
Reans, WOLVERHAMPTON,
West Midlands WV6 0UB
Tel: 01902 551564
Head: Ms F Pass
Category: BESD ADHD
(Coed Day 8-16)

Westcroft School

Greenacres Avenue, Underhill,
WOLVERHAMPTON, West
Midlands WV10 8NZ
Tel: 01902 558350
Head: Ms A Brown
Category: CLD (Coed Day 4-16)

NORTH YORKSHIRE

– SCARBOROUGH

The Woodlands Academy

Woodlands Drive, SCARBOROUGH,
North Yorkshire YO12 6QN
Tel: 01723 373260
Head: Mrs Annette Fearn
Category: MLD (2-16)

SCOTLAND

GLASGOW

Hollybrook Academy

135 Hollybrook Street,
GLASGOW G42 7HU
Tel: 01414 235937
Head: Ms Jaqueline Newell
Category: MLD (Secondary)

Linburn Academy

77 Linburn Road,
GLASGOW G52 4EX
Tel: 01418 832082
Head: Ms Lorna Wallace
Category: CLD (Secondary)

GREENOCK

Lomond View Academy

Ingleston Street, GREENOCK,
Inverclyde PA15 4UQ
Tel: 01475 714414
Head: Mr David Peden

Useful associations and websites

Action for Blind People

53 Sandgate Street
London SE15 1LE
Tel: 020 7635 4800
Helpline: 0303 123 9999
Email: helpline@rnib.org.uk
Website: www.actionforblindpeople.org.uk

A UK based charity (nos. 205913, SCO40050) that works to inspire change and create opportunities to enable blind and partially sighted people to have an equal voice and equal choice. They enable visually impaired people to transform their lives through work, housing, leisure and support. Part of the RNIB.

Action for Sick Children

32b Buxton Road
High Lane
Stockport SK6 8BH
Tel: 01663 763 004
Helpline: 0800 0744 519
Website: www.actionforsickchildren.org

Healthcare charity (no. 296295) formed in the 1960s to help parents whose children have to spend extended stays in hospital.

Action on Hearing Loss

19-23 Featherstone Street
London EC1Y 8SL
Tel: 020 7296 8000
Textphone: 020 7296 8001
Fax: 020 7296 8199
Email: informationline@hearingloss.org.uk
Website: www.actiononhearingloss.org.uk

Action on Hearing Loss, formerly the Royal National Institute for Deaf People, is the largest national charity (nos. 207720, SCO38926) representing the nine million deaf and hard of hearing people in the UK. As a membership charity we aim to achieve a radically better quality of life for deaf and hard of hearing people. We do this by campaigning and lobbying vigorously, by raising awareness of deafness and hearing loss, by providing services and through social medical and technical research.

Follow us on Twitter.

Action on Hearing Loss Cymru

Ground Floor,
Anchor Court (North)
Keen Road
Cardiff
CF24 5JW
Tel: 02920 333 034
Text: 02920 333 036
Fax: 02920 333 035
Email: cymru@hearingloss.org.uk

See main entry above.

Action on Hearing Loss Northern Ireland

4-8 Adelaide Street
Belfast
BT2 8GA
Tel: 028 9023 9619
Fax: 028 9031 2032
Textphone: 028 9024 9462
Email: information.nireland@hearingloss.org.uk

See main entry above.

Action on Hearing Loss Scotland

Empire House
131 West Nile Street
Glasgow
G1 2RXJ
Tel: 0141 341 5330
Text: 0141 341 5347
Fax: 0141 354 0176
Email: scotland@hearingloss.org.uk

See main entry above.

ADDISS – National Attention Deficit Disorder Information & Support Service

PO Box 340
Edgware
Middlesex HA8 9HL
Tel: 020 8952 2800
Fax: 020 8952 2909
Email: info@addiss.co.uk
Website: www.addiss.co.uk

ADDISS provides information and assistance for those affected by ADHD. Registered charity no. 1070827.

Advisory Centre for Education – (ACE)

72 Durnsford Road,
London
N11 2EJ
Tel: 0300 0115 142
Email: enquiries@ace-ed.org.uk
Website: www.ace-ed.org.uk

ACE is an independent national advice centre for parents/carers of children aged 5 to 16. Advice booklets can be downloaded or ordered from the website. Training courses and seminars for LA officers, schools and governors are available. As well as a training package for community groups advising parents on education matters. Has Facebook page and you can follow them on Twitter.

AFASIC – Unlocking Speech and Language

20 Bowling Green Lane
London EC1R 0BD
Tel: 020 7490 9410
Fax: 020 7251 2834
Helpline: 0300 666 9410
Website: www.afasicengland.org.uk

Helps children and young people with speech and language impairments. Provides: training/conferences for parents and professionals; a range of publications; support through local groups; and expertise in developing good practice. Registered charity nos. 1045617, SCO39170. Has a Facebook page.

AFASIC – Cymru

Titan House
Cardiff Bay Business Centre
Lewis Road
Ocean Park
Cardiff CF24 5BS
Tel: 029 2046 5854
Fax: 029 2046 5854
Website: www.afasiccymru.org.uk

See main entry above.

AFASIC – Northern Ireland

Cranogue House
19 Derry Courtney Road
Caledon
County Tyrone BT68 4UF
Tel: 028 3756 9611 (M-F 10.30am-2.30pm)
Email: mary@afasicnorthernireland.org.uk
Website: www.afasicnorthernireland.org.uk

See main entry above.

AFASIC – Scotland

42-44 Castle Street,
Dundee, DD1 3AQ
Tel: 01382 250060
Fax: 01382 568391
Email: info@afasicscotland.org.uk
Website: www.afasicscotland.org.uk

Registered charity no. SCO39170.

See main entry above.

Association of Blind and Partially-Sighted Teachers and Students (ABAPTAS)

BM Box 6727
London
WC1N 3XX
Tel: 0117 966 4839
Website: www.abapstas.org.uk

National organisation of visually impaired people that focuses on education and employment issues. Registered charity no. 266056.

Association of Sign Language Interpreters (ASLI)

Derngate Mews
Derngate
Northampton
NN1 1UE
Tel: 0871 474 0522
Textphone: 18001 0871 474 0522
Fax: 08451 70 80 61
Email: office@asli.org.uk
Website: www.asli.org.uk

Has a useful online directory of sign language interpreters.

Asthma UK

18 Mansell St
London E1 8AA
Tel: 0300 222 5800
Email: info@asthma.org.uk
Website: www.asthma.org.uk
Twitter: @AsthmaUK

Charity dedicated to helping the 5.2 million people in the UK who are affected by asthma. Registered charity nos. 802364, SCO39322.

Ataxia (UK)

Lincoln House, Kennington Park
1-3 Brixton Road
London SW9 6DE
Tel: 020 7582 1444
Helpline: 0845 644 0606
Email: office@ataxia.org.uk
Website: www.ataxia.org.uk
Twitter: @AtaxiaUK

Aims to support all people affected by ataxia. Registered charity nos. 1102391 and SCO406047. Has a Facebook page and you can follow them on Twitter.

BCS – IT Can Help

c/o Information Technologists
39a Bartholomew Close
London EC1A 7JN
Freephone & text phone helpline: 0800 269 545
Email: enquiries@abilitynet.org.uk
Website: www.itcanhelp.org.uk

Provides onsite volunteers to help individuals with disabilities who have computer problems Registered charity no. 292786.

BIBIC (British Institute for Brain Injured Children)

Old Kelways
Somerton Road
Langport
Somerset TA10 9SJ
Tel: 01458 253344
Fax: 01278 685573
Email: info@bibic.org.uk
Website: www.bibic.org.uk
Twitter: @bibic_charity

As a registered charity (no. 1057635) BIBIC helps children with a disability or learning difficulty caused by conditions such as cerebral palsy, Down's syndrome and other genetic disorders; acquired brain injury caused by trauma or illness; and developmental disorders such as autism, ADHD, Asperger syndrome and dyspraxia.

All children are assessed by a multi-professional team who put together a report and a therapy plan that is taught to the family by the child's key worker. This provides support for the family to learn about their child and how they can make a positive difference to their development. Sections of the plan are designed to be shared with the child's school and social groups to ensure a consistent approach in areas such as communication, behaviour and learning. Families return on a regular basis for reassessment and updated therapy programmes.

Blind Children UK

Hillfields
Reading Road
Burghfield Common
Reading
Berkshire RG7 3YG
Tel: 0800 781 1444
Email: services@blindchildrenuk.org
Website: www.blindchildrenuk.org
Twitter: @BlindChildrenUK

Formerly the National Blind Children's Society, Blind Children UK offers advice and support for blind and partially sighted children and their families and carers. Registered charity no. 1051607. Has a Facebook page.

Brain and Spine Foundation

LG01, Lincoln House
Kennington Park
1-3 Brixton Road
London SW9 6DE
Tel: 020 7793 5900
Helpline: 0808 808 1000
Fax: 020 7793 5939
Fax helpline: 020 7793 5939
Email: info@brainandspine.org.uk
Website: www.brainandspine.org.uk
Twitter: @brainspine

Registered charity (no. 1098528), which was founded in 1992 to help those people affected by brain and spine conditions.

British Blind Sport (BBS)

Pure Offices
Plato Close
Tachbrook Park
Leamington Spa
Warwickshire CV34 6WE
Tel: 01926 424247
Fax: 01926 427775
Email: info@britishblindsport.org.uk
Website: www.britishblindsport.org.uk
Twitter: @BritBlindSport

A registered charity (no. 271500) providing sport and recreation for blind and partially sighted people.

British Deaf Association England

356 Holloway Road
London N7 6PA
Tel: 020 7697 4140
Textphone: 05603 115295
Fax: 01772 561610
Email: bda@bda.org.uk
Website: www.bda.org.uk
Twitter: @BritishDeafNews

The BDA is a democratic, membership-led national charity (no. 1031687) campaigning on behalf of deaf sign language users in the UK. It exists to advance and protect the interests of the deaf community, to increase deaf people's access to facilities and lifestyles that most hearing people take for granted and to ensure greater awareness of their rights and responsibilities as members of society. The association has several main service areas, with teams covering education and youth, information, health promotions, video production and community services, offering advice and help. There is a national helpline that provides information and advice on a range of subjects such as welfare rights, the Disability Discrimination Act (DDA) and education.

British Deaf Association of Northern Ireland

Unit 5c, Weavers Court
Linfield Road
Belfast BT12 5GH
Tel: 02890 437486
Textphone: 02890 437480
Fax: 02890 437487
Email: northernireland@bda.org
Website: www.bda.org.uk

See main entry under British Deaf Association England.

British Deaf Association Scotland

1st Floor Central Chambers, Suite 58
93 Hope Street
Glasgow G2 6LD
Tel: 0141 248 5554
Fax: 0141 248 5565
Email: scotland@bda.org.uk
Website: www.bda.org.uk

See main entry under British Deaf Association England.

British Dyslexia Association

Unit 8, Bracknell Beeches
Old Bracknell Lane
Bracknell RG12 7BW
Tel: 0333 405 4567 (Helpline) or
0333 405 4555 (Admin)
Fax: 0845 251 9005
Email: helpline@bdadyslexia.org.uk
Website: www.bdadyslexia.org.uk

Helpline/information service open between 10am and 4.00pm (M-F) also open late on Wednesdays 5-7pm. Has a Facebook page. Registered charity no. 289243.

British Institute of Learning Disabilities (BILD)

Birmingham Research Park
97 Vincent Drive
Edgbaston
Birmingham B15 2SQ
Tel: 0121 415 6960
Fax: 0121 415 6999
Email: enquiries@bild.org.uk
Website: www.bild.org.uk

Registered charity (no. 1019663) committed to improving the quality of life of people with learning disabilities. They do this by advancing education, research and practice and by promoting better ways of working with children and adults with learning disabilities. BILD provides education, training, information, publications, journals, membership services, research and consultancy. Has a Facebook page and you can follow them on Twitter.

British Psychological Society

St Andrews House
48 Princess Road East
Leicester LE1 7DR
Tel: 0116 254 9568
Fax: 0116 227 1314
Email: enquiries@bps.org.uk
Website: www.bps.org.uk
Twitter: @BPSofficial

The representative body for psychology and psychologists in the UK. Has search facility for details on psychologists. Registered charity nos. 229642 & SCO39452.

Brunel Able Children's Education (BACE) Centre

Brunel University
School of Sport & Education,
Kingston Lane
Uxbridge, Middlesex UB8 3PH
Tel: 01895 267152
Fax: 01895 269806
Email: catherina.emery@brunel.ac.uk
Website: www.brunel.ac.uk/cbass/education/research/bace

Conducts research into all aspects of identification and provision for able and exceptionally able children. The centre has been involved in supporting the education of able children in inner city schools for a number of years. A number of courses are run for teachers to train them to make effective provision for able pupils.

Butterfly AVM Charity

Unit C2 Crispin Industrial Centre,
Angel Road Works
Advent Way
London
N18 3AH
Tel: 07811 400633
Fax: 0208 8037600
Email: support@butterflyavmcharity.org.uk
Website: www.butterflyavmcharity.org.uk/

Offers advice and support to anyone affected by an AVM

CALL Scotland

University of Edinburgh
Paterson's Land
Holyrood Road
Edinburgh
Midlothian EH8 8AQ
Tel: 0131 651 6235
Fax: 0131 651 6234
Email: call.scotland@ed.ac.uk
Website: www.callcentrescotland.org.uk
Twitter: @CallScotland

CALL Scotland provides services and carries out research and development projects across Scotland for people, particularly children with severe communication disabilities, their families and people who work with them in augmentative communication techniques and technology, and specialised computer use.

Cambian Group

Helpline: 0800 138 1418
Email: education@cambiangroup.com
Website: www.cambiangroup.com

Cambian Group is one of the UK's leading providers of specialist services in education, care, mental health and learning disabilities. Works with 140 public authorities.

Capability Scotland (ASCS)

Head Office, Westerlea
11 Ellersly Road
Edinburgh
Midlothian EH12 6HY
Tel: 0131 337 9876
Textphone: 0131 346 2529
Fax: 0131 346 7864
Website: www.capability-scotland.org.uk
Twitter: @capability_scot

ASCS is a national disability advice and information service, which provides free confidential advice and information on a range of disability issues including advice on cerebral palsy. Registered charity no. SCO11330.

Carers UK

20 Great Dover Street
London SE1 4LX
Tel: 020 7378 4999
Fax: 020 7378 9781
Adviceline: 0808 808 7777 or Email: advice@carersuk.org
Email: info@carersuk.org
Website: www.carersuk.org
Twitter: @CarersUK

For carers run by carers. Registered charity nos. 246329 & SCO39307.

Carers Northern Ireland

58 Howard Street
Belfast BT1 6PJ
Tel: 028 9043 9843
Email: info@carersni.org
Website: www.carersuk.org/northern-ireland
Twitter: @CarersNI

See main entry under Carers UK.

Carers Scotland

The Cottage
21 Pearce Street
Glasgow G51 3UT
Tel: 0141 445 3070
Email: info@carersscotland.org
Website: www.carersuk.org/scotland
Twitter: @CarersScotland

See main entry under Carers UK.

Carers Wales

Unit 5
Ynys Bridge Court
Cardiff
CF15 9SS
Tel: 029 2081 1370
Email: info@carerswales.org
Website: www.carersuk.org/wales
Twitter: @carerswales

See main entry under Carers UK.

Centre for Studies on Inclusive Education (CSIE)

The Park
Daventry Road
Knowle
Bristol BS4 1DQ
Tel: 0117 353 3150
Fax: 0117 353 3151
Email: admin@csie.org.uk
Website: www.csie.org.uk
Twitter: @CSIE_UK

Promoting inclusion for all children in restructured mainstream schools. Registered charity no. 327805.

Challenging Behaviour Foundation

c/o The Old Courthouse
New Road Avenue
Chatham
Kent ME4 6BE
Tel: 01634 838739
Family support line: 0300 666 0126
Email: info@thecbf.org.uk
Website: www.challengingbehaviour.org.uk
Twitter: @CBFdn

Supports families, professionals and stakeholders who live/work with people with severe learning disabilities who have challenging behaviour. Registered charity no. 1060714.

Child Brain Injury Trust (CBIT)

Unit 1, The Great Barn
Baynards Green Farm
Bicester
Oxfordshire OX27 7SG
Tel: 01869 341075
Email: info@cbituk.org
Website: www.childbraininjurytrust.org.uk
Twitter: @CBITUK

Formerly known as the Children's Head Injury Trust (CHIT) this organisation was originally set up in 1991. It offers support to children and families affected by brain injuries that happen after birth. Registered charity nos. 1113326 & SCO39703. Has Facebook page and you can follow them on Twitter.

Communication Matters

Leeds Innovation Centre
103 Clarendon Road
Leeds LS2 9DF
Tel/Fax: 0845 456 8211
Email: admin@communications.org.uk
Website: www.communicationmatters.org.uk

Support for people who find communication difficult.

Contact a Family

209-211 City Road
London EC1V 1JN
Tel: 020 7608 8700
Helpline: 0808 808 3555 Textphone: 0808 808 3556
Fax: 020 7608 8701
Email: helpline@cafamily.org.uk
Website: www.cafamily.org.uk
Twitter: @ContactAFamily

Registered charity (nos. 284912, SCO39169) that provides support, advice and information to families with disabled children. Has a Facebook page and you can follow them on Twitter.

Coram Children's Legal Centre

Riverside Office Centre
Century House North, North Station Road
Colchester,
Essex CO1 1RE
Tel: 01206 714 650
Fax: 01206 714 660
Email: info@coramclc.org.uk
Website: www.childrenslegalcentre.com

The Children's Legal Centre is an independent national charity (no. 281222) concerned with law and policy affecting children and young people. The centre runs a free and confidential legal advice and information service covering all aspects of law and the service is open to children, young people and anyone with concerns about them. The Education Legal Advocacy unit provides advice and representation to children and/or parents involved in education disputes with a school or a local education authority.

Council for Disabled Children

8 Wakley Street
London EC1V 7QE
Tel: 020 7843 1900
Fax: 020 7843 6313
Email: cdc@ncb.org.uk
Website: www.councilfordisabledchildren.org.uk
Twitter: @CDC_tweets

The council promotes collaborative work and partnership between voluntary and non-voluntary agencies, parents and children and provides a national forum for the discussion, development and dissemination of a wide range of policy and practice issues relating to service provision and support for children and young people with disabilities and special educational needs. Has a particular interest in inclusive education, special education needs, parent partnership services, play and leisure and transition. Registered charity no. 258825.

Council for the Registration of Schools Teaching Dyslexic Pupils (CReSTeD)

Old Post House
Castle Street
Whittington
Shropshire SY11 4DF
Tel: 01691 665783
Email: admin@crested.org.uk
Website: www.crested.org.uk

CReSTeD's aim is to help parents and also those who advise them choose an educational establishment for children with Specific Learning Difficulties (SpLD). It maintains a register of schools and teaching centres which meets its criteria for the teaching of pupils with Specific Learning Difficulties.

All schools and centres included in the Register are visited regularly to ensure they continue to meet the criteria set by CReSTeD. CReSTeD acts as a source of names for educational establishments which parents can use as their first step towards making a placement decision which will be critical to their child's educational future.

Cystic Fibrosis Trust

One Aldgate
Second floor
London EC3N 1RE
Tel: 020 3795 1555
Helpline: 0300 373 1000
Fax: 020 8313 0472
Email: enquiries@cftrust.org.uk
Website: www.cftrust.org.uk
Twitter: @CFtrust

The Cystic Fibrosis Trust is a national registered charity (nos. 1079049, SCO40196) established in 1964. It offers information and support to people with cystic fibrosis, their families, their carers and anyone affected by cystic fibrosis. It funds research, offers some financial support to people with cystic fibrosis and campaigns for improved services. It provides a wide range of information including fact sheets, publications and expert concensus documents on treatment and care for people with cystic fibrosis.

Disabled Living Foundation

4th Floor, Jessica House
Red Lion Square
191 Wandsworth High Street
London SW18 4LS
Tel: 020 7289 6111
Helpline: 0300 999 0004
Email: info@dlf.org.uk
Website: www.dlf.org.uk
Twitter: @DLFUK

This foundation provides free, impartial advice about products for disabled people. Registered charity no. 290069.

Down's Syndrome Education International

6 Underley Business Centre
Kirkby, Lonsdale
Cumbria LA6 2DY
Tel: 0300 330 0750
Fax: 0300 330 0754
Email: enquiries@downsed.org
Website: www.dseinternational.org
Twitter: @dseint

Down's Syndrome Education International works around the world to improve the development, education and social achievements of many thousands of people living with Down's syndrome. We undertake and support scientific research and disseminate quality information and advice widely through our websites, books, films and training courses.

Our education services support families and professionals to help people with Down's syndrome achieve sustained gains in all areas of their development.

For 30 years, we have disseminated the latest research findings in practical and accessible formats to the widest audiences, from birth to adulthood. Please visit our website for more information. Registered charity no. 1062823. We have a Facebook page and you can follow us on Twitter.

Down's Syndrome Association

Langdon Down Centre
2a Langdon Park
Teddington TW11 9PS
Tel: 0333 1212 300
Email: info@downs-syndrome.org.uk
Website: www.downs-syndrome.org.uk
Twitter: @DSAInfo

We provide information and support for people with Down's syndrome, their families and carers, and the professionals who work with them. We strive to improve knowledge of the condition. We champion the rights of people with Down's syndrome. Registered charity no. 1061474.

Down's Syndrome Association Northern Ireland

Unit 2, Marlborough House
348 Lisburn Road
Belfast BT9 6GH
Tel: 028 90666 5260
Fax: 028 9066 7674
Email: enquiriesni@downs-syndrome.org.uk

See main entry above.

Down's Syndrome Association Wales

Suite 1, 206 Whitchurch Road
Heath
Cardiff CF14 3NB
Tel: 0333 1212 300
Email: wales@downs-syndrome.org.uk

See main entry above.

Dyslexia Action

10 High Street,
Egham,
Surrey TW20 9EA
Tel: 0300 303 8357
Fax: 01784 222333
Email: info@dyslexiaaction.org.uk
Website: www.dyslexiaaction.org.uk
Twitter: @DyslexiaAction

Registered charity (nos. 268502, SCO39177) and the UK's leading provider of services and support for people with dyslexia and literacy difficulties. We specialise in assessment, teaching and training. We also develop and distribute teaching materials and undertake research.

Dyslexia Action is the largest supplier of specialist training in this field and is committed to improving public policy and practice. We partner with schools, LAs, colleges, universities, employers, voluntary sector organisations and government to improve the quality and quantity of help for people with dyslexia and specific learning difficulties.

Our services are available through our 26 centres around the UK.

Dyslexia Scotland

2nd floor – East Suite
Wallace House
17-21 Maxwell Place
Stirling FK8 1JU
Tel: 01786 446 650
Helpline: 0344 800 8484
Fax: 01786 471235
Email: info@dyslexiascotland.org.uk
Website: www.dyslexiascotland.org.uk
Twitter: @DyslexiaScotlan

Scottish association set up to support and campaign on behalf of people affected by dyslexia. They have a useful and easy to use website. Registered charity no. SCO00951.

Dyspraxia Foundation

8 West Alley
Hitchin
Hertfordshire SG5 1EG
Tel: 01462 455016
Helpline: 01462 454 986 (M-F 9am–5pm)
Fax: 01462 455052
Email: dyspraxia@dyspraxiafoundation.org.uk
Website: www.dyspraxiafoundation.org.uk
Twitter: @DyspraxiaFdtn

The foundation exists to support individuals and families affected by dyspraxia; to promote better diagnostic and treatment facilities for those who have dyspraxia; to help professionals in health and education to assist those with dyspraxia; and to promote awareness and understanding of dyspraxia. As well as various publications, the Dyspraxia Foundation organises conferences and talks and supports a network of local groups across the United Kingdom.

Registered charity no. 1058352.

Education Scotland

Denholm House
Almondvale Business Park
Almondvale Way
Livingston EH54 6GA
Tel: 0131 244 3000
Textphone: 01506 600236
Email: enquiries@educationscotland.org.uk
Website: www.educationscotland.gov.uk
Twitter: @EducationScot

Education Scotland is an executive non-departmental public body sponsored by the Scottish government. It is the main organisation for the development and support of the Scottish curriculum and is at the heart of all major developments in Scottish education, moving education forward with its partners.

ENABLE Scotland

Inspire House
3 Renshaw Place
Eurocentral
Lanarkshire ML1 4UF
Tel: 01698 737 000
Helpline: 0300 0200 101
Email: enabledirect@enable.org.uk
Website: www.enable.org.uk
Twitter: @ENABLEScotland

Contact the ENABLE Scotland Information Service about any aspect of learning disability. They offer jobs, training, respite breaks, day services, supported living, housing and support for people with learning disabilities in different parts of Scotland. Its legal service can assist families with wills and trusts. Registered charity no. SCO09024.

English Federation of Disability Sport

Sport Park, Loughborough University
3 Oakwood Drive
Loughborough
Leicestershire LE11 3QF
Tel: 01509 227750
Fax: 0509 227777
Email: info@efds.org.uk
Website: www.efds.co.uk
Twitter: @Eng_Dis_Sport

Charity (no. 1075180) that creates opportunities for disabled people to participate in sporting activities.

Epilepsy Action

New Anstey House
Gate Way Drive,
Yeadon
Leeds LS19 7XY
Tel: 0113 210 880
Helpline: 0808 800 5050
Fax: 0113 391 0300
Email: helpline@epilepsy.org.uk
Website: www.epilepsy.org.uk
Twitter: @epilepsyaction

Epilepsy Action is the UK's leading epilepsy organisation and exists to improve the lives of everyone affected by the condition. As a member-led association, it is led by and represent people with epilepsy, their friends, families and healthcare professionals.

GIFT

7 Tower Road
Writtle
Chelmsford
Essex CM1 3N
Tel: 01245 830321
Email: enquiries@giftcourses.co.uk
Website: www.giftltd.co.uk

GIFT aims to offer a value-for-money education consultancy of quality, which meets the needs of gifted and talented children and those working to support them in the excitement and challenge of achieving their full potential as human beings. Residential and non-residential courses are organised for exceptionally able children aged five to 18 throughout the year (see our website). INSET courses for schools on provision, identification and school policy are provided with a special emphasis on workshops for practical activities.

Haringey Association for Independent Living (HAIL)

Tottenham Town Hall
Town Hall Approach Road
Tottenham
London N15 4RY
Tel: 020 8275 6550
Fax: 020 8275 6559
Email: admin@hailltd.org
Website: www.hailltd.org

Haringey Association for Independent Living is a support service for adults with learning difficulties moving towards independent living. You can follow them on Twitter.

Headway

Bradbury House
190 Bagnall Road
Old Basford
Nottingham NG6 8SF
Tel: 0115 924 0800
Helpline: 0808 800 2244
Fax: 0115 958 4446
Email: enquiries@headway.org.uk
Website: www.headway.org.uk
Twitter: @HeadwayUK

Registered charity no.1025852 supporting people with brain injuries and their carers.

Helen Arkell Dyslexia Centre

Arkell Lane
Frensham
Farnham
Surrey GU10 3BL
Tel: 01252 792400
Email: enquiries@arkellcentre.org.uk
Website: www.arkellcentre.org.uk
Twitter: @ArkellDyslexia

A registered charity (no. 1064646) providing comprehensive help and care for children with specific learning difficulties including assessment, specialist tuition, speech and language therapy, summer schools and short courses. Initial consultation can be arranged in order to give advice on options for support. Professional teacher-training programmes and schools' support. Financial help available in cases of need.

Huntington's Disease Association

Head Office
Suite 24
Liverpool Science Park
Innovation Centre 1
131 Mount Pleasant
Liverpool L3 5TF
Tel: 0151 331 5444
Fax: 0151 331 5441
Email: info@hda.org.uk
Website: www.hda.org.uk
Twitter: @HDA_tweeting

Registered charity (no. 296453) offering support to people affected by Huntington's Disease (HD); which is sometimes referred to as Huntington's Chorea. Has a Facebook page.

Independent Panel for Special Education Advice (IPSEA)

Hunters Court
Debden Road
Saffron Walden CB11 4AA
Tel: 01799 582030
Adviceline: 0800 018 4016
Email: info@ipsea.org.uk
Website: www.ipsea.org.uk
Twitter: @IPSEAcharity

IPSEA offers free and independent advice and support to parents of children with special educational needs including: free advice on LAs' legal duties towards children with free accompanied visits where necessary, free support and possible representation for those parents appealing to the Special Educational Needs Tribunal, free second opinions on a child's needs and the provision required to meet those needs. Registered charity no. 327691.

Institute for Neuro-Physiological Psychology (INPP)

1 Stanley Street
Chester
Cheshire CH1 2LR
Tel: 01244 311414
Fax: 01244 311414
Website: www.inpp.org.uk

Established in 1975 to research into the effect central nervous system (CNS) dysfunctions have on children with learning difficulties, to develop appropriate CNS remedial and rehabilitation programmes, and to correct underlying physical dysfunctions in dyslexia, dyspraxia and attention deficit disorder (ADD).

Ivemark Syndrome Association

18 French Road
Poole
Dorset BH17 7HB
Tel: 01202 699824
Email: marcus.fisher@virgin.net

Support group for families with children affected by Ivemark Syndrome (also know as right atrial isomerism).

Jeans for Genes

199 Victoria Street
London SW1E 5NE
Tel: 0800 980 4800
Twitter: @JeansforGenes
Email: hello@jeanforgenes.com
Website: www.jeansforgenes.com

The first Friday of every October is Jeans for Genes Day. Their aim is to raise money to fund research into genetic disorders and their target figure is £3million each year. Registered charity no.1062206.

KIDS

7-9 Elliott's Place, London, N1 8HX
WC1N 2NY
Tel: 020 7359 3635
Website: www.kids.org.uk

KIDS was established in 1970 to help disabled children in their development and communication skills. Registered charity no. 275936. Has a Facebook page and you can follow them on Twitter.

Leonard Cheshire Disability England

66 South Lambeth Road
London SW8 1RL
Tel: 020 3242 0200
Fax: 020 3242 0250
Email: info@lcdisability.org
Website: www.lcdisability.org
Twitter: @LeonardCheshire

Leonard Cheshire – the UK's largest voluntary-sector provider of support services for disabled people. They also support disabled people in 52 countries around the world. Registered charity nos. 218186 and SCO05117.

Leonard Cheshire Disability Northern Ireland

Unit 5, Boucher Plaza
Boucher Road
Belfast BT12 6HR
Tel: 028 9024 6247
Fax: 028 9024 6395
Email: northernirelandoffice@lcdisability.org

See main entry – Leonard Cheshire Disability England.

Leonard Cheshire Disability Scotland

Murrayburgh House
17 Corstorphine Road
Edinburgh EH12 6DD
Tel: 0131 346 9040
Fax: 0131 346 9050
Email: scotlandoffice@lcdisability.org

See main entry – Leonard Cheshire Disability England.

Leonard Cheshire Disability Wales

Centre for Business
Office 3
12 Devon Place
Newport
Gwent NP20 4NN
Tel: 01633 263807

See main entry – Leonard Cheshire Disability England.

Leukaemia Care UK

1 Birch Court
Blackpole East
Worcester WR3 8SG
Tel: 01905 755977 Careline: 08088 010 444
Fax: 01905 755 166
Email: care@leukaemiacare.org.uk
Website: www.leukaemiacare.org.uk
Twitter: @LeukaemiaCareUK

Registered charity (nos. 259483, SCO39207) that exists to provide care and support to anyone affected by leukaemia.

Leukaemia Care Scotland

Regus Management
Maxim 1, Maxim Office Park
2 Parklands Way, Eurocentral
Motherwell ML1 4WR
Tel: 01698 209073
Email: scotland@leukaemiacare.org.uk

See main entry above.

Listening Books

12 Lant Street
London SE1 1QH
Tel: 020 7407 9417
Fax: 020 7403 1377
Email: info@listening-books.org.uk
Website: www.listening-books.org.uk
Twitter: @ListeningBooks

Registered charity (no. 264221) that provides a postal and internet based audio library service to anyone who is unable to read in the usual way due to an illness, disability or learning difficulty such as dyslexia.

Has a range of educational audio material to support all aspects of the National Curriculum, as well as thousands of general fiction and non-fiction titles for all ages. There is no limit to the number of titles you may borrow during the year.

Manx Dyslexia Asociation

Coan Aalin
Greeba Bridge
Greba
Isle of Man IM4 3LD
Tel: 07624 315724
Email: manxdyslexia@gmail.com
Website: manxdyslexia.org

Charity (no. IM706) founded in 1993 to help raise the awareness of dyslexia on the Isle of Man.

MENCAP England

123 Golden Lane
London EC1Y 0RT
Tel: 020 7454 0454
Helpline: 0808 808 1111
Fax: 020 7608 3254
Email: information@mencap.org.uk
Website: www.mencap.org.uk
Twitter: @mencap_charity

The Royal MENCAP Society is a registered charity (nos. 222377, SCO41079) that offers services to adults and children with learning disabilities. We offer help and advice in benefits, housing and employment via our helpline.

Helplines are open from Monday to Friday 9.30am-4.30pm; Wednesday – subject to change: (open am-closed pm). Language line is also used. Our office is open Monday-Friday 9-5pm.

We also offer help and advice to anyone who has any other issues or we can signpost them in the right direction. We can also provide information and support for leisure, recreational services (Gateway Clubs) residential services and holidays.

MENCAP Northern Ireland

Segal House
4 Annandale Avenue
Belfast BT7 3JH
Tel: 028 9069 1351
Email: helpline.ni@mencap.org.uk

See main entry – MENCAP England.

MENCAP Cymru

31 Lambourne Crescent
Cardiff Business Park
Llanishen, Cardiff CF14 5GF
Helpline: 02920 747588
Email: helpline.wales@mencap.org.uk

See main entry – MENCAP England.

MENSA

British Mensa Ltd
St John's House
St John's Square
Wolverhampton WV2 4AH
Tel: 01902 772771
Fax: 01902 392500
Email: enquiries@mensa.org.uk
Website: www.mensa.org.uk
Twitter: @BritishMensa

MENSA aims to bring about awareness that giftedness in a child is frequently a specific learning difficulty and should be recognised and treated as such, train teachers to recognise giftedness in a child, train teachers to teach gifted children, establish mutually beneficial relationships with other organisations having similar aims to our own and to devise and implement strategies aimed, at ministerial and senior civil servant levels, at bringing about recognition of the importance of catering for the needs of gifted children.

Mind, the National Association for Mental Health

15-19 Broadway
Stratford
London E15 4BQ
Tel: 020 8519 2122
Fax: 020 8522 1725
Email: contact@mind.org.uk
Website: www.mind.org.uk
Twitter: @MindCharity

Mind (the National Association for Mental Health) is the leading mental health charity (no. 219830) in England and Wales. Mind works for a better life for everyone with experience of mental or emotional stress. It does this by: advancing the views, needs and ambitions of people experiencing mental distress; promoting inclusion and challenging discrimination; influencing policy through effective campaigning and education; providing quality services that meet the expressed needs of people experiencing mental distress and which reflect the requirements of a diverse community; achieving equal legal and civil rights through campaigning and education.

With over 60 years of experience, Mind is a major national network consisting of over 200 local Mind associations, which cover most major towns and rural areas in England and Wales. These are separately registered charities operating under the Mind brand. The Mind network is the largest charitable provider of mental health services in the community. The work of the local associations is strengthened and supported by staff and activities through its many offices in England and Wales. This ensures that, as a national charity, Mind keeps a distinct local perspective to their work.

Mind believes in the individual and equipping them to make informed choices about options open to them. Mind's mental health telephone information service (Mindinfoline) deals with thousands of calls each year. We offer a vital lifeline to people in distress, their relatives and carers, as well as providing mental health information to members of the public, professionals and students.

Mind Cymru

3rd Floor, Quebec House
Castlebridge
5-19 Cowbridge Road East
Cardiff CF11 9AB
Tel: 029 2039 5123
Fax: 029 2034 6585
Email: contactwales@mind.org.uk

See main entry above.

Motability

City Gate House
22 Southwark Bridge Road
London SE1 9HB
Tel: 0300 4564566 Minicom/textphone: 0300 037 0100
Fax: 01279 632000
Website: www.motability.co.uk

Registered charity no. 299745. Motability helps disabled people to use their mobility allowance to obtain new transport.

MS Society

MS National Centre
372 Edgware Road
London NW2 6ND
Tel: 020 8438 0700
Fax: 020 8438 0701
Website: www.mssociety.org.uk
Twitter: @MSSocietyUK

Multiple Sclerosis Society. Registered charity nos. 207495 and SCO16433.

MS Society Cymru

Temple Court
Cathedral Road
Cardiff CF11 9HA
Tel: 029 2078 6676
See main entry above.

MS Society Northern Ireland

The Resource Centre
34 Annadale Avenue
Belfast BT7 3JJ
Tel: 02890 802 802

See main entry above.

MS Society Scotland

National Office, Ratho Park
88 Glasgow Road
Ratho Station
Newbridge EH28 8PP
Tel: 0131 335 4050
Fax: 0131 335 4051

See main entry above.

Muscular Dystrophy Campaign

61A Great Suffolk Street
London
SE1 0BU
Tel: 020 7803 4800
Email: info@musculardystrophyuk.org
Website: www.musculardystrophyuk.org
Twitter: @TargetMD

Registered charity (nos. 205395, SCO39445). Provides information and advice for families affected by muscular dystrophy and other neuromuscular conditions.

NAS – The National Autistic Society – England

393 City Road
London EC1V 1NG
Tel: 020 7833 2299
Autism Helpline: 0800 800 4104 (M-F 10-4)
Fax: 020 7833 9666
Email: nas@nas.org.uk
Website: www.autism.org.uk

The National Autistic Society is the UK's leading charity (nos. 269425, SCO39427) for people affected by autism. For more than 50 years we have worked to support children and young people with autism (including Asperger syndrome) to reach their goals. A well-rounded education, tailored to the needs of the individual, can help people to reach their full potential.

NAS Cymru

6/7 Village Way,
Greenmeadow Springs Business Park
Tongwynlais
Cardiff CF15 7NE
Tel: 02920 629 312
Fax: 02920 629 317
Email: wales@nas.org.uk

See main entry NAS – England.

NAS Northern Ireland

59 Malone Road
Belfast BT9 6SA
Tel: 02890 687 066
Fax: 02890 688 518
Email: northern.ireland@nas.org.uk

See main entry NAS – England.

NAS Scotland

Central Chambers
1st Floor
109 Hope Street
Glasgow G2 6LL
Tel: 0141 221 8090
Fax: 0141 221 8118
Email: scotland@nas.org.uk

See main entry NAS – England.

Nasen

4/5 Amber Business Village
Amber Close
Amington
Tamworth
Staffordshire B77 4RP
Tel: 01827 311500
Fax: 01827 313005
Email: welcome@nasen.org.uk
Website: www.nasen.org.uk

nasen promotes the interests of children and young people with exceptional learning needs and influences the quality of provision through strong and cohesive policies and strategies for parents and professionals.

Membership offers a number of journals, professional development and publications at a reduced cost, and provides a forum for members to share concerns and disseminate expertise and knowledge.

National Association for Able Children in Education (NAACE)

NACE National Office
The Core Business Centre
Milton Hill
Abingdon
Oxfordshire OX13 6AB
Tel: 01235 828280
Fax: 01235 828281
Email: info@nace.co.uk
Website: www.nace.co.uk

NAACE works with teachers to support able children in schools. The organisation also provides, publications, journals, booklets, courses and conferences. Registered charity no. 327230.

National Association of Independent Schools and Non-Maintained Special Schools (NASS)

PO Box 705
York YO30 6WW
Tel: 01904 624446
Email: krippon@nasschools.org.uk
Website: www.nasschools.org.uk

NASS is a voluntary organisation that represents the interests of those special schools outside the maintained sector of the education system.

Our commitment is to achieve excellence and to attain the highest professional standards in working with unique children and young people who have physical, sensory and intellectual difficulties. We exist to promote, develop and maintain the highest professional standards for non-maintained and independent special schools. We offer free information and advice on our member schools to families and professionals. Registered charity no. 1083632.

National Federation of the Blind of the UK

Sir John Wilson House
215 Kirkgate
Wakefield
Yorkshire WF1 1JG
Tel: 01924 291313
Fax: 01924 200244
Email: admin@nfbuk.org
Website: www.nfbuk.org

Registered charity no. 236629 set up to better the understanding between blind and sighted people.

Epilepsy Society

Chesham Lane
Chalfont St Peter
Gerrards Cross,
Buckinghamshire SL9 0RJ
Tel: 01494 601300
Helpline 01494 601400 (Mon-Fri 10am-4pm)
Fax: 01494 871927
Website: www.epilepsysociety.org.uk
Twitter: @EpilepsySociety

The Epilepsy Society provides information and support to those affected by epilepsy. Registered charity no. 206186.

NDCS – The National Deaf Children's Society

Ground Floor South, Castle House
37- 45 Paul Street
London
EC2A 4LS
Tel: 020 7490 8656
Minicom: 020 7490 8656
Fax: 020 7251 5020
Email: ndcs@ndcs.org.uk
Website: www.ndcs.org.uk
Twitter: @NDCS_UK

Leading provider of information, advice, advocacy and support for deaf children, their parents and professionals on all aspects of childhood deafness. This includes advice and information on education, including further and higher education, and support at Special Educational Needs Tribunals.

NDCS also provides advice on equipment and technology for deaf children at home and at school. Registered charity nos. 1016532 and SCO40779.

NDCS Cmyru

Ty-Nant Court, Morganstown, Cardiff, South Glamorgan CF15 8LW
Tel: 029 2037 3474
Minicom: 029 20811861
Fax: 029 2081 4900
Email: ndcswales@ndcs.org.uk

See main entry above.

NDCS Northern Ireland

38-42 Hill Street
Belfast BT1 2LB
Tel: 028 9031 3170 Text: 028 9027 8177
Fax: 028 9027 8205
Email: nioffice@ndcs.org.uk

See main entry above.

NDCS Scotland

Second Floor, Empire House
131 West Nile Street
Glasgow G1 2RX
Tel: 0141 354 7850 Textphone: 0141 332 6133
Fax: 0141 331 2780
Email: ndcs.scotland@ndcs.org.uk

See main entry above.

Network 81

10 Boleyn Way
West Clacton
Essex CO15 2NJ
Tel: 0845 077 4056 (Admin)
Helpline: 0845 077 4055
Fax: 0845 077 4058
Email: Network81@hotmail.co.uk
Website: www.network81.org

Network 81 offers practical help and support to parents throughout all stages of assessment and statementing as outlined in the Education Act 1996. Their national helpline offers an individual service to parents linked to a national network of local contacts.

NIACE – National Learning and Work Institute

Chetwynd House
21 DeMontfort Street
Leicester LE1 7GE
Tel: 0116 204 4200
Fax: 0116 204 6988
Email: enquiries@learningandwork.org.uk
Website: www.learningandwork.org.uk

Works across sectors and age groups to raise national standards and encourage adults in achieving literacy, numeracy and language skills. Registered charity no. 1002775. You can follow them on Twitter.

NOFAS – UK (National Organisation for Fetal Alcohol Syndrome)

165 Beaufort Park
London NW11 6DA
Tel: 0208 458 5951
Email: info@nofas-uk.org
Website: www.nofas-uk.org

Offers advice, support and information about Foetal Alcohol Spectrum Disorder. Registered charity no. 1101935.

Paget Gorman Signed Speech

PGS Administrative Secretary
43 Westover Road
Fleet GU51 3DB
Tel: 01252 621 183
Website: www.pagetgorman.org

Advice and information for parents and professionals concerned with speech and language-impaired children.

Parents for Inclusion (PI)

336 Brixton Road
London SW9 7AA
Tel: 020 7738 3888
Helpline: 0800 652 3145
Email: info@parentsforinclusion.org
Website: www.parentsforinclusion.org

A network of parents of disabled children and children with special needs. Registered charity no.1070675.

Physically Disabled and Able Bodied (PHAB Ltd)

Summit House
50 Wandle Road
Croydon
CR0 1DF
Tel: 020 8667 9443
Fax: 020 8681 1399
Email: info@phab.org.uk
Website: www.phab.org.uk

Registered charity (no. 283931) that works to promote and encourage people with and without physical disabilities to work together to achieve inclusion for all in the wider community.

Potential Plus UK

Suite 1-2
Challenge House
Sherwood Drive
Bletchley
Milton Keynes MK3 6DP
Tel: 01908 646433
Fax: 0870 770 3219
Email: amazingchildren@potentialplusuk.org
Website: www.potentialplusuk.org

Registered charity (no. 313182). It is a mutually supportive self-help organisation offering services both through local branches and nationally. Membership is open to individuals, families, education professionals and schools.

Royal National Institute of Blind People (RNIB)

105 Judd Street
London WC1H 9NE
Tel: 020 7388 1266
Fax: 020 7388 2034
Helpline: 0303 123 9999
Email: helpline@rnib.org.uk
Website: www.rnib.org.uk
Twitter: @RNIB

Every day another 100 people start to lose their sight – there are around two million people in the UK with sight problems, blindness being one of the major causes of disability in the UK. RNIB's pioneering work helps anyone with a sight problem – not just with Braille, Talking Books and computer training, but with imaginative and practical solutions to everyday challenges. They fight for equal rights for people with sight problems; fund pioneering research into preventing and treating eye disease and campaign to change society's attitudes, actions and assumptions so that people with sight problems can enjoy the same rights, freedoms and responsibilties as fully-sighted people.

RNIB promotes eye health by running public health awareness campaigns and their schools and colleges help educate hundreds of children and students with sight problems. They run campaigns on a wide variety of issues, from community care to the design of banknotes and coins, from legislation about broadcasting to accessible information. They lobby national and local government, hold public meetings, organise letter writing campaigns and work in coalitions to achieve their aims. Registered charity no. 226227.

Scope

6 Market Road
London N7 9PW
Helpline: 0808 800 3333 (Scope response)
Tel: 020 7619 7100
Text SCOPE plus message to 80039
Email: helpline@scope.org.uk
Website: www.scope.org.uk
Twitter: @Scope

Scope is a national disability organisation whose focus is people with cerebral palsy. We provide a range of support, information and campaigning services both locally and nationally in addition to providing opportunities in early years, education, employment and daily living. For more information about cerebral palsy and Scope services, contact Scope Response, which provides free information, advice and initial counselling. Open 9am-7pm weekdays and 10am-2pm Saturdays. Registered charity no. 208231.

Scope Cymru

4 Ty Nant Court
Morganstown
Cardiff CF15 8LW
Tel: 029 20 815 450
Email: helpline@scope.org.uk

See main entry above.

Scottish Society for Autism

Hilton House,
Alloa Business Park
Whins Road
Alloa FK10 3SA
Tel: 01259 720044
Advice line: 01259 222022
Twitter: @scottishautism
Email: autism@scottishautism.org
Website: www.scottishautism.org

The Scottish Society for Autism is a registered charity (no. SC009068) established in 1968. They aim to work with individuals of all ages with autism spectrum disorder (ASD), their families and carers, to provide and promote exemplary services and training in education, care, support and life opportunities.

Sense – The National Deafblind Charity

101 Pentonville Road
London N1 9LG
Tel: 0300 330 9250
Textphone: 0300 330 9252
Fax: 0300 330 9251
Email: info@sense.org.uk
Website: www.sense.org.uk
Twitter: @Sensetweets

Sense is the leading national charity that supports and campaigns for children and adults who are deafblind. We provide expert advice and information as well as specialist services to deafblind people, their families, carers and the professionals who work with them. We also support people who have sensory impairments with additional disabilities.

Our services include on-going support for deafblind people and families. These range from day services where deafblind people have the opportunity to learn new skills and Sense-run houses in the community – where people are supported to live as independently as possible. We also provide leading specialist advice, for example on education options and assistive technology. Registered charity no. 289868.

Shine

42 Park Road
Peterborough PE1 2UQ
Tel: 01733 555988
Fax: 01733 555985
Email: info@shinecharity.org.uk
Website: www.shinecharity.org.uk
Twitter: @SHINEUKCharity

The new name for the Association for Spina Bifida and Hydrocephalus (ASBAH). Europe's largest organisation dedicated to supporting individuals and families as they face the challenges arising from spina bifida and hydrocephalus.

Advisers are available to explain the problems associated with spina bifida and or hydrocephalus and may be able to arrange visits to schools and colleges to discuss difficulties. Registered charity no. 249338. Has a Facebook page and you can follow them on Twitter.

Useful associations and websites

Signature

Mersey House
Mandale Business Park
Belmont
Country Durham DH1 1TH
Tel: 0191 383 1155 Text: 07974 121594
Fax: 0191 3837914
Email: enquiries@signature.org.uk
Website: www.signature.org.uk
Twitter: @SignatureDeaf

Association promoting communication with deaf and deafblind people.

SNAP-CYMRU

Head Office
10 Coopers Yard
Curran Road
Cardiff CF10 5NB
Tel: 02920 348 990
Helpline: 0845 120 3730
Fax: 029 2034 8998
Email: enquiries@snapcymru.org
Website: www.snapcymru.org
Twitter: @SNAPCymru

An all-Wales service for children and families, which provides: accurate information and impartial advice and support for parents, carers, and young people in relation to special educational needs and disability; disagreement resolution service; casework service; independent parental support service; advocacy for children and young people in receipt of services; training for parents, carers, young people; training for professionals in relation to SEN/disability. Has a Facebook page.

Spinal Injuries Association

SIA House
2 Trueman Place
Oldbrook
Milton Keynes MK6 2HH
Tel: 01908 604 191
Adviceline: 0800 980 0501
Text: 81025
Email: sia@spinal.co.uk
Website: www.spinal.co.uk
Twitter: @spinalinjuries

Registered charity no.1054097 set up to provide services for people with spinal cord injuries.

The ACE Centre

Hollinwood Business Centre,
Albert Street
Hollinwood
Oldham OL8 3QL
Tel: 0161 358 0151
Fax: 0161 358 6152
Email: enquiries@ace-north.org.uk
Website: www.ace-north.org.uk
Twitter: @ACECentre

The centre offers independent advice and information, assessments and training in the use of assistive technology for individuals with physical and communication disabilities across the north of England. Registered charity no. 1089313.

The Alliance for Inclusive Education

336 Brixton Road
London SW9 7AA
Tel: 020 7737 6030
Email: info@allfie.org.uk
Website: www.allfie.org.uk

National network campaigning for the rights of disabled children in education.

The Association of National Specialist Colleges (NATSPEC)

c/o Derwen College
Oswestry
Shropshire SY11 3JA
Tel: 0117 923 2830
Email: chiefexecutive@natspec.org.uk
Website: www.natspec.org.uk

NATSPEC represents independent specialist colleges across England, Wales and Northern Ireland, providing for over 300 learners with learning difficulties and/or disabilities, often with complex or additional needs. Most colleges offer residential provision. Member colleges support learners in their transition to adult life, participation in the community and where possible employment. NATSPEC acts as a national voice for its member colleges and works in partnership with a range of other provider agencies and organisations. You can contact colleges directly via the website, or through your connexions/careers service.

The Brittle Bone Society

Grant-Paterson House
30 Guthrie Street
Dundee DD1 5BS
Tel: 01382 204446
Fax: 01382 206771
Email: bbs@brittlebone.org
Website: www.brittlebone.org
Twitter: @BrittleBoneUK

A UK registered charity (nos. 272100, SCO10951) providing support for people affected by Osteogenesis Imperfecta (OI).

The Disability Law Service

The Foundry, 17 Oval Way,
London, SE11 5RR
Tel: 020 7791 9800
Fax: 020 7791 9802
Email: advice@dls.org.uk
Website: www.dls.org.uk
Twitter: @DLS_law

The Disability Law Service (DLS) offers free, confidential legal advice to disabled people in the following areas: benefits; children; community care; consumer/contract; discrimination; further and higher education; and employment. In some cases they are able to offer legal representation. The Disability Law Service is made up of solicitors, advisers and trained volunteers who provide up-to-date, informed legal advice for disabled people, their families, enablers and carers. The advice they give is free, and the service offers complete confidentiality. They aim to offer a service that enables disabled people to access relevant information and clarify their rights. Registered charity no. 280805.

The Fragile X Society

Rood End House
6 Stortford Road
Great Dunmow,
Essex CM6 1DA
Tel: 01371 875 100
Fax: 01371 859 915
Email: info@fragilex.org.uk
Website: www.fragilex.org.uk

The aims of The Fragile X Society are to provide support and comprehensive information to families whose children and adult relatives have fragile X syndrome, to raise awareness of fragile X and to encourage research. There is a link network of family contacts, national helplines for statementing, benefits and family support for epilepsy. They publish information booklets, leaflets, a publications list, video and three newsletters a year. There are also national conferences four times a year. Family membership (UK) is free. Welcomes associate membership from interested professionals. Registered charity no. 1127861.

The Guide Dogs for the Blind Association

Burghfield Common
Reading
Berkshire RG7 3YG
Tel: 0118 983 5555
Fax: 0118 983 5433
Email: guidedogs@guidedogs.org.uk
Website: www.guidedogs.org.uk
Twitter: @guidedogs

The Guide Dogs for the Blind Association provides guide dogs, mobility and other rehabilitation services to blind and partially sighted people. Registered charity nos. 209617 and SCO38979.

The Haemophilia Society

Willcox House,
140 – 148 Borough High Street
London, SE1 1LB
Tel: 0207 939 0780

Email: info@haemophilia.org.uk
Website: www.haemophilia.org.uk
Twitter: @HaemoSocUK

Founded in 1950, this registered charity (nos. 288260, SCO39732) has over 4000 members and a network throughout the UK providing information, advice and support services to sufferers of haemophilia, von Willebrand's and related bleeding disorders. You can follow them on Twitter.

The Hyperactive Children's Support Group (HACSG)

71 Whyke Lane
Chichester
Sussex PO19 7PD
Tel: 01243 539966
Email: hacsg@hacsg.org.uk
Website: www.hacsg.org.uk

Support group. Will send information pack if you send a large SAE. Registered charity no. 277643.

The London Centre for Children with Cerebral Palsy

143 Coppetts Road
London
N10 1JP
Tel: 020 8444 7242
Fax: 020 8444 7241
Email: info@cplondon.org.uk
Website: www.cplondon.org.uk
Twitter: @lcccp

Provides education for young children with cerebral palsy using the system of Conductive Education. Registered charity no. 1124524.

The Makaton Charity

Westmead House
Farnborough
Hampshire GU14 7LP
Tel: 01276 606760
Fax: 01276 36725
Email: info@makaton.org
Website: www.makaton.org
Twitter: @MakatonCharity

Makaton vocabulary is a language programme using speech, signs and symbols to provide basic means of communication and encourage language and literacy skills to develop in children and adults with communication and learning difficulties. Training workshops, courses and a variety of resource materials are available and there is a family support helpline too. Registered charity no. 1119819.

The Planned Environment Therapy Trust (PETT)

Archive and Study Centre
Church Lane
Toddington
Cheltenham
Gloucestershire GL54 5DQ
Tel: 01242 621200
Fax: 01242 620125
Website: www.pettrust.org.uk
Twitter: @pettconnect

Founded to promote effective treatment for those with emotional and psychological disorders. Registered charity no. 248633.

The Social, Emotional and Behavioural Difficulties Association (SEBDA)

c/o Goldwyn School
Godinton Lane
Great Chart
Ashford
Kent TN23 3BT
Tel: 01233 622958
Twitter: @SebdaOrg
Email: admin@sebda.org
Website: www.sebda.org

SEBDA exists to campaign on behalf of and to provide information, training and a support service to professionals who work with children and young people with social, emotional and behavioural difficulties. Registered charity no. 258730.

Please note: they do not provide any services to parents.

The Stroke Association

Stroke House
240 City Road
London EC1V 2PR
Tel: 020 7566 0300
Helpline: 0303 3033 100
Fax: 020 7490 2686
Email: info@stroke.org.uk
Website: www.stroke.org.uk
Twitter: @thestrokeassoc

More than 250,000 people in the UK live with the disabilitie caused by a stroke. The association's website provides informatio and advice for free. Registered charity nos. 211015, SCO3778! IOM945, NP0369 (Jersey).

The Thalidomide Society

Tel: 020 8464 9048
Email: info@thalidomidesociety.org
Website: www.thalidomidesociety.org

Registered charity no. 231708 created in 1962. Support group for impaired adults whose disabilities are a result of the drug Thalidomide.

Together for Short Lives

New Bond House,
Bond Street, Bristol, BS2 9AG
Tel: 0117 989 7820
Helpline: 0808 8088 100
Email: info@togetherforshortlives.org
Website: www.togetherforshortlives.org.uk
Twitter: @Tog4ShortLives

The new name for the Association for Children's Palliative Care (ACT). Helps families with children who have life-limiting or life threatening conditions.

Tourette's Action

The Meads Business Centre,
19 Kingsmead, Farnborough,
Hampshire, GU14 7SR
Tel: 0300 777 8427
Email: admin@tourettes-action.org.uk
Website: www.tourettes-action.org.uk
Twitter: @tourettesaction

Registered charity no. 1003317 offering support and information about Tourette's.

U Can Do IT

Taylors Yard
7 Alderbrook Road
London SW12 8AD
Tel: 020 8673 3300
Fax: 020 8675 9571
Website: www.ucandoit.org.uk

U CAN DO IT is a London charity (no. 1070571) providing blind, deaf and physically disabled children and adults with the skills they need to utilise the internet. Tuition is one to one at home, by highly skilled police-vetted tutors (CRB level 2), with costs starting from £1 per lesson.

WheelPower – British Wheelchair Sport

Stoke Mandeville Stadium
Guttman Road
Stoke Mandeville
Buckinghamshire HP21 9PP
Tel: 01296 395995
Fax: 01296 424171
Email: info@wheelpower.org.uk
Website: www.wheelpower.org.uk
Twitter: @wheelpower

The British Wheelchair Sports Foundation is the national organisation for wheelchair sport in the UK and exists to provide, promote and develop opportunities for men, women and children with disabilities to participate in recreational and competitive wheelchair sport. Registered charity no. 265498.

Young Minds

Suite 11
Baden Place
Crosby Row
London SE1 1YW
Tel: 020 7089 5050
Parent Hotline: 0808 802 5544
Fax: 020 7407 8887
Website: www.youngminds.org.uk
Email: ymenquiries@youngminds.org.uk
Twitter: @youngmindsuk

National charity (nos. 1016968, SCO39700) committed to improving the mental health of young people and children in the UK. Their website has advice, information and details of how you can help.

Useful associations and websites

WEBSITES

www.abilitynet.org.uk
Ability Net is a charity (no. 1067673) that provides impartial, expert advice about computer technology for disabled people. You can follow them on Twitter.

www.abilityonline.net
Disability information and news and views online. Registered charity no. 1089117.

www.apparelyzed.com
Spinal cord injury peer support – has a forum with useful links.

www.ukdpc.net
United Kingdom's Disabled People's Council – a national umbrella organisation set up by disabled people to represent their interests at a national level. Registered charity no. 1067873.

www.cae.org.uk
Centre for Accessible Environments – a registered charity (no. 1050820), which is the leading authority on providing a built enviroment that is accessible for everyone, including disabled people.

www.choicesandrights.org.uk
CRDC – Choices and Rights Disability Coalition. Run for and by disabled people in the Kingston upon Hull and East Riding of Yorkshire area. Registered charity no. 1106462.

www.amyandfriends.org
Website set up to support those families affected by Cockayne Syndrome in the UK. Registered charity no. 1119746.

www.deafcouncil.org.uk
UK Council on Deafness. Has interesting list of member websites.

www.disabilitynow.org.uk
Disability Now – award winning online newspaper for everyone with an interest in disability.

www.focusondisability.org.uk
Focus on Disability – resource of general information regarding disability in the UK.

www.direct.gov.uk/disabledpeople
The UK government's web page for disabled people..

www.actionondisability.org.uk
Formerly HAFAD – Hammersmith and Fulham Action for Disability. Campaigning for rights of disabled people, the site is managed and controlled by disabled people.

www.heartnsoul.co.uk
Heart 'n' Soul Music Theatre – a leading disability arts group. Has a Facebook page.

www.mugsy.org
National Autistic Society – Surrey branch. Website has pages dedicated to all areas of the UK as well as international pages.

www.ncil.org
National Centre for Independent Living. A resource on independent living and direct payments for disabled people and others working in the field. Registered charity no. 1113427.

www.qefd.org.uk
Queen Elizabeth's Foundation – a national charity (no. 251051) supporting over 20,000 physically disabled people annually.

www.ssc.education.ed.ac.uk
Scottish Sensory Centre – for everyone who is involved in the education of children and young people with sensory impairment.

www.theark.org.uk
A registered charity (no. 1098204) set up to enhance the lives of people with multi-sensory impairment, learning difficulties and physical disabilities.

www.tuberous-sclerosis.org
Tuberous Sclerosis Association of Great Britain. Registered charity no. 1039549. Website provides information and support for people and families affected by TSC.

www.vitalise.org.uk
Vitalise (formerly The Winged Fellowship Trust) provides respite care for disabled children, adults and their carers. Registered charity no. 295072.

www.peoplefirstinfo.org.uk
WELDIS – an online information resource of services in and around Westminster for older people, adults and children with disabilities and their carers.

www.youreable.com
Information, products and services for the disabled community including news, shopping, pen pals and discussion forums.

Glossary

ACLD	Autism, Communication and Associated Learning Difficulties
ADD	Attention Deficit Order
ADHD	Attention Deficit and Hyperactive Disorder (Hyperkinetic Disorder)
AdvDip SpecEduc	Advanced Diploma in Special Education
AFBPS	Associate Fellow of the British Psychological Society
ALAN	Adult Literacy and Numeracy
ALCM	Associate of the London College of Music
ALL	Accreditation of Lifelong Learning
AOC	Association of Colleges
AQA	Assessment and Qualification Alliance/ Northern Examinations and Assessment Board
ASC	Autistic Spectrum Conditions
ASD	Autistic Spectrum Disorders
ASDAN	Qualifications for 11-16 age range
ASP	Asperger syndrome
AUT	Autism
AWCEBD	now SEBDA
BA	Bachelor of Arts
BDA	British Dyslexic Association
BESD	Behavioural, Emotional and Social Difficulties
BMET	Biomedical Engineering Technologist
BPhil	Bachelor of Philosophy
BSc	Bachelor of Science
BSL	British Sign Language
BTEC	Range of practical work-related programmes; which lead to qualifications equivalent to GCSEs and A levels (awarded by Edexcel)
C & G	City & Guilds Examination
C(Ed) Psychol	Certificate in Educational Psychology
CACDP	Council for the Advancement of Communication with Deaf People
CAMHS	Child and Adolescent Mental Health Service
CB	Challenging Behaviour
CD	Communcation Difficulties
CertEd	Certificate of Education
CF	Cystic Fibrosis
CLAIT	Computer Literacy and Information Technology
CLD	Complex Learning Difficulties
CNS	Central Nervous System
COPE	Certificate of Personal Effectiveness
CP	Cerebral Palsy

CPD	Continuing Professional Development
CRB	Criminal Records Bureau
CReSTeD	Council for the Registration of Schools Teaching Dyslexic Pupils
CSSE	Consortium of Special Schools in Essex
CSSIW	Care and Social Services Inspectorate for Wales
CTEC	Computer-aided Training, Education and Communication
D	Deaf
DDA	Disability Discrimination Act
DEL	Delicate
DfE	Department for Education
DIDA	Diploma in Digital Applications
DipAppSS	Diploma in Applied Social Sciences
DipEd	Diploma of Education
DipSEN	Diploma in Speial Educational Needs
DipSpEd	Diploma in Special Education
DT	Design and Technology
DYC	Dyscalculia
DYS	Dyslexia
DYSC	Dyscalculia
DYSP	Dyspraxia
EASIE	Exercise and Sound in Education
EBSD	Emotional, Behavioural and/or Social Difficulties
ECDL	European Computer Driving Licence
ECIS	European Council of International Schools
ECM	Every Child Matters (Government Green Paper)
EdMng	Educational Management
ELC	Early Learning Centre
ELQ	Equivalent or Lower Qualification
EPI	Epilepsy
EQUALS	Entitlement and Quality Education for Pupils with Learning Difficulties
FLSE	Federation of Leaders in Special Education
GCSE	General Certificate of Secondary Education
GLD	General Learning Difficulties
HA	High Ability
HANDLE	Holistic Approach to Newuro-DEvelopment and Learning Efficiency
HEA	Higher Educaiton Authority/Health Education Authority
HI	Hearing Impairment
HS	Hospital School
ICT	Information Communication Technology

Glossary

IEP	Individual Education Plan		PGCE	Post Graduate Certificate in Education
IIP	Investors in People		PGCertSpld	Post Graduate Certificate in Specific Learning Difficulties
IM	Idiopathic Myelofibrosis		PGTC	Post Graduate Teaching Certificate
ISI	Independent Schools Inspectorate		PH	Physical Impairment
IT	Information Technology		PhD	Doctor of Philosophy
KS	Key Stage		Phe	Partially Hearing
LA	Local Authority		PMLD	Profound and Multiple Learning Difficulties
LD	Learning Difficulties		PNI	Physical Neurological Impairment
LDD	Learning Difficulties and Disabilities		PRU	Pupil Referral Unit
LISA	London International Schools Association		PSHCE	Personal Social Health, Citizenship and Economics
MA	Master of Arts		RE	Religious Education
MAPA	Management of Actual or Potential Aggression		SAT	Standard Asessment Test
MBA	Master of Business Administration		SCD	Social and Communication Difficulties
MD	Muscular Dystrophy		SCLD	Severe and Complex Learning Difficulties
MDT	Multidisciplinary Team		SEAL	Social and Emotional Aspects of Learning
MEd	Master of Education		SEBD	Severe Emotional and Behavioural Disorders
MLD	Moderate Learning Difficulties			
MS	Multiple Sclerosis		SEBDA	Social, Emotional and Behavioural Difficulties Association
MSc	Master of Science		SEBN	Social, Emotional and Behavioural Needs
MSI	Multi-sensory Impairment		SHB	Sexually Harmful Behaviour
NAES	National Association of EBD Schools		SLCN	Speech, Language and Communicational Needs
NAS	National Autistic Society			
NASEN	Northern Association of Special Educational Needs		SLD	Severe Learning Difficulties
NASS	National Association of Independent Schools & Non-maintained Special Schools		SLI	Specific Language Impairment
			SLT	Speech and Language Teacher
			SP	Special Purpose/Speech Processing
NATSPEC	National Association of Specialist Colleges		SpEd	Special Education
NOCN	National Open College Network		SPLD	Specific Learning Difficulties
NPQH	National Professional Qualification for Headship		SP&LD	Speech and Language Difficulties
			STREAM	Strong Therapeutic, Restoring Environment and Assesssment Model
NVQ	National Vocational Qualifications		SWALSS	South and West Association of Leaders in Special Schools
OCD	Obsessive Compulsive Disorder			
OCN	Open Course Network		SWSF	Steiner Waldorf Schools Foundation
ODD	Oppositional Defiant Disorder		TAV	Therapeutic, Academic and Vocational
OT	Occupational Therapist		TEACCH	Treatment and Education of Autistic and related Communication Handicapped Children (also sometimes written as TEACHH)
P scales	method of recording the achievements of SEN students who are working towards the first levels of the National Curriculum			
PACT	Parents Association of Children with Tumours		TCI	Therapeutic Crisis Intervention
			ToD	Teacher of the Deaf
PACT	Parents and Children Together		TOU	Tourette syndrome
PCMT	Professional and Clinical Multidisciplinary Team		VB	Verbal Reasoning
			VIS	Visually Impaired
PD	Physical Difficulties		VOCA	Voice Output Communication Aid
PE	Physical Education		WMLG	West Midlands Lupus Group
PECS	Picture Exchange Communication System			

Index

Index